LRC - Batavia HS
Batavia, IL 60510

AMERICAN HEROES

MAGILL'S CHOICE

AMERICAN HEROES

Volume 1
Hank Aaron — Geronimo
1-350

from
The Editors of Salem Press

SALEM PRESS, INC.
Pasadena, California   Hackensack, New Jersey

Cover image: © Joseph Helfenberger/Dreamstime.com

Copyright © 2009, by SALEM PRESS, INC.
All rights in this book are reserved. No part of this work may be used or reproduced in any manner whatsoever or transmitted in any form or by any means, electronic or mechanical, including photocopy, recording, or any information storage and retrieval system, without written permission from the copyright owner except in the case of brief quotations embodied in critical articles and reviews. For information address the publisher, Salem Press, Inc., P.O. Box 50062, Pasadena, California 91115.

∞ The paper used in these volumes conforms to the American National Standard for Permanence of Paper for Printed Library Materials, Z39.48-1992 (R1997)

Some of the essays in this work originally appeared in the following Salem Press sets: *Great Lives from History: The 18th Century* (2006), *The 19th Century* (2006), and *The Twentieth Century* (2008), updated through 2008. New material has been added.

Library of Congress Cataloging-in-Publication Data
American heroes / from the editors of Salem Press.
    p. cm. — (Magill's choice)
    Includes bibliographical references and index.
    ISBN 978-1-58765-457-2 (set : alk. paper) — ISBN 978-1-58765-458-9 (v. 1 : alk. paper) — ISBN 978-1-58765-459-6 (v. 2 : alk. paper) — ISBN 978-1-58765-460-2 (v. 3 : alk. paper)   1. Heroes—United States—Biography. 2. Celebrities—United States—Biography. I. Salem Press.
    CT105.A47 2008
    920.02—dc22
2008017124

First Printing

PRINTED IN CANADA

Contents

Publisher's Note vii
List of Contributors ix
Complete List of Contents xvii
Key to Pronunciation xxiii

Hank Aaron 1
Ralph Abernathy 4
Abigail Adams 9
John Adams 14
Samuel Adams 19
Jane Addams 26
Muhammad Ali 31
Maya Angelou 38
Susan B. Anthony 43
Neil Armstrong 48

Robert D. Ballard 55
Benjamin Banneker 60
Clara Barton 64
Alexander Graham Bell 70
Mary McLeod Bethune 75
Black Hawk 80
Daniel Boone 84
Omar Nelson Bradley 89
Louis D. Brandeis 94
Joseph Brant 100
William J. Brennan 105
John Brown 109
Olympia Brown 115
Ralph Bunche 119
Richard Byrd 124

Frances Xavier Cabrini 129
Rachel Carson 133
Jimmy Carter 138
George Washington Carver 144
Mary Ann Shadd Cary 149
Carrie Chapman Catt 152
Wilt Chamberlain 158
César Chávez 161

Shirley Chisholm	164
Hillary Rodham Clinton	171
Ty Cobb	175
Bessie Coleman	179
Bill Cosby	183
Crazy Horse	187
David Crockett	194
Walter Cronkite	198
Clarence Darrow	201
Dorothy Day	207
Eugene V. Debs	212
Stephen Decatur	217
Jack Dempsey	221
Joe DiMaggio	227
Walt Disney	231
Dorothea Dix	238
Jimmy Doolittle	243
Helen Gahagan Douglas	247
William O. Douglas	251
Frederick Douglass	254
W. E. B. Du Bois	259
Amelia Earhart	265
Mary Baker Eddy	270
Marian Wright Edelman	277
Thomas Alva Edison	281
Albert Einstein	287
Dwight D. Eisenhower	292
Chris Evert	297
Louis Farrakhan	302
Betty Ford	305
Benjamin Franklin	309
John C. Frémont	315
Betty Friedan	322
William Lloyd Garrison	327
Marcus Garvey	333
Bill Gates	337
Lou Gehrig	341
Geronimo	346

Publisher's Note

Salem's *American Heroes* surveys more than 200 U.S. heroes from the American Revolution through today, in all areas of achievement. Whereas most reference works with a "heroes" theme focus on types of heroes (war heroes) or heroes by ethnicity (e.g., African American heroes), Salem's *American Heroes* combines heroes from all areas of achievement and all ethnicities into one comprehensive package, including all the standards taught from middle school through high school and four-year colleges.

In the twenty-first century, an age of global access to information and dwindling privacy, the term "hero" is more subjective than ever. Not all heroes are (or were) the spotless paragons envisioned in fiction or set forth in old history books. Today, many of our traditional heroes are silhouetted against their very human flaws—perhaps making their accomplishments all the more remarkable. All can agree, however, that a "hero" is a person who has placed others above self, who has invoked courage to undertake difficult and risky endeavors in order to better the world for others, who has breached the minimum of what is expected to reach for what can be. Such heroes come from all walks of life and can surprise not only others but also themselves in what they are able to accomplish, providing inspiration to others along the way. Many times they remain unnamed, from the single mother working to make ends meet to the soldier killed in service to country.

The 209 heroes covered in this three-volume set are individuals who, through their actions, have provided inspiration in all walks of society. Their contributions represent 40 areas of achievement, from Aviation and Space Exploration, Civil Rights, and Evangelism through Government and Politics, the Military, Religion, Social Reform, Sports, and Women's Rights. The broadly diverse coverage includes 42 African Americans, 152 Euro-Americans, 6 Jewish Americans, 3 Latino Americans, 15 Native Americans, 2 Pacific Islander Americans, and 64 women.

Each comprehensive, in-depth essay is arranged in a standard format. Essays open with the name of the individual and a famous quotation from that individual. Vital ready-reference data follow: identification (such as "Astronaut," "Baseball player," "Civil Rights activist," or "President of the United States"); a summary abstract of the person's key role and importance; dates and places of birth and (where applicable) death; a list of "also known as" names and nicknames; and a list of areas of achievement. The meat of each essay consists of several paragraphs covering "Early Life," on upbringing and education, which includes pronunciation guidelines for difficult-to-pronounce names; an in-depth overview of "Life's Work," addressing career and achievements; and a "Significance" section that summarizes the individual's major contributions. Every essay ends with a "Further

Reading" section that lists three to ten books and other print sources for further study; these bibliographies are up to date through 2007. All essays are signed by academicians and other expert contributors.

A comprehensive Subject and Personages Index is joined by a Category Index (arranging the heroes by area of achievement) and an Ethnicity Index (arranging them by ethnic group and including a list of the women in the set) to assist students and general readers in accessing the material for reports and areas of interest.

List of Contributors

Emily Alward
*Henderson, Nevada,
    District Libraries*

Eleanor B. Amico
University of Wisconsin—Oshkosh

Richard J. Amundson
Columbus College

Deborah Elwell Arfken
*University of Tennessee,
    Chattanooga*

Andy Argyrakis
Tribune Media Services

Mary Welek Atwell
Radford University

Bryan Aubrey
Maharishi International University

John W. Bailey
Independent Scholar

William J. Baker
University of Maine

Betty Balanoff
Roosevelt University

Carl L. Bankston III
Tulane University

Robert A. Becker
Louisiana State University

Milton Berman
University of Rochester

Robert L. Berner
University of Wisconsin—Oshkosh

Terry D. Bilhartz
Sam Houston State University

Cynthia A. Bily
Adrian College

Margaret Boe Birns
New York University

Gerhard Brand
*California State University,
    Los Angeles*

J. R. Broadus
University of North Carolina

Terrill Brooks
Baker College

Thomas W. Buchanan
Ancilla Domini College

Michael H. Burchett
Limestone College

William H. Burnside
John Brown University

Donald Burrill
*California State University,
    Los Angeles*

Larry W. Burt
*Southwest Missouri State
    University*

AMERICAN HEROES

Jack J. Cardoso
Clarence, New York

Elof Axel Carlson
State University of New York, Stony Brook

John Carpenter
University of Michigan

John M. Carroll
Lamar University

Diane S. Carter
Macomb Township, Michigan

Dennis W. Cheek
Ewing Marion Kauffman Foundation

Michael J. Clark
Calfornia State University, Hayward

Lesley Hoyt Croft
Arizona State University

Light Townsend Cummins
Austin College

Robert R. Davis, Jr.
Ohio Northern University

Rowena Wildin Dehanke
Altadena, California

Bill Delaney
San Diego, California

John E. DiMeglio
Mankato State University

Charles Duncan
Clark-Atlanta University

Harry J. Eisenman
University of Missouri, Rolla

Mark R. Ellis
University of Nebraska at Kearney

Paul F. Erwin
University of Cincinnati

Kimberly K. Estep
Wesleyan College

Kevin Eyster
Madonna University

Stephen C. Feinstein
University of Wisconsin—River Falls

Paul Finkelman
State University of New York, Binghamton

David G. Fisher
Lycoming College

Kirk Ford, Jr.
Clinton, Mississippi

Catherine Francis
Towson State University

Richard G. Frederick
University of Pittsburgh

John C. Fredriksen
Salem State College

List of Contributors

Francesca Gamber
Southern Illinois University at Carbondale

Cecilia M. Garcia
Washington, D.C.

Sheldon Goldfarb
University of British Columbia

Robert M. Goldman
Virginia Union University

Karen Gould
Austin, Texas

Lloyd J. Graybar
Eastern Kentucky University

Christopher E. Guthrie
Tarleton State University

Myra G. Gutin
Rider University

D. Harland Hagler
North Texas State University

William I. Hair
Georgia College

Lowell H. Harrison
Western Kentucky University

Fred R. van Hartesveldt
Fort Valley State College

John Harty
Independent Scholar

Karen L. Hayslett-McCall
University of Texas, Dallas

Diane Andrews Henningfeld
Adrian College

Anna Dunlap Higgins
Gordon College

Richard L. Hillard
University of Arkansas at Pine Bluff

Hal Holladay
Simon's Rock College of Bard

Pierre L. Horn
Wright State University

John Quinn Imholte
University of Minnesota, Morris

Carlton Jackson
Western Kentucky University

Robert Jacobs
Central Washington University

Duncan R. Jamieson
Ashland University

Willoughby G. Jarrell
Kennesaw State College

Maude M. Jennings
Ball State University

Lloyd Johnson
Campbell University

Charles L. Kammer
The College of Wooster

Leigh Husband Kimmel
Indianapolis, Indiana

Kenneth F. Kiple
Independent Scholar

Anne Klejment
University of St. Thomas

Carl E. Kramer
Clarksville, Indiana

Henry Kratz
University of Tennessee, Knoxville

Paul E. Kuhl
Winston-Salem State University

Karl G. Larew
Towson State University

Bruce L. Larson
Mankato State University

Thomas Tandy Lewis
St. Cloud State University

John L. Loos
Louisiana State University

Al Ludwick
Augusta Chronicle-Herald

Maxine N. Lurie
Independent Scholar

Richard B. McCaslin
High Point, North Carolina

Arthur F. McClure
Central Missouri State University

Robert McColley
University of Illinois

Mary McElroy
Kansas State University

Margaret McFadden
Appalachian State University

Jennifer McLeod
Independent Scholar

Sally Ward Maggard
West Virginia University

Barry Stewart Mann
Alliance Theatre

Henry S. Marks
Independent Scholar

Marsha Kass Marks
Independent Scholar

Annette Marks-Ellis
Antelope Valley College

John F. Marszalek
Xavier University of Louisiana

Elaine Mathiasen
Gaston, Oregon

Laurence W. Mazzeno
Alvernia College

Bernard Mergen
George Washington University

Eric Metchik
Salem State College

Richard D. Miles
Wayne State University

List of Contributors

Donna Mungen
Los Angeles Times

David Murphy
Kentucky State University

Parker Bradley Nutting
Framingham State College

James H. O'Donnell III
Independent Scholar

Keith W. Olson
University of Maryland, College Park

Gary B. Ostrower
Alfred University

Robert L. Patterson
Armstrong State College

Thomas R. Peake
King College

William Pemberton
University of Wisconsin—La Crosse

Andy Perry
West Hollywood, California

Barbara Bennett Peterson
California State University, San Bernardino

Michael Phillips
University of Texas, Austin

Steven J. Ramold
Eastern Michigan University

John David Rausch, Jr.
West Texas A&M University

James A. Rawley
University of Nebraska, Lincoln

Clark G. Reynolds
College of Charleston

Leo P. Ribuffo
George Washington University

Edward J. Rielly
Saint Joseph's College of Maine

J. Edmund Rush
Boise, Idaho

Wendy Sacket
Irvine, California

Dorothy C. Salem
Cuyahoga Community College

Stephen P. Sayles
University of La Verne

Elizabeth D. Schafer
Loachapoka, Alabama

J. Christopher Schnell
Southeast Missouri State University

Robert W. Sellen
Georgia State University

Brion Sever
Monmouth University

R. Baird Shuman
University of Illinois, Urbana-Champaign

Amy Sisson
University of Houston—Clear Lake

David Curtis Skaggs
Bowling Green State University

C. Edward Skeen
Memphis State University

Jane A. Slezak
*Fulton Montgomery
  Community College*

Christopher E. Smith
Michigan State University

Harold L. Smith
University of Houston-Victoria

Katherine Socha
St. Mary's College of Maryland

Joseph L. Spradley
Wheaton College

C. Fitzhugh Spragins
Arkansas College

David L. Sterling
University of Cincinnati

Leslie A. Stricker
Park University

James Sullivan
*California State University,
  Los Angeles*

Joseph E. Suppiger
Independent Scholar

Patricia E. Sweeney
Derby Neck Library

Glenn L. Swygart
Tennessee Temple University

James Tackach
Roger Williams University

Emily Teipe
Fullerton College

Brian G. Tobin
Lassen College

James H. Toner
Norwich University

Kenneth W. Townsend
Coastal Carolina University

David Trevino
Donna Klein Jewish Academy

Judith Ann Trolander
*University of Minnesota,
  Duluth*

Diane C. Vecchio
*University of Wisconsin -
  Whitewater*

Mary E. Virginia
Venice, Florida

Vernon L. Volpe
Texas A&M University

Harry M. Ward
University of Richmond

Robert P. Watson
Florida Atlantic University

William E. Watson
Immaculata University

Derrick Harper West
Davis, California

List of Contributors

Donna Glee Williams
*North Carolina Advance Center
   of Teaching*

Judith Barton Williamson
Sauk Valley Community College

Richard L. Wilson
University of Tennessee, Chattanooga

Michael Witkoski
University of South Carolina

Lisa A. Wroble
*Collier County Schools and
   Edison College*

Donald Yacovone
Florida State University

Lamont H. Yeakey
*California State University,
   Los Angeles*

Philip R. Zampini
Westfield State College

Robert F. Zeidel
Independent Scholar

Complete List of Contents

Volume 1

Publisher's Note vii
List of Contributors ix
Complete List of Contents. xvii
Key to Pronunciation xxiii

Hank Aaron 1
Ralph Abernathy 4
Abigail Adams 9
John Adams 14
Samuel Adams 19
Jane Addams 26
Muhammad Ali 31
Maya Angelou 38
Susan B. Anthony 43
Neil Armstrong 48

Robert D. Ballard 55
Benjamin Banneker 60
Clara Barton 64
Alexander Graham Bell 70
Mary McLeod Bethune 75
Black Hawk 80
Daniel Boone 84
Omar Nelson Bradley 89
Louis D. Brandeis 94
Joseph Brant 100
William J. Brennan 105
John Brown 109
Olympia Brown 115
Ralph Bunche 119
Richard Byrd 124

Frances Xavier Cabrini 129
Rachel Carson 133
Jimmy Carter 138
George Washington Carver 144

Mary Ann Shadd Cary	149
Carrie Chapman Catt	152
Wilt Chamberlain	158
César Chávez	161
Shirley Chisholm	164
Hillary Rodham Clinton	171
Ty Cobb	175
Bessie Coleman	179
Bill Cosby	183
Crazy Horse	187
David Crockett	194
Walter Cronkite	198
Clarence Darrow	201
Dorothy Day	207
Eugene V. Debs	212
Stephen Decatur	217
Jack Dempsey	221
Joe DiMaggio	227
Walt Disney	231
Dorothea Dix	238
Jimmy Doolittle	243
Helen Gahagan Douglas	247
William O. Douglas	251
Frederick Douglass	254
W. E. B. Du Bois	259
Amelia Earhart	265
Mary Baker Eddy	270
Marian Wright Edelman	277
Thomas Alva Edison	281
Albert Einstein	287
Dwight D. Eisenhower	292
Chris Evert	297
Louis Farrakhan	302
Betty Ford	305
Benjamin Franklin	309
John C. Frémont	315
Betty Friedan	322
William Lloyd Garrison	327
Marcus Garvey	333

Complete List of Contents

Bill Gates 337
Lou Gehrig 341
Geronimo 346

Volume 2

Complete List of Contents xxxiii
Key to Pronunciation xxxix

Althea Gibson 351
John Glenn 356
Emma Goldman 361
Al Gore 367
William Crawford Gorgas 371
Billy Graham 376
Nathanael Greene 380
Wayne Gretzky 387

Mary A. Hallaren 390
William F. Halsey 393
Fannie Lou Hamer 398
Alexander Hamilton 402
Learned Hand 408
Barbara Harris 413
Ernest Hemingway 417
Patrick Henry 422
Katharine Hepburn 426
Aileen Clarke Hernandez 432
Wild Bill Hickok 437
Oveta Culp Hobby 441
Bob Hope 446
Grace Murray Hopper 450
Sam Houston 455
Samuel Gridley Howe 460
Dolores Huerta 465
Charles Evans Hughes 471
Cordell Hull 478

Andrew Jackson 483
Jesse Jackson 488
Stonewall Jackson 494
Thomas Jefferson 498
Steve Jobs 503

Bobby Jones 507
John Paul Jones 513
Mother Jones 519
Barbara Jordan. 524
Michael Jordan 529
Chief Joseph 533

Kamehameha I. 538
Helen Keller 542
John F. Kennedy. 546
Robert F. Kennedy. 551
Billie Jean King 557
Martin Luther King, Jr. 562

Robert M. La Follette 569
Robert E. Lee 574
John L. Lewis 579
Meriwether Lewis and William Clark. 584
Liliuokalani 589
Abraham Lincoln 594
Charles A. Lindbergh 600
Belva A. Lockwood 606
Henry Cabot Lodge 610
Huey Long. 616
Joe Louis. 621
Juliette Gordon Low 627
Shannon W. Lucid 632

Douglas MacArthur 635
Dolley Madison 642
James Madison 646
Malcolm X. 650
Wilma Mankiller 655
Rocky Marciano 660
George C. Marshall 664
John Marshall 669
Thurgood Marshall 675
Golda Meir. 680
Thomas Merton 686
John R. Mott 690
John Muir 696
Edward R. Murrow 700

Complete List of Contents

Ralph Nader 705
Carry Nation 709
Martina Navratilova 714

VOLUME 3

Complete List of Contents xlix
Key to Pronunciation lv

Jack Nicklaus 719
Chester W. Nimitz 723

Barack Obama 728
Sandra Day O'Connor 733
Osceola 739
Jesse Owens 742

Thomas Paine 747
Rosa Parks 752
George S. Patton 758
Alice Paul 763
Robert Edwin Peary 768
John J. Pershing 774
Colin Powell 779

A. Philip Randolph 785
Jeannette Rankin 793
Ronald Reagan 798
Red Cloud 805
Walter Reed 809
Paul Revere 814
Sally Ride 819
Paul Robeson 824
Jackie Robinson 832
John D. Rockefeller 838
Knute Rockne 844
Eleanor Roosevelt 847
Franklin D. Roosevelt 852
Theodore Roosevelt 859
John Ross 864
Bill Russell 868
Babe Ruth 874

Sacagawea	880
Jonas Salk	885
Pete Sampras	889
Margaret Sanger	893
Junípero Serra	898
Alan Shepard	902
William Tecumseh Sherman	907
Sitting Bull	913
Margaret Chase Smith	917
Elizabeth Cady Stanton	922
Adlai E. Stevenson	928
James Stewart	934
Anne Sullivan	938
Ida Tarbell	942
Zachary Taylor	947
Tecumseh	952
Norman Thomas	956
Jim Thorpe	963
Harry S. Truman	968
Sojourner Truth	974
Harriet Tubman	979
Nat Turner	984
Earl Warren	988
Booker T. Washington	994
George Washington	1000
John Wayne	1005
Ida B. Wells-Barnett	1009
Elie Wiesel	1013
Hazel Wightman	1019
Oprah Winfrey	1023
Tiger Woods	1029
Orville and Wilbur Wright	1034
Chuck Yeager	1040
Babe Didrikson Zaharias	1044
Subjects by Category	1051
Ethnicity Index	1057
Subject and Personages Index	1061

Key to Pronunciation

Vowel Sounds

Symbol	*Spelled (Pronounced)*
a	answer (AN-suhr), laugh (laf), sample (SAM-puhl), that (that)
ah	father (FAH-thur), hospital (HAHS-pih-tuhl)
aw	awful (AW-fuhl), caught (kawt)
ay	blaze (blayz), fade (fayd), waiter (WAYT-ur), weigh (way)
eh	bed (behd), head (hehd), said (sehd)
ee	believe (bee-LEEV), cedar (SEE-dur), leader (LEED-ur), liter (LEE-tur)
ew	boot (bewt), lose (lewz)
i	buy (bi), height (hit), lie (li), surprise (sur-PRIZ)
ih	bitter (BIH-tur), pill (pihl)
o	cotton (KO-tuhn), hot (hot)
oh	below (bee-LOH), coat (koht), note (noht), wholesome (HOHL-suhm)
oo	good (good), look (look)
ow	couch (kowch), how (how)
oy	boy (boy), coin (koyn)
uh	about (uh-BOWT), butter (BUH-tuhr), enough (ee-NUHF), other (UH-thur)

Consonant Sounds

Symbol	*Spelled (Pronounced)*
ch	beach (beech), chimp (chihmp)
g	beg (behg), disguise (dihs-GIZ), get (geht)
j	digit (DIH-juht), edge (ehj), jet (jeht)
k	cat (kat), kitten (KIH-tuhn), hex (hehks)
s	cellar (SEHL-ur), save (sayv), scent (sehnt)
sh	champagne (sham-PAYN), issue (IH-shew), shop (shop)
ur	birth (burth), disturb (dihs-TURB), earth (urth), letter (LEH-tur)
y	useful (YEWS-fuhl), young (yuhng)
z	business (BIHZ-nehs), zest (zehst)
zh	vision (VIH-zhuhn)

AMERICAN
HEROES

HANK AARON

> *My motto was always to keep swinging. Whether I was in a slump or feeling badly or having trouble off the field, the only thing to do was keep swinging.*

Baseball player

Aaron, a perennial star of Major League Baseball, set several all-time records. His most famous record was surpassing Babe Ruth's career home-run mark of 714. Aaron also was well known for his tenacity in the face of racism both on and off the field.

Born: February 5, 1934; Mobile, Alabama
Also known as: Henry Louis Aaron (full name); Henry Aaron; Hammerin' Hank; the Hammer
Area of achievement: Sports

EARLY LIFE

Hank Aaron (EHR-uhn) was born to a large and loving family during the middle of the Great Depression. With his laborer father continually battling unemployment, and the family victimized by the odious Jim Crow laws of the time, the Aarons were facing challenging circumstances. Aaron grew up in the economically depressed area called Down the Bay, but, despite his introverted demeanor, he had many friends and enjoyed the company of his siblings. He was very athletic and enjoyed playing several sports, but he particularly excelled at football and baseball. The shy but fun-loving Aaron played baseball at two high schools, winning championships and gaining the interest of professional scouts. Even at this early age, Aaron showed a real talent for hitting hard line drives to all parts of the ballpark. With keen vision, strong wrists, and a beautiful swing, he was clearly an outstanding batter, but he also excelled at base running and had a strong and accurate throwing arm. Aaron was such an outstanding player that he usually competed against players several years older. His mother worried about the potentially harmful influences Aaron was encountering and tried vainly to keep him near home, but she was fighting a losing battle.

Aaron's adult career began with the local semiprofessional team, the Pritchett Athletics. Mobile, Alabama, had much baseball talent at the time and, in addition to Aaron, had produced or would produce major-league Hall of Fame players Satchel Paige, Willie McCovey, and Billy Williams. Aaron's next team was the Mobile Black Bears, but he clearly outclassed that level of competition quickly. Playing for the Bears was not a high-paying proposition, but it did lead him to meeting an agent who managed to land the young slugger a contract with a well-known and prestigious Negro League team, the Indianapolis Clowns.

After leading the Clowns to victory in the 1952 Negro League World Series, Aaron secured a tryout with one of the most successful and revered teams in Major League Baseball, the Brooklyn Dodgers. Incredibly, the Dodgers, who had brought integration to the major leagues in 1947 with Jackie Robinson and who now employed several

Hank Aaron.
(AP/Wide World Photos)

outstanding African American players, chose not to offer Aaron a contract. At this point, his meteoric rise in baseball appeared stalled, perhaps hopelessly so.

LIFE'S WORK

By 1952, only six of the eighteen major-league teams had African American players, and the Dodgers, the team with the strongest record in that area, had just rejected Aaron. Other teams, however, were interested, and he signed with another National League team, the Boston Braves. The team paid $10,000 for Aaron's contract, a fortune in the eyes of the young Alabaman, and he began preparing for his minor-league career. The Braves were about to abandon Boston, a city that for decades had been more enamored with the Braves' hometown rival, the Red Sox. By 1953, the team would be in Milwaukee.

Aaron spent the rest of the 1952 season playing for the Braves' farm, or minor-league, team in Eau Claire, Wisconsin, where he again outperformed his teammates and the competition and won an award for the best rookie in the league. At Eau Claire he encountered few examples of overt racism, but there were only three African Americans on the roster, and Eau Claire was a nearly all-white city. At Jacksonville, Florida, in 1953, the situation was substantially worse. This was the infamous Southern League, which had maintained the prohibition of black players long after the major leagues had integrated. African American players were refused at hotels and restaurants that welcomed their white teammates, and the crowd routinely hurled vile and hateful names at the black players from the stands. Nevertheless, Aaron had another outstanding season, and by 1954, the Milwaukee Braves could no longer deny him a space on its big-league team.

After Braves left fielder Bobby Thomson broke his ankle in a game, Aaron's place on the team was secured. Aaron's first major-league game was April 13, 1954, and the debut was inauspicious at best. Battling against Joe Nuxhall, the left-hander of the Cincinnati Reds, Aaron went without a hit in five at bats. The rookie remained confident and two days later achieved his first hit in the majors, a single against the St. Louis Cardinals and pitcher Vic Raschi. Later that month, Aaron connected for the first of his 755 career home runs, also against Raschi. Over the course of the 1954 season, he batted a very respectable .280 with 13 home runs before also suffering a broken ankle, which ended his year prematurely.

In the team's clubhouse, Aaron's reception was somewhat less than welcoming. Rookies usually were treated with an indifference bordering on hostility, but Aaron's treatment included comments made to him personally and to the press. Statements made by some of his veteran teammates showed they believed him to be lazy and not very bright. His manager, Charlie Grimm, was quoted as calling him "Stepanfetchit," and first baseman Joe Adcock questioned his work ethic. Aaron moved with a languid but athletic grace that seemed effortless to less-gifted players. Even at the major-league level, his graceful movement was interpreted as dilatory loping.

Nevertheless, through the 1950's and into the 1960's, Milwaukee embraced its slugging outfielder. Year after year, Aaron excelled. He led the league four times in home runs and twice in batting average. He won the award for National League Most Valuable Player in 1957. Aaron twice led the Braves to the World Series, helping them defeat the Yankees in 1957 (they lost to them the following year). In 1959, the Braves and Dodgers ended the season in a tie, but the Dodgers won the play-off series.

In 1966, after years of falling attendance, the Braves left Milwaukee for Atlanta, but Aaron's slugging continued. Babe Ruth's long-held career home-run mark of 714, which had stood since 1935, seemed in range for Aaron. After hitting 47 home runs in 1971, 34 in 1972, and 40 in 1973, Aaron trailed Ruth's mark by only one home run entering the 1974 season. The pressure of the pursuit wore Aaron down physically and emotionally, and he received a barrage of hate mail and death threats. The Braves opened the season in Cincinnati on April 4, and with his first swing of the year Aaron hit a three-run home run, tying Ruth's mark. By the time the Braves played their first home game against the Dodgers on April 8, the hype and media attention were overwhelming, yet Aaron connected for a home run off left-hander Al Downing. Finally, Aaron received the honors and recognition he had deserved for so long.

SIGNIFICANCE

Aaron played through 1976, spending his last two years in baseball as a player with the Milwaukee Brewers of the American League. He finished his career with 755 home runs, an elusive mark not matched until August 7, 2007, by Barry Bonds of the San Francisco Giants.

Both as a player and in retirement, Aaron never hesitated to speak out against any form of injustice. Through most of his career, he toiled in the shadows of flashier contemporaries such as Willie Mays and Mickey Mantle, but in the end his achievements outdistanced both of them. As great as that career was, however, it was dwarfed by his admirable personal traits such as concern for others, honesty, and diligence.

—Thomas W. Buchanan

Further Reading

Aaron, Hank, and Lonnie Wheeler. *I Had a Hammer: The Hank Aaron Story.* New York: HarperCollins, 1991. This illustrated autobiographical work excels particularly in covering Aaron's early years and provides a forum for his personal opinions.

Gutman, Bill. *It's Outta Here!* Lanham, Md.: Taylor Trade, 2005. This book consists of chapters dealing with various sluggers and home-run chases. The section on Aaron is clear, succinct, and interesting.

Tolan, Sandy. *Me and Hank: A Boy and His Hero, Twenty-Five Years Later.* New York: Free Press, 2000. This source offers a perspective from a longtime Aaron fan and admirer and relates well the impact Aaron's career had on fans of baseball.

Ralph Abernathy

" I don't know what the future may hold, but I know who holds the future. "

Civil rights leader

Abernathy, one of the greatest African American civil rights leaders of the twentieth century, led the Montgomery bus boycott with Martin Luther King, Jr., helped found the Southern Christian Leadership Conference (SCLC), and organized the Poor People's Campaign after King's assassination.

Born: March 11, 1926; near Linden, Marengo County, Alabama
Died: April 17, 1990; Atlanta, Georgia
Also known as: Ralph David Abernathy (full name)
Areas of achievement: Civil rights; religion and theology; social reform; oratory

Early Life

Ralph Abernathy (AB-ur-na-thee) was the son of William L. Abernathy and Louivery (Bell) Abernathy. He was one of twelve children in the Abernathy family and the grandson of a slave. Abernathy's early years were spent on the family farm, where he learned hard work and dedication from his father. William was an influential figure in his son's life. As the leader in the rural community of Linden, William served on the school board and was the first African American to serve on a jury in the county, according to later interviews given by his son. Abernathy recalled that his father was a tall, handsome man. Abernathy himself grew into a stocky man of five feet eight inches, weighing about 185 pounds.

Abernathy served overseas in the U.S. Army during World War II. This experience provided him with firsthand knowledge of segregation, since black soldiers were routinely treated as second-class citizens. However, his time in the Army also gave him access to the G.I. Bill. Through the money provided for education by the government, Abernathy was able to earn a bachelor of science degree in mathematics from Alabama

Ralph Abernathy.
(Library of Congress)

State College in 1950. He had already achieved his first goal in 1948 when he was ordained a Baptist minister. By 1951 Abernathy had completed a master's degree in sociology from Atlanta University. In the same year, he became the pastor of the First Baptist Church in Montgomery, Alabama.

While he was a graduate student in Atlanta, Georgia, Abernathy made the acquaintance of Martin Luther King, Jr., at a service at Ebenezer Baptist Church, where King's father served as pastor. The friendship grew when King was appointed pastor of the Dexter Avenue Church in Montgomery in 1954. The bond between King and Abernathy remained strong for the remainder of King's life.

Life's Work
Abernathy first rose to prominence for his role in the 1955-1956 Montgomery, Alabama, bus boycott. At the time, all buses in Montgomery had segregated seating: All African Americans were expected to sit at the rear of the bus. Whites and blacks were forbidden by law to sit next to each other or in the same parallel row. In addition, if there were no seats when a white person got on the bus, African Americans had to give up their seats for the white person.

Abernathy, Ralph

On December 1, 1955, Rosa Parks, a seamstress, was on her way home from work. She was tired, and her shoulders and neck hurt from working all day. When a white man got on the full bus, she refused to give up her seat. She was immediately arrested. The arrest mobilized the Montgomery African American leaders. Abernathy, a young but widely known minister, joined forces with the leaders the day after Parks's arrest. He immediately began planning a bus boycott as a nonviolent way of protesting the arrest. The reasoning behind the boycott was clear: The Montgomery bus company depended on its riders for income, and the vast majority of riders were African American. Therefore, if African Americans refused to ride the buses, they would hurt the company that enforced the laws of segregation.

At the same time, Abernathy suggested to fellow strategist Edward Nixon that King be included in their group. King's Dexter Avenue Baptist Church served as the headquarters and meeting place for the organizers. Abernathy, King, and Nixon, with other African American leaders, formed a group called the Montgomery Improvement Association to oversee the boycott. Plans for the boycott were finalized, and the protest was scheduled to begin on Monday, December 5, 1955, the day of Parks's trial. The organizers had hoped that most African Americans would not ride the buses, but they could not have predicted that the buses would remain 90 percent empty throughout the day.

What started as a one-day protest grew into a yearlong struggle. Abernathy and King emphasized the nonviolent nature of the protests. For one year, black citizens shared rides, walked to work, and found alternative means of transportation, shunning the city's nearly empty buses. During this time, black drivers and pedestrians were constantly harassed by police for real or imagined infractions; King himself went to jail when charged with driving thirty miles per hour in a twenty-five-mile-per-hour zone. Further, many African American leaders were arrested under an old antiboycott law. However, King was the only one who was brought to trial.

On November 13, 1956, at King's trial, word came from Washington, D.C., that the U.S. Supreme Court had decided that Alabama's bus segregation laws were unconstitutional. Finally, on December 21, 1956, more than one year after Parks's arrest, Abernathy and King rode on the first integrated bus in Montgomery.

In January, 1957, Abernathy, King, and African American leaders from other southern states met at Ebenezer Baptist Church in Atlanta to form a group that would coordinate existing protest groups and spread bus actions throughout the South. Known initially as the Southern Negro Leaders Conference on Transportation, this group soon took the name Southern Christian Leadership Conference (SCLC) and became one of the most important civil rights organizations in the country.

The Supreme Court's decision and the formation of the SCLC, however, led to violence in Montgomery. Abernathy's home and church, along with King's home and four additional homes, were bombed. The violence did not deter Abernathy and King from pursuing their goal of nonviolent protest. They organized sit-ins, marches, and voter-registration drives in cities such Selma and Birmingham, Alabama; St. Augustine, Florida; and Albany, Georgia, in their quest to desegregate the South. They were thrown in jail at least seventeen different times. Abernathy eventually gave up his church in Montgomery so that he could move to Atlanta to be closer to the SCLC headquarters. His ties to King became increasingly tight, and most acknowledge that Abernathy was King's closest friend and adviser. In 1965 Abernathy became the vice president of the SCLC at King's request.

In 1967 Abernathy and King turned their attention to the economic condition of most African Americans. In spite of great gains in legal rights, a disproportionate number of African Americans still lived in poverty. Even worse, as industry turned increasingly toward automation, many workers were being put out of their jobs. In response, King and Abernathy began planning the Poor People's Campaign, which they envisioned as a large-scale demonstration to be held in Washington, D.C. Although the campaign was scheduled to begin in March, 1968, King instead went to Memphis, Tennessee, in support of garbagemen on strike for higher wages. While there, he was assassinated on April 4, 1968, just outside the motel room he and Abernathy shared.

Abernathy became the new president of the SCLC on April 5, 1968, a role he fulfilled until 1977. As leader of the SCLC, he continued King's plans for the Poor People's Campaign and a march on Washington. King's death spurred many to volunteer for the march. Beginning in May, 1968, hundreds of protesters arrived in Washington and built a town of huts and shacks on federal land near the Lincoln Memorial. Dubbed Resurrection City, the shantytown finally housed about twenty-five hundred people. During the weeks of the campaign, Abernathy met with legislators and detailed the protesters' demands. On June 19, a large rally was held in support of legislation to end poverty. Some estimates put the total crowd at fifty thousand people. On June 24, 1968, when their permit expired, the demonstrators were forcibly evicted by the National Guard. Abernathy resisted the eviction and was put in jail.

Abernathy continued to lead the SCLC until 1977, when he resigned under pressure from other leaders. He decided to run for Congress but was unsuccessful in his bid. During the following years, he worked on his autobiography, *And the Walls Came Tumbling Down*, published in 1989. While the book offered readers an inside look at the Civil Rights movement, many were puzzled by Abernathy's allegations that King had engaged in extramarital affairs. The charges cast a pall over the book and Abernathy's last years. After a long career as a minister and fighter for civil rights, Abernathy died in Atlanta on April 17, 1990.

SIGNIFICANCE

Abernathy was at the heart of the Civil Rights movement, which lasted from 1954 to 1968. He was instrumental in assembling the talent needed for leadership in the Montgomery bus boycott and may have been partially responsible for bringing his friend, Martin Luther King, Jr., into the struggle. Perhaps Abernathy's greatest contribution to the movement was the counsel, advice, and friendship he gave King during the years when they led the SCLC together.

By all accounts, Abernathy did not have the poise or charisma that King had, and he remained overshadowed by King throughout his life. Even after King's death, he was subjected to comparisons with the fallen leader. Nevertheless, Abernathy's role at a crucial time in race relations in the United States was an important one, for even from the shadows, he worked to effect permanent change.

—*Diane Andrews Henningfeld*

Abernathy, Ralph

FURTHER READING

Abernathy, Donzaleigh. *Partners to History: Martin Luther King, Jr., Ralph David Abernathy, and the Civil Rights Movement.* New York: Crown, 2003. Abernathy's youngest daughter recounts how her father and King worked together in the Civil Rights movement, chronicling the Montgomery bus boycott, March on Washington, and other movement activities.

Abernathy, Ralph David. *And the Walls Came Tumbling Down.* New York: Harper & Row, 1989. Abernathy's autobiography is an important book that offers readers insight into Abernathy's understanding of his own position within the King circle. Unfortunately, Abernathy's decision to include material concerning King's alleged extramarital affairs overshadowed the rest of the book for most reviewers.

Garrow, David J. *Bearing the Cross: Martin Luther King, Jr., and the Southern Christian Leadership Conference.* New York: William Morrow, 1986. In this exhaustively researched 1987 Pulitzer Prize-winning autobiography, Garrow provides the benchmark biography of King. At the same time, he provides a close look at the founding and growth of the Southern Christian Leadership Conference, an important topic for any Abernathy student.

Kasher, Steven. *The Civil Rights Movement: A Photographic History, 1954-68.* New York: Abbeville, 1996. As the title suggests, this book is filled with stunning photographs of the Civil Rights movement. However, the book is also rich with well-documented text and a selected bibliography that will be invaluable to any student of the movement or Abernathy's life.

Murray, Paul T. *The Civil Rights Movement: References and Resources.* New York: G. K. Hall, 1993. An extremely useful book for any student who wants to know more about the movement and Abernathy. Contains bibliographic information for further study.

Robinson, Jo Ann Gibson. *The Montgomery Bus Boycott and the Women Who Started It.* Knoxville: University of Tennessee Press, 1987. The memoir of the founder of the Women's Political Council, one of the leading civil rights organizations in Montgomery at the time of the boycott.

Williams, Juan. *Eyes on the Prize: America's Civil Rights Years, 1954-1965.* New York: Viking, 1987. Journalist Juan Williams offers a highly readable account of the Civil Rights movement. The book ends before the death of King and the ascendancy of Abernathy to the head of the SCLC.

Young, Andrew. *An Easy Burden: The Civil Rights Movement and the Transformation of America.* New York: HarperCollins, 1996. Young, a close associate of King and Abernathy and an early leader of the SCLC, provides another insight into the Civil Rights movement and its leaders.

ABIGAIL ADAMS

❝ *If we mean to have heroes, statesmen and philosophers, we should have learned women.* **❞**

Educator, writer, and feminist

An early proponent of humane treatment and equal education for women, Abigail Adams wrote eloquent, insightful letters that provide a detailed social history of her era and her life with John Adams.

Born: November 22, 1744; Weymouth, Massachusetts
Died: October 28, 1818; Quincy, Massachusetts
Also known as: Abigail Smith (birth name)
Areas of achievement: Education; women's rights; social reform; literature

EARLY LIFE

Abigail Adams (AD-amz), born Abigail Smith, was one of four children of William Smith, minister of North Parish Congregational Church of Weymouth, and Elizabeth (Quincy) Smith from nearby Braintree, Massachusetts. Both parents were members of prominent New England families of merchants, statesmen, and ministers. From her parents, Abigail learned a conservative, rational Puritanism. She retained throughout her life a solid Christian faith and shared with her Puritan forebears a belief in the fundamental depravity of humankind. These religious convictions influenced her political opinions.

Observing her mother's example, Abigail learned her future roles as wife and mother, duties instilled in girls from an early age during this time in American history. As a minister's wife, Elizabeth Smith provided relief for the town's poor, nursed the town's sick, and presented herself as a model wife. She was nurturing and kind to her children.

In eighteenth century Massachusetts, education was prized. In government-supported schools, boys studied Latin, Greek, French, mathematics, and literary arts in preparation for higher education either at Harvard College or abroad. Girls, however, were educated almost exclusively at home, receiving only rudimentary training in reading and writing; some remained illiterate. They learned domestic skills such as sewing, fine needlework, and cooking, which were considered vital preparation for marriage. Abigail received only informal home instruction yet shared with her sisters the advantage of a keen intellect and unlimited access to her father's extensive library.

In her early adolescence, Abigail was encouraged in her studies by a young watchmaker and scholar, Richard Cranch. Although self-educated, Cranch conveyed his passion for scholarship to Abigail and to her sisters Mary and Elizabeth. It was through Cranch, who wedded Mary, that Abigail met her future husband.

Abigail proved a shrewd judge of character when at the age of nineteen she married Harvard-educated lawyer John Adams. Although they were not social equals—he was from a markedly less prominent family and practiced a profession that was poorly regarded—the match proved exceedingly profitable and satisfying for both parties. In

John, Abigail found a man who appreciated and even encouraged her forthrightness and her intellectual ability, while John in turn received emotional, financial, and intellectual support from Abigail.

LIFE'S WORK

Abigail Adams is best known for her remarkably detailed, eloquent letters. Although many creative outlets were considered unsuitable for women to pursue, letter writing was a socially sanctioned literary art for women in the eighteenth century. Abigail, who felt compelled to write, naturally selected that medium.

During her first ten years of marriage, however, Abigail's letter writing was not prolific, as she was kept extraordinarily busy with domestic affairs. Enduring five pregnancies in seven years, she also suffered the death of an infant daughter. In addition, she was plagued by several physical afflictions including frequent colds, rheumatism that caused acute swelling of her joints, and insomnia.

During these early years, she moved her household several times to remain with John in his work. The turmoil of their lives as they uprooted their family paralleled the contemporary political events in which John played a leading role. This was a pattern they would repeat throughout his working life and would include residences in Boston, Philadelphia, New York, Paris, and London. Abigail demonstrated repeatedly that

Abigail Adams.
(Library of Congress)

she was extraordinarily adaptable and found pleasure in observing foreign customs. She always, however, longed for the idealized pastoral life in Braintree that she had shared with John during their first few years of marriage.

In 1775, John embarked for Congress on the first of frequent extended absences from Abigail. With her husband away, Abigail weathered several personal tragedies, including a difficult pregnancy in 1777, during which she apparently suffered from toxemia and finally eclampsia, a condition that is usually fatal to the infant and often to the mother. A remarkable series of letters were written between John and Abigail during this period; in them, Abigail expressed loneliness and fear for her unborn child. The child, a girl, was indeed stillborn. John and Abigail's letters provide invaluable information on the social history of parent-and-child relationships.

The pattern of intimate and frequent letters continued over the next twenty-five years as John, an extraordinarily ambitious man, accepted political positions that removed him from home for periods often extending to years. While Abigail considered their separation as a patriotic sacrifice, she nevertheless frequently expressed her loneliness to John, imploring him to return home.

Because she was a married woman, Abigail was legally prevented from owning property in her own name. Notwithstanding, she repeatedly demonstrated her ingenuity and self-sufficiency. During their first ten years together, John's legal fees and the income from their farm supported the family. As events took him farther from home, his legal practice was largely abandoned and Abigail assumed most financial duties. She never welcomed the addition to her already burdensome domestic responsibilities, yet she consistently proved herself a competent manager. Abigail deplored debt and worked to ensure that her family avoided it. She successfully ran the farm for four years during which she was responsible for the odious chore of collecting rents from several tenants as well as supervising agricultural production. Scarcity of labor and acute inflation made the task a difficult one. After four years, she lessened her burden by renting the farm.

In 1778, Abigail began requesting luxury goods from John, who was then serving as a diplomat in France. She then profitably sold these items, which, because of war shortages and inflation, were scarce in Massachusetts. At the same time, Abigail also purchased land and speculated in currency. Through these endeavors, she kept her family solvent.

During the ten years in which she saw her husband only sporadically, Abigail expanded her literary interests, exploring, partly through John's guidance, political theory, biography, and history. She also wrote voluminously, to John, to other family members, and to friends. It was during this period that Abigail wrote to John of her political views regarding women's roles in the new nation. Her famous letter of March 31, 1776, in which she requested John to "Remember the Ladies," has established Abigail's reputation as an early proponent of women's rights. In context, however, it is clear that Abigail wrote not of political rights per se but of women's legal rights, specifically those that guaranteed them protection from physical abuse. At the time, divorce, although allowed in a few extreme instances, was generally unavailable. In addition, women abrogated all rights to property ownership upon marriage, which in turn made them ineligible to vote because property ownership was a key qualification for voting.

Abigail also advocated equal education for women. She argued for equal education within the context of her perception of women's traditional domestic roles. The concept of "Republican motherhood" held that, because women taught the sons who were destined to become leaders, women had an important role in maintaining the existence of an informed citizenry capable of supporting a republican government. To teach their sons successfully, these women required an education equal to that of boys and men, which Abigail hoped would be supported by law.

Although she is now considered an early advocate of women's rights, Abigail saw her own life as highly traditional. An adept manager of her family's resources, she nevertheless viewed her role as currency speculator, land purchaser, and farmer as aberrant and a patriotic sacrifice. She was comfortable only, it seems, in her domestic role, and in that, as in all else, she excelled. Abigail lived to see her son John Quincy establish a successful diplomatic and political career. Several personal tragedies marred her happiness, including the death of her son Charles from alcoholism when he was thirty years old and her daughter Nabby's brutally painful mastectomy and subsequent death from breast cancer.

Until 1800, when John retired from government office, Abigail functioned at times as host during his several years as a diplomat, first in England, then in France. She also served two terms as the vice president's wife during the George Washington administration and finally as First Lady during her husband's presidency from 1797 to 1801.

During the last eighteen years of her life, she retired with her husband to Quincy (formerly Braintree) and lived in relative domestic peace surrounded by children, grandchildren, sisters, nieces, and nephews. At the family's Quincy farm, Abigail pursued her lifelong hobby of gardening. Dying of typhoid fever in 1818, she was mourned by John, who, lamenting the loss of his "dearest friend," survived his wife by eight years.

Significance

Abigail Adams always functioned within the prescribed social roles for women of her time. She was an affectionate, protective mother who cared for her children physically and emotionally her entire life. She provided intellectual and emotional companionship as well as financial support for her brilliant but irascible husband John Adams. Although Abigail for a time functioned as merchant, farmer, and speculator, she viewed these roles as a patriotic sacrifice to support the political career of her husband.

While her own marriage provided her intellectual and emotional satisfaction, she condemned the tyranny of men over women and longed for legal protection for women. Women's education she hoped would one day rival that of men. She also yearned for the day when women would be able to limit the number of children they had. Nevertheless, her life must be viewed within the context of her eighteenth century world, where she functioned primarily within the domestic sphere. She was not a public advocate for women's rights; the term "women's rights" was not even used in her time. Yet, she did not view her role within her marriage as less valuable than that of her husband. To Abigail and to John, marriage was a true partnership.

She was a supremely shrewd, able woman who took every advantage available to her to expand her intellectual horizons, and she enjoyed a wide correspondence through her letters. In addition to providing an idea of this remarkable woman's psyche, Abigail Adams's copious letters give a detailed social history of her era and details into the character of her husband and of several other political leaders, including her close friend Thomas Jefferson.

—*Mary E. Virginia*

FURTHER READING

Adams, Abigail. *The Book of Abigail and John: Selected Letters of the Adams Family, 1762-1784*. Edited by L. H. Butterfield, Marc Friedlaender, and Mary-Jo Kline. Boston: Northeastern University Press, 2002. This revised text includes a foreword by David McCullogh, author of a best-selling biography of John Adams. Abigail's letters are her literary achievement—eloquent, informative, and illuminating.

Akers, Charles W. *Abigail Adams: An American Woman*. Boston: Little, Brown, 1980. Written specifically for the college undergraduate and high school student, Akers's work is admirably detailed and readable. Abigail's life is well grounded in historical context.

Gelles, Edith B. *Portia: The World of Abigail Adams*. Bloomington: Indiana University Press, 1992. An insightful biography of Adams, viewing her not only as John's wife and John Quincy's mother but also within the context of her domestic and predominantly female world. This work requires a knowledge of fundamental historical events, so it should be read in conjunction with a broader history, such as that of Akers. Includes an instructive introductory chapter, footnotes, a bibliography, and a chronology.

Levin, Phyllis Lee. *Abigail Adams: A Biography*. New York: St. Martin's Press, 1987. By far the most detailed biography of Adams, making extensive use of research sources. Unlike other biographers, Levin provides ample discussion of Abigail's life during the years after John Adams's retirement, although Levin does so against the backdrop of John Quincy's career. Similarly, Abigail's earlier life is viewed against John's career. Just shy of five hundred pages, the work contains footnotes, a bibliography, and a family tree.

Nagel, Paul C. *The Adams Women: Abigail and Louisa Adams, Their Sisters, and Daughters*. New York: Oxford University Press, 1987. While not exclusively about Abigail, Nagel's work is useful for placing Abigail's life within the context of her close female relations, including her sisters Mary and Elizabeth. Despite his admiration of her intellect, Nagel provides a portrait of Adams that is largely unsympathetic, making her appear domineering.

Withey, Lynne. *Dearest Friend: A Life of Abigail Adams*. New York: Simon & Schuster, 2001. Withey judges Adams by twentieth century standards rather than understanding her within her historical context. The author focuses extensively on Abigail's political views while paying scant attention to her more notable successes in her domestic roles, viewing Abigail as a "prisoner" in her world.

JOHN ADAMS

> *Democracy . . . while it lasts is more bloody than either aristocracy or monarchy. Remember, democracy never lasts long. It soon wastes, exhausts, and murders itself. There is never a democracy that did not commit suicide.*

President of the United States (1797-1801)

As a member of the Continental Congress, Adams helped bring the American colonies to the point of independence in 1776. As one of the new nation's first diplomats, he helped negotiate the treaty that ended the American War of Independence.

Born: October 30, 1735; Braintree (now Quincy), Massachusetts
Died: July 4, 1826; Quincy, Massachusetts
Areas of achievement: Government and politics; diplomacy

EARLY LIFE

John Adams (AD-amz) was born in Braintree, Massachusetts, where his family had lived for nearly a century. His father was a farmer and a town constable who expected his eldest son, John, to become a Congregational minister. The young Adams attended the Free Latin School in Braintree and then enrolled at Harvard College in 1751. On graduation in 1755, he taught school for a while at Worcester before deciding to abandon the ministry to take up law instead. In 1758, the intelligent, studious Adams returned to Braintree to practice law in what was still a country town only ten miles from Boston.

Six years later, he married Abigail Smith of Quincy, Massachusetts, a woman who matched him in intelligence and ambition and perhaps exceeded him in practicality. Short and already stocky (colleagues later called him rotund), Adams seemed to be settling into the life of a successful country courthouse lawyer who might, in time, aspire to a seat in the legislature when, in 1765, English parliament altered American colonial politics forever by passing the Stamp Act. The ensuing Stamp Act crisis offered to the ambitious Adams a quick route to popularity, influence, and public office. He did not miss his chance.

LIFE'S WORK

In 1765, John Adams denounced the stamp tax in resolutions written for the Braintree town meeting. When they were reprinted around the colony, his reputation as an opponent of English arrogance began to grow. Those in Boston who led the opposition to English taxes (including John Adams's distant relative, Samuel Adams) began to bring him more actively into their campaigns. He moved to Boston and won a seat in the Massachusetts General Court. He became, in effect, the local antigovernment party's lawyer, writing some of its more important public papers for the Boston town meeting and defending its members in court against charges brought by the Crown.

When Parliament answered the 1773 Boston Tea Party with the Coercive (or Intolerable) Acts in 1774, the general court chose Adams as a delegate to the intercolonial congress scheduled to meet in Philadelphia that fall, to discuss what the colonies should do. He wrote a "Declaration of Rights," adopted by the First Continental Congress, which based colonial rights to self-government not only on their charters and on the inherent rights of Englishmen but also on "the immutable laws of nature." Those were the grounds on which many colonists would soon challenge not merely England's right to tax them, but England's right to govern them at all. In good part, those were the grounds that underlay the Declaration of Independence.

Before the congress met again, war began at Lexington in April, 1775. When Adams arrived at the Second Continental Congress in the spring of 1775, he already believed that the only true constitutional connection between the colonies and England was through the king—a position he set out in newspaper essays signed "Novanglus." He had not yet, however, openly called for a severing of all ties to the mother country. He had seen the colonists' rage run out of bounds in the Stamp Act riots of 1765. He had been disturbed and angered by the joy with which some colonists greeted the closing of civil and criminal courts in Massachusetts when English authority collapsed in the colony. He was worried that a revolution might get out of hand and establish not liberty, but mob rule. Although such worries stayed very much in his mind, by the time the Second Continental Congress met, Adams realized that there were no practical alternatives left but armed resistance or submission to the Parliament. At the Congress, therefore, he worked both openly and by guile to bring reluctant and sometimes timid delegates to accept the inevitability of independence. When the Congress finally agreed to act, after more than one year of war, it was Adams who wrestled Thomas Jefferson's declaration through to adoption on July 4, 1776.

Adams had applauded Thomas Paine's *Common Sense* when it appeared in January, 1776, but he disliked the very democratic plan of government advocated by Paine. The kind of government Adams favored can be seen most clearly in the plan he drew up for Massachusetts's revolutionary constitution. Adams thought the purpose of the American Revolution was to preserve old liberties, not to establish new ones, and that the new Constitution ought to conserve as much of England's admirable constitutional heritage as possible. The constitution he drafted included relatively high property qualifications for voting and holding office (to ensure stability); it left the structure of Massachusetts's government much as it had been before independence, except for replacing English officials with elected American ones.

For more than a year after independence, Adams served on a variety of committees in Congress and in Massachusetts, doing work that was as exhausting as it was important. In October, 1777, he withdrew from Congress and returned to Massachusetts, but in November, Congress named him one of its emissaries to France, charged with raising loans for the republic across Europe and with negotiating treaties of friendship, trade, and alliance, especially with the French nation.

That alliance was concluded before Adams arrived at Paris, but he stayed on and was immediately caught up in the roiling jealousies that were endemic at the American mission there. Adams especially disliked and distrusted Benjamin Franklin, whose demeanor, integrity, honesty, and morals he judged inferior to his own. Adams returned to Massachusetts in August, 1779, but by December he was back in France to help ne-

Adams, John

gotiate a peace treaty with England. He feuded with Franklin almost constantly over which of them was responsible for what in conducting the republic's diplomacy, but ultimately all three peace commissioners (Adams, Franklin, and John Jay) agreed to negotiate a separate treaty between the United States and England, a treaty that did not directly involve France.

Though Franklin was responsible for the broad outlines of the agreement, Adams worked out some crucial compromises, without which the treaty may well have failed. Adams persuaded the English, for example, to concede to American fishing rights off the Newfoundland and Nova Scotia coasts in return for the new nation agreeing to open its courts to Loyalists. Adams stayed on for a year in France after the war ended in 1783, and then moved to London as the United States' first minister to the Court of St. James in 1785. He spent three years there, trying with little success to iron out problems between the United States and England (mostly involving noncompliance with the peace treaty).

While in London, he wrote the three-volume *A Defense of the Constitutions of the United States of America* (1787-1788), in which he explained his conservative and primarily English approach to the proper constitution of civil governments. The work was frank in its praise of the basic principles of the English constitution and earnest in its cautions about the risks of letting government rely too heavily on popular majorities to determine policy and law. Indeed, some Americans began to consider Adams soft on aristocracy and even monarchy. The first volume of *A Defense of the Constitutions of the United States of America* appeared in time to influence the thinking of delegates at the Constitutional Convention.

Adams returned home in 1788, and he was chosen as George Washington's vice president under the new Constitution of 1787. He did not like the job. "My country," he wrote to his wife, "has in its wisdom contrived for me the most insignificant office that ever the invention of man contrived or his imagination conceived." For the next eight years, nevertheless, he served Washington loyally, presiding over the Senate and breaking tie votes in favor of Federalist policies. His reward came in 1797, when, as Washington's chosen successor, Adams defeated Jefferson and became the second president of the United States.

Adams's presidency was at best only a partial success. He had hoped, as Washington had in 1789, to become president of a united people. By the time he took office, however, the people had already divided themselves into two rival political parties: the Federalists (ostensibly led by Adams) and the National (or Jeffersonian) Republicans, led by Adams's vice president and old friend, Thomas Jefferson.

Furthermore, world affairs all but guaranteed that his presidency would be troubled. As Adams took office, for example, the United States was already dangerously close to war with France. The French, who had already fought their own revolution and created a republic of sorts, were at war with England and were angry that the United States had refused to aid France, a conflict called the XYZ affair. By 1797, the French were beginning to seize American ships on the high seas. When American peace commissioners, whom Adams had sent to France to try to work things out short of war, reported that the French had demanded bribes to begin serious negotiations, Americans reacted angrily. Adams asked Congress to prepare for a war that seemed inevitable, but, at the same time, he refused to abandon his efforts to avoid it if possible. For the remainder of his presidency, Adams stuck to the same policy—prepare for war but work for peace—until (just as he left office) it yielded a new treaty of amity between the United States and France.

In the meanwhile, the Federalist Party, influenced by Alexander Hamilton more than by Adams, forced through Congress very high (and very unpopular) taxes to pay for the war they confidently expected to begin at any moment. Moreover, Federalist congressmen passed, and Adams signed, the unpopular Alien and Sedition Acts in 1798. The first act raised to fourteen the number of years an immigrant had to live in the country before becoming a citizen and was evidently designed to prevent recent Irish immigrants from voting against Federalists, whom they rightly believed to be pro-English. The second, the Sedition Act, made the publication of virtually all criticism of federal officials a crime. Both laws lost whatever legitimacy they may have had in the eyes of the public when the supposedly imminent war, which might have justified them as national defense measures, failed to come.

Federalist judges and prosecutors enforced the laws anyway, jailing, for example, several prominent Republican newspaper editors for violating the Sedition Act by criticizing Adams (though no Federalist editor ever went to jail for vilifying Jefferson). The partisan application of the law left Adams and the Federalists saddled with a reputation as opponents of free speech as the election of 1800 approached. Adams was further crippled by growing divisions in his own party (Hamilton actually campaigned against him) and by the slow pace at which his diplomacy worked. Most voters did not know, for example, until after they had voted, that Adams's policy had succeeded and that a lasting peace with France had been arranged.

In the election of 1800, Adams lost to Jefferson by eight electoral votes. Exhausted, bitterly disappointed, and tired as well of the constant bickering and criticism, public and private, of the last four years, Adams retired from public life on the day Jefferson was inaugurated. He returned to his home in Quincy to spend his time farming, reading, and writing an occasional essay on law or history. He died on July 4, 1826, a few hours after his great antagonist and greater friend, Jefferson, died in Virginia.

SIGNIFICANCE

Throughout his life, John Adams never got the praise he thought was his due. He was an important writer in the years preceding independence, but none of his writings had the broad impact of John Dickinson's *Letters from a Farmer in Pennsylvania, to the Inhabitants of the British Colonies* (1767-1768) or the great popular appeal of Thomas Paine's *Common Sense*. In the long run, however, through his writings on government and constitutions, Adams contributed as much or more to the development of republican constitutional thought than all but two or three of the founders.

His work in Europe negotiating the Treaty of Paris (1783) was at times brilliant, but it was the colorful and cunningly rustic Benjamin Franklin who caught the public's eye. Adams was president of the United States, but he immediately followed Washington in that office and inevitably Americans compared the two and found Adams the weaker president. Adams claimed that he did not seek the people's praises, but all of his life he watched men who were no more intelligent than he, no more dedicated to the

Adams, John

republic, and no more successful in serving it, win the kind of warm public applause that seemed beyond his grasp. He was respected but not revered, and he knew it.

Broadly speaking, Adams made three major contributions to the revolution and the new republic. First, he worked in Massachusetts and in Congress to keep the revolution from running amok and destroying what was good in the English political tradition. He demonstrated to skeptical Tories and doubtful rebels, by both his words and his work, that independence need not be an invitation to anarchy, despotism, or mob rule, and so he helped make independence an acceptable alternative to submission. Second, with Jay and Franklin, he protected American interests in the double-dealing diplomatic atmosphere of Paris and London during the war and won for the republic a treaty that secured its independence as well as the vast undeveloped territories and other economic resources it needed to survive and develop. Third, as president, he kept the new republic out of what would have been a bitter, divisive war fought under a new, untested Constitution; thanks to Adams's skillful foreign policy, the republic did not have to face its first war under the Constitution for another twelve years.

Yet Adams never completely accepted the more democratic implications of the revolution, and so, by the end of his career, he was both one of the most important of the republic's founders and one of the least appreciated.

—*Robert A. Becker*

FURTHER READING

Adams, Abigail. *The Book of Abigail and John: Selected Letters of the Adams Family, 1762-1784*. Edited by L. H. Butterfield, Marc Friedlaender, and Mary-Jo Kline. Boston: Northeastern University Press, 2002. This revised text includes a foreword by David McCullogh, author of a best-selling biography of John Adams. John and Abigail's letters illustrate their remarkable relationship and the private and public worlds in which they lived.

Adams, John. *The Portable John Adams*. Edited by John Patrick Diggins. New York: Penguin Books, 2004. A collection of Adams's writings, containing portions of his diary and autobiography, and some of his political works, including "A Dissertation on Canon and Feudal Law" and "Thoughts on Government."

Cappon, Lester J., ed. *The Adams-Jefferson Letters: The Complete Correspondence Between Thomas Jefferson and Abigail and John Adams*. 2 vols. Chapel Hill: University of North Carolina Press, 1959. Covers the years 1777 to 1826. Excellent in conveying the revolutionary and early national periods through Adams's eyes. The letters following 1812 are remarkable, with the two aging rebels reminiscing about the revolution and their presidencies and speculating about the nation's future.

Ferling, John E. *Adams vs. Jefferson: The Tumultuous Election of 1800*. New York: Oxford University Press, 2004. Ferling describes how this "contest of titans" marked a turning point in American history, with Adams's Federalists and Jefferson's Republicans battling over two different ideas of how the new nation should be governed.

Grant, James. *John Adams: Party of One*. New York: Farrar, Straus, and Giroux, 2005. A compact, well-written biography, examining Adams's early life and public career. Grant bases his biography on Adams's diaries, letters, and unfinished autobiography.

Jensen, Merrill. *The Founding of a Nation: A History of the American Revolution, 1763-1776*. New York: Oxford University Press, 1968. One of the best accounts of the origins and events of the revolution from the Grenville Program of 1763 to the Declaration of Independence. Narrative in form, scholarly, and nicely written.

McCullogh, David. *John Adams*. New York: Simon & Schuster, 2001. A highly praised, best-selling biography. Offers a clearly written, comprehensive, and balanced account of Adams's life, with detailed descriptions of events and prominent personalities of the time.

Morris, Richard B. *The Peacemakers: The Great Powers and American Independence*. New York: Harper & Row, 1965. Still the best account of the negotiations leading to peace in 1783. An extremely detailed work.

Shaw, Peter. *The Character of John Adams*. Chapel Hill: University of North Carolina Press, 1976. Examines Adams's ideas in the light of his (especially Puritan) background and his personal experiences at each stage of his life and career. Controversial but interesting and insightful.

Smith, Page. *John Adams*. 2 vols. Garden City, N.Y.: Doubleday, 1962. One of the most complete and detailed accounts of Adams's life. Especially helpful on particular incidents or periods of Adams's life.

SAMUEL ADAMS

> *Our contest is not only whether we ourselves shall be free, but whether there shall be left to mankind an asylum on earth for civil and religious liberty.*

Boston politician and Revolutionary War hero

A resident of the strategic city of Boston, which was the center of resistance to English colonial policies, Adams was one of the most significant organizers of the American Revolution.

Born: September 27, 1722; Boston, Massachusetts
Died: October 2, 1803; Boston, Massachusetts
Area of achievement: Government and politics

EARLY LIFE

The American ancestry of Samuel Adams (AD-amz) began with Henry Adams, who emigrated from Devonshire, England, to Quincy, Massachusetts, in the early seventeenth century. One branch of the family included John Adams, who became second president of the United States. Samuel Adams's grandfather was a sailor, Captain John Adams. His father, Samuel Adams, Sr., lived his entire life in Boston, operating a malt house, or brewery, and was an active member of the old South Church. He was also active in local politics, establishing the first of the Boston Caucus Clubs, which played a vital role in the early upheavals of the revolutionary period.

Samuel Adams.
(Library of Congress)

Samuel Adams, then, was born into an active and influential, civic-minded Boston family. He grew up familiar with and keenly interested in local politics and knew most Boston political leaders through their friendship with his father. Many of those leaders were prominent in Massachusetts colonial politics as well. Samuel absorbed the traditional independent-mindedness of Boston and thought of Massachusetts as autonomous and largely self-governing within the broader parameters of the British Empire.

Educated in the small wooden schoolhouse in the rear of King's Chapel, Samuel received a traditional grounding in Latin and Greek grammar, preparatory to entering Harvard College. When he received the A.B. degree in 1740 and the master of arts in 1743, his interest in politics was already clear. He titled his thesis, "Whether It Be Lawful to Resist the Supreme Magistrate, if the Commonwealth Cannot Otherwise Be Preserved."

Life's Work

Samuel Adams thus embarked upon his life's work in colonial politics, but he also had to make a living for his family. To that end, his father gave him £1,000 to help him get started in business. He promptly lent £500 to a friend (who never repaid the loan) and lost the other £500 through poor management. His father then took him into partnership in his malt house, from which the family made a modest living.

Adams lived an austere, simple life and throughout his life had little interest in making money. At a time of crisis just before the war, General Thomas Gage governed Massachusetts under martial law and offered Adams an annuity of £2,000 for life. Adams promptly rejected the offer; "a guinea never glistened in my eyes," he said. A man of integrity, he would not be bribed to refrain from doing what he believed to be right. His threadbare clothing was his trademark, reflecting his austerity and lack of interest in material things.

In 1748 his father died, leaving him one-third of his modest estate. Adams gradually sold most of it during the busy years of his life and was rescued from abject poverty in his retirement years only by a small inheritance from his son. During most of his life, his only income was a small salary as a clerk of the Massachusetts General Assembly.

Adams married Elizabeth Checkley, the daughter of the minister of New South Congregational Church, in 1749. She died eight years later, survived by only two of their five children, a boy and a girl. Adams reared the children and managed alone for seven years but remarried in 1764 to Elizabeth Wells. He was then forty-two years old, and she was twenty-four.

Adams was of average height and muscular build. He carried himself straight in spite of an involuntary palsied movement of his hands and had light blue eyes and a serious, dignified manner. He was very fond of sacred music and sang in the choir of New South Church. Personable, he maintained a close relationship with his neighbors and was constantly chatting with those he met along the street. He had a gift for smoothing over disputes among his friends and acquaintances and was often asked to mediate a disagreement. Adams was a hard worker, and through the years his candle burned late at night as he kept up his extensive correspondence, much of which does not survive today. His second cousin, John Adams, likened him to John Calvin, partly because of his deep piety but also because of his personality: He was "cool . . . polished, and refined," somewhat inflexible, but consistent, a man of "steadfast integrity, exquisite humanity, genteel erudition, obliging, engaging manners, real as well as professed piety, and a universal good character."

Samuel Adams was interested in political philosophy and believed strongly in liberty and Christian virtue and frugality. He helped organize discussion clubs and the *Public Advertiser*, a newspaper to promote understanding of political philosophy. He served in political offices large and small, as fire ward, as moderator, and as tax collector. An orthodox Christian, he warned of the political implications of the "fallen" nature of humans, susceptible as most individuals were to self-aggrandizement, if not corruption. Colonial Americans believed that power had the tendency to corrupt, and Adams was no exception. Speaking for the Boston town meeting, Adams said,

> [Such is] the depravity of mankind that ambition and lust of power above the law are . . . predominant passions in the breasts of most men. [Power] converts a good man in private life to a tyrant in office.

Despite mythology to the contrary, Adams was not a mob leader, though he was popular with the common workers of Boston. He was opposed to violence and sought

Adams, Samuel

to achieve his aims by political means. No evidence has ever been found placing Adams at any of the scenes in Boston involving mob violence such as the Boston Massacre, the wrecking of Lieutenant Governor Thomas Hutchinson's house, or the physical harassment of merchants. He has often been charged with "masterminding" these events, but only by conjecture, not on the basis of historical evidence.

In his early forties, Adams was well known in Boston politics when the Stamp Act crisis occurred in 1765-1766, the beginning of the revolutionary period. Along with his friend James Otis, Adams spoke out strongly and wrote much against the dangers of the Stamp Act. Before the Boston town meeting, Adams denied the right of the British parliament to tax the colonists. The Massachusetts charter gave Americans the right "to govern and tax ourselves." If Parliament could tax the colonies, then the English living in America would become "tributary slaves" without representation. Adams called for a unified resistance to this "tyranny" throughout the colonies. The Boston town meeting then elected Adams to a seat in the Massachusetts General Assembly, where he was soon elected to the position of clerk, a position he held for ten years.

This principle of opposing taxation without representation became one of the most significant rallying points for resisting British control of the colonies. Adams nevertheless stressed that he had no desire for colonial representation in the British parliament. Since the colonists would be considerably outnumbered and since travel to England was so slow, it would be "impracticable for the subjects in America" to have a tiny voice in Parliament. Instead, Adams and most of his fellow American strategists wanted to be able to make their own laws in their own American "parliaments." "All acts," wrote Adams,

> made by any power whatever other than the General Assembly of this province, imposing taxes on the inhabitants, are infringements of our inherent and unalienable [inalienable] rights as men and British subjects. . . .

On November 1, 1765, the day the Stamp Act was to go into effect, Boston buildings were draped in mourning black and the church bells tolled slowly. Governor Francis Bernard ordered the Boston militia to muster as a precautionary peacekeeping measure. Yet the men would not respond; one drummer sounded the call only to have his drum promptly broken. The rest of the drummers preserved their instruments by not using them. In direct violation of the Stamp Act, the Massachusetts General Assembly voted 81 to 5 to open the law courts of the province without using stamped papers, as required by the act.

In 1772, Adams sought and received the authorization of the Boston town meeting to create a Committee of Correspondence to inform and consult with other towns in the province, with a view to concerted and coordinated action. This was not a new idea. It had been customary for many years in Europe and in America for legislative bodies to use committees to handle official correspondence with other such governing authorities. As early as 1768, Richard Henry Lee had suggested to the Virginia House of Burgesses the formation of an intercolonial system of correspondence among the provincial assemblies. It was in Boston, however, that the idea was finally implemented.

As clerk of the Massachusetts General Assembly, Adams expanded the circular-letter type of correspondence to include all the colonies. In time, those letters contributed significantly to the unified action of the colonies. Realizing the potential strength in such an arrangement, the British secretary of state for the colonies, Lord Hillsborough, instructed the governor of Massachusetts to order the General Assembly to rescind a circular letter sent to other colonies. Instead, the General Assembly, in a heated debate, voted 92 to 17 to refuse to rescind the letter. The governor dissolved the legislature, but Adams—a pioneer in realizing the enormous importance of communication and information in sustaining any cause—published the names of the seventeen who had voted against the measure, impairing their political future. Britain now sought to obtain evidence to arrest and deport to England for prosecution those who resisted British law. Adams also published that letter, and the effect was electrifying, because it showed the clear intention of the British government to bypass the cherished English right of trial by jury of one's peers.

The political year of 1773 began with now-governor Hutchinson's opening speech to the Massachusetts General Assembly on the issue of parliamentary supremacy. Did the British parliament have authority over the elected assembly of Massachusetts, and, if so, to what extent? Adams headed the committee of the assembly designated to reply to the governor. He simply and cleverly took Hutchinson's own famous book, *History of Massachusetts Bay* (1760), and compared what he had written earlier with the current message. Adams found many inconsistencies and contradictions. The governor's book, for example, acknowledged that the founders of the Massachusetts Bay Colony had been assured by the Crown that "they were to be governed by laws made by themselves" and not by Parliament.

Adams also had a hand in the Boston Tea Party later that same year. The British East India Company was partially owned by the British government but, because of mismanagement, had stockpiled a great quantity of tea that needed to be sold before it spoiled. The Tea Act of spring, 1773, gave the company a monopoly on tea sales in America but sharply cut the price of tea. The controversial tea tax (set by the Townshend Acts of 1767) would continue to be levied, but the actual price, including the tax, paid in America for tea would only be about one-half that paid by a Londoner for his or her tea.

This monopoly on the tea trade was potentially seriously damaging to American free enterprise. Without competition, merchant trade could not prosper, and the Americans would eventually pay unnecessarily high prices for imports. Moreover, a precedent would be set regulating trade excessively instead of following more of a free market system. Adams, however, chose to focus on the taxation issue rather than the monopoly issue, because the former could be defended more emotionally and symbolically. When American patriots refused to allow the tea to be landed, the governor refused to allow the merchant ships to return with their cargoes of tea. The stand-off ended when colonists destroyed thousands of pounds of tea by dumping it into the bay.

The response of the British government inflamed the angry Americans. The Boston Port Act closed the port of Boston and threatened to ruin the city as a commercial center. Salem and Marblehead merchants responded by inviting the merchants of Boston

Adams, Samuel

to use their docks and warehouses free of charge. Contributions of food and supplies came from many colonies. Adams asked the people of Massachusetts to support a "Solemn League and Covenant" not to buy British goods. (The wording of the boycott was significant, reminiscent to American colonists of the English Civil War and of the heroism of the later Scottish Covenanters.)

General Gage in effect established martial law in Boston and even dissolved the General Assembly. The assembly, however, was in the process of selecting delegates to the First Continental Congress in Philadelphia. When General Gage's messenger arrived to order the assembly to disband, Adams, who was the clerk, locked the doors to keep the messenger out until the delegation process was completed. The elected delegates included both Samuel Adams and John Adams. General Gage considered arresting Samuel Adams but did not want to provoke a violent reaction, which such a measure would assuredly incite.

The 300-mile trip to Philadelphia was the longest of Adams's life. Even there, however, he found himself influential politically, becoming the key member of the newly organized Committee of Safety, a coordinating group. Adams was also the chairman of the Donation Committee, which distributed gifts of food and supplies collected along the Atlantic seaboard for the aid of the unfortunate people of the Boston area. The Committee of Safety began collecting weapons and supplies, and it even stored cannon at Concord.

An active member of the Continental Congress, Adams played a significant political role throughout the Revolutionary War. After the war, he approved of the new U.S. Constitution, but only after assurances were given him that a bill of rights was to be added. Adams became lieutenant governor of Massachusetts in 1789 and governor in 1793, retiring from that office in 1797. He died on October 2, 1803, at the age of eighty-one, having devoted his life to the cause of liberty and independence in a new nation, the United States of America.

Significance

It would be difficult to overestimate the importance of Samuel Adams to the American Revolution. Along with Virginia, New York, and Pennsylvania, Massachusetts led the way to independence. There was no center of power quite so volatile, however, as Massachusetts. It was there that the events that sparked the revolution occurred, events that included resistance to the Stamp Act, the Boston Massacre, the *Liberty* incident, and organized boycotts, as well as letters of protest.

Adams was involved in all of these events. His importance, moreover, was recognized in the very highest echelons of the British government. When King George III ordered Governor Hutchinson to London for consultation, one of the questions he asked him was what accounted for the importance of Adams in the colonies. Hutchinson's reply reflected his frustration with Adams: "A great pretended zeal for liberty and a most inflexible natural temper. He was the first that publicly asserted the independency of the colonies upon the kingdom."

It is true that Adams was a principal advocate of complete independence from the British, but not until 1775. All that he had advocated for years following the Stamp Act crisis was self-government within the British system. He did not push for independence until it became obvious to him that the king was a "tyrant [with] an unalterable determination to compel the colonies to absolute obedience."

—*William H. Burnside*

FURTHER READING

Adams, Samuel. *The Writings of Samuel Adams*. Edited by H. A. Cushing. 4 vols. New York: G. P. Putnam's Sons, 1904-1908. Indispensable primary material, including letters, newspaper articles, and official correspondence of the Massachusetts General Assembly.

Alexander, John K. *Samuel Adams: America's Revolutionary Politician*. Lanham, Md.: Rowman & Littlefield, 2002. In this biography, Alexander argues that Adams was America's first professional, modern politician, who fought to protect constitutional liberties.

Bailyn, Bernard. *The Ideological Origins of the American Revolution*. Cambridge, Mass.: Belknap Press, 1967. Not much on Adams directly, but essential for understanding his ideological milieu. Bailyn finds, as did Adams, that the war was fought over constitutional issues.

Chidsey, Donald Barr. *The Great Separation: The Story of the Boston Tea Party and the Beginning of the American Revolution*. New York: Crown, 1965. Written in a popular novelist's style, this book brings to life the issues and actions surrounding the Boston Tea Party, including Adams's role.

Fowler, William M., Jr. *Samuel Adams: Radical Puritan*. Edited by Oscar Handlin. New York: Longman, 1997. A brief biography that places Adams's life within the context of Boston politics. Fowler argues that Adams was the revolutionary leader most concerned with upholding the Puritan values of Massachusetts.

Galvin, John R. *Three Men of Boston*. New York: Thomas Y. Crowell, 1976. Recounts the events leading up to the revolution in Boston by focusing on Samuel Adams, Thomas Hutchinson, and James Otis. Galvin captures the complexity of the period and shows how the issues and events were interrelated.

Hosmer, James K. *Samuel Adams*. Boston: Houghton Mifflin, 1885. A standard nineteenth century biography of Adams.

Maier, Pauline. *The Old Revolutionaries: Political Lives in the Age of Samuel Adams*. New York: Alfred A. Knopf, 1980. The chapter "A New Englander as Revolutionary: Samuel Adams" brilliantly analyzes Adams's historical significance. Maier analyzes the interpretive data on Adams and introduces many fresh insights.

Montross, Lynn. *The Reluctant Rebels: The Story of the Continental Congress, 1774-1789*. New York: Harper and Brothers, 1950. This work examines the critical role of the Continental Congress in the American Revolution, discussing Adams's contributions to the Congress.

JANE ADDAMS

" America's future will be determined by the home and the school. The child becomes largely what he is taught; hence we must watch what we teach, and how we live. "

Social reformer and educator

Addams, a writer of hundreds of books and articles and a cofounder and director of the Hull House settlement in Chicago, promoted a variety of social reforms designed to facilitate the adjustment to urban, industrial America from 1890 to 1935.

Born: September 6, 1860; Cedarville, Illinois
Died: May 21, 1935; Chicago, Illinois
Area of achievement: Social reform

EARLY LIFE

Jane Addams (AD-amz) was born in the village of Cedarville in northern Illinois. Her father, John Huy Addams, owned a local mill and had investments in land and other enterprises in several states; his belief in civic responsibility led him to represent his district in the Illinois senate from 1854 to 1870. Her mother, Sarah, died when Jane was barely two years old, and an older sister supervised the Addams household until John Addams remarried in 1868. Anna Haldeman Addams, the widow of a Freeport merchant, was a self-educated woman with a high regard for social position, travel, dress—in general, the cultural aspects of life. Jane received tutelage from her stepmother in these areas, which supplemented the information she gleaned from books in the local subscription library, conveniently located in John Addams's house. Her formal education began in the village school in Cedarville; in 1877, she entered nearby Rockford Female Seminary (of which her father was a trustee), an institution dedicated to instilling in young women religious piety, cultural awareness, and domesticity. That Jane became president of her class, valedictorian, and editor of the class magazine attests her popularity and intellectual qualities.

Shortly after Jane's graduation from the seminary, in 1881, John Addams died. This shock combined with Jane's indecision about a career to produce several years of irresolution and depression. She began medical study at the Woman's Medical College in Philadelphia, but poor health forced her to leave after a few months. She was then bedridden for six months following an operation on her spine to correct the slight curvature caused by childhood spinal tuberculosis. At the urging of her stepmother, she toured Europe for twenty-seven months from 1883 to 1885, absorbing Old World culture with Anna and a few college classmates. Her purposelessness persisted after her return. She accompanied her stepmother to Baltimore for two winters and engaged in some charity work there, but her nervous depression continued. It was not until her second trip to Europe, in 1887-1888, in the company of her former teacher, Sarah Anderson, and college friend, Ellen Gates Starr, that she perceived a means to reconcile her intellectual and cultural interests with a useful career. In London she visited

Toynbee Hall, a social settlement in the city's East End, and discussed the institution's social and cultural activities with its founder, Canon Samuel A. Barnett. She also toured the People's Palace, an institute for the working class. These experiences acquainted her with the attempts of other educated men and women to deal with the problems of modern society by living and working in a poor neighborhood. Before leaving Europe she discussed her plan for founding a Chicago settlement with Starr; a few months after arriving home, the two women opened Hull House, on September 18, 1889.

Life's Work

While the model of Toynbee Hall initially influenced Addams's establishment of Hull House, the ethnically mixed population around the Halsted Street settlement had a greater impact on its development in the 1890's. When the two women residents moved into the old Hull mansion, they had no formal program of activities and sought to establish contact with their neighbors by sharing their literary enthusiasms in a series of "reading parties." Soon, however, the needs of area residents dictated programs. A wide variety of activities evolved in the first decade, including classes, clubs, social and cultural events, and a day nursery. Many of these activities drew on the cultural backgrounds of immigrants; Greeks staged classical Greek dramas at the Hull

Jane Addams.
(Library of Congress)

House Theater, and Italian and German immigrants discussed Dante and Johann Wolfgang von Goethe. As the functions of the settlement multiplied and Hull House added new buildings, Addams stood as the central figure—still a young woman, her brown hair drawn back into a bun, her pleasant face distinguished by pensive dark eyes—radiating goodwill and competence.

Her changed awareness of the nature of urban problems began to emerge in the 1890's. While her original impulse in establishing Hull House had reflected the religious and humanitarian principles of her early years, a combination of circumstances now led her to consider the causes of poverty and maladjustment to industrial society. Florence Kelley, who came to Hull House as a resident in the early 1890's, contributed her infectious interest in scientific investigations of the neighborhood as a basis for reform proposals. Her work culminated in the 1895 publication of *Hull-House Maps and Papers: A Presentation of Nationalities and Wages in a Congested District of Chicago, Together with Comments and Essays on Problems Growing Out of the Social Conditions*, a series of essays by Hull House residents, including "The Settlement as a Factor in the Labor Movement," by Addams. Addams was critical of current labor practices, an outgrowth of her involvement in the unsuccessful mediation of the Pullman strike in 1894. She also criticized the response to the depression of 1893-1894 by existing charitable organizations, which too often stressed laziness and other individual vices as the determinants of poverty. Her developing view was to consider the underlying causes of labor problems and social ills: the dislocation caused by modern industrial organization. Her promotion of scientific inquiry was abetted by members of the new Department of Sociology at the University of Chicago, particularly Albion Small, who encouraged her to publish in the *American Journal of Sociology*, which he began editing in 1896.

Addams's far-flung activities of the early 1900's aimed at achieving harmony between industrialism, on one hand, and traditional ideas of morality and culture, on the other. She was particularly interested in children and their development through educational and social activities. She promoted public parks and playgrounds in Chicago, established a kindergarten at Hull House, and set up a Hull House camp for neighborhood children outside the city. She promoted reform in education, believing that traditional educational methods and subjects insufficiently prepared children for modern life. She served on the Chicago Board of Education from 1905 to 1908 and was a founder of the National Society for the Promotion of Industrial Education. (Founded in 1906, the society's efforts culminated in the 1917 Smith-Hughes Act, which provided federal support for vocational education in high schools.) She was also a founding member of the National Child Labor Committee, which supported compulsory education laws as well as restrictive legislation for child labor in factories.

By the time she published her autobiographical masterpiece, *Twenty Years at Hull House* (1910), Addams was widely recognized as an expert in social problems and a spokesperson for major programs for progressive reform. A leading suffragist (and officer of the National American Woman Suffrage Association from 1911 to 1914), she was attracted by the woman's suffrage and industrial justice planks of the Progressive Party in 1912. She delivered a stirring speech seconding Theodore Roosevelt's nomination at the party's convention in Chicago and subsequently traveled more than seven thousand miles campaigning for the party. When Woodrow Wilson won the election, she opined that he would pursue a program of Progressive democracy. The war in Europe in 1914 impaired Progressive aspirations for reform, however, and directed Addams's attention to the cause she would pursue for the rest of her life: world peace.

During the period of American neutrality, until April, 1917, Addams worked for international arbitration, believing that neutral nations could resolve the war's causes and mediate with the belligerents. With Carrie Chapman Catt, she issued a call to women to attend a conference in Washington in January, 1915, resulting in the formation of the Woman's Peace Party, with Addams as its chair. Later in the year, she was elected president of the International Conference of Women at the Hague. (When the group reorganized after the war as the Women's International League for Peace and Freedom, she was elected president and retained the post until 1929.) When mediation did not materialize and the United States entered the war, she did not support the war effort, although in 1918 she worked for Herbert Hoover's Department of Food Administration, which she viewed as a humanitarian response to the upheaval of war. Her patriotism came under attack, and the Daughters of the American Revolution withdrew her lifetime honorary membership. In the years following the war, she continued to search for ways to ensure lasting peace; her efforts were recognized by the award of the Nobel Peace Prize in 1931, which she shared with Nicholas Murray Butler.

Her final years were marked by tributes and honors from organizations throughout the world. Her activities were hampered, however, by failing health. She underwent major surgical operations and suffered a heart attack in the early 1930's; she died on May 21, 1935. Following services at Hull House, she was buried in the cemetery at Cedarville.

SIGNIFICANCE

Jane Addams was in the vanguard of Progressive reformers. Rather than exhibiting a populist-type aversion to modern industrial conditions, she shared with other urban reformers a belief that social, political, and economic relationships could be modified in a democratic fashion to deal with changed conditions. The belief in evolutionary change toward a new "social morality" was the theme of her first book, *Democracy and Social Ethics* (1902), a collection of essays on such diverse topics as charity organizations, family relationships, women in domestic employment, labor-management relations in industry, education, and the roles of bosses and reformers in politics.

Her experiences at Hull House provided her with a vantage point that few other reformers enjoyed. Observations of the ordinary led her to formulate social theories. For example, her reflections on the activities of neighborhood children led to a remarkable book, *The Spirit of Youth and the City Streets* (1909), in which she discussed the importance of the natural instinct toward play among children and the "urban democracy" exhibited on the playground.

The neighborhood was also a place where social experimentation could occur, where ideas could be translated to practice, for Addams was a rare combination of social theorist and pragmatic reformer. As such, she attracted other educated and talented people to join the settlement, many of whom were young women who faced the same career quandary with which she had dealt in the 1880's. She was willing to draw

Addams, Jane

on the observations and ideas of this group in formulating her own programs. This open-minded deference to ideas, including those of William James and John Dewey, may have been her greatest strength in attempting to apply democratic idealism to an urban industrial setting in new ways that represented a profound break from the genteel tradition in which she was reared and educated.

Her attitude toward war rested on the same ideal of Progressive democracy as her social theories. Like other Progressives, she believed that war destroyed social progress and moral civilization. Unlike most other Progressives, however, she could not support U.S. involvement in the war, citing as her reasons the sanctity of human life and the irrationality of war as an instrument of change. As a practical idealist, she supported such postwar initiatives as the League of Nations, the World Court, and the Kellogg-Briand Pact, hoping that they would serve as instruments to direct world public opinion against war. In international affairs, as well as in industrial relations, Addams was always willing to pursue numerous programs, never losing her faith in achieving human progress through social change.

—*Richard G. Frederick*

FURTHER READING

Addams, Jane. *Democracy and Social Ethics.* Edited by Anne Firor Scott. New York: Macmillan, 1902. Reprint. Cambridge, Mass.: Belknap Press, 1964. Originally published in 1902, this book was a compilation of earlier magazine articles (revised for the book), which addressed the problem of applying ethics to an evolving democratic system. This edition includes an excellent introduction to the life and thought of Addams by the editor.

———. *The Social Thought of Jane Addams.* Edited by Christopher Lasch. Indianapolis: Bobbs-Merrill, 1965. An excellent introduction to Addams through her published and unpublished writings. Following a biographical introduction by Lasch, the material is organized under five subject headings, which reflect Addams's diverse interests.

———. *Twenty Years at Hull House with Autobiographical Notes.* New York: Macmillan, 1910. A good source for understanding Addams and the Progressive reform movement, as the book is at once autobiography, publicity for Hull House, and a consideration of reform ideas in the twenty years preceding its publication.

Davis, Allen F. *American Heroine: The Life and Legend of Jane Addams.* New York: Oxford University Press, 1973. A balanced biography that establishes Addams's writing and other activities in a broader cultural context. The most realistic appraisal of her accomplishments.

Farrell, John C. *Beloved Lady: A History of Jane Addams' Ideas on Reform and Peace.* Baltimore: Johns Hopkins University Press, 1967. The first study to analyze the thought of Addams rather than concentrate on her humanitarian sentiments or involvement in settlement activity. Particularly good in demonstrating that her ideas often conflicted with later historical accounts of the "average" Progressive reformer.

Joslin, Katherine. *Jane Addams: A Writer's Life.* Urbana: University of Illinois Press, 2004. Joslin argues that Addams's emergence as a public figure stemmed from her books and essays. She describes how Addams rejected scholarly writing in favor of a combination of fictional and analytical prose that appealed to a wide readership.

Knight, Louise W. *Citizen: Jane Addams and the Struggle for Democracy*. Chicago: University of Chicago Press, 2005. An insightful account of the early years of Addams's life, from 1860 through 1899, which depicts her personality flaws as well as her compassion.

Lasch, Christopher. *The New Radicalism in America, 1889-1963: The Intellectual as a Social Type*. New York: Alfred A. Knopf, 1965. In a perceptive essay on Addams, Lasch examines her early life and motivation for reform; he finds that her gradual emergence as an adherent to the "new radicalism" (marked by interest in educational, cultural, and sexual reform) was based on the conflict between the genteel values of her parents' generation and her own perceptions of life and society.

Levine, Daniel. *Jane Addams and the Liberal Tradition*. Madison: State Historical Society of Wisconsin, 1971. An intellectual biography of Addams, which asserts that she was a radical in urging rapid change. The book deals with three facets of her life: Hull House, her publicizing of social problems, and activism in national affairs.

Linn, James Weber. *Jane Addams: A Biography*. New York: D. Appleton-Century, 1935. An admiring but thorough biography by Addams's nephew. Not interpretive, but valuable for detail, as the author had access to all of Addams's manuscripts and files prior to her death, and discussed with her the proposed biography.

Muhammad Ali

> *Only a man who knows what it is like to be defeated can reach down to the bottom of his soul and come up with the extra ounce of power it takes to win when the match is even.*

Boxer

Ali was probably the greatest as well as the best-recognized sports personality of the twentieth century. He brought heavyweight boxing matches to areas of the world never before regarded as important in boxing circles.

Born: January 17, 1942; Louisville, Kentucky
Also known as: Cassius Marcellus Clay, Jr. (birth name); Cassius Clay; The Greatest
Area of achievement: Sports

Early Life

Muhammad Ali (muh-HAH-mahd ah-LEE) was born Cassius Marcellus Clay, Jr., in Louisville, Kentucky, to Cassius Marcellus Clay, Sr., and Odessa Lee Grady Clay. His father was a commercial artist specializing in sign painting; he also painted murals for churches and taverns. His mother sometimes worked as a domestic for four dollars a day to help support the family. Some of the Clays trace their name to Ali's great-great-grandfather, who was a slave of Cassius Marcellus Clay, a relative of Henry Clay and ambassador to Russia in the 1860's.

Known during boyhood as a mischievous child and lover of practical jokes, Ali was considered indolent by his father. He often remarked that eating and sleeping were Ali's two most strenuous activities. That changed when Ali became involved in boxing at the age of twelve. Unlike most boxers, however, he was reared in a lower-middle-class environment. When, at age twelve, Ali's bicycle was stolen, he reported the theft to a Louisville police officer who gave boxing lessons in a gymnasium operated in Ali's neighborhood. This white police officer, Joe Elsby Martin, was to guide Ali through most of his amateur boxing career. After six weeks of boxing lessons, Ali had his first fight, weighing in at eighty-nine pounds. He won a split decision and was regarded as an average boxer at that time. Yet two characteristics had already manifested themselves in Ali: his dedication to his newfound interest, a dedication to make himself into "The Greatest" (a slogan he adopted relatively early in his career), and his propensity to talk back to people, particularly his detractors. He was known as a smart aleck, a sassy person.

Ali attended Du Valle Junior High School and was graduated from Central High School in Louisville, 376th in his class of 391. He was known more for his marble-shooting and rock-throwing prowess than for any interest in academics. Ali's first public exposure came in Louisville, when he was booked for fights on *Tomorrow's Champions*, a local weekly television boxing show. By this time, he was also training four hours a day under Fred Stoner, a black trainer at the Grace Community Center, a gymnasium in the all-black section of Louisville. Ali later said that Stoner molded his style, his stamina, and his system.

During his illustrious amateur career, Ali won 100 of 108 fights, six Kentucky Golden Gloves championships, and two national Amateur Athletic Union championships. During his last two years as an amateur, he lost only once, to Amos Johnson in the 1959 Pan-American Games trials. By this time, he wanted to box professionally, but Martin convinced him to remain an amateur and enter the 1960 Olympics, as this would give him national recognition and ensure his professional success. Ali, who was already advertising himself as the next heavyweight champion of the world, stopped off in New York City on the way to the Olympic Games in Rome and visited Madison Square Garden, then the mecca of professional boxing. He won the light-heavyweight title at the Olympics and returned to the United States in triumph. Soon afterward, however, he was refused service in a restaurant in his hometown and had to fight a white motorcycle gang leader to escape from the restaurant. This incident so embittered him that he threw his Olympic Gold Medal into the Ohio River.

When Ali turned to professional boxing in 1960, he was already six feet three inches tall. In his heyday, he weighed more than 200 pounds, usually weighing in at around 220 pounds. Ali did not look like a boxer. His rather large, round face was unmarked, and he was not muscle-bound. Bodybuilding has long been an anathema to boxers; heavy surface muscles restrict the movement of hands and arms, and Ali's forte already was speed and defense in the ring. Indeed, one of his most celebrated slogans was "Float like a butterfly, sting like a bee."

Ali, Muhammad

Muhammad Ali. (AP/Wide World Photos)

    Three days before his first professional fight, on October 29, 1960, Ali signed a contract with eleven white businessmen from Louisville and New York City. These men were willing to invest in a potential heavyweight champion. Known as the Louisville Sponsoring Group, it was headed by William Faversham, Jr., vice president of the Brown-Forman Distillers Corporation. Ali received a ten-thousand-dollar bonus for signing, a salary of four thousand dollars annually for the first two years and six thousand dollars annually for the following four years, as well as having all of his expenses paid. He was also to receive 50 percent of all of his earnings.
    Ali began his professional training under former light-heavyweight champion Archie Moore. Angelo Dundee soon supplanted Moore, also becoming Ali's de facto manager during Ali's early professional career. Angelo was calm under fire and saved Ali's championship at least twice. He was an excellent cornerman who had come up through the ranks. His brother, Chris Dundee, was at the time promoting a weekly fight card in Miami Beach. Angelo joined Chris, and they established their training headquarters on the second floor of a two-story building on the corner of Fifth Street and Washington Avenue, in Miami Beach. This gymnasium later became known as the Fifth Street Gym and was probably the best-known and most respected training center in the United States.

Ali, Muhammad

Ali won his first seven fights as a professional, beginning with the defeating of Tunney Hunsaker. Some of his early fights were held in Louisville, and his first national television exposure was against Alonzo Johnson. Johnson was then twenty-seven years old and an experienced boxer. The bout, televised by the National Broadcasting Company (NBC) on the Gillette Cavalcade of Sports, was a difficult one for Ali, but he won and was on his way.

Ali was soon showing all the braggadocio for which he became noted: talking constantly to confuse his opponents, writing short ditties deriding them, and predicting the round in which he would stop them. There was, however, a method to his madness. His behavior increased the spectators' enthusiasm for his fights and brought him fame and fortune, along with derision. It is said that Ali had watched the antics of Gorgeous George, one of the first truly flamboyant wrestlers to appear on television, noting his ability to enrage most of the spectators at his matches. Yet these same spectators paid as much money for tickets to see George lose as his fans paid to see him win. Fifty percent of all revenue from fights was still coming to Ali. More than twelve thousand people came to see him knock out Alejandro Lavorante in California in five rounds, and his fight with Archie Moore in California in November, 1962, drew more than sixteen thousand people. In March, 1963, he fought Doug Jones in Madison Square Garden, filling it for the first time in more than a decade; more than eighteen thousand people came to see him fight, paying $105,000 for this privilege. Ali then went to England to box British heavyweight champion Henry Cooper. Ali predicted a victory by a fifth-round knockout of Cooper, but late in the third round, Cooper knocked Ali down and stunned him. Dundee, however, noticed that one of Ali's gloves was split, and the extra minutes needed to fix it enabled Ali to clear his head. Cooper's propensity to be cut easily allowed Ali to win by a technical knockout in the fifth round, as he had predicted.

Life's Work

Ali finally had the opportunity to fight for the heavyweight championship of the world. Sonny Liston was then regarded as the quintessential champion and was a prohibitive favorite to retain his crown. Yet at the weigh-in before the fight in Miami Beach on February 25, 1964, Ali distracted Liston with a carefully rehearsed display of hysteria and paranoia. During the fight, he taunted Liston and, using his superior speed and longer reach, peppered Liston with long-range jabs and right-hand punches. He so wore down his opponent that Liston was unable to answer the bell for the seventh round. Ali was declared the heavyweight champion of the world. In a return match with Liston, held in Lewiston, Maine, on May 25, 1965, Ali knocked him out with a very quick right-hand punch in the first round. He next defeated the former champion, Floyd Patterson, winning a technical knockout in the twelfth round, in Las Vegas, Nevada. Many believed that Ali could have ended the fight earlier but instead chose to bait and mock Patterson unmercifully. In 1966, he stopped all five of his challengers. Only one, George Chavallo, went the distance. Early in 1967, he defeated Ernie Terrell and was recognized as the undisputed heavyweight champion. Only one month later, he knocked out Zora Folley.

By this time, Ali's activities beyond the ring were receiving more notoriety than

Ali, Muhammad

were his successful title defenses. Immediately after he won the championship from Liston, he announced that he had joined the black nationalist Nation of Islam and changed his name from Cassius Clay to Muhammad Ali. Popularly known as the Black Muslims, the sect was then regarded by white America as a dangerous and subversive antiwhite group. (Ali converted to mainstream Sunni Islam in 1975.) Also, Ali had been married twice by this time. His first marriage to Sonje Roi was dissolved in 1966. His second marriage was to Belinda Boyd (Khalilah Toloria), with whom he had four children. He wooed Belinda when she was seventeen years old and working in a Chicago Nation of Islam bakery. They were divorced in 1977. He was married a third time, to Veronica Porsche, in 1977. This third marriage produced two children.

Many whites began to compare Ali to the former champion Jack Johnson, a black boxer who had defied the stereotypes of his time by living a fast and integrated life. This comparison was odd, for Ali was probably the best-trained heavyweight champion of all time, and he neither smoked nor drank. In 1966, the Selective Service Board reclassified him as 1-A, thus removing his deferred status of 1-Y. Ali then appealed, citing conscientious-objector status on religious grounds. He formally refused induction into the Army on April 18, 1967. The World Boxing Association then stripped him of his championship, as did the New York Athletic Commission. Therefore, for three years, during what was the prime of his athletic life, Ali was unable to fight. In 1970, however, a federal court ruled that the revocation of his license was arbitrary and unreasonable, and Ali was able to resume his career.

In 1971 Ali lost his bid to regain the title when Joe Frazier knocked him down in the fifteenth round of a fight in Madison Square Garden; the decision went unanimously to Frazier in what was dubbed as the fight of the century. Against all odds, on October 30, 1974, Ali again won the heavyweight crown. After two losses and fifteen wins, he faced George Foreman (who in the meantime had won the title from Frazier) in Kinshasa, Zaire (now Democratic Republic of the Congo), Africa, on October 30, 1974, in what became known as the Rumble in the Jungle. Here he used his "rope-a-dope" tactics, lying back on the ring ropes and letting Foreman tire himself out. Only his superior hand speed and movement enabled him to do this. Foreman was knocked out in the eighth round. During this period, Ali lived very well, with Belinda, his second wife, on what was described as a baronial, four-and-a-half-acre estate, with a three-car garage containing his-and-hers Rolls Royces. During this period, Ali successfully defended his title against Frazier in the Philippines, in what became known as the Thrilla in Manila. However, Ali's skills were waning; after barely defeating two mediocre boxers, he lost his crown to Leon Spinks in Las Vegas, Nevada, on February 15, 1978. Summoning all of his strength, Ali trained hard for a rematch, winning the title for an unprecedented third time on September 15, 1978. He lost his last major fight to Larry Holmes in October, 1980, but his final match was against twenty-seven-year-old Trevor Berbick in the Bahamas, which he lost in a unanimous decision.

During his career, Ali earned more than fifty million dollars. Much of this money went for taxes, an expensive lifestyle, and divorces; a third of it went to Herbert Muhammad, who became Ali's manager of record in 1966. By the 1980's Ali was showing signs of mental and physical decay, the result of Parkinson's disease, not, as some conjectured, from brain damage resulting from his fights. Ali retired permanently in

1981 with a career record of fifty-six wins (thirty-seven of them by knockouts) and five losses. The formal diagnosis of Parkinson's disease came in 1982. At the time Ali could claim, with justice, that he was the most famous man in the world.

In retirement Ali became an iconic sports figure, receiving recognition in many forms. *Forbes Magazine* placed him thirteenth on its Celebrity One Hundred list, the Kentucky Athletic Hall of Fame picked him as Kentucky Athlete of the Century, and both *Sports Illustrated* and the British Boxing Association selected him as sportsman of the twentieth century. He was inducted into the International Hall of Fame and the Olympic Hall of Fame. He received the Spirit of America Award, the Otto Hahn Peace Medal in Gold from the United Nations Association of Germany, and the Presidential Medal of Freedom. In 1996 he was accorded the honor of lighting the Olympic flame at the Summer Games in Atlanta, Georgia, where he was presented a gold medal to replace the one that he had lost. In 2007 Princeton University awarded him an honorary doctorate of humanities.

In retirement Ali involved himself in humanitarian programs. The Muhammad Ali Center in Louisville, which opened in 2005, not only preserves the boxing memorabilia of Ali but also his ideals: peace, social responsibility, and personal growth. The Muhammad Ali Parkinson Center at the Barrow Neurological Institute in Phoenix, Arizona, provides treatment, research, and education for patients and families. Ali has supported delivery of food and medical services to places such as the Ivory Coast, Indonesia, Mexico, and Morocco, often traveling to these countries to promote the humanitarian effort, and he has lobbied before state legislatures and Congress for laws to protect children and to regulate professional boxing. In *The Soul of a Butterfly: Reflections on Life's Journey* (2004), Ali discusses the meaning of religion and forgiveness as he reflects on turning points in his life.

Ali lives in Scottsdale, Arizona, with his fourth wife, Yolanda, whom he married following his divorce from Porsche in 1986. He has nine children. Despite the slurring of speech, tremors, and muscular stiffness from Parkinson's disease, he travels frequently.

Significance

Ali was America's premier heavyweight champion of all time. He is credited with reviving interest in boxing and helping promote international acceptance of the sport. His fights in the Congo and Manila made him history's most recognized boxer, and in 1998 a documentary film about the African bout, *When We Were Kings*, won an Academy Award; in 2001 actor Will Smith re-created Ali's youthful exuberance in the biographical film *Ali*. Nevertheless, Ali's stand for the principles in which he believed cost him dearly. Most Americans came to admire him for his courage if not for his beliefs. George Plimpton captured Ali's standing in writing of his appearance during the 1996 Olympic Games opening ceremony: "It was a kind of epiphany that those who watched realized how much they missed him and how much he had contributed to the world of sport."

—*Henry S. Marks*

Further Reading

Ali, Muhammad, with Hana Yasmeen Ali. *The Soul of a Butterfly: Reflections on Life's Journey*. New York: Simon & Schuster, 2004. Ali's memoir focuses on his spiritual evolution, recounting his life from his childhood to his eventual role as an activist for peace and for wider understanding of Parkinson's disease.

Brenner, Teddy, and Barney Nagler. *Only the Ring Was Square*. Englewood Cliffs, N.J.: Prentice-Hall, 1981. Typical breezy sports biography, but with interesting sidelights into Ali's career.

Brunt, Stephen. *Ali: The Opposition Weighs In*. Guilford, Conn.: Lyons Press, 2002. Brunt tells of Ali's fights from the perspective of fifteen of his opponents, including Joe Frazier, Ken Norton, George Foreman, and Larry Holmes. Provides many insights into Ali's style and character. Includes photographs.

Greene, Bob. "Muhammad Ali Is the Most Famous Man in the World." *Esquire*, December, 1983. Tidbits of Ali's later life and a synopsis of Ali's career in an appendix labeled "Dossier."

Marqusee, Mike. *Redemption Song: Muhammad Ali and the Spirit of the Sixties*. 2d ed. New York: Verso, 2005. Marqusee describes Ali's conversion from a prizefighter to a cultural icon and how this transformation was influenced by the rebellious decade of the 1960's.

Massaquoi, Hans J. "The Private World of Muhammad Ali." *Ebony*, September, 1972. Depicts the opulent lifestyle of Ali when he was still fighting. Provides many examples of Ali's personal beliefs, especially on women's rights.

Muhammad Ali. New York: Harry N. Abrams, 2004. There is little text in this coffee-table book, but its dozens of black-and-white and color photographs by Magnum photographers testify wonderfully to the spirit and skill of Ali during his heyday as a boxer.

Pacheco, Freddy. *Fight Doctor*. New York: Simon & Schuster, 1983. Pacheco was Ali's physician until splitting with him shortly before Ali's first fight with Leon Spinks. He was the first to notice deterioration in Ali's physical and mental well-being and the first to advise Ali to quit fighting.

Remnick, David. *King of the World: Muhammad Ali and the Rise of an American Hero*. New York: Random House, 1998. Remnick's biography focuses on Ali's character, describing how Ali created himself as a new type of boxing champion who defied the traditional stereotypes of his profession.

Angelou, Maya

MAYA ANGELOU

" Bringing the gifts that my ancestors gave,/ I am the dream and the hope of the slave./ I rise. . . . "

American poet and writer

Angelou's rhythmic, gospel-inspired poetry and candid autobiographical works express a philosophy that celebrated the African American community and Americans in general.

Born: April 4, 1928; St. Louis, Missouri
Also known as: Marguerite Annie Johnson (birth name)
Areas of achievement: Literature; education; women's rights; civil rights

EARLY LIFE

Maya Angelou (MI-ah AN-jeh-lew) was born Marguerite Annie Johnson in St. Louis, Missouri, to Vivian Baxter and Bailey Johnson. Following her parents' divorce when she was three years old, Angelou and her brother were sent to live with their paternal grandmother, Annie Henderson, in Stamps, a poor rural section of Arkansas. Angelou's grandmother, whom she called Momma, was the stable force in Angelou's early life. Annie was a strong, religious woman who made sure that the family went to church regularly. Religion and spiritual music were important factors in the Johnson family life. Angelou also enjoyed a close relationship with her brother, Bailey, who gave her the name Maya.

Angelou and her brother lived with their grandmother and Uncle Willie in the rear of the Johnson store, which Annie had owned for twenty-five years. Because the store was the center of activity for the local black community, Angelou saw at first hand the indignities that black residents suffered as a result of the prejudices of whites in Stamps.

Angelou faced a severely traumatic experience when she was just seven and a half years old. During one of her visits to her mother in St. Louis, a friend of Angelou's mother raped her. When her mother's brothers found out about the rape, they killed the man responsible. Believing that she had caused the man's death by speaking his name, Angelou refused to speak for five years following these traumatic events. With the encouragement of Mrs. Flowers, an educated black woman from Stamps, Angelou regained her speech. Under Mrs. Flowers's further guidance, Angelou began to read the works of William Shakespeare, Edgar Allan Poe, Langston Hughes, and Paul Laurence Dunbar.

After graduating at the top of her eighth grade class in Stamps, she went to Los Angeles to pass the summer with her father, but after being attacked by his girlfriend, she lived for a month in a junkyard with runaways from many races. The experience, she later wrote, deeply affected her views of race. Angelou and her brother continued their education in San Francisco, living with their mother. While still in high school, she worked as the first black woman streetcar conductor in San Francisco.

At the age of seventeen, having just graduated from George Washington High

School and unmarried, Angelou gave birth to her son, Guy Johnson. To support herself and Guy, she took jobs as a waitress, cook, and nightclub singer. In 1950, she married Tosh Angelos, a former sailor of Greek ancestry, but they were divorced after a few years. (Angelou's surname was derived from that of her former husband.)

Angelou continued her early interest in music and dance by studying with Martha Graham. She went on to tour twenty-two countries during 1954 and 1955 as the premier dancer in *Porgy and Bess*. Her travels with the cast took her to Italy, France, Greece, Yugoslavia, and Egypt. During the late 1950's, Angelou and Guy lived in a houseboat commune in California, where they went barefoot, wore jeans, and let their hair grow long. These experiences brought Angelou into contact with a variety of people from different countries and of different races.

As Angelou became interested in a writing career, she moved to New York in 1958 and joined the Harlem Writers Guild. In addition to working on her writing, she starred in the New York production of Jean Genet's *The Blacks* (1960) with Godfrey Cambridge and collaborated with Cambridge to produce, direct, and star in *Cabaret for Freedom* (1960).

In 1960, Angelou and Guy moved to Cairo, Egypt, with a South African freedom fighter, Vusumzi Make. In Egypt, she served as an editor for *Arab Observer*, an English-language newspaper. Two years later, she and Guy moved to the West African nation of Ghana, where she worked for three years as a writer, as an assistant administrator for the University of Ghana, and as a feature editor for *African Review*.

LIFE'S WORK

Angelou's firsthand knowledge of the harmful effects of racism led her to political activism in the 1960's, working for civil rights and for a wider understanding of African American culture. In the 1960's, at the request of Martin Luther King, Jr., Angelou served as the northern coordinator of the Southern Christian Leadership Conference. Her knowledge of black traditions and cultures went beyond political activism as well. She produced *Blacks, Blues, Black* (1968) for National Educational Television, a ten-part series that explores African traditions in American life. Other television credits include *Assignment America* (1975), *The Legacy* (1976), *The Inheritors* (1976), and *Trying to Make It Home* (1988).

In the first volume of her now-classic autobiographical novel, *I Know Why the Caged Bird Sings* (1970), Angelou shares her experience of growing up as a poor black female in the segregated rural South. The book is candid about issues of racism, sexism, child rape, sexuality, and other topics, and it remains a target of censors opposed to its explicitness and seeking to ban it from public schools and libraries. The book has been one of the most frequently challenged books in the United States, according to the American Library Association. Throughout her career, however, and despite these challenges, Angelou continued to draw on her own experiences as the subject matter for her work. She published five more volumes of her personal narrative showing how she was able to overcome obstacles such as racism and sexism to achieve personal success.

In *Gather Together in My Name* (1974), Angelou writes about a difficult period in her life, a time when she was forced to work at menial jobs to support herself and her son. In *Singin' and Swingin' and Gettin' Merry Like Christmas* (1976), Angelou describes her life as a dancer and actor, including her travels with the cast of *Porgy and Bess*. The next two volumes, *The Heart of a Woman* (1981) and *All God's Children Need Traveling Shoes* (1986), describe the rise of her career. *A Song Flung Up to Heaven* (2002) concerns her return to the United States and involvement in the Civil Rights movement. Angelou told George Plimpton in an interview for the *Paris Review* that the prevailing theme running through all the autobiographies was her love for her son; she also placed these works in the tradition of the slave narrative that extends back into the early nineteenth century.

An early exposure to spirituals and gospel music deeply influenced Angelou's poetry, which displays a clear rhythm of gospel music and which reveals a woman whose faith sustained her in difficult times. She published several volumes of poetry: *Just Give Me a Cool Drink of Water 'fore I Diiie* (1971), which earned a Pulitzer Prize nomination; *Oh Pray My Wings Are Gonna Fit Me Well* (1975), whose title came from a nineteenth century spiritual; *And Still I Rise* (1978); *Shaker, Why Don't You Sing?* (1983); *Now Sheba Sings the Song* (1987); *I Shall Not Be Moved* (1990); *A Brave and Startling Truth* (1995); *Amazing Peace* (2005); *Mother: A Cradle to Hold Me* (2006); and *Celebrations: Rituals of Peace and Prayer* (2006).

Angelou began publishing books for children in 1986 with *Mrs. Flowers: A Moment of Friendship*, which is a selection from *I Know Why the Caged Bird Sings*. Nine more followed, illustrated with drawings or photographs: *Life Doesn't Frighten Me* (1993, an extended poem), *Soul Looks Back in Wonder* (1993, with others), *My Painted House, My Friendly Chicken, and Me* (1994), and *Kobe and His Magic* (1996). In 2004 she published *Angelina of Italy*, *Isaac of Lapland*, *Renee Marie of France*, and *Michael of Hawaii*.

The diversity of Angelou's experiences and considerable talents led her into dance, theater, and film as well. As an actor, she is probably best known for her portrayal of Kunta Kinte's grandmother in the television production of Alex Haley's *Roots* (1977). She played the role of the grandmother in the 1993 television film *There Are No Children Here*. In addition to her acting career, she produced and directed for the stage and screen. She also wrote the screenplays for *Georgia, Georgia* (1972) and *All Day Long* (1974) and collaborated on the teleplay for *Sister, Sister* (1982). In 1995 she had a cameo role in *How to Make an American Quilt*, and in 1998 she directed her first film, *Down in the Delta*, making her the first African American woman to be a Hollywood director. She also appeared in the television version of *Down in the Delta* (1999), *The Amen Corner* (1999), and *The Runaway* (2000) and served as a host for the show *Oprah & Friends* on the AM Satellite Radio in 2006.

In 2005, Angelou published a cookbook, *Hallelujah: The Welcome Table*. Two volumes of essays appeared in the 1990's: *Wouldn't Take Nothing for My Journey Now* (1993) and *Even the Stars Look Lonesome* (1997). According to *The New Yorker* writer Hilton Als, these works are collections of "homilies strung together with autobiographical texts" that stress Angelou's inner journey.

Angelou received many honors. *Ladies' Home Journal* named her Woman of the Year in Communications in 1976. She received honorary doctorates from the University of Arkansas, Claremont Graduate University, Ohio State University, Atlanta Uni-

Angelou, Maya

versity, Wheaton College, Occidental College, Columbia College, Kean College, Smith College, Mills College, Lawrence University, and Wake Forest University, and others. At the request of U.S. president Bill Clinton, Angelou wrote and delivered the commemorative poem at his inauguration on January 20, 1993. This poem, "On the Pulse of Morning," was later published by Random House and is perhaps her best-known work among American readers.

Angelou won a Grammy Award for Best Spoken Word or Non-Musical Album (1995), North Carolina's Woman of the Year Award from the Black Publishers Association (1997), the Humanitarian Contribution Award (1997), the Alston/Jones International Civil and Human Rights Award (1998), the Christopher Award (1998), and the National Medal of Arts (2000). In 2001, *Ladies Home Journal* named her among the thirty most powerful women in the nation.

Angelou also spent much of her career as a teacher, beginning with a lectureship at the University of California, Los Angeles, in 1966. She was writer-in-residence at the University of Kansas in 1970 and distinguished visiting professor at Wake Forest University, Wichita State University, and California State University, Sacramento. Since 1981, Angelou has held a lifetime appointment as Reynolds Professor of American Studies at Wake Forest. During her travels abroad, and through much study, Angelou became fluent in French, Spanish, Italian, Arabic, and Fante, a West African language.

Significance

In *I Know Why the Caged Bird Sings*, Angelou evokes an authentic portrait of what it was like to be black, poor, and female in the segregated South during the 1930's. In the autobiographical novel, she reveals herself as a strong, determined black woman who overcomes adversities and emerges triumphant. These personal evocations, with their candor and sincerity, are Angelou's legacy.

Angelou was consistent in producing a literature that spoke to other black women who struggled to live their lives and to support their families, all while trying to maintain a positive outlook on life. As she matured as a writer, Angelou extended her message of hope and possibility to include all persons, regardless of race or color.

—*Judith Barton Williamson*

Further Reading

Angelou, Maya. *I Know Why the Caged Bird Sings: The Collected Autobiographies of Maya Angelou.* New York: Modern Library, 2004. A hefty but handy collection of all six of Angelou's memoirs, the central source for any study of her life and milieu.

Bloom, Harold, ed. *Maya Angelou.* Philadelphia: Chelsea House, 2001. A collection of essays about Angelou, including analyses of her poetry and the autobiographical content of her work. Includes an introduction by Bloom, a noted literary critic.

Braxton, Joanne M. *Black Women Writing Autobiography: A Tradition Within a Tradition.* Philadelphia: Temple University Press, 1989. Discusses how Angelou employs the image of the protecting mother as a primary archetype within her work. Traces Angelou's development of themes common to black female autobiography: the centrality of the family, the challenges of child rearing and single parenthood, and the burden of overcoming negative stereotypes of African American women.

Angelou, Maya

Cud Joe, Selwyn. "Maya Angelou and the Autobiographical Statement." In *Black Women Writers (1950-1980)*, edited by Mari Evans. Garden City, N.Y.: Anchor Press, 1983. Cud Joe discusses the importance of Angelou's biographical work, arguing that she represents "the condition of Afro-American womanhood in her quest for understanding and love rather than for bitterness and despair." Cud Joe stresses that by telling the story of her own life in *I Know Why the Caged Bird Sings*, Angelou has shown readers what it means to be a black woman or girl in the United States.

Elliott, Jeffrey M., ed. *Conversations with Maya Angelou*. Jackson: University Press of Mississippi, 1989. A collection of more than thirty interviews with Angelou that originally appeared in various magazines and newspapers, accompanied by a chronology of her life. Provides a multifaceted perspective on the creative issues that have informed Angelou's work as an autobiographer and a poet.

Hilton, Als. "Songbird." *The New Yorker*, August 5, 2002. Written soon after the publication of Angelou's last volume of autobiography, *A Song Flung Up to Heaven*, this well-written, substantial article discusses, sometimes critically, her early life and the literary value, inspiration, and social impact of each autobiography.

Lupton, Mary Jane. "Singing the Black Mother: Maya Angelou and Autobiographical Continuity." *Black American Literature Forum* 24 (Summer, 1990): 257-275. A scholarly assessment of Angelou's literary contributions to the genre of autobiography, placing her within the rich context of African American narratives.

O'Neal, Sondra. "Reconstruction of the Composite Self: New Images of Black Women in Maya Angelou's Continuing Autobiography." In *Black Women Writers (1950-1980)*, edited by Mari Evans. Garden City, N.Y.: Anchor Press, 1983. O'Neal argues that Angelou's primary contribution to the canon of African American literature lies in her realistic portrayal of the lives of black people, especially black women. O'Neal goes on to demonstrate the ways in which Angelou successfully destroys many of the stereotypes of black women.

Tate, Claudia, ed. *Black Women Writers at Work*. New York: Continuum, 1989. In this collection of interviews, Tate explores the personal lives and works of such contemporary African American writers as Gwendolyn Brooks, Alice Walker, and Toni Morrison. In the interview, Angelou discusses the importance of black role models.

Susan B. Anthony

> *I shall earnestly and persistently continue to urge all women to the practical recognition of the old Revolutionary maxim. Resistance to tyranny is obedience to God.*

Feminist and social reformer

A gifted and tireless worker for feminist causes, Anthony was for five decades the preeminent voice and inspiration of the women's suffrage movement.

Born: February 15, 1820; Adams, Massachusetts
Died: March 13, 1906; Rochester, New York
Also known as: Susan Brownell Anthony (full name)
Area of achievement: Women's rights

Early Life

Susan Brownwell Anthony (AN-thah-nee) was the second child of Daniel and Lucy Read Anthony. Her mother, a sullen, withdrawn woman, grudgingly accepted her domestic role as housewife and mother of six. Susan loved but pitied her mother and learned from her more what to avoid than emulate. Her father, in contrast, always loomed large in his daughter's eyes. A radical Quaker, Daniel Anthony was liberal in creed and illiberal toward those who tolerated the social evils that he so adamantly despised. Strong-willed and independent of mind, Daniel Anthony taught his children to be firm in their convictions and to demonstrate their love for God by working for human betterment.

As an owner of a small cotton mill, Daniel Anthony had the means to provide for his daughter's education. A precocious child, Anthony took full advantage of her opportunities, first attending the village school and later receiving private instruction from a tutor hired by her father. At the age of seventeen, Anthony left with her older sister Guelma for a Quaker boarding school in Philadelphia. Anthony's seminary training, however, was cut short by the Panic of 1837. With mounting business debts, Daniel Anthony was forced to auction his cotton mill, homestead, furniture, and even his personal belongings, and to relocate as a dirt farmer on a small tract of land outside Rochester, New York.

In response to the family crisis, Susan Anthony left boarding school, secured a teaching position, and began sending half of her two-dollar weekly salary home to the family. For the next decade, Anthony remained in the classroom, instructing her pupils in the three R's, even as she augmented her own education with extensive reading and study. Intelligent yet unpretentious, Anthony matured into an athletic, tall, and slender woman with thick brown hair and warm blue eyes. Hardly the ugly, unsexed "battle-ax" her future enemies portrayed her to be, Anthony was courted by several suitors and remained single largely because none of her admirers, in her opinion, equaled her father in character or conviction.

Like her father, Anthony was a reformer who yearned for a society free from the

Anthony, Susan B.

Susan B. Anthony.
(Library of Congress)

evils of slavery and alcoholism. An idealist but not a dreamer, Anthony worked actively in these reform efforts, serving during her twenties as president of the Canajoharie Daughters of Temperance. In 1849, at her father's request, Anthony resigned from teaching to take over management of the family farm near Rochester. This relocation enabled Daniel Anthony to devote his full attention to a new business venture (an insurance agency that eventually made him prosperous again). The move also allowed Anthony to commit herself more fully to reform activity.

Life's Work
While still a teacher in Canajoharie, Anthony read a newspaper account of a meeting in nearby Seneca Falls, where a group of sixty-eight women and thirty-two men issued a Declaration of Women's Rights. This declaration demanded free education, equality of economic opportunity, free speech, the right to participate in public affairs, and the right to vote. As a schoolteacher making only one-third the salary of her male colleagues, Anthony sympathized with many of these demands for equal rights. Her Quaker upbringing, however, had convinced her that no person should participate in a government that waged war or condoned slavery, and she was thus not yet ready to take up the cause of women's suffrage.

In 1851, while attending an antislavery lecture in Seneca Falls, Anthony met the

Anthony, Susan B.

renowned Elizabeth Cady Stanton. The two women developed an instant friendship that led to a strong partnership in reform work. Together they organized the Woman's State Temperance Society of New York and petitioned the state legislature for a prohibition law. On numerous occasions during the 1850's, Anthony left Rochester for Seneca Falls to care for Stanton's children while their mother was away on speaking tours.

Although agreeing with Stanton on most issues, Anthony for several years refrained from embracing Stanton's call for women's suffrage. Gradually, however, the arrogance and disregard of many male reformers for the rights of women altered Anthony's view. Finally, in 1853, after the male delegates of the New York Woman's Temperance Society monopolized the annual convention and rudely ousted Stanton as president, Anthony declared her full allegiance to the women's crusade for equal rights and political equality.

Anthony's political conversion brought new life to the fledgling women's movement. An experienced worker willing to assume the time-consuming chores that no one else wanted, Anthony labored around the clock for feminist causes, organizing women into local associations, scheduling conventions and arranging speakers, seeking contributions, and paying administrative expenses. During the winter of 1854-1855, Anthony personally visited fifty-four of the sixty New York counties, collecting signatures in support of legal rights for married women.

When the legislature failed to act, Anthony promised to return with petitions every year until the inequities were rectified. For five years the tireless Anthony kept her promise, and in 1860, following a stirring address by coworker Stanton, the New York legislature granted property and guardian rights to married women. Much to Anthony's and Stanton's dismay, however, two years later the same body repealed portions of the marriage reform bill. This setback confirmed what Anthony had been saying for a decade: Benevolent legislation alone was insufficient; women would be fully protected only when they enjoyed full political powers.

For Anthony and her associates, the decade of the 1860's was eventful but largely disappointing. Before the Civil War, Anthony campaigned hard for the American Anti-Slavery Society, and during the war she helped establish the Women's Loyalty League to lobby for a constitutional amendment that would abolish slavery and guarantee civil and political rights for all Americans. Nevertheless, despite her lifelong commitment to black rights, after the war Anthony opposed both the wording of the Fourteenth Amendment, because it inserted the word "male" in reference to citizen's rights, and the Fifteenth Amendment, for its failure to include the word "sex" in protecting voting rights for all citizens.

Berated by her former allies, who insisted that women must not endanger the long-awaited liberation of slaves with additional demands for women's rights, Anthony countered the accusations by asserting that if reformers linked these two great causes, then the moment in history called by some "the Negro's hour" could be the woman's hour as well. This controversy ultimately split the women's movement. Following an explosive Equal Rights Association convention in 1869, Anthony and Stanton organized the National Woman Suffrage Association (NWSA), a "for women only" organization committed to the passage of a national woman's suffrage amendment, while the

Anthony, Susan B.

more conservative reformers established the American Woman Suffrage Association (AWSA), a rival body that focused its efforts at the state rather than the national level.

At this time, Anthony's commitment to feminist goals did not deter her from other reform activities. In 1868, Anthony organized the Working Woman's Association in a futile attempt to unionize woman workers and build female solidarity across class lines. In the same year, Anthony and Stanton allied themselves with the eccentric millionaire George Francis Train and began publishing a radical newspaper entitled *The Revolution*. On its masthead was the motto: "Principle, not policy; justice, not favors. Men, their rights, and nothing more: Women, their rights and nothing less." This paper, which opened its columns to editorials on greenback currency, divorce laws, prostitution, and a variety of other controversial issues, survived only two years and left Anthony with a debt of ten thousand dollars. It took six years, but Anthony ultimately repaid the entire debt from income she gained delivering suffrage lectures on the Lyceum circuit. Following this experience, Anthony determined to disassociate herself from other controversial reforms and focus all of her energy on the crusade for woman suffrage.

In 1872, Anthony gained national media attention when she registered and voted in the presidential election. Several weeks later, a federal marshal issued her an arrest warrant for illegal voting. While awaiting trial, Anthony went on a whirlwind tour delivering the lecture, "Is It a Crime for a U.S. Citizen to Vote?" Her defense was that the Fourteenth Amendment made her a citizen, and citizenship carried with it the right to vote. During her trial, the judge refused to allow her to testify on her own behalf, demanded the jury to render a guilty verdict, and fined her one hundred dollars. Outraged by this travesty of justice, thousands sent contributions to the NWSA treasury. Although she lost the trial, Anthony (who never paid the fine) won added respect for herself and her cause.

Anthony spent the last three decades of her life recruiting and training a new generation of suffragist leaders, including, among many others, Anna Howard Shaw and Carrie Chapman Catt. In 1889, at the age of sixty-nine, Anthony worked to secure a merger of the rival NWSA and AWSA. Three years later, she accepted the presidency of the unified National American Woman Suffrage Association, and served in this capacity until 1900, when she passed on her mantle of leadership to her hand-picked successors. As honorary president emeritus, Anthony remained the dominant figure in the movement until the time of her death in March, 1906.

SIGNIFICANCE

When Anthony joined the women's rights movement at the age of thirty-three, women held little social, professional, or educational standing. They were denied the right to vote, to hold office, or to be tried by their peers. As wives, they lost their legal individuality, having no rights to inherit property, keep earnings, sign contracts, or claim more than one-third of their husbands' estates. As mothers, they lacked legal custody or control over their own children. By the time of Anthony's death, however, 80 percent of American colleges, universities, and professional schools admitted women. In many states women had legal control over their own earnings and property and, in case of divorce, generally were awarded custody of their children. Although much discrimina-

Anthony, Susan B.

tion remained, reform legislation along with advances in the medical treatment of women had increased the life expectancy of women from forty to fifty-one years. In four states, women enjoyed full suffrage rights, and in the majority of the remaining states, women voted in school or municipal elections.

Many of these changes were in part a consequence of the Industrial Revolution, which freed many women from a portion of their domestic chores, created new opportunities for employment, and provided increasing numbers with the wealth and leisure to sponsor reform work. The improved status of American women, however, was also a result of the heroic efforts of individuals who endured decades of hardship and ridicule in their quest for equal rights. For more than half a century, Anthony campaigned tirelessly for feminist goals. A radical visionary, the "Napoleon of Feminism" was also a shrewd, practical politician who did more than any other reformer to change the minds of men toward women, and of women toward themselves. Although vilified throughout much of her career, by the time of her death Anthony was the heroine of a second generation of suffragists, who in 1920 would win the victory she had fought so hard to achieve.

—*Terry D. Bilhartz*

FURTHER READING

Barry, Kathleen. *Susan B. Anthony: A Biography of a Singular Feminist*. New York: New York University Press, 1988. Scholarly but readable biography, explaining how Anthony's family background, education, Quaker upbringing, and the early temperance movement produced a woman with a striving for social justice. Outlines Anthony's involvement in the abolition and suffrage movements.

Buhle, Mary Jo, and Paul Bulhe. *A Concise History of Woman Suffrage: Selections from the Classic Works of Stanton, Anthony, Gage, and Harper*. Urbana: University of Illinois Press, 1978. An abridged volume of the basic sources of the women's suffrage movement. Provides useful selections from the writings of Anthony and other eminent suffrage leaders.

DuBois, Ellen Carol, ed. *The Elizabeth Cady Stanton-Susan B. Anthony Reader: Correspondence, Writings, Speeches*. Boston: Northeastern University Press, 1992. Collection of letters, speeches, and other written works tracing the relationship and political development of the two women. DuBois provides critical commentary to illuminate the women's writings and experiences.

Edwards, G. Thomas. *Sowing Good Seeds: The Northwest Suffrage Campaigns of Susan B. Anthony*. Portland: Oregon Historical Society, 1990. Anthony traveled to Oregon in 1871, 1896, and 1905 to campaign for women's suffrage. Edwards uses newspaper accounts of her trips to describe how Anthony organized her campaign and obtained publicity and support for women's right to vote.

Flexner, Eleanor. *Century of Struggle: The Woman's Rights Movement in the United States*. Cambridge, Mass.: Harvard University Press, 1959. An overview of the women's rights movement that offers insights into the intellectual origins of American feminism. It remains the standard history of the suffrage crusade.

Harper, Ida H. *The Life and Work of Susan B. Anthony*. 3 vols. Indianapolis: Bowen-Merrill, 1898-1908. The authoritative biography, written with Anthony's assis-

Armstrong, Neil

tance. The only source for numerous Anthony papers that were destroyed after its publication.

Lutz, Alma. *Susan B. Anthony: Rebel, Crusader, Humanitarian.* Boston: Beacon Press, 1959. A well-documented, straightforward biography. Informative, but, like the other dated biographies, it makes no attempt to penetrate beyond the surface record of events.

Sherr, Lynn. *Failure Is Impossible: Susan B. Anthony in Her Own Words.* New York: Times Books, 1995. Excerpts from Anthony's speeches and letters. Sherr provides commentary about Anthony's life and career.

Truman, Margaret. *Women of Courage.* New York: William Morrow, 1976. A popular collection of biographical sketches of noted American women. The Anthony essay concentrates on her arrest, trial, and conviction for illegal voting in the 1872 presidential election.

NEIL ARMSTRONG

❝ *I think we're going to the moon because it's in the nature of the human being to face challenges. . . . we're required to do these things just as salmon swim upstream.* ❞

Test pilot and astronaut

Armstrong was the first person to walk on the Moon. He was commander of the Apollo 11 spacecraft, which made the first piloted lunar landing mission in history, and he had an early career as a test pilot.

Born: August 5, 1930; Wapakoneta, Ohio
Also known as: Neil Alden Armstrong (full name)
Areas of achievement: Aviation and space exploration; business

EARLY LIFE

Neil Armstrong (ARM-strong), the first person to set foot on the Moon, was born on a farm in Auglaize County near Wapakoneta, Ohio. He was the elder son of Stephen Armstrong and Viola Armstrong; his younger brother, Dean Alan, was born in Jefferson, Ohio, and had a long career with the Delco Division of General Motors Corporation at Anderson, Indiana; Neil also had a sister, June Louise. Stephen Armstrong was an auditor for the state of Ohio, and his work took the family across the state to many towns. The Armstrongs moved from Warren to Jefferson, to Ravenna, to St. Mary's, Upper Sandusky, and finally to a more permanent home in Wapakoneta. The Armstrongs were descendants of Scotch-Irish immigrants, while the mother's ancestors were of German background. Neil's father eventually was made the assistant director of mental hygiene and corrections of the state of Ohio.

Armstrong began his formal education in the public schools of Warren, Ohio, where he attended Champion Heights Elementary School. His advanced reading abil-

Neil Armstrong.
(NASA/USAF)

ity (he had read ninety books in the first grade) permitted him to skip the second grade. Known as a shy and modest boy, he played baseball and football with friends and enjoyed school activities.

Influenced by his father, Armstrong had an early interest in aviation. His family attended the National Air Races at the Cleveland airport, and as a six-year-old boy he accompanied his father in a plane called a Tin Goose (Ford TriMotor) that provided air rides near their home in Warren. During the Great Depression, Armstrong developed a deep interest in building model airplanes, a hobby that soon filled his room with the smell of glue and balsa wood. He quickly advanced from hobby kits to creating bigger and more powerful models of his own, which he tested at the town park. During his high school years, to improve his homemade planes, Armstrong built a seven-foot-long wind tunnel in the basement of his family's house. He was also an enthusiastic fan of science fiction, especially that of H. G. Wells.

One neighbor, Jacob Zint, owned a powerful telescope and often invited youngsters to look at the Moon, stars, and planets. Armstrong remembered these stargazing experiences as awe inspiring and began more study of the universe. He loved to learn; his schoolbooks, which his parents saved, reflect his thorough study and wide reading in the fields of science and mathematics. With his collection of the popular *Air Trails* magazine, he kept pace with aviation advancements. As a high school student, at the age of fifteen, he worked in stores to earn enough money to take flying lessons. On his sixteenth birthday, even before he had a driver's license, he was granted a student pilot's license. He later said that he had decided to become an aircraft designer and thought that a good designer needed to know how to fly.

Armstrong rode his bicycle day after day in 1946 to the Auglaize Flying Field at Wapakoneta, where flight instructor Aubrey Knudegard trained him to fly in an Aeronca 7AC Champion, built in Middletown, Ohio. The Aeronca Airplane Company had been a pioneer in the production of light, single-wing aircraft for private flying, and Armstrong learned to fly the plane with skill. Since the initial flights in 1903 of the Wright brothers at Kitty Hawk, North Carolina, the growth of aerospace research had been concentrated at the Wright-Patterson Air Force Base in Dayton, Ohio, and the Miami Valley had become a center of postwar aviation development and testing. Armstrong was flying from a local airfield not far from this national air base. He also became an Eagle Scout in the Boy Scouts of America.

In the fall of 1947, following his graduation from Wapakoneta High School, Armstrong entered Purdue University at Lafayette, Indiana, on a United States Navy scholarship. Enrolled in the College of Engineering, he had completed about two years of study when the navy ordered him to report to Pensacola, Florida, for special flight training. After the outbreak of the Korean War in July, 1950, Armstrong was the youngest member of his unit, Fighter Squadron 51, when it was sent overseas for active duty. He flew seventy-eight combat missions from the flight deck of the aircraft carrier the USS *Essex*. One mission nearly cost him his life: His Panther jet, damaged by antiaircraft fire, nicked a cable stretched across a North Korean valley; with grim determination and skill, he guided the plane back into South Korea before parachuting to safety. Armstrong won three Air Medals for his combat duty. (Author James Michener modeled his classic 1953 novel *The Bridges of Toko-Ri* after Armstrong and some other fliers in the squadron.)

On completion of his navy service in 1952, Armstrong returned to Purdue to finish his bachelor of science degree in aeronautical engineering and was graduated in 1955. On campus, he met Janet Shearon of Evanston, Illinois, who shared his love for flying; their college courtship led to marriage on January 28, 1956. Three children were born to the Armstrongs: Eric, born in 1957; Karen, born in 1959 (she died near the age of three); and Mark, born in 1963.

Armstrong had by then matured into a handsome aviator with a strong physical stature, standing nearly six feet tall. Reserved in speech but quite able to express himself, Armstrong had keen blue eyes that reflected the intensity of concentration and the good judgment of his mind. Always a good listener, he had absorbed a remarkable amount of information about airborne flight and often drew vital information from that reservoir.

LIFE'S WORK

Armstrong went to work at the Lewis Flight Propulsion Laboratory in Cleveland, serving as a research pilot. After six months at Lewis, he transferred to the High Speed Flight Station at Edwards Air Force Base in California, where he served as an aeronautical research pilot testing many pioneering aircraft, including the X-15 rocket airplane (he took it to more than 200,000 feet above Earth's surface and flew at speeds of nearly four thousand miles per hour), the X-1, F-100, F-101, F-102, F-104, F5D, B-47, and the paraglider. In all, he flew more than two hundred different kinds of aircraft. While in California, he began his master of science degree in aerospace engineering at the University of Southern California, completing it in 1969.

Spurred by the Soviet Union's successful launching of the first Earth-orbiting satellite, *Sputnik 1*, on October 4, 1957, the United States in 1958 established the National Aeronautics and Space Administration (NASA) to coordinate all space research projects sponsored by the federal government. Soon the United States was sending its satellites skyward, and NASA began training spacecraft pilots called "astronauts" for orbital flights. *Explorer 1* became the first successful American data-gathering space satellite, launched in January, 1958. It was Soviet cosmonaut Yuri Gagarin, however, who became the first human in space orbit, in April, 1961, aboard the *Vostok 1*; the United States sent its first piloted capsule into suborbital flight in May, 1961, with Alan B. Shepard, Jr., flying in *Freedom 7*. That month, President John F. Kennedy, in an address to Congress, called for the nation to land the first person on the Moon by the end of the decade, a goal that was achieved.

While still working at NASA's facility at Edwards Air Force Base (consolidated into NASA), Armstrong applied to be one of the United States' astronauts. The requirements favored men from military units, but Armstrong was accepted in 1962; he was the first civilian admitted to the astronaut program by NASA. The Armstrongs moved to El Lago, Texas, and Armstrong joined the nation's second recruit class of astronauts in training at the new NASA Manned Spacecraft Center in Houston for a two-year intensive program of classroom study and training for space travel.

NASA developed three space programs while Armstrong worked as an astronaut. The first, designated Project Mercury, was to develop the technology and experience to send a person into Earth orbit. On February 20, 1962, the first piloted orbital flight launched by the United States carried John Glenn as pilot of a three-orbit space trip. The Gemini program, created in 1962, launched a series of two-person spacecraft in Earth orbit during 1965 and 1966, including two unpiloted and ten piloted ventures. Project Apollo, created in 1960, was redirected in 1962 to land on the Moon by 1970, using a three-person crew. Nine crewed Apollo missions of lunar orbit or landings were made by the end of that program in 1972.

Armstrong was assigned as a command pilot for the Gemini 8 mission launched on March 16, 1966. He successfully performed the first docking of two vehicles (one piloted, the other unpiloted) in space. He and David R. Scott found the two crafts pitching and spinning out of control; Armstrong detached their Gemini capsule, and then, as it began to roll even faster, brought it back under control and made an emergency landing in the Pacific Ocean. He also served as commander of the backup crew for *Gemini 11* and late in 1966, at the request of President Lyndon B. Johnson, went on a twenty-four-day goodwill tour of South America with other astronauts.

It was as spacecraft commander of Apollo 11, the first piloted lunar landing mission in history, that Armstrong gained the distinction of being the first to land a craft on the Moon and the first to step on its surface, an event that was achieved on July 20, 1969, four days after the craft's launch. Michael Collins served as command module pilot of the *Columbia*, which orbited the Moon while Armstrong and Colonel Edwin E. Aldrin, Jr., aboard the four-legged lunar module called the *Eagle*, landed near the Sea of Tranquillity (at about 4:18 P.M., eastern daylight time) and explored the surface before the rendezvous with the *Columbia* for the return trip.

The next day, *The New York Times* ran the headline, "MEN WALK ON MOON: Astronauts Land on Plain; Collect Rocks, Plant Flag." Relating one of humanity's most historic moments, a journalist recounted:

> About six and a half hours [following the lunar landing], Mr. Armstrong opened the landing craft's hatch, stepped slowly down the ladder and declared as he planted the first human footprint on the lunar crust: "That's one small step for man, one giant leap for mankind."
>
> His first step on the moon came at 10:56:20 P.M., as a television camera outside the craft transmitted his every move to an awed and excited audience of hundreds of millions of people on Earth.
>
> Colonel Aldrin soon joined Armstrong and, in a two-and-a-half-hour stay outside the *Eagle*, the two set up a camera for live television transmission, conducted seismographic and laser experiments, planted a United States flag, and collected samples of Moon soil and rocks. After twenty-two hours, they blasted off to rejoin the *Columbia*, climbed back into the command module, jettisoned the lunar *Eagle*, and returned to earth to splash down southeast of Hawaii and were personally welcomed by President Richard M. Nixon aboard the USS *Hornet*. Nixon said: "You have taught man how to reach for the stars."

For eighteen days after the splashdown, the three lunar astronauts were kept in isolation to avoid any contamination from the Moon's environment. New York City welcomed them with the greatest ticker-tape parade since Charles A. Lindbergh's solo flight to Paris in 1927. At the White House, they received the nation's highest civilian honor: The Medal of Freedom was given to each of them. In the next months, they visited twenty-two nations and were awarded medals and citations from governments and scientific organizations around the world.

Armstrong was reassigned to the position of deputy associate administrator for aeronautics, Office of Advanced Research and Technology, NASA Headquarters, Washington, D.C. He was responsible for the coordination and management of NASA research and technology work related to aeronautics. Warned in his correspondence with Charles A. Lindbergh of the dangers of fame, he resolutely shunned the limelight and evaded reporters and photographers. From then on, his name was among the best known on the planet, but he could travel anywhere without being recognized.

In the fall of 1971, at the urging of his friend, Paul Herget, astronomer and professor of space science, whose work in the field of minor planets and in satellite orbits had won world recognition, Armstrong accepted an appointment as professor of engineering at the University of Cincinnati, an interdisciplinary post he retained until 1980. After their return to Ohio, the Armstrongs lived on a farm near Lebanon, Warren County, where their sons were graduated from high school.

Between 1979 and 1981, Armstrong worked part-time for the Chrysler Corporation and appeared in a national advertising campaign for the Detroit car manufacturer. For a short time, he and his brother Dean owned and operated the Cardwell International Corporation, a producer and exporter of oil field equipment. He later headed CTA, an aviation company based in Charlottesville, Virginia. Sought by many major corporations, Armstrong accepted positions on the board of directors of several companies, including Gates Learjet and United Airlines. In the 1980's, although carefully guarding his schedule, he became a popular speaker at national conventions and trade associations as well as a commencement speaker for many universities, some of which awarded him honorary degrees. He turned down offers from both major political parties to run for office.

Following the explosion of the *Challenger* orbiter on January 28, 1986, in which seven astronauts lost their lives, President Ronald Reagan named William Rogers chair and Neil Armstrong vice chair of a presidential commission to investigate the causes of the *Challenger*'s failure. For the next six months, Armstrong served as an active member of that commission, appearing on television and before Congress with the chair to report on the findings of the body. After the Rogers Commission disbanded, Armstrong served on the board of directors of Thiokol, the corporation that had manufactured the rocket booster that caused the disaster.

In 1989 he was divorced from Janet. During a golf tournament in 1992, Armstrong met Carol Held Knight; they married two years later. In addition to creating difficulties in his first marriage, his fame sometimes caused him embarrassment and problems. He stopped signing autographs in 1994 after learning that the autographed items were being sold for thousands of dollars on such venues as the Internet company eBay, and he twice initiated lawsuits against those who used his name, words, or—in one case—hair without his permission or knowledge. He donated the settlements to charities.

Armstrong retired from business on May 7, 2002, resigning as chair of the board of EDO Corporation, an advanced technology firm serving defense, intelligence, and commercial markets in New York. He had become chair in 2000.

In 2005 a long-standing controversy was revived over what exactly Armstrong had said when he first stepped onto the Moon's surface. He always maintained that he had said "That's one small step for a man, one giant leap for mankind"; however, the "a" went unheard and the resulting statement, seemingly a mere redundancy, was sometimes ridiculed. A computer programmer in Australia, Peter Shann Ford, reprocessed the audio recording with advanced computer equipment and discovered that Armstrong was correct; an "a," only 35 milliseconds long, emerged from the reprocessing. Hidden in the static of the original transmission, the correct version reflected Armstrong's modest attempt to deflect attention from himself and include all humanity in the event.

Honors came early to Armstrong for his Moon landing and continued throughout his life. The Boy Scouts gave him the Distinguished Eagle Scout Award and Silver Buffalo Award. He also received the Congressional Space Medal of Honor, the Robert H. Goddard Memorial Trophy, and the National Aeronautics Association's Collier Trophy. Many places have been named after him, including a moon crater near his landing site, schools, streets, and, in 2004, the new engineering building at his alma mater.

Armstrong, Neil

Significance

When the three astronauts of *Apollo 11* addressed a joint session of the United States Congress on September 16, 1969, Armstrong recalled how they had left a bronze plaque on the *Eagle*'s remnants. It declared: "Here men from the planet Earth first set foot upon the Moon. July 1969, A.D. We came in peace for all mankind." Such sentiments reflect the noble convictions of Armstrong: He saw his individual role in the gigantic space exploration mission as that of only one member of the nation's great team; his accomplishment as a victory for the whole of human endeavor: "a giant leap for mankind," "in peace for all mankind." Hence, he was able to return quietly to university and business activities after becoming the greatest explorer of all time.

Governor James A. Rhodes led a drive for the erection of a globelike museum honoring Armstrong on the edge of his hometown at Wapakoneta, which houses a vast collection of the awards, citations, gifts, and honors given the Ohio native. As a new American hero, a skillful and courageous commander in the tradition of Christopher Columbus, Ferdinand Magellan, and others, Armstrong confidently walked on the Moon first and confidently returned to work among his fellows. Through it all he remained unassuming about his achievement. He said in 2005, "I was elated, ecstatic and extremely surprised that we were successful."

—*Paul F. Erwin*

Further Reading

Brinkley, Douglas. "The Man and the Moon." *American History* 39 (August, 2004): 26-78. A substantial, enjoyable article that discusses Armstrong's famous reticence and shyness, reluctant participation in the Johnson Space Center Oral History Project, ferocious ability to concentrate on whatever he is doing, and role in U.S. aerospace programs.

Crouch, Tom D. *The Giant Leap: A Chronology of Ohio Aerospace Events and Personalities, 1815-1969*. Columbus: Ohio Historical Society, 1971. A graphic story of human flight from the time of early balloons, aircraft, and dirigibles through to Apollo 11's splashdown in 1969.

Hansen, James R. *First Man: The Life of Neil A. Armstrong*. New York: Simon & Schuster, 2005. Highly acclaimed biography that recounts Armstrong's career in flying, portraying him as a great but reluctant hero.

Mallon, Thomas. "Moon Walker." *The New Yorker*, October 3, 2005. A shrewd, provocative review of Armstrong's career and examination of his character that came out, in part, as a review of James R. Hansen's biography.

Wagener, Leon. *One Giant Leap: Neil Armstrong's Stellar American Journey*. New York: Forge, 2004. A well-researched, balanced, and updated biography of Armstrong.

Westman, Paul. *Neil Armstrong: Space Pioneer*. Minneapolis, Minn.: Lerner, 1980. A preliminary biography of Armstrong in conversational style packed into sixty-four pages with fine black-and-white photographs largely supplied by NASA. Contains an appendix of all United States piloted spaceflights from Mercury 3 through Project Apollo.

ROBERT D. BALLARD

❝ All kids dream a marvelous image of what they want to do. But then society tells them they can't do it. I didn't listen. I wanted to live my dream. ❞

Undersea explorer

As a pioneering undersea explorer, Ballard made several remarkable discoveries, including the resting place of the Titanic *and other ships, new life-forms along hot spots in the undersea Earth crust, and evidence supporting the theory of plate tectonics.*

Born: June 30, 1942; Wichita, Kansas
Also known as: Robert Duane Ballard (full name)
Area of achievement: Exploration

EARLY LIFE

Robert D. Ballard (BAL-lurd) was born in Wichita, Kansas, a distant relative of the gunslinger William "Bat" Masterson, who was for a time in the nineteenth century the sheriff of Wichita. When Ballard was still a young boy, his family resettled to Pacific Beach, a suburb of San Diego, California, where his father worked developing the Minuteman missile. Ballard began what would become a lifelong fascination with the world under the sea. He spent countless hours exploring along the shore, dreaming of submarines, and poring over the illustrations in an edition of his favorite book, Jules Verne's science-fiction novel *Vingt mille lieues sous les mers* (1869-1870; *Twenty Thousand Leagues Under the Sea*, 1873). When he was a senior in high school, he won a competition that enabled him to spend a summer training at the Scripps Institute of Oceanography in La Jolla, California.

Ballard's parents taught him to work hard to set and achieve his goals, and that lesson served him well while he was still a college student. At the University of California, Santa Barbara, he earned a degree in both chemistry and geology and completed the university's Reserve Officer Training Corps (ROTC) program, earning a commission as an Army lieutenant doing intelligence work.

After graduation, Ballard began graduate study in oceanography in Hawaii, where he also took a part-time job as a dolphin trainer at Sealife Park. This job helped him develop his skills as a writer and public speaker. In 1966 he transferred to the Navy and took a job helping to design and develop missions for submersibles for the Ocean Systems Group of his father's employer, North American Aviation. Ballard liked this work because it combined his passions for applied science, or technology, and pure science. The next year the Navy sent him to Boston to serve as an oceanographic liaison officer in the Office of Naval Research. His duties included serving as the Navy's liaison to the Woods Hole Oceanographic Institution on Cape Cod, Massachusetts.

LIFE'S WORK

On his first tour of Woods Hole, Ballard was attracted to *Alvin*, an experimental miniature research submarine capable of taking three divers to a depth of 6,000 feet, where

55

Ballard, Robert D.

the water pressure exceeds one ton per square inch. Ballard spent as much time as his position allowed at Woods Hole, helping map the geology of the ocean floor in the Gulf of Maine. In September, 1969, he left the Navy and joined the staff at Woods Hole; three months later he descended in a submersible for the first time as part of a team studying the continental shelf off the coast of Florida.

During these years, Ballard was also a student in the Ph.D. program in marine geology and geophysics at the University of Rhode Island. For his doctoral dissertation research, Ballard attempted to advance the plate tectonics theories of Professor Patrick Hurley of the Massachusetts Institute of Technology. He used *Alvin* to make some forty dives in the Gulf of Maine and surrounding areas, helping develop the techniques that made it possible to use the vessel's remote manipulator arm to drill for and collect samples of bedrock. With data taken from these samples and the results of his earlier mapping work, he provided hard evidence that the continents sit on movable tectonic plates and that the American, European, and African continents were once connected. At the same time, his work helped the *Alvin* team demonstrate and expand the capabilities of the submersible, thus attracting much-needed interest and funding from both government and private agencies.

By the fall of 1971, *Alvin* had been rebuilt with a titanium pressure sphere, making it capable of descending to 12,000 feet, the average depth of the seafloor. This improvement made it possible for Ballard and others to explore the undersea mountain range known as the Mid-Atlantic Ridge in 1973 and 1974, in a project called the French American Mid-Ocean Undersea Study, or Project FAMOUS. With the French scientist Jean Francheteau, Ballard posited a new theory about the composition and activity of the Mid-Atlantic Ridge. By this time the capabilities of both Ballard and the submersibles were drawing scientific and popular attention, and Ballard found himself something of a celebrity. He was now chief scientist on many expeditions and was able to obtain the funding he needed for further exploration.

In 1977 Ballard led a team from Woods Hole in an exploration of the Galapagos Rift area of the Pacific Ocean near Ecuador. The team intended to study the vents that expelled warm water from beneath the ocean floor. These vents were so far beneath the ocean's surface that no sunlight could penetrate to them, and it was supposed that no living things would be found there. Surprisingly, the researchers discovered various forms of life, including clams, crabs, bacteria, and giant tube worms, many more than eight feet long, living near underwater geysers. Oceanographers were excited by the discovery, which spurred extensive research to learn more about the chemical and biological processes that make life possible in this unlikely environment.

Ballard's next major expedition took him to the ocean floor off the coast of Baja California, Mexico. There, in 1979, he was part of a research team that discovered "black smokers," underwater volcanoes spewing black fluids reaching temperatures of 350 degrees Celsius through chimneys made of sulfide mineral deposits.

With improvements to *Alvin* continually being made, Ballard began to think that an old dream of his might become a reality: He might be able to locate the giant ship *Titanic* on the ocean floor. *Titanic*, which had sunk in 1912 on its first voyage from England to New York City, was thought to lie some thirteen thousand feet below the surface—too far for divers or previous submersibles to go. Government and industry figures were eager to find the sunken ship, knowing the publicity would provide a tremendous public relations boost to the finders. The military hoped that technology developed for undersea exploration could also be used for submarine warfare. Private adventurers had been searching for the ship for years. Ballard was able to gather funding and the support of the Navy, and in 1982 he established the Woods Hole Deep Submergence Laboratory (DSL). The lab team developed *Argo*, a sophisticated video sled about the size of a car, with floodlights and three cameras, and *Jason*, a smaller tethered robot vehicle that could be sent into tighter spaces than *Argo* could enter. The *Argo-Jason* system enabled a research crew onboard a ship to send and steer cameras out into the dark depths and to receive and interpret video pictures.

When testing of the *Argo-Jason* system was completed, Ballard and a team of French scientists launched a joint effort to locate the *Titanic*. The French, who had sophisticated sonar technology, would map the ocean floor in the area where the *Titanic* was thought to lie and determine a smaller area for *Argo* to search. For five frustrating weeks, the French covered a 100-mile target area but did not locate the ship. A few days before the French left the area, Ballard and his team arrived. Drawing on the French data, the Americans limited their search to a narrower area and located the *Titanic* late in the night of August 31, 1985. A year later, Ballard returned to *Titanic*, and this time he sent the smaller *Jason* robot into the ship itself to photograph the interior. The pictures of the ship, with its recognizable central staircase and unopened bottles of wine, captured the imaginations of viewers around the world.

Ballard continued his exciting work, in 1989 establishing the JASON Project, a program that sent live images from *Jason* video robots to students at museums and science centers so that they could experience through "telepresence" some of the wonders of the undersea world. Greatly expanding the possibilities of distance learning, Ballard made it possible for more than a million students each year in thousands of classrooms around the world to work interactively with underwater cameras and other equipment far below the surface of the ocean. Ballard also pursued the interest in undersea archaeology he had demonstrated in his search for the *Titanic*: In the 1990's he located and photographed the German battleship *Bismarck*, American and Japanese warships sunk during World War II at Guadalcanal, the luxury ship *Lusitania*, and several trading ships from the Roman Empire, some as old as two thousand years.

Ballard retired from Woods Hole in 1997 and founded the Institute for Exploration, dedicated to expanding the fields of underwater archaeology and deep-sea geology. Two years later, the institute merged with the Mystic Aquarium in Connecticut to form the Sea Research Foundation's Institute for Exploration, with Ballard as president. The institute developed underwater vehicles that carry sensing and imaging equipment to depths far beyond where humans could safely go and that send data back to researchers at the surface.

In 1998, Ballard again set out to locate sunken ships, this time in the Pacific Ocean near the island of Midway, where an important battle was fought between the Japanese and the Allies during World War II. Using the latest technology for undersea exploration, Ballard and his crew found and photographed four Japanese carriers and the American aircraft carrier the USS *Yorktown* more than three miles below the surface.

Ballard, Robert D.

Ballard's explorations continued into the twenty-first century. In 2002, working with the National Geographic Society, he located wreckage from John F. Kennedy's *PT-109*, which was sunk off the Solomon Islands during World War II. Ballard also managed to find and interview the two Solomon Island natives who rescued Kennedy and his crew after they had been shipwrecked. He and archaeologist George Bass led a group of marine archaeologists to explore ancient artifacts and mollusk remains 7,000 feet down in the Black Sea, using *Argus*, a remotely operated tethered underwater vehicle with optical cameras. The presence of shells from freshwater species identified during this expedition lent support to a much-debated theory that the Black Sea was settled by human beings before a large-scale flood devastated the area. In 2003 Ballard returned to the wreck of the *Titanic* to document the decay that had befallen the ship in the eighteen years since Ballard had found it on the ocean floor.

Ballard's twin passions for exploration and for teaching led him to an active parallel career as a public speaker, television host, and teacher. He was awarded the Cairn Medal of the National Maritime Museum in 2002 and was invited to speak at the John F. Kennedy Presidential Library in 2005. In 2004, he became a professor of oceanography and director of the Institute for Archaelogical Oceanography at the University of Rhode Island.

Significance

Throughout a career of more than thirty years, Ballard participated in more than one hundred dives and ventured out in more deep-diving submersibles than anyone else in the world. His explorations contributed greatly to knowledge of what lies beneath the surface of the oceans. Some discoveries, such as evidence in support of plate tectonic theory or the finding of life near hot vents on the ocean floor, were primarily of interest to other scientists and were presented in dozens of articles Ballard contributed to scientific journals. Ballard's discovery of the *Titanic* and the other lost ships thrilled people all over the world—both scientists and nonspecialists alike—in part because of his talent for making science and technology accessible to general audiences. Ballard wrote or cowrote more than a dozen books (including a juvenile biography and a children's pop-up book), as well as magazine articles and television programs.

Ballard also made great technological contributions, helping develop and refine submersibles, underwater video cameras, and robots to hold and move the cameras. Through his writing, speaking, and photography, and through the telepresence of the JASON Project, Ballard shared his discoveries with the world.

—*Cynthia A. Bily*

Further Reading

Allen, Christina G., Pat Cummings, and Linda C. Cummings, eds. *Talking with Adventurers: Conversations with Christina Allen, Robert Ballard, Michael Blakey, Ann Bowles, David Doubilet, Jane Goodall, Dereck and Beverly Joubert, Michael Novacek, Johan Reinhard, Rick West, and Juris Zarins*. Washington, D.C.: National Geographic Society, 1998. Ballard and the other scientists explain their jobs, including a typical working day and their most frightening experiences. This volume is intended for younger readers; the information it contains is useful and accessible.

Ballard, Robert D., and Rick Archbold. *The Lost Ships of Robert Ballard*. San Diego, Calif.: Thunder Bay Press, 2005. A large coffee-table book that celebrates several glorious sunken ocean liners and warships, including the *Titanic*, *Bismarck*, *Lusitania*, and *Andrea Doria*, that Ballard located on the ocean floor. Includes high-tech underwater photographs, as well as paintings and historical images.

_____. *Return to Midway*. Washington, D.C.: National Geographic Society, 1999. Ballard's exploration of ships sunk during the World War II battle at Midway, including the aircraft carrier USS *Yorktown*, which was found more than three miles below the surface of the ocean. Richly illustrated with photographs and paintings.

Ballard, Robert D., with Will Hively. *The Eternal Darkness: A Personal History of Deep-Sea Exploration*. Princeton, N.J.: Princeton University Press, 2000. Ballard provides an account of his own explorations and the efforts of other twentieth century explorers to investigate the ocean depths. Includes photographs, charts, and maps.

Ballard, Robert D., with Malcolm McConnell. *Explorations: My Quest for Adventure and Discovery Under the Sea*. New York: Hyperion, 1995. A complete account of Ballard's entire career in marine geology, this best-selling autobiography offers accessible explanations of his scientific achievements. This volume is more memoir than science and is thought by many to exaggerate Ballard's contributions to some projects, but it is lively reading, telling its story with dialogue and beautiful descriptive passages.

Hecht, Jeff. "20,000 Tasks Under the Sea." *New Scientist* 147 (September 30, 1995): 40-45. A description of Ballard's post-*Titanic* explorations of the Mediterranean Sea, looking for more than two-thousand-year-old sunken ships from the Roman Empire. For this feat of underwater archaeology, Ballard had the use of a U.S. Navy nuclear submarine, the NR-1, designed originally for deep-sea military surveillance and able to withstand high pressure and stay underwater for up to one month.

BENJAMIN BANNEKER

> *" I am of the African race, and in the colour which is natural to them of the deepest dye; and it is under a sense of the most profound gratitude to the Supreme Ruler of the Universe. "*

Mathematician and astronomer

Banneker's calculations provided the essential data for almanacs published from 1792 through 1797. A free black in a slave state, Banneker overcame obstacles of rural isolation, little formal education, and racial prejudice to establish himself as a respected scientist, earn a place on the crew that surveyed the District of Columbia, and become a symbol of racial equality in the abolitionist movement. He is also known for his letter to Thomas Jefferson calling on him to end slavery in America.

Born: November 9, 1731; Baltimore County, Maryland
Died: October 9, 1806; Baltimore, Maryland
Areas of achievement: Astronomy; mathematics; social reform

EARLY LIFE

Benjamin Banneker (BA-neh-kur) was born into a family whose American antecedents came in bonds to colonial Maryland. His grandmother, Molly Welsh, was a convict transported from England to Maryland in about 1683. After completing a period of servitude, she became a free landowner in the western part of Baltimore County near the Patapsco River. In 1692, Molly bought two Africans and in a few years restored freedom to both. One of the men, named Bannka, claimed to be the kidnapped son of an African king. In defiance of laws that forbade miscegenation, Molly married the prince and took Banneky as her surname.

The Bannekys had four daughters. The oldest, Mary, born in about 1700, married an African who had been given freedom as a baptismal gift. He had chosen Robert as his Christian name and, when married, took Banneky as his surname. The name's spelling varied until the mid-eighteenth century, when it settled at Banneker. Three of the four children born to Robert and Mary grew to maturity. The oldest, and the only son, was Benjamin, born in 1731.

In about 1729, Robert bought 25 acres of land close to Molly's farm. On March 10, 1737, when Benjamin was five years old, Robert purchased 100 acres from the nearby Stout plantation. The title was in Robert's and Benjamin's names to assure that the family could protect its freedom should Robert die suddenly. Maryland laws were not sympathetic to free blacks and authorized reenslavement of those who did not own property.

Banneker's education was rudimentary. His grandmother taught him to read from the Bible. For a few months, he attended a country school where the schoolteacher, probably a Quaker, taught both black and white children. Benjamin learned to write a very clear, even beautiful, script and mastered the fundamentals of mathematics through basic algebra. At some point, he also learned to play the flute and the violin. Though meager, this education powerfully shaped the course of Banneker's life. He purchased his own Bible in 1763, read it diligently, and sprinkled his writings with scriptural quotations. He never formally joined a Christian denomination, but he often attended Quaker, and sometimes Methodist, services. His reading interests went beyond the Bible to literature in general. He painstakingly compiled a small library, composed essays in his own commonplace book, and wrote poetry.

Mathematics, though, was the subject that most stimulated his intellectual curiosity. He had unusual abilities with numbers. As a young man, he became locally famous for being able to solve fairly complex computations in his head. He had a special fondness for mathematical puzzles and liked to trade tricky problems with his neighbors.

It was probably during such an exchange with a neighbor that Banneker first saw and then borrowed a watch. The timepiece fascinated him, and he dismantled it to observe its moving parts. Using the watch as a model, Banneker produced a clock made entirely of hand-carved hardwoods. The clock kept accurate time, struck the hours, and was the wonder of the Patapsco valley.

Banneker completed the clock in 1753, when he was twenty-two. His father died six years later, leaving Benjamin the sole owner of the Stout acreage. The rest of the property was divided among Benjamin and his two married sisters. Banneker lived with his mother until she died in 1775. He never married and lived the rest of his life on his well-kept, productive farm. He might have died in obscurity had not the Ellicott brothers bought land adjoining the Banneker farm.

LIFE'S WORK

Joseph, Andrew, and John Ellicott brought their large families and the families of several workers to the Patapsco valley in 1771, when Benjamin Banneker was forty years old. Before they were fully settled, the Ellicotts and their workers bought food from the existing farms. Andrew Ellicott's young son George developed a special friendship with Banneker. At age fifteen in 1775, George was recognized as a mathematical prodigy, an accomplished surveyor, and a gifted astronomer. With George's encouragement and assistance, Banneker rapidly mastered advanced mathematics and became fascinated with astronomy. In the fall of 1788, George loaned Banneker books on mathematics and astronomy, a telescope, a set of drafting instruments, a lamp, and a large, oval drop-leaf table.

Banneker soon spent clear nights in open fields observing the heavens. When recording his observations in cold weather he dressed heavily and wrapped himself in blankets. At dawn he returned to his cabin and slept for a few hours. He spent most of the rest of the day at the oval table studying the borrowed books and plotting the movements of the stars. The calculation of a star's location for a particular date could involve as many as ten different algebraic and logarithmic operations.

As he gained a sure grasp of astronomy, Banneker began the ambitious project of calculating an ephemeris—a table showing the positions of the Earth, Moon, planets, and stars throughout the year. The ephemeris was the basis for projecting eclipses and predicting weather conditions. It was, therefore, the major component of an almanac, a compilation of astronomical and weather-related data for a given year. He was encouraged in this project by his mentor George and by George's cousin, Major Andrew Ellicott. Major Ellicott had prepared ephemerides for publication from 1781 through 1786, but the demands of his work as a surveyor forced him to abandon the time-consuming calculations. In the summer of 1790, Banneker submitted completed ephemerides for 1791 to three publishers, but none of the editors bought his work. Although discouraged, Banneker began an ephemeris for 1792.

In January of 1791, President George Washington instructed Secretary of State Thomas Jefferson to have the District of Columbia surveyed. On February 2, 1791, Jefferson named Major Ellicott the chief surveyor. Ellicott was to find the true meridian and longitude of the future capital and to prepare a topographical map of the 10-mile-square tract of land. Because he was shorthanded, Ellicott turned to Banneker for help. Banneker had no practical experience as a surveyor, but he had mastered the mathematics involved and knew how to work with most of the astronomical instruments.

On February 7, 1791, Banneker, at age fifty-nine, made his first trip outside Baltimore County. During his three-month stay at the site of the future capital, he gained valuable experience as assistant to Ellicott. He learned to use the astronomical clock and other instruments new to him. He also kept a resolution to abstain from drinking wine and hard liquor while working with the surveying crew.

Upon his return home, he finished the ephemeris for 1792. Meanwhile, Joseph and George Ellicott had interested members of the Society of Friends and the antislavery societies in Baltimore and Philadelphia in Banneker. Through their assistance, Banneker's 1792 ephemeris was published by the Baltimore firm of Goddard and Angell. The almanac, *Benjamin Banneker's Pennsylvania, Delaware, Maryland and Virginia Almanack and Ephemeris for the Year of Our Lord, 1792.* was sold in Baltimore, Philadelphia, and Alexandria beginning in December, 1791. The editors of the almanac included a note in the work's front matter, stating that the almanac was "an extraordinary Effort of Genius—a COMPLETE and ACCURATE EPHEMERIS . . . calculated by a sable Descendant of Africa. . . ." The editors argued that the almanac was proof that skin color had no relationship to mental or intellectual capacity, that all people were alike, and that slavery should be ended. The first four thousand copies quickly sold out, as did a second printing by Goddard and Angell and a condensed edition printed by William Young in Philadelphia.

Banneker prepared an ephemeris that was published in an almanac each year through 1797. The almanacs were extremely popular and sold well. At least twenty-eight editions of these almanacs appeared in those six years. Starting in 1794, Banneker computed tide tables for Chesapeake Bay, a feature that competing almanacs did not contain.

The elderly astronomer was of average height and had a full head of thick, white hair. Though portly, his posture, gentlemanly behavior, and staff gave him a dignified air. Banneker continued to calculate ephemerides through 1802, the year he turned seventy-one. His capacity for work had diminished, and he was unable to complete the rigorous computations. He died quietly in his home four years later on October 9, 1806.

SIGNIFICANCE

Benjamin Banneker's abilities as a mathematician and astronomer made him famous in his lifetime. There was, however, much more to his fame than his scientific accomplishments themselves. Banneker was the son and grandson of Africans. He was a free black in a predominantly white society that almost universally regarded black people as mentally inferior to whites. Banneker's best-known act—in his lifetime and since—was his correspondence with Thomas Jefferson.

On August 19, 1791, Banneker sent the author of the Declaration of Independence a handwritten copy of his ephemeris and a long letter. He introduced himself as a black man and then eloquently pleaded with Jefferson to use his influence to end the slavery that still kept some from enjoying their "inalienable rights." Jefferson responded by expressing the hope that people would soon recognize that circumstances, not natural endowments, kept blacks in a condition that suggested inferiority, but he made no pledge to do anything more than to send Banneker's almanac to abolitionists in France.

Those two letters were printed in the 1793 almanac and reprinted frequently in abolitionist literature in the nineteenth century. Benjamin Banneker had become a symbol of racial equality because he was an example of black achievement. His name has been invoked over the years in black educational efforts, such as Benjamin Banneker College of Prairie View A&M University at Prairie View, Texas.

—*Paul E. Kuhl*

FURTHER READING

Allen, Will W., comp. *Banneker: The Afro-American Astronomer.* Washington, D.C.: Black Heritage Library, 1921. Reprint. Freeport, N.Y.: Books for Libraries Press, 1971. This work is based largely on primary sources. However, the book contains a paper by Daniel Murray that advances the oft-repeated, undocumented claim that Banneker worked with Major Pierre Charles L'Enfant and had a copy of the city's plans for use after L'Enfant left the capital site in a rage.

Allen, William G. *Wheatley, Banneker, and Horton.* Boston: D. Laing, 1849. Reprint. Freeport, N.Y.: Books for Libraries Press, 1970. A condensation of an earlier work on records held by the Ellicott family.

Armistead, Wilson. *A Tribute for the Negro: Being a Vindication of the Moral, Intellectual, and Religious Capabilities of the Colored Portion of Mankind, with Particular Reference to the African Race.* 1848. Reprint. Miami, Fla.: Mnemosyne, 1969. A collection of abolitionist literature. The material on Banneker consists of a brief biographical sketch and a reprint of the Jefferson correspondence.

Baker, Henry E. "Benjamin Banneker, the Negro Mathematician and Astronomer." *Journal of Negro History* 3 (April, 1918): 99-118. A fine sketch based upon a rare work prepared by George Ellicott's daughter Martha Ellicott Tyson.

Bedini, Silvio A. *The Life of Benjamin Banneker: The First African-American Man of Science.* 2d rev. ed. Baltimore: Maryland Historical Society, 1999. An excellent study of Banneker, based on careful review of secondary materials, previously unused material from private archives, and Banneker's commonplace book and journal. Originally published in 1971, this expanded edition includes new photographs and information on Banneker's African roots.

Cerami, Charles. *Benjamin Bannecker: Surveyor, Astronomer, Publisher, Patriot.* New York: J. Wiley, 2002. A clearly and simply written biography that examines Banneker's life and the breadth of his career.

Miller, John Chester. *The Wolf by the Ears: Thomas Jefferson and Slavery.* New York: Free Press, 1977. Miller treats the correspondence between Banneker and Jefferson in the context of Jefferson's life and slavery in the United States.

CLARA BARTON

> *I may be compelled to face danger, but never fear it, and while our soldiers can stand and fight, I can stand and feed and nurse them.*

Nursing pioneer

After devoting half of her life to humanitarian pursuits, Barton became the key figure in establishing the American Red Cross.

Born: December 25, 1821; North Oxford, Massachusetts
Died: April 12, 1912; Glen Echo, Maryland
Also known as: Clarissa Harlowe Barton (full name)
Areas of achievement: Nursing; public health

EARLY LIFE

Clarissa Harlowe Barton (BAR-tuhn), known as Clara, was influenced by her parents' liberal political attitudes. The youngest child, Clara had identity problems that worsened when she showed interests in academic and other pursuits considered masculine. Farmwork and nursing relatives who were ill, however, led her increasingly to connect approval and praise to helping others.

In 1836, Barton began teaching school. She was a gifted teacher who chose to enforce discipline through kindness and persuasion at a time when physical force was the standard. During the next decade, Barton developed quite a reputation as she moved from town to town, taming obstreperous students and leaving for another challenge. As she gained self-confidence, she began to have an active social life, though she never married. Tired of teaching and concerned that her own education was inadequate, she enrolled at the Clinton Liberal Institute in Clinton, New York, at the end of 1850. She studied for a year, but as an older student she felt out of place and made few friends.

Unable to afford more school and unwilling to be dependent on her family, Barton went to live with friends in New Jersey. In 1852, she persuaded authorities to offer free public education by allowing her to open a free school. Although she was initially unpaid, Barton eventually made the school such a success that she was offered a salary and the opportunity to expand her program. As the school grew, however, the school board decided that a man should be placed in charge and paid more than any women involved. Frustrated and angry, Barton moved to Washington, D.C., in search of new opportunities in 1854.

Clara Barton.
(Library of Congress)

Barton found work as a clerk in the Patent Office, where the commissioner was willing to give women positions. For several years Barton made good money and earned respect for her efficiency despite the resentment of her male colleagues. Shifting political fortunes forced Barton to leave her post in 1857. For three years, she lived at home in Massachusetts before returning to the Patent Office in 1860.

Life's Work

With the outbreak of the Civil War in 1861, Clara Barton began the humanitarian work that would occupy the rest of her life. Federal troops were arriving in Washington without baggage or food. She began to gather and distribute supplies to ease their distress. Her efforts quickly grew to include battlefield assistance in helping the wounded at the beginning of the war. Because the military had badly underestimated medical needs, Barton's individual efforts at gathering supplies and caring for the wounded at battles such as Fredericksburg proved immensely valuable. By the end of 1862, however, the Army was becoming better organized and the work of amateurs was no longer significant. Barton also had problems getting official support and recognition because, unlike Barton, most volunteers were more harm than help. The Army could not accept one volunteer while denying others. Barton, as she often did, became defensive, taking every rebuke, regardless of the source, personally.

Barton, Clara

After the war, Barton undertook a project to identify missing soldiers and inform their families of their fates. Her efforts included a trip to Andersonville prison where, with the help of a former inmate who had kept the death roll, Barton supervised the identification and marking of some 13,000 graves. Despite some success, Barton's work in tracing missing soldiers resulted in identification of less than 10 percent of the missing.

During her pursuit of these activities, Barton confronted two difficulties of a sort typical of her career. One problem arose because the Army was also attempting to find missing soldiers. Barton sought sole control of the whole effort, but this control was not granted and she feuded with the officer in charge. Barton possessed a zeal for efficiency that made her reluctant to share responsibility or credit. This attitude prevented her from delegating authority and provoked hostility among many people who actually wanted to help her. The second problem was a result of poor accounting. She could not provide details of expenses, leaving herself open to charges of malfeasance.

Although she was always more interested in field work than administration, Barton was unwilling to share power with someone who would handle paperwork. She paid little attention to tracking the disbursement of donated funds and poured her own limited resources into her projects even though she could produce no receipts. There is no evidence that she sought personal gain. Nevertheless, her poor accounting resulted in repeated complaints that ultimately came back to haunt her during her work with the Red Cross.

Barton's involvement with the Red Cross began in Europe, where she met some of the organization's leaders and learned that the United States had not ratified the Treaty of Geneva (1864) that had created the organization. Barton was invited to assist in the work of the International Red Cross during the Franco-Prussian War of 1870-1871. Her experiences gave her a new perspective on the suffering of civilians during war—she had worked almost entirely on behalf of soldiers in the Civil War. Friendship with Grand Duchess Louise of Baden, a Red Cross leader, resulted in Barton working six months in Strasbourg. She was convinced of the value of the Red Cross and determined that supporting self-help was better than handouts. She held these convictions the rest of her life.

In 1872, Barton returned to the United States, after suffering a nervous breakdown that some regarded as partially psychosomatic. Retiring from public life to stay in a sanatorium eventually improved her health. In 1877, she decided to form an American Red Cross society to gather funds to help victims of the Russo-Turkish War. She received permission from the International Red Cross and began a campaign to secure American ratification of the Treaty of Geneva. U.S. government officials, however, insisted that because the country observed the tenets of the treaty, there was no reason for a formal alliance.

Barton lobbied diligently for ratification. She sought help from friends in Washington, D.C., cultivated the press, and relied upon her friendship with members of the Grand Army of the Republic, a Civil War veterans group that had honored her. To increase awareness of the work of the Red Cross, Barton made peacetime disaster relief a priority. Progress was slow, but the treaty was ratified in 1882. Her group was officially recognized by the government, paving the way for it to be associated with the International Red Cross. This recognition helped Barton launch her next campaign: to make the American Association of the Red Cross the central relief agency in the United States.

The 1880's and 1890's were times of heroic effort for Barton. Her labor was certainly greatly increased by her refusal to yield any share of control, and, during the decades of her presidency, she and the Red Cross were essentially synonymous. She wanted the national agency to be the center of a network of state groups, but she was frequently drawn away from organizing to oversee field work and was hampered by continual shortages of funds. She also spent much of 1883 running a women's prison at the request of Benjamin Butler, the former Union general who had become governor of Massachusetts. Assisting Butler with his political problems concerning the funding of the progressive prison, Barton established that the costs were mostly appropriate, despite sloppy administrative work. Unfortunately, her efforts on Butler's behalf diverted Barton's attention from the urgent demands of Red Cross work.

For the rest of her life, however, Barton devoted herself almost exclusively to Red Cross work. She traveled, seeking funds and public support—sometimes for herself as well as her cause—and attended annual meetings of the International Red Cross, where she was accepted as a delegate when no other woman was even allowed on the convention floor. She was a hero to feminists, whose cause she supported, although never so vigorously as to cause hostility toward the Red Cross. Field work continued to beckon, including relief efforts in the wake of floods in the Ohio and Mississippi River valleys in 1884 and an earthquake in Charleston, South Carolina, in 1886. She allowed the head of the New Orleans chapter to lead an effort in a yellow fever epidemic around Jacksonville, Florida, only to find that the nurses he took resembled camp followers more than caregivers. This incident confirmed her determination to do everything herself.

Barton received praise from the press for relief efforts in the wake of the 1889 Johnstown flood, but she was later greatly criticized for not keeping track of expenditures. Some of the expenses appear to have been inappropriate, though not fraudulent, but her lack of receipts made defense against such criticism almost impossible. Barton hoped to parlay the Johnstown success into government funding for the Red Cross as the official agency for coordinating wartime relief. This effort stalled, however, and she turned her attention to efforts to alleviate a Russian famine.

By the mid-1890's, relief funds were at a low ebb, and criticism of her poor accounting hampered the activities of both the American and international organizations. Although Barton was in her seventies and her energy was beginning to decline, she repudiated every criticism, attacked critics, and continued. In 1896, she went to Turkey to aid Armenians suffering from Turkish atrocities. She secured permission from the Turkish sultan to send Dr. Julian Hubbell, one of her most loyal collaborators, into Armenia, where he had significant success.

Back in the United States, she found appeals from Cuban civilians suffering in the struggle against Spain. Because the U.S. government wanted to keep out of the conflict, little was being done to provide relief. Eventually, Barton went to survey the situation with a committee of relief agencies. When the head of another agency criticized her work and tried to supplant her, Barton returned to the United States and got her ri-

Barton, Clara

val discredited. By the time she returned to Cuba, however, the Spanish-American War had begun. The New York Red Cross chapter, which, along with several others, had been acting almost autonomously, provided necessary assistance to stateside military hospitals, and the California chapter sent aid to the Pacific front in the Philippines. Barton headed for Cuba, eventually leaving without official sanction. Although intending to help civilians, her team stumbled into a battle fought by the Rough Riders. To her delight, Barton found herself nursing soldiers again. Important work with civilians followed, and the Red Cross proved its value.

The organization's efforts during the Spanish-American War and its aftermath did lead to legislation granting a federal charter to the American Red Cross in 1900. In the end, however, this success was also Barton's downfall. Concerned that donations were in decline, some members of the Red Cross organized independent efforts during Barton's absence and were reluctant to relinquish control to her. The crisis came after a hurricane in Galveston, Texas, in September of 1900.

Barton launched relief efforts without consulting the organization's new board of directors, and her bookkeeping was so lackadaisical that the national treasurer resigned rather than defend her expenditures. The struggle went on for several years, becoming more acrimonious because Barton came to regard her critics as personal foes. Finally, Barton was forced to resign all ties to the Red Cross in 1904. She did retain quarters at a house in Maryland that had been built largely with her own money and had served as Red Cross headquarters during the final years of her presidency. Continuing to support public health efforts and the women's rights movement, Barton alternated living in Maryland and in North Oxford, Massachusetts, until her death in April, 1912.

Significance

Clara Barton established the American Red Cross almost single-handedly. Earlier efforts to do so had failed, and the nation lacked a major disaster relief agency. Rival organizations did arise, but most were launched later in imitation of Barton's efforts. Barton's prodigious labor and self-sacrifice on behalf of establishing the American Red Cross ultimately earned for her the recognition she desired, yet she never allowed her ego to prevent her from giving unstintingly of her work and wealth to those who needed help.

That ego did, however, cause problems. The combination of childhood insecurity and individual success in the Civil War rendered Barton incapable of working equally with others. She preferred to work with trusted aides who deferred to her authority, and she seemed to interpret any initiative outside her control as a personal affront. This caused Barton much disquiet and slowed the growth of the Red Cross. Although most if not all the charges made against her personally were without merit, it cannot be denied that, had she shared leadership with someone who was willing to do the vital paperwork, much more progress could have been made. Furthermore, Barton's reputation would not have been sullied. Nevertheless, her crusading spirit on behalf of nursing reform created for Barton an impressive legacy.

—*Fred R. van Hartesveldt*

FURTHER READING

Barton, Clara. *The Story of My Childhood*. Reprint. New York: Arno Press, 1980. Although it was intended to be the first chapter of an autobiography and hence covers only Barton's first years, this work is a valuable source given the influence of her childhood on her character.

Barton, William E. *The Life of Clara Barton*. 2 vols. Boston: Houghton Mifflin, 1922. An old-fashioned and uncritical biography but filled with details and information often missing in modern studies.

Burton, David H. *Clara Barton: In the Service of Humanity*. Westport, Conn.: Greenwood Press, 1995. Sympathetic yet critical biography, which suggests that Barton's dedication to helping people in need was not entirely selfless. While he recounts the many examples of Barton's heroism and generosity, the author also portrays his subject as a self-centered and thin-skinned personality.

Dulles, Foster Rhea. *The American Red Cross*. New York: Harper & Brothers, 1950. Written by an excellent historian, this valuable work provides background on Barton and her work with the Red Cross.

Oates, Stephen B. *A Woman of Valor: Clara Barton and the Civil War*. New York: Free Press, 1994. Best known for his biographies of Abraham Lincoln, Oates provides a vivid account of Clara Barton's early career during the Civil War years. While revealing Barton's drive to succeed and her skill in generating public support for her relief efforts, Oates's detailed narrative also illuminates her difficult personality and strained emotional life, thus providing a welcome corrective to older, less critical accounts.

Pryor, Elizabeth B. *Clara Barton: Professional Angel*. Philadelphia: University of Pennsylvania Press, 1987. Although informed by the author's research into numerous primary sources, this biography suffers somewhat from a lack of critical distance in its approach, as suggested by its subtitle.

Ross, Ishbel. *Angel of the Battlefield: The Life of Clara Barton*. New York: Harper & Brothers, 1956. A reasonable biography, though somewhat dated. Like most of the work on Barton, this volume is adulatory in its approach.

ALEXANDER GRAHAM BELL

" Great discoveries and improvements invariably involve the cooperation of many minds. "

Educator and inventor

One of the major inventive geniuses of modern times, Bell created and perfected the telephone and greatly advanced the teaching of the deaf.

Born: March 3, 1847; Edinburgh, Scotland
Died: August 2, 1922; Baddeck, Cape Breton Island, Nova Scotia
Areas of achievement: Telecommunications; invention and technology

EARLY LIFE

The second of three boys, Alexander Graham Bell was born into a Scottish family prominent in the field of elocution. Both his grandfather Alexander Bell and his father, Alexander Melville Bell, taught the subject. The former invented a technique to check stammering, while the latter became a major innovator and author in corrective speech. His mother, Eliza Grace Symonds Bell, a portrait painter and musician, educated her son until his tenth year. After three years of formal schooling, he spent a year in London with his grandfather, who inspired the young Bell with his deep commitment to the study of the science of sound. Bell then taught music and elocution as a student teacher in Elgin, in the midst of which he spent a year at the University of Edinburgh. During 1866-1867, he taught at a college in Bath, England. Thus, he was largely family-taught and self-taught; his black, penetrating eyes and intense, though modest, manner attested his inquiring mind.

LIFE'S WORK

Bell's genius had begun to reveal itself in 1864, when, at the age of seventeen, he undertook his first experiments in the science of sound, followed the next year by initial work in the application of electricity to transmitting speech via sound waves. Upon the death of his grandfather, Bell's father replaced the former in London and published his major tract *Visible Speech: The Science of Universal Alphabetics* in 1867, the year that young Alexander became his assistant. From his father, Bell had inherited the notion of visible speech—that is, a visual-symbolic alphabet for use in producing spoken sounds—and therefore also his father's dedication to improving methods for teaching the deaf to talk. During 1868-1870, father and son established an equal partnership, even as Bell studied anatomy and physiology at University College, London, and applied his father's techniques of visible speech at a school for the deaf at Kensington.

Such a heavy workload began to undermine Bell's health, alarming his parents, inasmuch as they had recently lost both their other sons to tuberculosis. In 1870, they immigrated to Canada, settling in the countryside near Brantford, Ontario. There, Bell's health was quickly restored, and he resumed his work in Boston, tutoring and teaching at schools for the deaf, opening his own school for other teachers, continuing his experiments in sound, and making an improvement in the system of visible speech that has remained a standard technique ever since. He also invented an audiometer. Formal

Bell, Alexander Graham

recognition came early in 1873 when Boston University made him professor of vocal physiology and the mechanics of speech, a post he held for four years.

During 1873-1876, Bell brought together his disparate studies of the science of sound and its electrical telegraphic transmission. Ever since his first experiments with the latter in 1865, Bell spent whatever spare time he had in attempting to invent a device by which oral sounds could be transmitted via electrical wires: the telephone. Concurrently, he studied the human ear to discover the importance of the membrane for such a device, and he learned to transmit multiple electrical messages over a single wire. In applying the key element of acoustics to telegraphy, Bell sought and received the counsel and encouragement of the venerable experimental physicist Joseph Henry, who had worked along similar lines.

Basically a scientist, Bell was fortunate to hire as his technical assistant Thomas A. Watson, an adept mechanic who shared his long nights of experiments on electrical sound transmission. Unable to fund this work himself, Bell found two patrons in the fathers of deaf children he was teaching. These men were Thomas Sanders and Gardiner G. Hubbard. Only rest, however, could restore Bell's physical strength from occasional fatigue resulting from these considerable labors, and Bell obtained it at his parents' home in Canada.

The first, though unintelligible, human sounds, Bell's to Watson, came through their wire in June, 1875, but it was not until March 10, 1876, that a twenty-foot-long wire carried the monumental, though unanticipated, first message: "Mr. Watson, come here; I want to see you." The two men rapidly improved their invention, and Bell astounded the scientific world with his first public demonstration of the telephone at the International Centennial Exposition at Philadelphia in June, 1876. The following spring, he demonstrated the first long-distance telephone conversation, between Boston and New York.

In July, 1877, Bell, Hubbard, and Sanders created the Bell Telephone Company. Having patented all the related inventions, Bell finally began to enjoy the resulting financial rewards, although some six hundred lawsuits ensued, with rivals claiming credit—until 1888, when the Supreme Court ruled in Bell's favor as sole inventor of the telephone.

Though his fame was assured through his epic creation, Bell remained equally dedicated to the education of the deaf, especially after he married Hubbard's daughter Mabel, one of his deaf students, in July, 1877. She became an important source of encouragement and inspiration for the rest of his life and gave him two daughters. During their subsequent trip to Europe, where he introduced the telephone, Bell lectured on the teaching of the deaf at Oxford University. After settling in Washington in 1878, Bell enlarged his study of the physical nature of deafness and in 1880 founded the Volta Laboratory upon receiving the French Volta Prize of fifty thousands francs (about ten thousand dollars).

Bell used the Volta Laboratory in the spirit of scientific philanthropy; instead of patenting new discoveries made there, he allowed their general use for the public good. Most important were the photophone to send words by light ray and an induction balance or electric probe to locate metal objects in the human body, the latter first used to find the assassin's bullet that mortally wounded President James A. Garfield.

Bell, Alexander Graham

Bell became an American citizen in 1882 and soon thereafter built a summer home and research laboratory at Baddeck, Cape Breton Island, Nova Scotia. Among many honors he received from European countries was a Ph.D., awarded by the University of Würzburg in Bavaria.

Bell's restless, inquisitive mind seemed to accelerate as he grew older, and his black hair, beard, and sideburns turned a striking, billowy white. At the Volta Laboratory, he improved upon Thomas Alva Edison's phonograph during the mid-1880's; proceeds from the sale of some of the patents were used to transform the Laboratory into the Volta Bureau for the Increase and Diffusion of Knowledge Relating to the Deaf. His prize pupil the next decade became Helen Keller.

In 1890, Bell founded and became first president of the American Association to Promote Teaching of Speech to the Deaf (renamed the Alexander Graham Bell Association for the Deaf in 1956). An early study of marriage among the deaf led into eugenics and the problems of longevity, research that emerged as a major book in 1918. He also supported Albert A. Michelson's first measurements of the speed of light. Bell continued to improve upon the telephone, and he and Watson inaugurated the first transcontinental phone call when, in 1915, they conversed between San Francisco and New York.

Alexander Graham Bell.
(Library of Congress)

Bell, Alexander Graham

The possibilities of manned powered flight held the greatest fascination for Bell from before 1891, when he supported the pioneering work of Samuel P. Langley, until the end of his life. Bell believed that tetrahedron-shaped cells could be joined for lift and experimented with them in immense kites. During 1907-1909, he teamed up with aviation pioneer Glenn H. Curtiss and three other young men in the Aerial Experiment Association (AEA), the brainstorm of his wife, who also funded its work. Among the aircraft the five men created at Bell's Nova Scotia laboratory and Curtiss's facility at Hammondsport, New York, was Bell's own tetrahedral plane. Though it finally flew in 1912, it proved too unwieldy, but where the tetrahedron failed as an aeronautical device, it eventually proved highly successful in architecture (as, for example, in R. Buckminster Fuller's geodesic dome).

In 1916, Bell advocated American preparedness in military air power, and inasmuch as the AEA operated their craft from the water and the ice, Bell during and after World War I developed a high-speed hydrofoil motorboat for riding above the water at speeds of up to seventy miles per hour.

At his Nova Scotia laboratory and in Washington, Bell carried on his manifold experiments, which also included a home air-cooling unit, an artificial respirator, the breeding of sheep, improved methods of lithography and sonar detection, and a vertical-propelled, aircraft-type engine that anticipated the helicopter and jet propulsion. His extensive notebooks were filled with other ideas that he never had time to develop; he was working on a means to distill saltwater when he died. His chief fame, however, rests on the invention of the telephone, of which thirteen million existed worldwide at the time of his death on August 2, 1922. Two days later, on the day of his funeral, all telephones in the United States and Canada fell silent for one minute in tribute to him.

SIGNIFICANCE

Alexander Graham Bell typified the remarkable generation of American inventor-scientists of the late nineteenth century whose ability to apply scientific discoveries to everyday practical technological uses played a major part in the rise of contemporary urban civilization. Driven by an insatiable curiosity and endowed with sheer experimental (though not theoretical) genius—and perfect pitch—Bell was able to focus his many interests on two or three projects simultaneously, often complementing one another. Thus, his humanitarian work on helping the deaf to learn to speak was wedded early to his efforts to invent the practical telephone. He never lost interest in either project, although aviation commanded equal attention the second half of his life. This was a fascination shared by many prominent peers in the scientific and technological worlds, among them, for example, explorer Robert Edwin Peary, yacht designer W. Starling Burgess, and naval inventor Bradley A. Fiske.

An immensely generous person, Bell was completely selfless in his devotion to the deaf, to whose improvement he committed many of the profits from the telephone. Because he championed the diffusion of scientific knowledge, he became a major catalyst in the cause of popular science. With Hubbard, in 1883, he founded and operated for eleven years *Science* magazine, subsequently taken over by the American Association for the Advancement of Science.

In 1888, Bell was a founder of the National Geographic Society, ten years later suc-

Bell, Alexander Graham

ceeding Hubbard as its president, until 1904. Under his presidency, in 1899, the *National Geographic* magazine began publication. One of his daughters married the editor Gilbert H. Grosvenor; Bell's grandson, Melville Bell Grosvenor, succeeded to the editorship half a century later. In 1891, Bell funded the creation of the Astrophysical Observatory of the Smithsonian Institution and seven years after that became a regent of the Smithsonian, a post he held the rest of his life. Largely through Bell's efforts, the remains of James Smithson were returned from Genoa, Italy, to Washington, D.C., in 1904.

Like other major inventors of his day, Bell had to protect his patents from challengers and did so by keeping copious notes and having numerous photographs taken. His love of nature was embodied in his summer home and laboratory, named Beinn Bhreagh, the commanding view of the Bras d'Or Lakes in this "New Scotland" (Nova Scotia) reminding him of his native land. Such an idyllic environment proved especially conducive to his experiments over the last thirty-five years of his life. There he died, and there—in a mountainside—he was buried. He had shared the wonders of nature with the world at large through the pages of the *National Geographic*. The full legacy of Alexander Graham Bell is beyond measure.

—*Clark G. Reynolds*

FURTHER READING

Bruce, Robert V. *Bell: Alexander Graham Bell and the Conquest of Solitude.* Boston: Little, Brown, 1973. The standard biography, this heavily annotated work focuses on the development of the telephone but offers a good general treatment of Bell's life before and after its invention.

Casey, Louis S. *Curtiss: The Hammondsport Era, 1907-1915.* New York: Crown, 1981. Though a biography of pioneer aviator and manufacturer Glenn H. Curtiss in his early years of aviation, the book discusses Bell's role in the AEA, utilizing among its sources the AEA *Bulletin*.

Costain, Thomas B. *Chord of Steel.* Garden City, N.Y.: Doubleday, 1960. A popular account of the invention of the telephone.

Grosvenor, Edwin S., and Morgan Wesson. *Alexander Graham Bell: The Life and Times of the Man Who Invented the Telephone.* New York: Harry N. Abrams, 1997. A biography of Bell, focusing on the early history of the telephone, enlivened by more than four hundred color and black-and-white illustrations.

Mackay, James. *Alexander Graham Bell: A Life.* New York: John Wiley & Sons, 1997. Mackay depicts Bell as a man of great intelligence and curiosity and describes his varied interests and inventions. Provides new information on Bell's early years and how these years influenced his later life.

Mackenzie, Catherine Dunlap. *Alexander Graham Bell: The Man Who Contracted Space.* Boston: Houghton Mifflin, 1928. This early biography is a sound though dated work.

Parkin, J. H. *Bell and Baldwin.* Toronto: University of Toronto Press, 1964. Centers on the association of Bell with the Canadian F. W. "Casey" Baldwin during the AEA period with Glenn H. Curtiss.

Waite, Helen E. *Make a Joyful Sound: The Romance of Mabel Hubbard and Alexander*

Graham Bell. Philadelphia: MacRae Smith, 1961. A moving account of the relationship between Bell and his wife, who, though twelve years his junior, emerges as a key figure in her own right and proof positive of Bell's success in overcoming the disability of deafness. She died in 1923.

Watson, Thomas A. *Exploring Life.* New York: D. Appleton, 1926. This biography by Bell's main assistant (1854-1934) illuminates the great inventor's character and methods.

Mary McLeod Bethune

❝ *Invest in the human soul. Who knows, it might be a diamond in the rough.* **❞**

Educator and social reformer

A leading voice and activist for democratic ideals before World War I and up to the early years of the Civil Rights movement, Bethune was instrumental in founding organizations to advance the education and rights of African Americans, inspiring others as she was herself inspired.

Born: July 10, 1875; Mayesville, South Carolina
Died: May 18, 1955; Daytona Beach, Florida
Also known as: Mary Jane McLeod (birth name)
Areas of achievement: Education; social reform; civil rights

Early Life

Mary McLeod Bethune (meh-CLOWD bay-THYEWN) was born in Mayesville, South Carolina, to Sam and Patsy McLeod, who were former slaves. She was the seventeenth child to be born to the couple and the first to be born free. Her father was a farmer and her mother probably did laundry to supplement the family income in addition to her own work on the family farm. Many of the older McLeod children were either married or on their own, but the younger children assisted with the support of the family by picking cotton. By her own report, Bethune, at nine years of age, could pick 250 pounds of cotton a day.

One incident in particular is reputed to have inspired Bethune's determination to become educated. While she was in a neighboring house being shown around by the white family's young daughters, they happened into a room with books. Bethune picked up one of the books and was examining it when one of the girls spoke sharply to her about putting the book down, reportedly telling her, "You can't read, so you shouldn't even handle a book!" Shocked at this response and perhaps vaguely aware of the insult, Bethune became determined to read. As it happened, a young black woman was in the neighborhood to start a school for black children. This teacher approached the McLeods about having Bethune attend. The likelihood of one of the children of this poor family being allowed to go to school seemed remote. Nevertheless, Bethune's de-

Bethune, Mary McLeod

sire to go was so strong and apparently so heartfelt that her mother convinced her father to let her go. When she was able to read the Bible to her parents as a result of this schooling, they all, parents and child, came to appreciate the benefits of education.

Bethune did well at the little country school. Her teacher recommended her for further schooling, and her tuition was paid in part by Mary Chrissman, a white dressmaker from Denver, Colorado. The new school, known as Scotia School, was located in Concord, South Carolina. Bethune contributed to her education by doing odd jobs at the school. Having done well in her studies at Scotia, she was again recommended by her teachers for scholarships to continue her studies. She was accepted as a student at the Moody Bible Institute in Chicago, Illinois, and received additional financial support from Chrissman.

At the Moody Institute, Bethune became a member of the Gospel Choir Team that preached and sang throughout Illinois. She had hoped to become a missionary in Africa on completion of her studies, but because she was so young she was not considered a suitable candidate. Instead, she took a teaching assignment at Haines Normal and Industrial Institute in Augusta, Georgia, where she met a black woman who was to affect her life in important ways: Lucy Laney, the school's principal and founder and a trailblazer in the education of blacks. Sympathizing with Bethune's compassion for the uneducated black children of the neighborhood around the school, Laney allowed Bethune to teach them on Sunday afternoons. Soon, Bethune had the children singing familiar songs, and she encouraged them to listen to Bible stories later.

The sponsoring Presbyterian Board of Haines Institute sent Bethune to other schools nearby. One of those schools was the Kendall Institute in Sumter, South Carolina. It was here that she met Albertus Bethune, also a teacher, whom she married in May of 1898. Their son, Albert McLeod Bethune, was born a year later. The family soon moved to Palatka, Florida, where Mary Bethune established a Presbyterian mission school. Her husband did not share her enthusiasm for missionary work, however, and the couple was eventually separated.

LIFE'S WORK

Having been born in the South during Reconstruction undoubtedly saddled Bethune with many adversities. She was black, poor, and female, none of which made her more remarkable than other young women alive during the same period. What did distinguish her was her ability to conquer those misfortunes, to share her accomplishments with others, and to choose to devote her life to acts of service to others. From the time she read the Bible to her parents, she seemed to recognize and become inspired by the power of words and their effects on others.

Bethune's lifework began in Daytona Beach when she saw other young black women in need of all varieties of education. Her ambition to provide a place for their schooling took the form of grasping at any possibilities, becoming inventive as the need arose: Discarded, crumpled paper could be smoothed out to write lessons on; burned wooden twigs could become charcoal for pencils; cracked plates or broken chairs could be repaired. Anything that could be salvaged was recycled and returned to useful service. Her crowning achievement in these salvage operations was an area in the city that had been used as a garbage dump, but which she saw could be used for a

Mary Mcleod Bethune.
(Library of Congress)

school. Selflessness and determination proved to be the hallmarks of Bethune's character. She had $1.50 as her original budget, but she made do and found creative ways to recruit both students and community assistance for her projects.

The years following the founding of the school with five students on October 3, 1904, led to the rapid growth of her program of education for blacks. By 1906, Bethune had 250 students and employed a few teachers who worked for salaries of $15 to $25 a month. To lessen the drain on the meager finances and to become more independent, she stopped renting and began to buy land for her needs. By 1925, Bethune School merged with the Cookman School for boys to become Bethune-Cookman College. The merged institution included a grade school, high school, and college. Because southern policies of segregation at the time extended to the care of hospital patients, Bethune was led to erect a hospital near the college in 1911 to provide better treatment for the black community. It was named for her father and proved to be another example of her vision.

During the years of the Wilson administration, Bethune became more active in social organizations devoted to protest and social reform. She served on the executive board of the Urban League as well as on committees resisting the discriminatory policies of the Young Women's Christian Association (YWCA). Since many of the positions taken by the YWCA were either condescending or blatantly biased, Bethune became one of several women opposing the racist stance of that association. She was also active in the formation of the National Association of Wage Earners, an organization dedicated to informing women of their rights as workers.

In 1921, Bethune was one of the executive leaders of the International Council of Women of the Darker Races of the World. The intention of this group was to raise the esteem and awareness of darker peoples about themselves and others from what has been called the Third World and what is best called the developing world.

She continued her activities on behalf of black children and women to combat the injustices and inequities they faced. Founding the National Association of Negro Women in 1935 and working with the Franklin D. Roosevelt administration, Bethune directed the Negro branch of the National Youth Administration. She was also founder and president of the National Association of Colored Women's Clubs.

Although she served as president of Bethune-Cookman College from 1904 to 1942 and was one of its trustees until her death in 1955, her influence was not exclusively focused on education. She was a special assistant to the secretary of war during World War II and served on the Committee for National Defense under President Harry S. Truman. She also served as a consultant to the conference that drafted the United Nations charter. These activities and her many honorary degrees and medals never caused her to abandon her main concern: the education of every black child.

Bethune's imagination was not restricted to what she, or anyone, could see immediately. She was known to say "just because you can't see a thing, does not mean that it does not exist." During many of her talks, Bethune would frequently compare the peoples of the world to flowers. Some students would remark that there were no black flowers in the world's gardens. At first, she had only her visionary remark to offer, since there appeared to be no way to rebut the observation. On one of her trips to Europe, however, she was presented with a "black" tulip by one of her hosts in the Netherlands. She later planted the tulips on her campus as proof of her maxim.

Bethune's ability to maintain her lofty vision allowed her to endure in the face of great challenges. The black community was hard hit by the era's wars, economic depressions, riots, and lynchings. For the most part, there was little government intervention on behalf of black victims. Protests by black organizations went unheard, were ignored, or were suppressed. The activities of racist organizations such as the Ku Klux Klan were accepted, permitted, or even encouraged, while blacks were denied their civil rights despite their achievements as responsible citizens. Poverty and ignorance, combined with racism, did much to inhibit black people. None of these conditions could dampen Bethune's spirit. Working with Eleanor Roosevelt and some of the nation's top businesspeople, Bethune enhanced her effectiveness as a representative of the black community and as an individual educator. She died of a heart attack in 1955 and was buried on the campus of her beloved college.

Significance

During times when being an African American often meant being invisible, disheartened, and denied chances to achieve intellectually, especially if female, Bethune became a person whose entire life disproved such stereotypes. By white American standards, she possessed little physical beauty, but by any standards her spirit, energy, and compassion were evidence of great inner beauty. Bethune's drive to give women access to worlds that had been closed to them, to give all blacks intellectual choices that had been denied them, and to give children an example to follow in providing service to others made her one of the most notable African American leaders of her time. Before her death, she had lived to see Bethune-Cookman become one of the finest of the historically black colleges in the country. She had left her mark on the administrations of two American presidents. Using her keen understanding of human behavior and harnessing her ability to negotiate change in the face of great opposition, Bethune became one of the most influential voices in the struggle for racial equality.

—*Maude M. Jennings*

FURTHER READING

Bethune, Mary McLeod. *Mary McLeod Bethune: Building a Better World—Essays and Selected Documents*. Edited by Audrey Thomas McCluskey and Elaine M. Smith. Bloomington: Indiana University Press, 1999. Contains seventy of Bethune's writings and other documents dating from 1902 through 1955.

Carruth, Ella Kaiser. *She Wanted to Read: The Story of Mary McLeod Bethune*. New York: Abingdon Press, 1966. A biography written for juveniles that presents a portrait of Bethune's early years. Also includes some coverage of her involvement as a presidential adviser as well as her activities as an organizer and founder of groups concerned with women's rights and labor relations.

Hanson, Joyce A. *Mary McLeod Bethune and Black Women's Political Activism*. Columbia: University of Missouri Press, 2003. Hanson examines Bethune's political activism in the context of the activism of African American women in her time.

Lerner, Gerda, ed. *Black Women in White America: A Documentary History*. New York: Pantheon Books, 1972. Contains excerpts of works and speeches by notable black women including Bethune. Extremely useful for accurate firsthand accounts of her life and her activities in entries such as "A College from a Garbage Dump," "Another Begging Letter," and "A Century of Progress of Negro Women."

McKissack, Patricia, and Fredrick McKissack. *Mary McLeod Bethune: A Great Teacher*. Hillside, N.J.: Enslow, 1991. Another biography directed at juvenile readers that provides an excellent introduction, broadly describing Bethune's life and achievements in fighting bigotry and racial injustice. Focuses much of its attention on Bethune's courage in overcoming adversity. Illustrated.

Salem, Dorothy. *To Better Our World: Black Women in Organized Reform, 1890-1920*. New York: Carlson, 1990. Salem's work is the fourteenth volume in Carlson's Black Women in United States History series. Provides a chronological narrative of the efforts made by black women's organizations to improve the lives of African Americans in the United States. A well-researched historical account that provides insights into the backgrounds of black women reformers, highlighting their resiliency of character in the face of failures as well as successes.

Smith, Elaine M. "Mary McLeod Bethune and the National Youth Association." In *Clio Was a Woman: Studies in the History of American Women*, edited by Mabel E. Deutrich and Virginia C. Purdy. Washington, D.C.: Howard University Press, 1980. An excellent assessment of Bethune's work in supervising the activities of the National Youth Administration with respect to African Americans. Although aimed at a scholarly audience, this essay is accessible to general readers and helps place Bethune's accomplishments within the context of her own time as well as the larger field of women's studies.

BLACK HAWK

> *Courage is not afraid to weep, and she is not afraid to pray, even when she is not sure who she is praying to.*

Native American leader

Black Hawk was a leader in the last Indian war of the old Northwest, and he dictated one of the most revealing and enduring Native American autobiographies of his time.

Born: 1767; Saukenak, Virginia Colony (now near Rock River, Illinois)
Died: October 3, 1838; near the Des Moines River, Iowa
Also known as: Ma-ka-tai-me-she-kia-kiak
Area of achievement: Native American affairs

EARLY LIFE

Known as Ma-ka-tai-me-she-kia-kiak in his native language, Black Hawk was the adopted brother of a chief of the Foxes and was brought up by the Sauk (Sacs)—"Sac" was the original French spelling. The Sauk and Foxes were small tribes that formed an alliance, sometimes including the Potawatomi and Winnebago, to defend themselves against larger neighboring nations. Black Hawk was already a warrior and a leader among his people at the age of fifteen.

In his autobiography, *Life of Ma-ka-tai-me-she-kia-kiak: Or, Black Hawk* (1834), Black Hawk described how he became chief at the death of his father when they were fighting together against the Cherokee near the Meramec River, a short distance below modern St. Louis. Black Hawk fell heir to the chieftainship but was obliged to mourn, pray, and fast for five years in what he called a "civil capacity," hunting and fishing. When he was twenty-one, he became head chief of the Sauk and Foxes. The two tribes were united and lived together as a single group.

Black Hawk's early years were spent in warfare against neighbors, primarily the Osage, Kaskaskia (a member of the Illinois Confederacy), and Chippewa. According to Black Hawk, there were two major reasons for warfare among the Indians: preservation of hunting grounds and revenge for the deaths of relatives. Despite Black Hawk's renown as a warrior, there was a highly developed ethical and spiritual side of his character, and he tried to do what the Supreme Spirit directed.

LIFE'S WORK

Black Hawk's personality was complex, and it would be a mistake to oversimplify the main events in his life. Probably he should not be considered a great leader. He was highly individualistic, often impulsive, colorful, and emotional. His policies did not significantly help his nation, and other Indian leaders such as Pontiac and Crazy Horse were greater than he. It could be argued that his leadership was shortsighted and brought disaster on his people. The Black Hawk War could have been avoided.

Black Hawk never liked the American settlers, and for this he may be easily forgiven—during his lifetime the Sauk continually suffered from white armies, white officials, white traders, and white settlers. His adopted son was murdered by white American settlers. He liked the British. He was on good terms with a British trader and with Robert Dixon, British agent in the War of 1812, during which Black Hawk took an active role against the Americans. Most of Black Hawk's life prior to his capture in 1832 was marked by his dislike of Americans. The experience that contributed to this attitude more than any other was the St. Louis treaty of 1804, which Black Hawk rejected. In his own words, "It has been the origin of all our difficulties."

Napoleon sold Louisiana to the United States in 1803; soon after, American officials arrived in St. Louis to claim control and sign treaties with Indian tribes in the area. According to Black Hawk, the treaty with the Sauk was fraudulent. The Sauk had sent four representatives to St. Louis to obtain the release of a Sauk imprisoned there for killing an American—these were negotiators with a specific mission, not diplomats or chiefs. Much later they returned dressed in fine coats and wearing medals, and they could not remember much of what had happened. They were drunk most of the time they were in St. Louis. They also signed a treaty ceding all the Sauk lands east of the Mississippi to the United States.

Black Hawk and the rest of the Sauk were indignant. Not long after, a United States Army detachment came to erect Fort Madison near the Sauk villages. Black Hawk was scandalized by the treaty, asserting that the Sauk and Fox signers of the treaty had no authority from their nations. Twentieth century historian Milo Milton Quaife, however, claims that "no more than the usual cajolery of the Indians was indulged in by the white representatives in securing the cession." The rejection of this treaty by the Indians and the acceptance of its legality by the United States say much about the quality of American law during this period.

The second major event in Black Hawk's life prior to his battles during the 1830's against the Illinois militia and the United States Army was his rivalry with another Sauk chief, Keokuk. Although not a chief by birth, Keokuk rose by the exercise of political talents to a position of leadership in his tribe. He was more of a realist than Black Hawk, and although he may not have liked the Americans any more than Black Hawk did, he tried not to antagonize them. As a nation the Sauk were divided, some favoring Black Hawk and others, Keokuk. In 1819, Keokuk and other members of the nation were persuaded by American authorities to leave the Sauk home on Rock Island and go to the western side of the Mississippi. Keokuk ultimately triumphed over Black Hawk after the war of 1832, which placed Black Hawk under the governance of Keokuk.

The rivalry between Black Hawk and Keokuk had a long history. Throughout the 1820's, Black Hawk resisted the encroachments of white settlers, and he tried to hold on to the Sauk's ancestral home on Rock Island. At first Black Hawk favored negotiation with the white Americans no less than Keokuk. Eventually, however, having exhausted all means of peaceful resistance, Black Hawk took up arms and tried to recruit

Black Hawk

allies among the Potawatomi. He led his entire nation—warriors, women, and children—on a long anabasis from Rock Island to Bad Axe River, winning some battles and losing others, culminating in the final attempt to reach the safety of the western bank of the Mississippi. The most pitiful aspect of the tragedy was the fate of the Sauk women and children. In the words of historian Reuben G. Thwaites,

> Some of the fugitives succeeded in swimming to the west bank of the Mississippi, but many were drowned on the way, or cooly picked off by sharpshooters, who exercised no more mercy towards squaws and children than they did towards braves—treating them all as though they were rats instead of human beings.

Black Hawk led the last great war between Indians and whites on the eastern side of the Mississippi; if it terrified numerous white settlers in the frontier regions of the old Northwest—what is now Illinois and Wisconsin—it should be stressed that the Indian civilian populations living on ancestral lands had been terrorized by whites for a far longer period of time. Although Black Hawk initiated the battle, the final tragedy was not his doing. The deliberate killing of noncombatants was an act of the United States, not an Indian act. A few Sauk managed to reach the western bank only to be attacked by a war party of Lakota (Sioux) Indians under the orders of General Atkinson.

Black Hawk would have been the first to condemn these military practices, and he fully expressed his indignation in his autobiography. These massacres went far beyond his conception of the conduct of war. Some historians have been hasty to blame him, failing to consider the requirements of defensive warfare at the time. Although the Indians received few favorable settlements in their negotiations with the whites, those who suffered the most were perhaps the most pacific—those who, because they never fought the whites, never signed treaties with them either, and consequently never received rights or privileges. Most of these nations have completely disappeared, leaving no survivors. In one of Black Hawk's most telling critiques of Keokuk, he said: "I conceived that the *peaceable disposition* of Keokuk and his people had been, in a great measure, the cause of our having been driven from our village."

Black Hawk had a quixotic, romantic temperament. He could be impulsively emotional and also ethical, courageous, even idealistic and chivalrous in battle. Some of these traits might surprise a modern reader accustomed to clichés about Indians. Repeatedly Black Hawk complimented the braver of his adversaries, whether enemy Indians or whites. If he encountered an enemy group that had less than half his number, he declined to do battle. He admired both determination and heroism in war, and the traits he came to admire in his white conquerors after 1832 were largely military virtues.

It was probably not a coincidence that Black Hawk struck up a spontaneous friendship with Lieutenant Jefferson Davis in 1832; these two leaders of rebellion had traits in common. Jefferson Davis was to repeat Black Hawk's act of defiance against superior military forces twenty-five years later as president of the Confederate States, and the results would be comparable.

Black Hawk's autobiography was dictated and translated on the spot in 1833; there is no extant text in the Sauk language. The book has a seemingly childish quality that is probably more attributable to the interpreter and editor than to Black Hawk himself. There are many exclamation points, underlinings, and expressions of delight, and much reveling in the good fight. Nevertheless, the document gives an ample, three-dimensional portrait of a man spontaneously describing his thoughts and feelings, trying to account for what he has done and what has happened to him.

Black Hawk died a broken man on an Indian reservation in Iowa in 1838. A decade later, his rival Keokuk died a wealthy man in Kansas, where he had moved after selling the Sauk and Fox lands in Iowa.

SIGNIFICANCE

After the Black Hawk War, the combined population of the Sauk and Foxes was greatly diminished. They were finally resettled in an area west of the Mississippi in a segment of what was known as "the Permanent Indian Frontier of 1840." It adjoined the Potawatomi to the west, the Lakota to the north, and the Winnebago to the northeast. The Sauk and Foxes would still need military virtues as well as diplomacy when they jostled with these Indians and, later, with whites in their new habitat. Military abilities did not immediately become obsolete—far from it. Soon, however, the Indians' greatest adversaries were to become alcoholism, diseases such as cholera, and starvation.

Black Hawk's major weakness was probably diplomacy. In his war against the whites he did not secure the adherence of a significant number of other Indian nations, nor did he spend much time or effort in attempting it. Seventy years earlier, Pontiac had been more successful in forging an antiwhite alliance. Whether Black Hawk could have been more successful if he had put more effort into negotiations, especially with other Indian nations, is a matter of speculation. Black Hawk thought in broad ethical categories. He believed the Great Spirit would reward him if he fought for justice. Patient diplomacy, with its concomitant drudgery and uncertainty, was not for him.

—*John Carpenter*

FURTHER READING

Black Hawk. *Life of Ma-ka-tai-me-she-kia-kiak: Or, Black Hawk.* Edited by Milo Milton Quaife. New York: Dover, 1994. Originally published during the 1830's, Black Hawk's autobiography is a fascinating document. However, it has many inaccuracies and biases and should be read with critical skepticism. His account of the British is naïve, as well as his description of the "prophet" White Cloud. Black Hawk grossly understates his own losses in the battles of 1832. Still, a vivid picture of an admirable human being emerges from the pages of his autobiography.

Drake, Benjamin. *The Life and Adventures of Black Hawk.* Cincinnati: G. Conclin, 1844. Half history and half fiction, written shortly after the events described.

Eby, Cecil. *"That Disgraceful Affair": The Black Hawk War.* New York: W. W. Norton, 1973. Perhaps the best book about the Black Hawk War. Very thoroughly documented and at the same time a readable narrative, as well as an incisive critique of the major actors in the war.

Nichols, Roger L. *Black Hawk and the Warrior's Path.* Arlington Heights, Ill.: H. Davidson, 1992. Biography of Black Hawk, focusing on the wars he waged against rival tribes, white pioneers, and others. Nichols seeks the reasons for Black Hawk's actions, particularly his involvement in the war that bears his name.

Quaife, Milo Milton. *Chicago and the Old Northwest, 1673-1833*. Chicago: University of Chicago Press, 1913. Well-documented and thorough general history that draws somewhat specious conclusions.

Slotkin, Richard. *Regeneration Through Violence: The Mythology of the American Frontier, 1600-1860*. Middletown, Conn.: Wesleyan University Press, 1973. A critical or "revisionist" account of the frontier. A welcome antidote to earlier sentimental accounts of the frontier wars but obsessively overstated.

Stevens, Frank E. *The Black Hawk War*. Chicago: F. E. Stevens, 1903. A thorough account, still useful.

Thwaites, Reuben G. *Story of the Black Hawk War*. Madison: Wisconsin State Historical Society, 1892. A narrative by one of the best American historians of the period; Thwaites combines great erudition with a keen critical spirit.

DANIEL BOONE

> *" I had gained the summit of a commanding ridge, and, looking round with astonishing delight, beheld the ample plains, the beauteous tracts below. "*

Explorer and settler

In addition to opening Kentucky to settlement, an area earlier considered part of the West, Boone became a legendary symbol of the early American frontier and is considered a national hero.

Born: November 2, 1734; Berks County, Pennsylvania
Died: September 26, 1820; near St. Charles, Missouri
Area of achievement: Exploration

EARLY LIFE

Daniel Boone (bewn) was the sixth of eleven children. His father, Squire Boone, was the son of an English Quaker who came to Philadelphia in 1717; his mother, Sarah Morgan, was of Welsh ancestry. Young Boone received little, if any, formal schooling, but he learned to read and write, although his spelling was erratic. His real interest was in the forest, and as a boy he developed into an excellent shot and superb woodsman.

Squire Boone left Pennsylvania in 1750, and by 1751 or 1752, the family was settled on Dutchman's Creek in North Carolina's Yadkin Valley. Daniel hunted and farmed, and he was a wagoner in General Edward Braddock's ill-fated 1755 expedition against Fort Duquesne. He may have been a wagon master three years later, when General John Forbes took the fort. During the 1750's, Boone met John Finley, who captivated him with tales of the lovely land called Kentucky.

Boone, Daniel

In young adulthood, Boone was about five feet nine inches in height, and had broad shoulders and a broad chest. Strong and quick, he possessed marvelous endurance and calm nerves. He had blue eyes, a Roman nose, a wide mouth with thin lips, and dark hair that he wore plaited and clubbed. Boone detested coonskin caps and always wore a hat. Mischievous and fun-loving, he was a popular companion, but Boone was happiest when alone in the wilderness. Honest, courageous, quiet, and unpretentious, he inspired confidence, and he accepted the leadership roles thrust upon him.

On August 14, 1756, Daniel married Rebecca Bryan, four years his junior. Between 1757 and 1781, they had ten children, and Rebecca carried much of the burden of rearing them during Daniel's long absences. One child died in infancy, and sons James and Israel were killed in Kentucky by American Indians. Rebecca ended Daniel's interest in Florida by refusing to move there in 1766. Boone, sometimes accompanied by brother Squire and brother-in-law John Stuart, explored westward, always tantalized by stories of the fine lands and bountiful game to be found in Kentucky.

LIFE'S WORK
On May 1, 1769, Daniel Boone, John Finley, John Stuart, and three hired hands left Boone's cabin for his first extended visit into Kentucky. A successful hunt was spoiled by a band of Shawnee, who took their catch and most of their equipment. Stuart was later killed, and when the rest of the party went back for supplies in 1770, Boone remained behind to hunt and explore westward. In 1771, some hunters investigated a strange sound and found Boone, flat on his back, singing at full volume for sheer joy. The seizure of another catch by Native Americans was a small price to pay for such delights.

In September, 1773, Boone attempted to take his family and other settlers into Kentucky, but they turned back after an American Indian attack in which Boone's son James was among those killed. On the eve of Lord Dunmore's War in 1774, Boone and Michael Stoner were sent to warn hunters and surveyors in Kentucky of the impending danger. In sixty-one days, they covered more than 800 miles of wilderness, although Boone paused at the incipient settlement at Harrodsburg long enough to claim a lot and throw up a cabin. During the short Indian war, Boone's role as a militia officer was to defend some of Virginia's frontier forts.

During these years, Boone became associated with Judge Richard Henderson, who dreamed of establishing a new colony (to be called Transylvania) in the western lands claimed by the North Carolina and Virginia colonies. Boone helped persuade the Cherokees to sell their claim to Kentucky, and agreement was reached at Sycamore Shoals on March 17, 1775. Anticipating that result, Boone and thirty axmen had already started work on the famed Wilderness Road that brought thousands of settlers into Kentucky and helped destroy the wilderness solitude that Boone loved.

Boonesborough was soon established on the south bank of the Kentucky River, and crops were planted in hastily cleared fields. When Henderson arrived with a larger party, a government was set up with representatives from the tiny, scattered stations. Boone introduced measures for protecting game and improving the breed of horses. American Indian raids frightened many of the settlers into fleeing eastward, but during the summer of 1775, Boone brought his family to Boonesborough. Had he joined the exodus, the settlements probably would have been abandoned. Even the capture of a daughter and two other girls by American Indians did not shake his determination to hang on. Henderson's grandiose scheme failed when Virginia extended its jurisdiction over the region by creating a vast Kentucky County in December, 1776.

The American Revolution was fought largely along the seaboard, but the British used American Indians to attack the Kentucky settlements; the war in the West was fought for survival. Boone accepted the new nation created in 1776, but he was later charged with Toryism and treasonable association with the enemy. A court-martial cleared him of all charges, and he received a militia promotion.

During a raid led by Shawnee chief Blackfish, Boone's life was saved by young Simon Kenton, one of his few peers as a woodsman. The indigenous peoples' incursions brought the settlers near starvation, given the danger of both hunting and farming. When Boone was captured near Blue Licks by a large Shawnee raiding party on February 7, 1778, he persuaded his twenty-six salt makers to surrender to save their lives. Boone then convinced Blackfish to return home, and that Boonesborough would capitulate in the spring. Boone was adopted by Chief Blackfish, who refused to sell him to the British in Detroit. Big Turtle, as Boone was called by the Shawnee, enjoyed American Indian life, but he escaped in June, 1778, to warn Kentuckians of an impending attack. First by horse, and then on foot, Boone covered 160 miles in four days with only one meal, and upon his arrival Boonesborough's defenses were hastily improved. In any event, the attacking party of four hundred American Indians and twelve French Canadians did not arrive until September 7. The settlers prolonged negotiations, hoping help would arrive, and the nine-day siege was one of the longest in American Indian warfare. All hostile stratagems failed, and Boonesborough survived.

George Rogers Clark's 1778-1779 campaign in the Illinois country and later expeditions against American Indian towns eased some of the danger. Indeed, Boonesborough was becoming too crowded for Boone, and in October, 1779, he moved to Boone's Station, a few miles from the fort. Boone had acquired some wealth, but he and a companion were robbed of between $40,000 and $50,000 when they went east in 1780 to purchase land warrants. Boone felt honor-bound to repay the persons who had entrusted money to him.

His hunting exploits, escapes from American Indians, and other feats of skill and endurance made him a legend in his own time. Kentucky was divided into three counties in November, 1780, and Boone's importance was recognized by appointments as Fayette's sheriff, county-lieutenant, lieutenant-colonel of militia, and deputy surveyor, and by election to the Virginia legislature. Captured by the British in Charlottesville in 1781, Boone soon escaped or was paroled.

In August, 1782, after a failed American Indian attack on Bryan's Station, Boone's warnings went unheeded, and the rash pursuers were ambushed near Blue Licks; Boone's son Israel was among the sixty-four non-Indian casualties. Boone participated in expeditions across the Ohio River to curb the indigenous, but he criticized Clark for not moving his headquarters to the eastern settlements for better protection. This criticism failed to take into account Clark's responsibilities for the Illinois country as well as for Kentucky: Louisville was a central location from which Clark could move quickly in either direction.

About 1783, Boone moved to Livestone (Maysville) on the Ohio River, where he opened a store, surveyed, hunted, and worked on prisoner exchanges with the indigenous. His fame spread throughout the nation and to Europe after 1784, following John Filson's addition of a thirty-four-page Boone "autobiography" to *The Discovery, Settlement, and Present State of Kentucke* (1784). In 1789 or 1790, Boone moved to Point Pleasant, in what became West Virginia, but he was in the Blue Licks area by 1795. By then, defective land titles had cost him most of his good lands, and Boone ceased to contest any claims brought against him. Disappointed by his treatment and convinced that Kentucky, a state since 1792, was becoming too crowded, Boone decided to move to Missouri, where Spanish officials welcomed him. In 1799, just before he was sixty-five years old, Boone led a party across the Mississippi River and settled on land some sixty miles west of St. Louis.

The next few years were happy ones. Despite rheumatism, Boone could still hunt, and the wilderness lured him into long journeys westward, perhaps as far as Yellowstone. He received large land grants, and as a magistrate he held court under a so-called Justice Tree. The old pioneer was incensed in 1812, when he was rejected as a volunteer for the War of 1812; he was seventy-eight years old but ready to fight. His wife Rebecca died in 1813, and Boone probably made his last long hunt in 1817. He had a handsome coffin made and stored for future use. After the Louisiana Purchase, through carelessness and a series of misunderstandings, he lost most of his Missouri land, just as he had earlier lost his holdings in Kentucky.

Boone probably made his last visit to Kentucky in 1817; he was reputed to have only fifty cents left in his pocket after he paid the last of his creditors. Two years later, Chester Harding painted Boone's only life portrait. Boone died at a son's home near St. Charles on September 26, 1820, after a brief illness. In 1845, his and Rebecca's remains were reinterred on a hill above Frankfort, Kentucky.

Significance

Despite his preference for the wilderness, Daniel Boone contributed mightily to the end of the Kentucky frontier—by opening roads, building settlements, surveying land, and fighting American Indians. Without his leadership, Kentucky's settlement would have been delayed, for he inspired trust that kept settlers from fleeing to safety. This clash between the idea of wilderness as paradise and the restrictions of civilization has been a common theme in the history of the American frontier; it remains an issue still.

In addition to his notable accomplishments, Boone became the symbol of the American frontier during the first half-century of nationhood. James Fenimore Cooper and Lord Byron were only two of many authors whose work includes depictions of Boone. Both his character and his exploits made Boone a natural hero, and they marked a way of life, believed virtuous, that was rapidly vanishing.

—*Lowell H. Harrison*

Further Reading

Boone, Nathan. *My Father, Daniel Boone: The Draper Interviews with Nathan Boone.* Edited by Neal O. Hammon, with an introduction by Nelson L. Dawson. Lexington: University Press of Kentucky, 1999. Historian Lyman Draper interviewed

Boone, Daniel

Boone's only surviving child, Nathan, and Nathan's wife, Olive, in 1851, as part of Draper's research for a biography of Boone. This is an updated transcript of those interviews.

Chaffee, Allen. *The Wilderness Trail: The Story of Daniel Boone*. New York: T. Nelson and Sons, 1936. An account that tells much more about Boone than his connection with the Wilderness Trail, one of the major routes for pioneers who entered Kentucky.

Draper, Lyman C. *The Life of Daniel Boone*. Edited by Franklin Belue. Mechanicsburg, Pa.: Stackpole Books, 1998. Historian Draper died in 1891, leaving a massive but unfinished biography of Boone. Belue has transcribed and annotated Draper's manuscript. Although Draper presents a hagiographic account of Boone, his work was based on extensive research and interviews, and he vividly re-creates many details of Boone's life. Belue's chapter notes correct Draper's romanticism, and the seventy-six period drawings, engraving, photos, and maps enhance the text.

Eckert, Allan W. *The Court Martial of Daniel Boone*. Boston: Little, Brown, 1973. This well-researched and well-written historical novel reconstructs the charges brought against Boone and his successful defense. The trial record disappeared, but Eckert's version sounds plausible.

Filson, John. *The Discovery, Settlement, and Present State of Kentucke: . . . To Which Is Added . . . the Adventures of Col. Daniel Boon*. Wilmington, Del.: James Adams, 1784. This rare book has been reprinted many times. Although the "autobiography" was written by Filson and contains many errors, he did interview Boone and a number of other Kentuckians.

Lofaro, Michael A. *Daniel Boone: An American Life*. Lexington: University Press of Kentucky, 2003. Lofaro published an excellent biography, *The Life and Adventures of Daniel Boone*, in 1979. This updated biography is more detailed and is based upon thirty years of research. Lofaro explains why Boone is considered the quintessential frontiersman and why the idea of the frontier remains a part of the American experience.

Thwaites, Reuben Gold. *Daniel Boone*. New York: D. Appleton, 1902. Despite its years, this book provides a generally accurate biography. The author was one of the first Boone biographers to make use of the Lyman Draper manuscripts.

OMAR NELSON BRADLEY

> *We are given one life, and the decision is ours whether to wait for circumstances to make up our mind, or whether to act, and in acting, to live.*

U.S. Army general and chairman, Joint Chiefs of Staff (1949-1953)

Bradley provided stability and continuity within the U.S. military establishment during the critical period following the end of World War II and the onset of the Cold War.

Born: February 12, 1893; Clark, Missouri
Died: April 8, 1981; New York, New York
Also known as: Omar N. Bradley; G.I. General
Area of achievement: Military

EARLY LIFE

Omar Nelson Bradley (BRAD-lee) was born to John Smith Bradley, a schoolteacher, and Sarah Elizabeth Hubbard Bradley, a homemaker. Though "desperately poor," to use Bradley's words, his family took in the two daughters of his mother's sister when the latter died, and they became his "sisters." A second son was born to the Bradleys but died of scarlet fever before his second birthday.

Bradley's father, who supplemented the modest income he received from his teaching with what odd jobs he could find, contracted pneumonia and died in January, 1908. The family moved to Moberly, where Bradley attended high school and became interested in Mary Quayle, the daughter of his Sunday school teacher and his future wife. Having been graduated in 1910 with good grades, "but not the highest," Bradley planned to become a lawyer, though he was uncertain as to how he would fund his education. His Sunday school superintendent suggested that he consider the U.S. Military Academy at West Point in New York.

Bradley took the advice, competed for and won an appointment to West Point, and entered the academy in 1911. In later life, he would remark that the four years spent at West Point were "among the most rewarding of my life." Considering the subsequent career that sprang from those four years, one might say that the country as a whole was handsomely rewarded as a result of Bradley's decision.

When he was graduated from West Point in 1915, Bradley stood forty-fourth in a class of 164. He later confessed that his affinity for sports—Bradley played on the varsity football and baseball teams—might have detracted from his academic performance. Bradley's class would gain fame as the one that "the stars fell on." Bradley, who would ultimately wear five of those stars, was always proud of a complimentary entry in his senior yearbook, which described "his most promising characteristic" as "getting there...." The words of praise came from fellow classmate Dwight D. Eisenhower, who was himself destined to wear five stars and be twice elected president of the United States.

Bradley, Omar Nelson

Omar Nelson Bradley.
(Library of Congress)

Life's Work

Following graduation, Bradley was assigned to duty with the Fourteenth Infantry Regiment at Fort Laughton near Seattle, Washington. He was later transferred to Douglas, Arizona, but did not join the Pershing expedition into Mexico. On December 28, 1916, Bradley, by then a first lieutenant, married his high school sweetheart, Mary Quayle. Four months later, the United States entered World War I. Convinced that his career would suffer irreparable harm if he did not see duty in France, Bradley desperately tried to secure assignment to a combat unit. He never succeeded; instead he spent the war guarding copper mines in Montana. When he was finally ordered to report for overseas duty, his destination was not France but Siberia. Fortunately, those orders were canceled, and Montana suddenly looked much better than it had before.

Like most career officers, Bradley found duty in the peacetime army to be rather routine and advancement quite slow. He spent five years teaching in one capacity or another: one year as an instructor in the ROTC program at South Dakota State University and four years in the math department at West Point. He became a father during his tour at West Point, when Mary gave birth to a daughter, Elizabeth. An earlier stillborn birth and complications arising during the second pregnancy convinced the Bradleys that they should have no more children.

Bradley, Omar Nelson

After completing his tour at West Point in 1923, Bradley attended infantry school at Fort Benning, Georgia, for one year and was then assigned to duty in Hawaii for three years. While there he met George S. Patton, then serving as chief intelligence officer of the Hawaiian Division and described by Bradley as "one of the most extraordinary men—military or civilian—I ever met."

Returning to the United States in 1928, Bradley attended the Command and General Staff School at Fort Leavenworth, Kansas, after which he had a choice of assignments between Fort Benning and West Point. He chose the former, later recalling that it was "the most important decision of my life." While at Benning he attracted the attention of George C. Marshall, who would later, as chief of staff of the Army, prove to be instrumental in Bradley's rapid rise to high command during World War II. In fact, after attending the Army War College and serving another four years at West Point, Bradley served under Marshall following Marshall's appointment as chief of staff in April, 1939. When, in late 1940, Marshall offered Bradley command of the Eighty-second Division, he became the second in his class to get two stars and the first to command a division.

Like so many of his colleagues, Bradley first attracted widespread public attention during World War II. Though he never reached the pinnacle of command achieved by Eisenhower or assumed the almost legendary proportions of the flamboyant Patton, he carved his own special place in United States military history as the "G.I. General." Newsman Ernie Pyle, whose cartoons and reports made household names of many wartime personalities, confessed that it was a challenge to write about Bradley because he was so "damn normal." Rather tall and solidly built, Bradley was never described as handsome. In his late forties when the United States entered the war, he was balding and bespectacled, conveying a congeniality not usually associated with a combat general.

Bradley was not assigned to overseas duty until February, 1943, when he joined Eisenhower in North Africa. For a brief time he served as deputy commander of the United States II Corps under George S. Patton and later assumed command of that unit when Patton was called to head Seventh Army operations in the Sicilian campaign. Bradley again served under Patton in Sicily, where he became disillusioned with his superior's methods both on and off the battlefield. Patton's involvement in the infamous slapping incidents in Sicily, in which he struck two enlisted men who were suffering from battle fatigue, cost him any chance he might have had for immediate advancement. Consequently, when Sicily was safely in Allied hands, it was Bradley who was chosen to command American forces in the next major operation of the war—Normandy—while Patton remained behind.

Bradley played a key role in Operation Overlord, first as commander of the American First Army and later as head of the Twelfth Army Group, on an equal footing with Britain's field marshal Bernard Law Montgomery. In an ironic twist, Patton, who assumed command of the newly activated Third Army on August 1, 1944, was now subordinate to Bradley. This proved to be a workable combination when Bradley the strategist and Patton the tactician combined to parlay Operation Cobra into a theaterwide breakout, leading to the eventual liberation of most of northern France. Bradley proved to be an asset to Eisenhower in more ways than one. He not only demonstrated great competence as a strategist and battlefield manager but also held a tight rein on Patton and frequently served as a buffer between him and the equally irascible Montgomery.

As the war in Europe drew to a close, Bradley did not have to worry about a new assignment. Marshall, Eisenhower, and President Harry S. Truman were unanimous in the opinion that he should be made head of the Veterans Administration. In August, 1945, Bradley assumed the new duties of his office and all the headaches that went with it—chief among them being administration of the G.I. Bill and upgrading the quality of medical care for veterans. He found his job to be challenging and rewarding, deriving the greatest satisfaction from the improvements made in the quality of medical care that veterans received.

In February, 1948, Bradley left the Veterans Administration to become chief of staff of the Army, a post he held for about eighteen months before becoming chairman of the Joint Chiefs of Staff in August, 1949. This was the position he held when the so-called Cold War turned hot in Korea in June, 1950. Bradley's view that the United States was right to intervene in Korea while not seeking to expand the war in Asia represented a consensus within the military; his often quoted statement that a wider war in Asia would be "the wrong war, at the wrong place, at the wrong time, and with the wrong enemy" succinctly summarized the military's position. This conviction put him at odds with General Douglas MacArthur, then commander of United Nations forces in Korea, but ultimately it was Bradley's viewpoint that prevailed.

The Korean War ended in 1953 during Bradley's tour as chairman of the Joint Chiefs of Staff, and shortly thereafter he resigned from full-time active service. Ceremonial duties as one of the nation's senior military statesmen took some of his time, but most of it was devoted to his business interests. He served for a while as chair of the board of the Bulova Watch Company and was a director on several other corporate boards. In 1965, Bradley's wife died, and for several months he suffered from severe depression. In September, 1966, he married Kitty Buhler, a gregarious Hollywood screenwriter, who, despite being thirty years his junior, remained devoted to him until his death in April, 1981.

SIGNIFICANCE

Bradley was the product of rural, midwestern America—the values of which were always reflected in his career. Cognizant of his own modest beginnings, he identified and sympathized with the plight of the common soldier. He successfully made the transition from combat general to administrator and from total war, as required by World War II, to the concept of limited war, as imposed by the constraints of the Cold War. His career spanned two world wars and the Korean conflict. During World War II, his professional military talents had carried him to the position of Army Group command. He ultimately wore five stars as general of the Army and served as head of the Veterans Administration, chief of staff of the Army, and chairman of the Joint Chiefs of Staff. Who could doubt, to paraphrase Eisenhower, that the farm boy from Missouri had truly "gotten there"?

—*Kirk Ford, Jr.*

FURTHER READING

Blumenson, Martin. *Patton: The Man Behind the Legend, 1885-1945*. New York: William Morrow, 1985. This book offers insights into Patton's candid assessment of Bradley, first as a subordinate and later as a superior. Patton displays great respect for Bradley while objecting strenuously to some of his military decisions.

Bradley, Omar N. *A Soldier's Story*. New York: Henry Holt, 1951. Published during Bradley's tenure as chairman of the Joint Chiefs of Staff, these wartime memoirs, though informative, reflect the restrictions imposed on Bradley by his official position and government classification of many World War II documents.

Bradley, Omar N., and Clay Blair. *A General's Life*. New York: Simon & Schuster, 1983. Begun as an autobiography and subsequently completed by Blair after the general's death, this is the only work that entirely covers Bradley's life and career.

Chandler, Alfred D., Jr., and Louis Galambos, eds. *The Papers of Dwight David Eisenhower*. 11 vols. Baltimore: Johns Hopkins University Press, 1970-1979. Bradley and Eisenhower confronted many common problems from different perspectives both during and after World War II. These volumes are useful and illuminating for both periods.

Eisenhower, Dwight D. *Crusade in Europe*. Garden City, N.Y.: Doubleday, 1948. Eisenhower's wartime memoirs contain much information on Bradley and the major campaigns in which he participated. Eisenhower's appreciation of Bradley's talents is apparent.

Jordan, Thomas M. "Battle Command: Bradley and Ridgway in the Battle of the Bulge." *Military Review* 90, no. 2 (March-April, 2000): 95. Describes the role of Bradley and Lieutenant General Matthew Ridgway in the Battle of the Bulge in Germany in 1944.

Muench, James F. *Five Stars: Missouri's Most Famous Generals*. Columbia: University of Missouri Press, 2006. Profiles five American generals from Missouri, including Bradley.

Pogue, Forrest C. *Ordeal and Hope, 1939-1943* and *Organizer of Victory, 1943-1945*. Vols. 2-3 of *George C. Marshall*, 3 vols. New York: Viking Press, 1963-1966. Perhaps more than any other, Marshall was instrumental in Bradley's rapid climb to Army Group command in 1944. The works cited here cover only the war years.

Weigley, Russell F. *Eisenhower's Lieutenants: The Campaigns of France and Germany, 1944-1945*. Bloomington: Indiana University Press, 1981. A brilliant work describing the last major military campaigns of the European war. This book evaluates Bradley's skills as a strategist while inviting comparisons with his colleagues, British and American.

Brandeis, Louis D.

LOUIS D. BRANDEIS

> *America has believed that in differentiation, not in uniformity, lies the path of progress. It acted on this belief; it has advanced human happiness, and it has prospered.*

Associate justice of the United States (1916-1939)

Brandeis was a leading social reformer from 1897 to 1916, gaining the unofficial title of the "people's attorney." He was the leader of the American Zionist movement, and he served as associate justice of the United States. In protecting intellectual and personal freedom, Brandeis thought it was the duty of the Court to protect minority views from a tyranny of the majority. It was in this area of law that Brandeis made his mark as one of the Court's greatest justices and as one of the most important American legal philosophers.

Born: November 13, 1856; Louisville, Kentucky
Died: October 5, 1941; Washington, D.C.
Also known as: Louis Dembitz Brandeis (full name)
Areas of achievement: Law and jurisprudence; social reform

EARLY LIFE

Louis D. Brandeis (BRAN-dis) was the son of Adolph Brandeis and Frederika (Dembitz) Brandeis, refugees from Prague, Czechoslovakia. His parents and relatives had fled the failed liberal revolutions of 1848, and he grew up in an atmosphere that was intellectual, open-minded, progressive, and dedicated to freedom. This heritage was evident throughout his career.

At age fifteen, Brandeis was graduated from Louisville public schools and then lived and studied in Europe for three years. In 1875, he entered Harvard Law School. Although lacking a college degree, he completed the three-year program in only two years, being graduated in 1877 with the highest grades in the law school's history.

LIFE'S WORK

Brandeis's career centered on the law and public service. His law practice was enormously successful, and his early clients included major railroads and manufacturing companies. In 1889, Brandeis argued, and won, his first case before the U.S. Supreme Court, on behalf of the Wisconsin Central Railroad. In 1890, Brandeis and his former partner Samuel Warren jointly published a path-breaking article in the *Harvard Law Review*, "The Right to Privacy." The article helped create a new concept in law, one that Brandeis later supported from the bench.

By the mid-1890's, Brandeis was earning more than seventy thousand dollars a year—a large sum in those days. Through frugal living and careful investments, he became a millionaire by 1900. As his wealth grew, so did his generosity; between 1905 and 1939, he gave away approximately one and one-half million dollars. Brandeis also used his wealth to free himself from the necessity of taking on paying clients. In 1891, when he married his second cousin Alice Goldmark, the two decided to dedicate their

Brandeis, Louis D.

lives to public service. By 1895, he had begun to devote most of his energies to public interest work. Brandeis not only worked without a fee but also paid money to his law firm so that his partners would not suffer from his pro bono activities. Brandeis brought his expertise as a corporate lawyer to social causes.

In 1892, Brandeis was profoundly affected when plant owners used armed guards against workers in the Homestead Steel Strike. Brandeis later wrote,

> I think it was the affair at Homestead which first set me to thinking seriously about the labor problem. It took the shock of that battle, where organized capital hired a private army to shoot at organized labor for resisting an arbitrary cut in wages, to turn my mind definitely toward a searching study of the relations of labor to industry.

After 1892, Brandeis became known as the "people's attorney" for his willingness to take public interest cases for free or for a very small fee. In 1904, as the unpaid counsel, Brandeis convinced Boston officials and the gas company to adopt a sliding scale for gas prices that guaranteed the company a minimum of 7 percent profit on its assets while lowering rates to consumers from a dollar to ninety cents per thousand cubic feet of gas. The sliding scale formula allowed the company to raise its dividends by 1 percent for every five cents it reduced the price of gas. This built-in incentive for increased efficiency and lower prices brought the cost of gas to eighty cents within a year, while the return on the gas company's investment rose to 9 percent.

In 1906, Brandeis resigned from the board of directors of the United Shoe Manufacturing Company when the company tried to monopolize the industry and used illegal methods to stop competition. Years later, Brandeis testified against United Shoe at public hearings and served as counsel for competitors seeking to prevent a monopoly of the industry. Eventually, the shoe monopoly was broken and fair competition restored. Brandeis also investigated corruption in the life insurance industry. Brandeis helped create savings-bank life insurance in Massachusetts, which provided low-cost life insurance through state-regulated banks. As with gas prices, Brandeis showed that enlightened and regulated capitalism could work for the benefit of all. The banks made money from selling the insurance, the customers gained safe insurance at reasonable prices, and to compete, the major insurance companies lowered their premiums. Other states adopted the program, and by 1914 Brandeis estimated that the various reforms saved Americans twenty million dollars a year.

Starting in 1905, Brandeis led a coalition of businesspeople, civic leaders, and reformers in fighting the New Haven Railroad's attempt to monopolize all rail traffic in New England by acquiring its main competition, the Boston and Maine Railroad. Brandeis opposed monopolies because he believed they were inefficient and harmful to consumers. The struggle against the New Haven monopoly lasted until 1914, when the Wilson administration forced the New Haven Railroad to give up the Boston and Maine. During this struggle, public attacks on Brandeis became personal. Newspapers controlled by those with financial interests in the New Haven Railroad pictured him as "King Louis of New England." Anti-Semitic caricatures of Brandeis falsely accused him of corruption.

In 1914, Brandeis published *Other People's Money and How the Bankers Use It*.

Brandeis, Louis D.

This extremely influential book stimulated the passage of some banking regulations. Brandeis's major recommendations were ignored, however, until after the failure of thousands of banks in the 1930's. Only at that point did Congress adopt the kind of legislation for which Brandeis argued in 1914.

The pro bono cases profoundly affected Brandeis's life. *Muller v. Oregon* (1908) involved an Oregon statute that limited the working day to ten hours for women employees. This statute reflected a national movement to limit hours for all workers, prohibit child labor, and create minimum wages. In 1905 the Supreme Court, in *Lochner v. New York*, had struck down a similar statute regulating working hours for men.

In arguing the Muller case, Brandeis had few legal precedents with which to work. *Lochner v. New York*, the most obvious precedent, was something Brandeis had to overcome. Brandeis brilliantly met the challenge. His brief was more than one hundred pages long. Only two of those pages, however, were devoted to legal precedents and principles. The rest of the brief discussed the social facts of industrial employment. Using statistics from numerous American and foreign sources, Brandeis demonstrated the physical costs of the industrial employment of women. The brief was a masterful combination of economics, sociology, and public health data. Without overruling *Lochner v. New York*, a unanimous Supreme Court upheld the Oregon statute as a reasonable exercise of the state's police powers. The Court took the unusual step of noting the importance of "the brief filed by Mr. Louis D. Brandeis." The "Brandeis brief," as it was called, revolutionized legal argument by legitimizing a court's use of social science data. The Court's decision was a personal triumph for Brandeis and a major victory for the Progressive movement in America.

In 1910, Brandeis successfully mediated a New York garment industry strike. During these negotiations, Brandeis came in contact with large numbers of immigrant Eastern European Jews. This led Brandeis to rediscover his own Jewish roots and the Zionist movement. Although born and reared Jewish, Brandeis had never been actively involved in his faith. Of his relatives, only his uncle Louis Dembitz had been a practicing Jew. Dembitz had also been an ardent Zionist even before Theodor Herzl organized the World Zionist Congress. Brandeis had obviously been influenced by his uncle, because as a young man he had changed his middle name from David to Dembitz, in honor of his uncle. In 1912, Brandeis met with representatives of the World Zionist Congress.

As a democratic movement striving to provide liberty and opportunity for an oppressed minority, Zionism was consistent with Brandeis's own social goals. From 1914 until 1921, Brandeis was the leader of the Zionist Organization of America. Zionism was Brandeis's only extrajudicial activity after he joined the Supreme Court in 1916. As the Holocaust loomed on the horizon, Brandeis increased his donations to the cause, giving more than a quarter of a million dollars between 1933 and 1939.

Brandeis was gradually drawn into politics. He never sought elective office and was never a regular party man. In 1912, he campaigned for Woodrow Wilson and served as an adviser to the candidate. After Wilson's victory, Brandeis worked with the administration on antitrust matters and drafted legislation creating the Federal Reserve System (1913) and the Federal Trade Commission (1914).

In 1916, President Wilson nominated Brandeis to the Supreme Court. As the "people's attorney," Brandeis had offended moneyed interests throughout the country. The American Bar Association and some elite reformers opposed Brandeis because he was not "one of the boys." Former president William H. Taft opposed Brandeis because Taft himself wanted to be on the Court and foolishly believed that Wilson might appoint him. The Boston establishment adamantly opposed the man who had exposed the greed of the insurance and banking industries and had successfully prevented monopolies in the shoe manufacturing and railroad industries. Executives from United States Steel, the United Shoe Manufacturing Company, the New Haven Railroad, various Wall Street law firms and Boston banks, the president of Harvard University, and *The Wall Street Journal* opposed Brandeis. Those who had financial interests in these industries hated him because he had so often defeated them in court. They also disliked him because Brandeis was not "one of them." Throughout the confirmation hearings, there were undertones of anti-Semitism. Brandeis was the first Jew appointed to the Supreme Court. For many Americans, particularly the elite in Boston, this alone disqualified Brandeis.

Brandeis was supported by Progressives from around the nation. While the incumbent president of Harvard, A. Lawrence Lowell, the son of a Massachusetts industrialist, opposed the institution's alumnus, the university's president emeritus, Charles Eliot, a renowned scholar, supported Brandeis. Many of the Republican supporters of

Louis D. Brandeis.
(Library of Congress)

Brandeis, Louis D.

Theodore Roosevelt rallied to Brandeis. The four-month confirmation struggle was the longest in American history. In the end, Brandeis received support from all but one Senate Democrat as well as five Progressive Republicans.

Brandeis was sixty years old when he joined the Court. He remained until he was eighty-two. Except for his last few years on the bench, Brandeis was almost always in the minority—a Progressive voice on the conservative, or even reactionary, Court. Thus, for much of his career Brandeis was a dissenter. As a lawyer Brandeis had defended legislative regulation of the economy; as a justice he usually deferred to the will of the people, as reflected in legislation. Two exceptions to Brandeis's deference to legislatures involved early New Deal legislation and all civil liberties cases.

Brandeis supported President Franklin D. Roosevelt, but in 1935 he joined a unanimous Court in striking down the National Industrial Recovery Act because he found that Congress had exceeded its constitutional authority. This did not signal that Brandeis had become an economic conservative. Rather, he thought the act was poorly drafted and overbroad. After 1936, Brandeis consistently supported Roosevelt.

When it came to the protection of individual liberty and rights, Brandeis never deferred to a legislature. In protecting intellectual and personal freedom, Brandeis believed it was the Court's duty to protect minority views. It was in this area of law that Brandeis made his mark as one of the Court's greatest justices and as one of the most important legal philosophers in U.S. history.

Brandeis's career was marked by his desire to protect human liberty and dignity. In *Whitney v. California* (1927), Brandeis argued that free speech allowed a society to find truth. He declared,

> Those who won our independence by revolution were not cowards. They did not fear political change. They did not exalt order at the cost of liberty. To courageous, self-reliant men, with confidence in the power of free and fearless reasoning applied through the processes of popular government, no danger flowing from speech can be deemed clear and present, unless the incidence of that evil apprehended is so imminent that it may befall before there is opportunity for full discussion. If there be time to expose through discussion the falsehood and fallacies, to avert the evil by the processes of education, the remedy to be applied is more speech not enforced silence.

In *Olmstead v. United States* (1928), Brandeis wrote a powerful and prophetic dissent, arguing that wiretapping without a warrant constituted a "search" in violation of the Fourth Amendment. Brandeis brilliantly refuted Chief Justice Taft's majority opinion that a wiretap did not constitute a search because there was no physical invasion of the property. Brandeis argued that the framers "knew that only a part of the pain, pleasure and satisfactions of life are to be found in material things." Thus, the framers "sought to protect Americans in their beliefs, their thoughts, their emotions and their sensations. They conferred, as against the government, the right to be left alone—the most comprehensive of rights and the right most valued by civilized men." Brandeis declared that "men born to freedom are naturally alert to repel invasion of their liberty by evil-minded rulers. The greatest dangers to liberty lurk in insidious encroachment by men of zeal, well-meaning, but without understanding." Brandeis further asserted that "to declare that in the administration of the criminal law the end justifies the means—to declare that the government may commit crimes to secure the conviction of a private criminal—would bring terrible retribution." Not four years following his retirement from the Court, Brandeis died, in 1941.

Significance

By his own example, Brandeis set a modern standard for high-priced lawyers taking pro bono cases. In the Brandeis brief, he gave lawyers a new tool and helped liberate the legal profession from a dependence on stale and dry precedents to deal with the realities of the world. He worked to make the legal profession a servant of the people and the public good and not simply the servant of the rich and powerful. As an adviser to state and federal officials, Brandeis helped shape progressive reforms. Insurance regulation, antimonopoly statutes, and banking reform all benefited from his wisdom and ideas.

On the Court, Brandeis left an unsurpassed legacy of support of civil liberties and social justice. His confirmation in the face of a widespread anti-Semitic opposition helped break down barriers for minorities in the United States. His dissents on freedom of speech and criminal law later became precedents for a more enlightened Court. People meeting Brandeis for the first time often noticed his eyes, penetrating and deep, like his mind. While of only average height, Brandeis resembled a beardless Lincoln in his sharp features. As an aging justice, he looked the part of a philosopher and prophet. President Roosevelt referred to him as "old Isaiah," and, like the biblical prophet, Brandeis was a foe of injustice and a friend of liberty.

—*Paul Finkelman*

Further Reading

Brandeis, Louis D. *The Family Letters of Louis D. Brandeis*. Edited by Melvin I. Urofsky and David W. Levy. Norman: University of Oklahoma Press, 2002. An annotated collection of Brandeis's letters to his wife, daughters, brother, and other family members that provides insight into his personality and character.

Freund, Paul A. "Mr. Justice Brandeis." In *Mr. Justice*, edited by Allison Dunham and Philip B. Kurland. 2d ed. Chicago: University of Chicago Press, 1964. Essay on Brandeis by a former law clerk who later became a distinguished law professor at Harvard Law School.

Konefsky, Samuel J. *The Legacy of Holmes and Brandeis: A Study of the Influence of Ideas*. New York: Macmillan, 1956. Traces the influence of the two great dissenters on the Court.

Mason, Alpheas Thomas. *Brandeis: A Free Man's Life*. New York: Viking Press, 1946. A classic biography of Brandeis by a leading scholar in constitutional history. This is the best introduction to Brandeis.

Purcell, Edward A., Jr. *Brandeis and the Progressive Constitution: Erie, the Judicial Power, and the Politics of the Federal Courts in Twentieth-Century America*. New Haven, Conn.: Yale University Press, 2000. Examines Brandeis's opinion in *Erie Railroad Co. v. Tompkins*, a 1938 Supreme Court decision that transferred power from the federal to the state courts. Describes how the decision led to legal, politi-

Brant, Joseph

cal, and ideological battles over the role of the federal court system.

Todd, Alden L. *Justice on Trial: The Case of Louis D. Brandeis.* Chicago: University of Chicago Press, 1964. A prizewinning study of the struggle to confirm Brandeis as a Supreme Court justice. Excellent for its details and descriptions.

Urofsky, Melvin I. *American Zionism from Herzl to the Holocaust.* Garden City, N.Y.: Anchor Press, 1975. This book details the importance of Brandeis to the Zionist movement in the United States.

_____. *Louis D. Brandeis and the Progressive Tradition.* Boston: Little, Brown, 1980. Places Brandeis in the context of the Progressive movement. Includes a useful biography.

_____. *A Mind of One Piece: Brandeis and American Reform.* New York: Charles Scribner's Sons, 1971. Excellent study of the role of Brandeis in twentieth century reform.

JOSEPH BRANT

❝ *The Mohawks have on all occasions shown their zeal and loyalty to the Great King; yet they have been very badly treated by his people.* ❞

Mohawk chief and military leader

Brant demonstrated the impact an educated Native American leader could have on his people's destiny, as he led the way for a great Mohawk migration to Canada after the American Revolution, in which he fought for the British against American revolutionaries.

Born: 1742; Ohio Country
Died: November 24, 1807; near Brantford, Ontario, Canada
Also known as: Thayendanegea (birth name); Kayendanegea; Two Sticks of Wood Bound Together
Area of achievement: Native American affairs

EARLY LIFE

Known to his Mohawk kin as Thayendanegea, meaning "he who places two bets," Joseph Brant was the son of Argoghyiadecker (also known as Nickus Brant), a prominent leader on the New York Indian frontier during the mid-eighteenth century. He had an older sister known as Molly Brant who became an extremely influential tribeswoman. She combined her own political acumen with her role as consort to the American Indian superintendent for the British, William Johnson, to build a powerful network within the tribe. Some observers believed she was capable of influencing tribal decisions in a major way. Major Tench Tilghman, an American observer in the Iroquois Country in 1776, observing Molly Brant and the other Iroquois women, reflected that "women govern the Politics of Savages as well as the refined part of the world."

Brant, Joseph

Brant grew up in the Mohawk village of Canojohare, where he enjoyed the traditional teachings of the tribal elders as well as the efforts of Anglican missionaries who came to convert the indigenous peoples to Christianity and to teach them basic educational skills. So bright was the young Brant, however, that this village education was insufficient. Accordingly, when David Fowler and Samson Occum visited the Mohawk Country as representatives of the Reverend Eleazar Wheelock's school in Lebanon, Connecticut, Brant was one of three young Mohawks designated to return eastward for additional education.

Upon their arrival in Lebanon, Brant and his Mohawk companions were so frightened by their surroundings that they kept their horses ready at a moment's notice for flight back to their village. Of the three new students, the schoolmaster had the highest praise for Brant: "The other being of a family of distinction among them, was considerably cloathed, Indian-fashion, and could speak a few words of English."

Within three months, Brant's two companions returned to the safety of their home country, but Brant remained to study and to help teach the Mohawk language to a young missionary named Samuel Kirkland. When Kirkland went west in November on a recruiting mission, Brant went along to interpret and help persuade two more Mohawks to attend school. During his sessions in Lebanon, Brant improved his written Mohawk and his English skills, which would serve him well as both interpreter and then spokesman for his people. As early as March of 1768, he assisted Ralph Wheelock in conferring with an Onondaga chief, to the visitor's obvious approval: "By Joseph Brant's help I was able to discourse with him, and delivered to him my discourse to this nation."

Brant's stay at school was curtailed by the outbreak of war in the West. When Pontiac and his followers attempted to drive the British out of the Ohio Country, Brant's sister Molly urged her brother to come home, lest some revenge-seeking colonist murder him.

Although he never returned to Wheelock's school, Brant retained not only his literary skills but also his belief that education was the key to success and survival for his people. In time he was regarded as the most able interpreter in the British northern American Indian department. He had the advantage of being a respected Mohawk who could attend such important meetings as the tribal council at Onondaga, where he could take notes on the proceedings and then report them accurately to the British officials.

In the years before the American Revolution, Brant married Margaret, daughter of the Oneida chief Skenandon. At her death, he married her sister Susanna, who cared for Brant and his young children until her death. His third wife was Catherine Croghan, the Mohawk daughter of George Croghan, a member of the British Indian department and a confidant of William Johnson.

LIFE'S WORK

The coming of the American Revolution turned the world of Joseph Brant and the Mohawks upside down. He would emerge from his position as an official in the British Indian department to become the most feared Mohawk warrior of the time. Indeed, some historians have since described him as the most ferocious American Indian leader of the colonial period. Such accusations, however, were largely frontier hyperbole.

What Brant did during the American Revolution was accompany Guy Johnson,

Brant, Joseph

who had succeeded to the office of Indian superintendent at the death of his uncle in 1774, to London in 1775-1776. Feted by the royal court, Brant dined with the famous and had his portrait painted, both alone and as a figure in the background when Benjamin West painted Colonel Guy Johnson. In both cases, the depiction of a powerful and dignified young man suggests the sagacity Brant would use to lead the Mohawks through the difficult war years.

When Brant finally made his way back to America, he had to slip through the countryside in disguise to avoid capture. To his dismay he found the Mohawk Country in an uproar over the war, with many Mohawks already planning to immigrate to the British post at Niagara. Brant first went to Niagara to secure the safety of his family and then recruited warriors to return with him to the Mohawk Country, where they might attempt to drive out American invaders and aid British expeditions coming through American Indian country. Despite the accusations of frontiersmen in later years, there is no evidence to support the contention that Brant was a bloodthirsty killer. For most of 1777 and 1778, Brant was active in the Mohawk Country with his band of warriors. In 1779, however, they had to withdraw toward Niagara in the face of the major expedition launched through the Iroquois Country by the Americans under General John Sullivan.

After he had a disagreement with his old friend Guy Johnson in 1780, he withdrew to the Ohio Country in an attempt to rally the indigenous peoples of that territory. In 1781 he joined an attack on an American flotilla on the Ohio River, destroying supplies destined for George Rogers Clark in the Illinois Country. This success, however, did not change the plight of the Ohio Indians, for as Brant heard in Detroit late in 1781, many of the western tribal leaders believed the British would walk away from them when the end of the war came. As Brant soon came to know, the fear was well-founded, for the rumors of peace first heard in late 1781 were confirmed in early 1782.

Immediately, Brant wrote to General Frederick Haldimand in Canada, seeking to hold the British officer to his promise of sanctuary in Canada for the Mohawks. A man of his word, Haldimand agreed that Brant and his people had sacrificed too much. By March, 1783, Brant and Haldimand agreed on a Mohawk homeland along the Grand River in present-day Ontario. As a reward for his faithful service, Brant was commissioned by Haldimand as captain of the Northern Confederate Indians.

With this commission in hand and with the general's help in clearing title to the land, Brant began leading the Mohawks and others to Canada. By virtue of his newfound rank, Brant assumed the role of spokesman for all the pro-British Iroquois, especially those migrating to Canada. In his role as tribal leader and frontier entrepreneur, Brant would have his critics. Some accused him of profiting from the establishment of the Mohawks in Canada, and his opponents were especially bitter when he opened unused Mohawk lands for settlement by whites, from whom he collected a kind of real estate commission. Others may have resented the baronial style he had copied from William Johnson, as the following attests:

> Captain Brant . . . received us with much politeness and hospitality. . . . Tea was on the table when we came in, served up in the hansomest China plate and every other furniture in proportion. After tea was over, we were entertained with the music of an elegant hand or-

gan on which a young Indian gentleman and Mr. Clinch played alternately. Supper was served up in the same gentel stile. Our beverage, rum, brandy, Port and Maderia wines... our beds, sheets, and English blankets, equally fine and comfortable.... Dinner was just going on the table in the same elegant stile as the preceding night, when I returned to Captain Brant's house, the servants dressed in their best apparel. Two slaves attended the table, the one in scarlet, the other in coloured clothes, with silver buckles in their shoes, and ruffles, and every other part of their apparel in proportion.

In the face of criticism, Brant often countered by using his support system within the traditional Iroquois matriarchy, the mothers and aunts who dominated village politics, nominated the sachems, and influenced the councils. With their assistance, he silenced opposition. Since his sister was the brilliant and powerful Molly Brant and his wife, Catherine, was from a prominent Iroquois family, he well understood the most effective means of playing politics within the Iroquois council.

Two of Brant's long-term goals were advancing the cause of Christianity and advancing education among the Iroquois. Within a few years after his relocation in Canada, he was joined by his longtime friend and supporter, Daniel Claus, in editing the Prayer Book of the Anglican Church in Mohawk. This new volume, published in 1786, contained not only the Mohawk version of the Book of Common Prayer but also the Gospel of Mark.

In the 1780's, funds were obtained to build a church in the Grand River settlement. Then, in 1788, the former Anglican missionary at Canojohare, the Reverend John Stuart, came to visit, bringing with him some of the silver communion plates that once had been in the Mohawk church at Fort Hunter in New York. According to Stuart, the church Brant had seen constructed "in the Mohawk village is pleasantly situated on a small but deep River—the Church [is] about sixty feet in length and forty-five in breadth—built with squared logs and boarded on the outside and painted—with a handsome steeple & bell, a pulpit, reading-desk, & Communion-table, with convenient pews." Stuart had no great love for Brant; he was convinced that Brant would accept no clergyman for the Mohawk church whom he could not dominate. Indeed, believed Stuart, the Mohawks "were afraid of the restraint which the continued residence of a Clergyman would necessarily lay them under." Evidently there was some substance to this belief, since the number of white missionaries at Grand River remained quite low as long as Brant was in a position of influence there.

Brant remained the active frontier speculator until the last years of his life. Constantly involved in land transactions, travel, and farming, he never lacked for activity, yet his home was always the place of choice for visitors. As many callers pointed out, he lived in a grand style, and when he decided to build a new home early in the nineteenth century, it closely resembled Johnson Hall, the home of Sir William Johnson in New York where Brant had spent so much time as a child and as a young adult. From youth to death, Brant lived in two worlds.

SIGNIFICANCE

Joseph Brant's life was a success story, judged by most standards. He grew up among the elite of the Iroquois. His father was a prominent leader and his sister Molly Brant a respected woman among the Mohawks. Because of his intellectual ability, he was of-

Brant, Joseph

fered a chance for an education enjoyed by few of his contemporaries. Once he had acquired that education, he chose to walk the extremely narrow path between the two worlds of his own people and the neighboring new Americans and the European immigrants.

One of the most powerful role models in his life was Sir William Johnson, whose splendid home was the center of conviviality, diplomacy, and trade in the Mohawk Valley. Watching the success with which Johnson played patron to the Iroquois, military leader, land speculator, colonial politician, and wilderness baron had to have an impact on Brant. During the course of his travels, Brant was always careful to cultivate his patrons and the right politicians. Such adroitness served him well in maintaining his leadership position in the face of all opposition.

While Brant had his enemies and his detractors, he succeeded in surviving and in guaranteeing the survival of the Mohawks who followed him. While a strictly traditionalist tribal leader might not have approved of Brant's feet being in two worlds, others might agree that he found the only way for Native American peoples to survive in a world of rapid change.

—*James H. O'Donnell III*

FURTHER READING

Fenton, William N. *The Great Law and the Longhouse: A Political History of the Iroquois Confederacy*. Norman: University of Oklahoma Press, 1998. A comprehensive history that also examines Brant's role in Iroquois relations with the British and with American revolutionaries from 1760 to 1794.

Fischer, Joseph R. *A Well-Executed Failure: The Sullivan Campaign Against the Iroquois, July-September 1779*. Columbia: University of South Carolina Press, 1997. A military analysis of the Continental army's first expedition against the American Indians, focusing on field operations.

Graymont, Barbara. *The Iroquois in the American Revolution*. Syracuse, N.Y.: Syracuse University Press, 1972. An overview of the Iroquois in the American Revolution by the leading student of Six Nations affairs. While a bit naïve about the motives of the missionaries, it is extremely useful for its accounts of the battles in which the Iroquois took part.

Johnson, Charles. *The Valley of the Six Nations*. Toronto, Ont.: Champlain Society, 1964. An indispensable source for understanding Brant and the Mohawks in Canada. Reprints a number of sources that reveal the tensions with which Brant had to contend.

Mintz, Max M. *Seeds of Empire: The American Revolutionary Conquest of the Iroquois*. New York: New York University Press, 1999. Focuses on the military campaigns against the Iroquois and their Tory allies from 1777 through 1779. Mintz contends the American Revolution was not only a struggle for freedom but also a battle for American Indian lands, "and the jewel was the upstate New York domain of the Iroquois' Six Nations."

O'Donnell, James H., III. "Joseph Brant." In *American Indian Leaders: Studies in Diversity*, edited by R. David Edmunds. Lincoln: University of Nebraska Press, 1980. An analysis of Brant, his role models, and his career.

Stone, William L. *The Life of Joseph Brant, Thayendanegea.* New York: G. Dearborn, 1838. The classic nineteenth century account in which the author tries to unearth every story and scrap of evidence, both real and imagined, about Brant. It is still the place to start for anyone doing serious research on Brant.

WILLIAM J. BRENNAN

> *Those whom we would banish from society or from the human community itself often speak in too faint a voice to be heard above society's demand for punishment.*

Associate justice of the United States (1956-1990)

The most influential liberal voice of the U.S. Supreme Court during the second half of the twentieth century, Brennan wrote many of the Court's landmark opinions in the areas of criminal procedures, First Amendment freedoms, equal protection, gender equality, and personal autonomy.

Born: April 25, 1906; Newark, New Jersey
Died: July 24, 1997; Arlington, Virginia
Also known as: William Joseph Brennan, Jr. (full name)
Area of achievement: Law and jurisprudence

EARLY LIFE

The second of eight children whose parents were Irish immigrants, William J. Brennan (BREHN-nehn) was profoundly influenced by his hardworking father, who rose from a coal shoveler in a brewery to become a city commissioner and director of public safety. Growing up in a working-class milieu, Brennan identified with poor people and favored labor unions. Adopting his father's liberal social philosophy and work ethic, Brennan made excellent grades in school while he worked at a large number of jobs, beginning in grade school and continuing through his college years.

Brennan majored in business and finance at the University of Pennsylvania, graduating with honors in 1928. The week before graduation, he married Marjorie Leonard, who worked in order to finance his legal education at the Harvard Law School, where he graduated in 1931. Admitted to the New Jersey bar the next year, he embarked on a career as a labor lawyer at a prominent law firm, where he was named a partner in 1937. Following the outbreak of World War II, he entered the U.S. Army as a major in 1942 and left the service as a colonel in 1945.

LIFE'S WORK

Returning to civilian life, Brennan was a leading voice in the court reform movement of New Jersey. In 1949, he was appointed a trial judge, and three years later he was appointed to the Supreme Court of the state. As a judge, he was a strong supporter for the rights of criminal defendants, and he criticized McCarthy-period excesses in speeches around the state. In 1956, President Dwight D. Eisenhower nominated Brennan as as-

Brennan, William J.

William J. Brennan.
(Library of Congress)

sociate justice of the U.S. Supreme Court. Eisenhower's advisers convinced him that the appointment of a Roman Catholic Democrat from the Northeast would help Republicans gain votes in some of the closely divided states. In the Senate, Senator Joseph McCarthy was the person to oppose the nomination. Eisenhower would later refer to his choice of Brennan as one of his two major mistakes, the other being the selection of Chief Justice Earl Warren.

Despite Brennan's junior status, he quickly emerged as one of the most brilliant and influential of the justices. Quickly joining the Court's liberal wing, he would write a large percentage of the Warren Court's landmark decisions. However, Brennan usually took a more cautious and nuanced approach than did his liberal colleagues, avoiding absolute statements in favor of a "balancing" of competing legal values. Even his critics acknowledged the care and thoughtfulness of his writings.

Many of Brennan's more important judicial opinions dealt with issues of equal protection. In *Cooper v. Aaron* (1958), he asserted federal judicial supremacy in reaction to the "massive resistance" to desegregation orders in the South. His opinion for the Court in *Baker v. Carr* (1962) provided the foundation for the "reapportionment revolution," based on the principle of "one person, one vote." In the case of *Green v. School Board* (1968), Brennan rejected a "freedom of choice" plan that preserved racially segregated schools, and he insisted that school districts had the obligation to bring about desegregated schools. Brennan's *Green* ruling provided the basis for later decisions approving court-ordered busing plans, which he would consistently endorse.

Brennan also wrote many of the landmark First Amendment opinions, particularly in the area of free expression. His opinion in *Roth v. U.S.* (1957), for example, explicitly recognized for the first time that some forms of pornography were constitutionally protected. Although the opinion recognized that states might criminalize obscenity, he defined "obscenity" so narrowly that it became very difficult to prosecute. In *New York Times v. Sullivan* (1964), Brennan's opinion for the Court recognized the constitutional right to criticize public officials without the threat of libel suits, based on "the principle that debate on public issues should be uninhibited, robust, and wide open." Rejecting the idea of absolute immunity from libel, however, he allowed officials to sue for "actual malice," which he defined as reckless and deliberate disregard for the truth. His majority opinion in *Goldberg v. Kelly* (1970) recognized welfare as a form of property for constitutional purposes, which meant that it could not be terminated except through fair procedures.

Beginning in the 1970's, as the Supreme Court became more conservative, Brennan and Thurgood Marshall were the strongest proponents of judicial liberalism. In *Gregg v. Georgia* (1976), they were the only justices to dissent and argue that capital punishment was inherently unconstitutional. On most constitutional and statutory issues, the two justices disagreed with the conservative William H. Rehnquist, who was appointed chief justice in 1986. In an increasingly polarized Court, Brennan worked tirelessly to attempt to achieve a liberal majority. In *Texas v. Johnson* (1989), he spoke for a 5 to 4 majority in striking down laws that criminalized the desecration of the flag of the United States.

Brennan was the Court's most outspoken proponent of gender equality. In the landmark case of *Craig v. Boren* (1976), his opinion for the majority recognized gender-based classifications would be subject to heightened scrutiny, which meant that any discrimination against women was likely to be found unconstitutional. Brennan, nevertheless, was a consistent defender of affirmative action programs that involved preferences on the basis of gender or race in order to counteract the effects of prior discrimination. He was also a strong supporter of the controversial "right of privacy," which included a woman's right to obtain an abortion, despite his active membership in the Catholic Church, which opposes abortion.

Brennan sometimes wrote very caustic dissents, and he occasionally became involved in public controversy. In the *South Texas Law Review* (1986), he responded to Attorney General Edwin Meese and other critics who accused him of "judicial activism," or rendering judgments based on ideological preferences rather than the literal words of the U.S. Constitution or the original intent of the Framers. Referring to these criticisms as "little more than arrogance cloaked as humility," he argued the Court should uphold the fundamental purpose of the Constitution, which was to promote the "human dignity of every individual." His approach was based on the concept of a "living Constitution," which assumes that the meaning of the Constitution changes as culture evolves. His conservative colleague Antonin Scalia described his jurisprudence as "results-oriented."

Brennan, William J.

SIGNIFICANCE

Brennan exercised a profound impact on the Supreme Court during the second half of the twentieth century. During his tenure of thirty-four years, he authored 1,360 opinions, second in number only to those written by Justice William O. Douglas. In addition to his contributions as a researcher and writer, he was recognized as being unusually effective in negotiating with other justices to form a majority. Chief Justice Warren described him as "a prodigious worker and a master craftsman" who served as "a unifying influence on the bench and in the conference room."

Brennan was strongly committed to an activist Court that would not hesitate to take a strong stand in favor of the principles and values of judicial liberalism. While he avoided absolutist positions, he could be counted on to vote in favor of individual liberties, equality for minorities, the rights of criminal defendants, and personal autonomy in matters such as marriage and sexuality. Few of his opinions have been overturned, and he is widely recognized as one of the most articulate and thoughtful writers in the history of the Court.

—*Thomas Tandy Lewis*

FURTHER READING

Goldman, Roger, and David Gallen. *Justice William J. Brennan, Jr.: Freedom First.* New York: Carroll & Graf, 1994. A scholarly and sympathetic analysis of Brennan's life and his career in jurisprudence.

Irons, Peter. *Brennan vs. Rehnquist: The Battle for the Constitution.* New York: Alfred A. Knopf, 1994. Written by a prominent liberal lawyer, this book presents an excellent comparative analysis of two strong ideological voices that dominated the Supreme Court for many years.

Marion, David. *The Jurisprudence of Justice William J. Brennan: The Law and Politics of "Libertarian Dignity."* New York: Rowman & Littlefield, 1997. A close analysis arguing that Brennan's career represented the most important judicial force of the century, promoting an expansion of individual rights and human dignity.

Michelman, Frank. *Brennan and Democracy.* Princeton, N.J.: Princeton University Press, 1999. Written by an admiring former law clerk, this rather difficult book analyzes Brennan's views on the substantive and procedural aspects of modern democratic theory.

O'Brien, David M., ed. *Judges on Judging: Views from the Bench.* 2d. ed. Washington, D.C.: CQ Press, 2004. A collection of writings on judicial processes by justices of various courts in the United States. Includes two essays by Brennan: "The Constitution of the United States: Contemporary Ratification" and "Guardians of Our Liberties—State Courts No Less than Federal."

Richards, Robert D. *Uninhibited, Robust, and Wide Open: Mr. Justice Brennan's Legacy to the First Amendment.* Boone, N.C.: Parkway, 1994. A relatively short account of Brennan's opinions on the major categories relating to freedom of expression, which he considered the "cornerstone of the democracy."

Schwartz, Bernard, and E. Joshua Rosenkranz, eds. *Reason and Passion: Brennan's Enduring Influence.* New York: W. W. Norton, 1997. Collection of interesting essays on a variety of topics written by journalists, legal scholars, and six Supreme Court justices.

Urofsky, Melvin I. *The Warren Court: Justices, Rulings, and Legacy.* Santa Barbara, Calif.: ABC-CLIO, 2001. An examination of the Supreme Court with Warren as chief justice. Includes profiles of the justices, including Brennan; the Court's discussions of its decisions; and an appraisal of its influence.

JOHN BROWN

> *I, John Brown, am now quite certain that the crimes of this guilty land will never be purged away but with Blood.*

Militant abolitionist

Thanks to the notoriety Brown gained in a single dramatic act of rebellion, he has come to symbolize the struggle over the abolition of slavery in the United States. He was the catalyst for change from polite debate and parliamentary maneuvering aimed at modification of the institution to physical violence and a direct onslaught on southern territory and the supporters of slavery.

Born: May 9, 1800; Torrington, Connecticut
Died: December 2, 1859; Charles Town, Virginia (now in West Virginia)
Also known as: Shubel Morgan
Areas of achievement: Civil rights; social reform

EARLY LIFE

A native Connecticut John Brown was born in a state that, like many others in New England in 1800, was agriculturally exhausted and in religious turmoil. His parents, Owen and Ruth (Mills) Brown, were affected by both problems at his birth. Economically, the Brown family was barely at the subsistence level. John's father moved from job to job: farmer, carpenter, handyman. Though the family descended from the early Mayflower settlers, they were never able to capitalize on their ancestry. Religiously, Owen Brown was a harsh practitioner of the piety of his Puritan forebears, and he instilled in his son a lifelong fear and adoration of a militant and volatile God.

The elder Brown had been married twice and fathered sixteen children. His first wife, John's mother, suffered from mental disease as did others in her family. According to some accounts, John did not take well to his stepmother, but there is little evidence to support this conjecture. The peripatetic life of the family was probably more disturbing to him. When John was five, his father moved to Hudson, Ohio, following the line of the moving frontier. Again, the family was without the necessary capital to take advantage of the opportunities available in the rich Ohio Valley. His father became a herdsman and then a tanner, a vocation that the son quickly mastered. His father had some plans for his son which included sending him to Plainsfield, Massachusetts, to study for the ministry. John did not stay long, however, either because of poor preparation or because of his poor eyesight.

John Brown returned to Hudson to help his father with the cattle and the tanning shop. At the age of twenty, he married Dianthe Lusk, who bore him seven children in twelve years of married life. She, like his mother, had mental problems. Dianthe Brown died in 1831, and within a year of her passing, Brown married Mary Anne Day, then sixteen, who bore him thirteen more children in twenty-one years. Brown, possessing a modicum of education in a frontier region, became a surveyor as well as a tanner like his father. Also like his father, Brown was a mover. In 1825, he moved to Pennsylvania, cleared land, and set up what was to become a successful farm and tannery. He also became a postmaster, but still he was unsatisfied. Quick fortunes were being made in land and business speculation, and Brown sold off his holdings and moved back to Ohio. There he hoped to take advantage of land speculation and canal building contracts. He lost heavily and began pyramiding debt while turning to cattle and sheep selling. His creditors moved in on him and he was compelled to declare bankruptcy.

LIFE'S WORK

Brown's work in the woolen business brought him a partnership with another man, Simon Perkins, to establish a wool brokerage in Springfield, Massachusetts. Fluctuating prices and market instability, however, confounded his efforts to make a success of the business. He was also accused of "weighting" the packs of hides, which were sold by weight to English markets. The collapse of this last business venture was followed by numerous lawsuits, one involving sixty thousand dollars for breach of contract. Brown settled his affairs as best he could. He was fifty years old and virtually penniless, with a large family to support.

Even as a young man, Brown had learned from his father the biblical precept that it was sinful to earn one's living from the sweat of others and that slavery was wrong. In Ohio both he and his father had lent their resources to aiding the underground movement of runaway slaves. John Brown's barn at his farm in Pennsylvania was a station in that movement, and he formed a League of Gileadites among black people in Springfield to encourage them to defend both themselves and fugitive slaves.

Brown's activity in New England brought him in touch with men whose lives would never be the same after meeting him. Gerrit Smith, a New York benefactor of abolitionism who owned much of the Adirondack Mountains, was attracted to Brown. He had given land for use by runaway slaves in a small community known as North Elba. He gave Brown a farm from which he could train and educate the former slaves. Given the severe climate, short growing season, and lack of arable land in the region, not to mention Brown's spotty record as a farmer, problems developed. Brown himself declared that he felt "omnipotent" in his new role as guide and exemplar to the black people in his charge.

Within two years, however, he was in Akron, Ohio. His mind was turned to developing a grand plan for an attack on slavery. As early as 1847, he had talked about gathering a band of men from the free states to make forays into slave territory to rescue black slaves from bondage. He talked of setting up a mountain stronghold as a base of terrorist activity, but the ideas did not take coherent form until the Fugitive Slave Act, part of the Compromise of 1850, was passed. The Kansas-Nebraska Act, four years later, further agitated him and his sons, five of whom moved to the territory to help make Kansas a free state. In May, 1855, John Brown, Jr., wrote a mournful letter to his father explaining the conditions and imploring him to send arms to battle proslavery forces. Brown dispatched his family to North Elba again and set out for Kansas with a wagonload of guns and ammunition.

Brown found his sons impoverished and ill when he arrived at Osawatomie. Though he was to join the colony as a surveyor, he quickly assumed leadership of the local militia and made Free Soil a vengeance-wreaking crusade. His group fought in the ineffectual Wakarusa War and then, after the sacking of Lawrence by proslavery forces, he and his party, which included four sons and two others, ritually slaughtered five settlers at Pottawatomie. He had reached a personal turning point, viewing himself as an instrument in the hands of an angry god.

Brown's own colony was overrun and burned and one of his boys killed in retaliation. Brown now was gray in hair and features, with a bent back and glittering gray-blue eyes; he had grown a full beard that was streaked with gray, which made him appear older than his fifty-six years. His fervent attitude toward slavery fired his listeners, many of whom, such as Franklin Sanborn, Thomas W. Higginson, Theodore Parker, Gerrit Smith, G. L. Stearns, and Samuel Gridley Howe, were ripe for the leadership that Brown promised. He met with these members of the Massachusetts State Kansas Committee, and they responded with some arms, ammunition, and money to take with him to Kansas again.

Kansas had no stomach for bloodshed in 1857 as it moved closer to voting the issue of free or slave, and Brown now thought of a daring plan to liberate slaves in the South itself. In the spring of 1858, he visited the colony of runaway slaves in Catham, Canada, to gain volunteers. His money gone, he turned again to Smith and the Massachusetts group. They argued for a delay, gave him some money and supplies, and Brown again headed for Kansas, this time under the name of Shubel Morgan. There he led a raid on some plantations in Missouri in which one planter was killed and some slaves liberated. Brown was now a wanted man with a bounty on his head. He headed for Canada with the slaves in tow and then proceeded east, making speeches in Cleveland and Rochester to solicit funds. Again the old group came through with thirty-eight hundred dollars, knowing full well that Brown was bent on violence.

It was Harpers Ferry that became fixed in Brown's mind; to the commander in chief of a provisional army for liberation it was an ideal objective. The federal arsenal in the town was noted for the quality of arms and its technology since its creation in 1798. The complex of forges, shops, tool and die works, and assembly areas turned out rifles and handguns in an assembly line process that foretold mass production. John Hall of Maine had gained a contract in 1819 to turn out breech-loading rifles using his idea of interchangeable parts, and his contract was renewed yearly until 1844, when a totally new rifle plant was built to produce the Standard United States Model military rifle. The skilled workers were mostly transplanted northerners who were regarded as "foreigners" by local southerners. A canal and a railroad as well as a macadam road led to the town of three thousand, which included 1,250 free blacks and some 88 slaves.

Brown, John

    The Brown contingent of both white and black people established themselves in a farm five miles from the Ferry to lay plans for their attack. On Sunday, October 16, 1859, they marched by night down the dirt road leading to the town. By mid-morning, the men had taken both the town and its leading citizens.

    Brown did not know what to do with his victory. He had control of the engine house, the federal armory, the railroad, and the town of Harpers Ferry, and the very magnitude of his success overwhelmed and confused him. He let a train continue, certainly with the knowledge that the passengers would alarm state and federal officials. He did nothing about searching out possible followers from the town population or the countryside. He had guns, powder and shells, and a well-situated natural fortress, as well as a small though very devout band of followers. Brown lost his revolutionary compass at this critical moment. His willingness to fight was not in question. Shots were fired and lives were taken until Lee's troops stormed the engine house and cut Brown down. Though he was not severely wounded, there was little recourse for his men but to surrender.

    The military quickly restored order and moved Brown to prison while dispatching squads to investigate the farm that had been the band's headquarters. There they found letters and documentation that implicated Brown's northern associates in the Harpers Ferry venture. Why Brown had kept, let alone brought with him, these damning materials is uncertain. He certainly treasured his association with successful and influential men, and, given his life on the margin of society, this connection was important enough to be sustained with physical evidence. Furthermore, Brown was concerned about the shifting commitment of antislavery reformers and therefore by keeping documentation he could hold them to the course. The discovery of these materials, however, proved the conspiracy case against Brown and his men and threw fear into those who had aided them.

    Of the men who had followed Brown to Harpers Ferry on October 16, only eleven remained alive. Brown had seen two of his sons killed in the melee that followed the arrival of the militia from Charles Town and Lee's marines. On October 18, he was jailed in Charles Town to await indictment, which came a week later.

    Brown, Aaron Stevens, Edwin Coppoc, Shields Green (the black man who had chosen to go with Brown despite the admonition and concerns of Frederick Douglass), and John Copeland were all indicted on October 25 for treason against Virginia, for conspiring with slaves to rebel, and for murder. All of them pleaded not guilty and requested separate trials. The court agreed and determined that Brown would be tried first.

    The prosecution was headed by Charles Harding, state attorney for Jefferson County, and Andrew Hunter, a seasoned Charles Town attorney. The court was presided over by Judge Richard Parker, who had just begun the semiannual term of his circuit court and already had a grand jury seated. Turner had just gaveled the court to order when Brown's defense attorney read a telegram from one A. H. Lewis of Akron, Ohio, declaring that Brown's family was suffering from hereditary insanity. It proceeded to list the people on his mother's side who were known to have severe mental problems. The inference was that Brown himself was insane and therefore not fit for trial. His attorney had shown Brown the telegram, and Brown admitted to his mother's death by insanity and the fact that his first wife and two of his sons were afflicted. Brown, however, rejected the plea of insanity on his behalf, though he apparently gave his attorney permission to use the document. The judge ruled out the plea on the basis that the evidence was in unreliable form. He also rejected a delay to enable Brown to get a new attorney.

Brown's trial began on October 27, 1859, and lasted less than four days. He was carried to the court each day in a litter, and with each day, he became more irritated with his court-appointed attorneys. They had been joined by a twenty-one-year-old Boston attorney, George Hoyt, who had been retained by some Brown supporters who hoped to learn more about the case on behalf of the group of backers who were facing possible indictment as coconspirators. Botts and Green gratefully withdrew from the defense team, leaving the inexperienced Hoyt alone. Legal help soon came in the form of Samuel Chilton of Washington and Hiram Griswold of Cleveland, who were persuaded to take up what Brown himself realized was a lost cause.

The prosecution's case was devastating. Brown's request that he be tried as commander in chief of a provisional army, according to the laws governing warfare, was rejected. Brown's vision of himself as a messianic leader of a noble crusade against slavery was ignored. On October 31, at 1:45 P.M., the case went to the jury, which, after only forty-five minutes, declared Brown guilty on all counts. The verdict cast a pall on the audience, which days before had been vociferous in its rage against Brown. Brown himself said nothing as he lay quietly on his cot. The sentence of death by hanging was passed on November 2, with the date for execution set for December 2.

The coconspirators captured with Brown were tried as well and all sentenced to the same fate. Brown had visited with them in jail, calling on them to be firm and resolute and to implicate no one. Friends of Brown had sought to bring his wife from North Elba, but Brown insisted that she remain at home. Only on the afternoon before his execution did she visit with him and then stand by to claim his body.

Governor Henry Wise was besieged with demands for clemency, threats, and warnings of plots to free Brown. Martial law was proclaimed in Charles Town, and fifteen hundred soldiers, including a company of cadets from Virginia Military Institute commanded by Stonewall Jackson, ringed the gallows on December 2.

John Brown's death on a rope in Charles Town was but the end of a beginning. The larger crisis that Brown had foreshadowed soon came with a character of violence and death that would have perhaps given even Osawatomie pause. The South, by insisting on dealing with Brown's case, had arrogated to itself police authority over what was a crime against federal property. It thereby threw down a gauntlet of defiant sectionalism and states' rights.

None of this was lost on Brown's supporters in the North, who, after suffering gag rules in Congress blocking their petitions against slavery, after almost thirty years of relentless electioneering, pamphleteering, lecturing, haranguing, debating, and propagandizing against slavery, and after suffering dismaying defeats at the hands of every branch of government and in virtually every attempt to work within the system, were ready to exploit John Brown's fateful end.

Antislavery reformers took charge of the body, and by wagon, train, and steamer they took it to the hills where Brown had felt "omnipotent." It was a cortege that would

Brown, John

be duplicated six years later on the death of Abraham Lincoln—a slow, somber taking of martyred remains home. Through Lake Placid and on to the little village of North Elba they took Brown, and near his little home they buried him. Gerrit Smith, the man who had given him the land, was not with him at the burial. Smith had become mentally deranged after Brown's capture and was institutionalized. Others who were closely involved with Brown, such as Frederick Douglass, found it convenient to flee to Canada or travel abroad. Brown, the guerrilla fighter and terrorist who had taken the struggle against slavery beyond rhetoric, had made clear that the approaching confrontation would be violent.

SIGNIFICANCE

John Brown was a tragic figure central to the great tragedy of Civil War America. Whether he was a hero in that era is, at best, controversial. There seems little doubt that had his earlier ventures been successful, he would have melded with other entrepreneurs of the moving frontier and probably been lost as another subject representing an enterprising nation. A failure as a businessperson, he turned all of his energies to what became for him a holy mission: rooting out the evil of slavery. Social, economic, and political displacement encouraged many in his region to seek redress. Brown, however, personalized these conflicts to an extreme degree and placed himself at a point from which there was no turning back.

—*Jack J. Cardoso*

FURTHER READING

Boyer, Richard O. *The Legend of John Brown: A Biography and a History*. New York: Alfred A. Knopf, 1972. This is a fine biography that takes the story of Brown up to his arrival in Kansas in 1855. Boyer died before he could complete the second volume.

Malin, James C. *John Brown and the Legend of Fifty-Six*. Philadelphia: American Philosophical Society, 1942. Malin's work is highly critical of Brown's activities in Kansas and of Brown personally. It is useful, however, for its detail of that period of Brown's life.

National Park Service. *John Brown's Raid*. Washington, D.C.: Superintendent of Documents, 1974. Here is an outstanding piece of work based on reports by William C. Everhart and Arthur L. Sullivan that gives sweep and substance to Brown and his men at Harpers Ferry in the space of sixty-eight pages.

Oates, Stephen B. *To Purge This Land with Blood: A Biography of John Brown*. New York: Harper & Row, 1970. Oates's book is a full biography of Brown and establishes the point of view that Brown's puritanical heritage was at the base of his thought and action. He also has something to say in a bibliographical essay. See also his article: "John Brown and His Judges: A Critique of the Historical Literature." In *Civil War History* vol. 17, 1971, pp. 5-24.

Reynolds, David S. *John Brown, Abolitionist: The Man Who Killed Slavery, Sparked the Civil War, and Seeded Civil Rights*. New York: Alfred A. Knopf, 2005. Reynolds's biography is generally sympathetic toward Brown. He portrays Brown as a Puritan in the tradition of Oliver Cromwell and Jonathan Edwards—a man who saw the world as a battle of good versus evil, and who sought to avenge the evil of slavery.

Sanborn, Franklin B., ed. *The Life and Letters of John Brown*. New York: Negro Universities Press, 1891. This is a book to be used carefully as it is biased toward Brown. However, the gathering of Brown's letters makes this a valuable resource.

Stauffer, John. *The Black Hearts of Men: Radical Abolitionists and the Transformation of Race*. Cambridge, Mass.: Harvard University Press, 2002. During the 1850's, Brown, Gerrit Smith, and two African Americans, Frederick Douglas and doctor/scholar James McCune Smith, formed an interracial alliance to abolish slavery. Stauffer describes how the men worked to promote abolition and other social issues, and how their revolutionary zeal waned after Brown's 1859 raid on Harpers Ferry.

Villard, Oswald Garrison. *John Brown, 1800-1859: A Biography Fifty Years After*. Gloucester, Mass.: Peter Smith, 1910. Villard's biography is still a standard work on Brown and his time. It cannot be ignored in any study.

OLYMPIA BROWN

> *How natural that the errors of the ancient should be handed down and, mixing with the principles and system which Christ taught, give to us an adulterated Christianity.*

Protestant cleric and social reformer

Among the first Americans to demand that higher education be opened to women, Brown managed to graduate from college and become one of the first women ordained a minister. She was also prominent in the woman suffrage movement.

Born: January 5, 1835; Prairie Ronde, Kalamazoo County, Michigan Territory
Died: October 23, 1926; Baltimore, Maryland
Also known as: Olympia Brown Willis
Areas of achievement: Social reform; education; women's rights

EARLY LIFE

Olympia Brown was the first of four children born to Asa and Lephia Brown. Her parents were pioneers who made the eight-hundred-mile trip from their native Vermont to live on the frontier in Michigan Territory during the year before she was born. In contrast to many of their neighbors, the Brown family was one in which education played a vital role. When the children were young, they were taught by their mother, a woman passionate about education, who pasted together articles from newspapers and journals to make books for her children.

Lephia and Asa Brown were also strong in their religious faith, Universalism. They taught their children the main tenants of this religion—a detail that would greatly influence Olympia's later life. In 1837, when Michigan attained statehood and began a statewide public school system, the Browns built a one-room schoolhouse on their property and took the necessary steps to secure pupils and teachers. After attending Cedar Park Seminary in nearby Schoolcraft, Michigan, the fifteen-year-old Olympia taught at the family schoolhouse. At time in her life, she experienced sexual discrimination for the first time: She wanted to continue her education, but few colleges admitted women.

After many debates with her father, Olympia and her younger sister left home in 1854 to attend Mount Holyoke Female Seminary in South Hadley, Massachusetts. Although the courses she took deepened her hunger for learning, she left Mount Holyoke after only one year because of its rigid Calvinistic atmosphere and the sexual discrimination she perceived behind the facade of female education. Once again, she struggled to find an institution that would admit women, and she suffered many rejections. Finally, when she was twenty years old, she was accepted at Antioch College in Yellow Springs, Ohio. Antioch was an institution that imposed no religious conversion on its students.

LIFE'S WORK

As had been the case in Brown's education up to that moment, Antioch's educational system was discriminatory, as male and female students were given different assignments. Brown's religious background told her that all humans were created equal, so she refused to accept the system and became the only female student to complete the men's assignments, orations on various topics, a discipline taboo at that time for American women. Brown also was responsible for bringing to the school other women speakers. It was, in fact, while listening to one of the few women ministers in America that Brown sensed her own destiny.

After graduating from Antioch in 1860, Brown struggled for entrance into a theological college. Once admitted, she again endured sexual harassment. She also struggled to perfect her speaking voice and had to fight for ordination. She finally was ordained at the Universalist Divinity School of St. Lawrence University in 1863. Within a year, she received the call to her first full-time parish in Weymouth Landing, Massachusetts. This assignment began a series of assignments to parishes struggling so hard that male ministers turned them down or gave up on them.

Although Brown's first official work for the women's movement began while she was attending Antioch College, it was not until her tenure at Weymouth Landing that she began winning national prominence for her role in the movement's 1867 Kansas campaign, which sought to secure the vote for women in that newly settled territory. Although she had been given many promises concerning arrangements and accommodations that would be in place during the campaign, Brown faced disorganization, a collapsing support base in the Republican Party, and sweltering heat. She also worked almost entirely on her own, as the promised arrangements for a traveling companion also fell through. In Kansas, she was alone, an unmarried woman, hundreds of miles from home and within fifty miles of deadly wars between settlers and Native Americans. She was completely dependent on pioneer farmers for her conveyance, housing, support, and, at times, the means of escape in the face of sometimes hostile crowds. Although the Kansas campaign ultimately failed to achieve its objective, Elizabeth Cady Stanton was so impressed with the fear that the ninety-pound Olympia Brown aroused among opposition speakers that she began trying to persuade Brown to work full-time in the suffrage movement.

Brown chose to remain in her field for the time being, accepting her next religious call to the Universalist Church in Bridgeport, Connecticut, in 1870. Three years later, she married John Henry Willis. Although those around her had feared that marriage would distract her from both the ministry and the women's cause, Brown discovered in her husband one who supported her on every front. He changed his own job to meet the demands of hers and relocated when her work made it necessary. He also supported her then-radical decision to keep her maiden name, Brown.

In 1874, Brown gave birth to her first child, John Parker Willis, and then discovered that while she had been on maternity leave some members of her congregation had begun lobbying for a male minister. Although the majority of the congregation supported Brown, she resigned. By 1876, Brown had given birth to a second child, Gwendolen Brown Willis. In 1878, she was appointed to a struggling church in Racine, Wisconsin. In her hands, the Racine parish flourished as an educational and cultural center. The Racine church would prove, however, to be Brown's last full-time ministerial position.

Although Brown never completely quit the ministry, she dedicated her final decades to full-time work within the fight for women's equality. She was active in many organizations, including the Wisconsin Suffrage Association, the Wisconsin Federation of Women's Clubs, the Federal Suffrage Association, the National Woman Suffrage Association, and the Woman's Party.

During the winter of 1917, when she was more than seventy years old, Brown participated in a march on Washington, D.C., in support of woman suffrage. She was among the people who witnessed several men attacking the marchers and then saw President Woodrow Wilson have the women arrested, instead of their attackers. The following year, she again marched in Washington, this time personally burning some of the president's speeches before the crowds. Finally, in 1920, when she was eighty-five years old, she was able to vote in her first election. She then dedicated her remaining six years to worldwide equality by active participation in the Women's League for Peace and Freedom, the League of Nations, the League of Women Voters, and the American Civil Liberties Union.

SIGNIFICANCE

Although Olympia Brown had relatives who ran an Underground Railroad station in their home, she herself never knew the plight of American slaves at first hand. She also had no firsthand knowledge of the abuses of factory workers or of the hardships of immigrants. Nevertheless, hers is an important story in American history. She lived on the American frontier; she shocked college administrators by wearing the costume named after Amelia Bloomer and refusing chaperones; she was ordained into the ministry at a time when the mere idea of such a thing was heresy to many; she knew and was respected by some of the most important leaders in the woman suffrage movement; and she was one of the few prominent figures of the movement still alive in 1920 when the Nineteenth Amendment was passed.

Brown, Olympia

Olympia Brown experienced sexual discrimination both within the educational system and within churches. During her lifetime, she argued against prevailing notions of womanhood, accused novelists of portraying women as insipid, and railed against the notion that young girls should be taught to be "little ladies." At a time in American history when women of her class were expected to be "quiet angels" in their homes, she was politically astute and vocal, taking on the weaknesses in the political positions of prominent figures, such as Ralph Waldo Emerson and Frederick Douglass, in their presence. Through it all, she refused to let go of her personal doctrine that all people are created equal and that women are people, too.

—Anna Dunlap Higgins

FURTHER READING

Baker, Jean H., ed. *Votes for Women: The Struggle for Suffrage Revisited.* Oxford, England: Oxford University Press, 2002. A solidly researched work that places Brown in the national struggle for woman suffrage.

Brown, Olympia. *Suffrage and Religious Principle: Speeches and Writings of Olympia Brown.* Edited by Dana Greene. Metuchen, N.J.: Scarecrow Press, 1983. Collection of some of Brown's major writings and speeches.

Buhle, Mari Jo, and Paul Buhle, eds. *The Concise History of Woman Suffrage: Selections from the Classic Work of Stanton, Gage, and Harper.* Urbana: University of Illinois Press, 1978. Like Baker's book, this is an important work that helps place Brown in the larger picture of woman suffrage. Many readers should find this updated version more reader-friendly than the original source, which was published in 1868.

Coté, Charlotte. *Olympia Brown: The Battle for Equality.* Racine, Wis.: Mother Courage Press, 1988. A full-length biography, this book also includes two of Brown's best-remembered addresses and lists the whereabouts of most of the other documents by and about Brown, most of which are located at Radcliffe College in Cambridge, Massachusetts.

Emerson, Dorothy May, ed. *Standing Before Us: Unitarian Universalist Women and Social Reform, 1776-1936.* Boston: Skinner House Books, 2000. This work contains a biographical sketch of Brown and Brown's own "The Higher Education of Women." The book also confirms Brown's status as the first woman ordained to the Universalist ministry.

Ralph Bunche

> *Hearts are the strongest when they beat in response to noble ideals.*

Diplomat

Bunche played a major role in making Americans conscious of the contradictions between their racial policies and their democratic aspirations. He helped bring better understanding between nations, participating in the drafting of the United Nations Charter, and through diplomatic negotiations helped to maintain peace in the Middle East and Africa, winning the Nobel Peace Prize for his efforts.

Born: August 7, 1904; Detroit, Michigan
Died: December 9, 1971; New York, New York
Also known as: Ralph Johnson Bunche (full name)
Area of achievement: Diplomacy

Early Life

Ralph Bunche (buhnch) was born to Fred Bunche, a barber, and Olive Agnes Johnson Bunche, who named him for his grandfather, Ralph Johnson, who was born a slave. The family moved frequently during Ralph's early life, and he remembered that in each community a different ethnic group was singled out for contempt: the Italians in Detroit; the blacks in Knoxville, Tennessee, where he spent a winter when he was six; the Mexicans in New Mexico, where the family moved because of his mother's poor health; and the Chinese and the Japanese in California, where he and his younger sister, Grace, lived with their grandmother after their mother's death. These early memories of the different faces of prejudice clearly influenced his later interests and outlook on life.

In the fall of 1916, Bunche's father left home, never to be heard from again. The following February, his mother, who suffered from rheumatic fever, died. His maternal grandmother, Lucy Johnson, kept the family together, but within a few months his favorite uncle, who suffered from tuberculosis, committed suicide. In less than a year, Bunche had lost three of the most significant adults in his life. His grandmother, widowed early in life, had reared her children alone and now became his anchor. A light-skinned woman who could have passed for white, she was a dominant influence in her family. Her husband, Ralph's grandfather, had been a schoolteacher, and education was a value she continued to uphold for her grandchildren.

Even as a child, Bunche was accustomed to hard work. By the age of seven he was selling newspapers, and before his mother died he worked in a bakery after school until nearly midnight every day. In Los Angeles, where he went to live with his grandmother, he graduated as valedictorian from Jefferson High School. He attended the University of California, Los Angeles (UCLA), on an athletic scholarship, where he was also a teaching assistant in the political science department, and was graduated magna cum laude in 1927. He received an M.A. degree from Harvard in 1928 and in June, 1930, married Ruth Ethel Harris, one of his students, with whom he had three children: two daughters, Jean and Jane, and a son, Ralph.

Bunche, Ralph

A handsome man of medium height and build, Bunche was destined to attract favorable attention for his accomplishments and pleasing personality. On a Rosenwald field fellowship, he toured Europe, England, and North and West Africa in 1931-1932 and in 1934 received a Ph.D. from Harvard, winning the Tappen Prize for the best doctoral dissertation in the social sciences for that year. His dissertation was a study of colonial administration in French West Africa; the transition of the former African colonies to independent statehood was one of his abiding concerns through the remainder of his life. His Harvard years were followed by postdoctoral work in anthropology and colonial policy at Northwestern University, the London School of Economics, and the University of Capetown, South Africa, in 1936-1937. A Social Science Research Council postdoctoral fellowship allowed him to visit Europe, South and East Africa, Malaya, and the Netherlands East Indies between 1936 and 1938.

During these years, Bunche was also teaching. He began teaching political science at Howard University in 1928 and served as chair of the department from 1929 to 1950, when he left Howard to teach government at Harvard. He codirected the Institute of Race Relations at Swarthmore in 1936 while on leave from Howard. By his early thirties, his brilliance, hard work, and breadth of interests made him one of the most highly educated, well-informed men in the United States.

Ralph Bunche.
(Library of Congress)

Bunche, Ralph

LIFE'S WORK

In 1939, Bunche became a member of the staff of the Carnegie Corporation Survey of the Negro in America. This project was headed by a Swedish economist, Gunnar Myrdal, and resulted in a two-volume work, *An American Dilemma: The Negro Problem and Modern Democracy* (1944). Bunche was one of a half dozen staff men who helped Myrdal with this massive project, based primarily on hundreds of interviews and personal observations of the participating scholars. He toured the South by automobile in 1939 with Myrdal, and most of the interviews were conducted by his assistants in 1939 and 1940.

Bunche's part of the study dealt mainly with black organizational life, leadership, and ideology. He emphasized the extent to which disfranchisement of black voters had corrupted politics in the South, cutting off reform possibilities at the grass roots. He castigated the use of the poll tax and the white primary and pointed out the lack of secrecy in voting, which made political independence unlikely for poor people of either race in the South. Bunche emphasized the glaring inconsistencies between democracy and discrimination, stating,

> If democracy is to survive the severe trials and buffetings to which it is being subjected in the modern world, it will do so only because it can demonstrate that it is a practical, living philosophy under which all people can live the good life most abundantly. It must prove itself in practice or be discredited as a theory.

Bunche's work on race relations in the United States was followed by work for the United States government, in which he dealt with race relations on a global scale. In 1941, he was asked to serve as a senior social science analyst on Africa and the Far East areas of the British Empire section of the Office of Strategic Services. He became chief of the African section in 1943 and then became a territorial specialist in the Division of Territorial Studies of the United States State Department in 1944-1945. In 1945, he was the first black division head in the State Department. He also helped draft the United Nations Charter.

Bunche was made director of the Division of Trusteeship of the United Nations from 1946 to 1948, and then principal director of the Department of Trusteeship from 1948 to 1954. In 1947, he became special assistant to representatives of the secretary general of the United Nations Special Committee on Palestine. Tensions were very high in Jerusalem as the question of the partition of Palestine was being considered. The Arab high command forbade Arabs to testify before the special United Nations commission, so Bunche and others met with them secretly in Syria and Lebanon. After meeting separately with each side, Bunche composed both the majority and minority reports to the satisfaction of both parties. His ability to grasp the problems involved and his empathy for the opposing factions made him a unique diplomat, trusted and acceptable to Jews and Arabs alike.

When the Arabs declared war on Israel in 1948, Bunche was sent as the chief representative of the secretary general of the United Nations to help mediate the dispute, along with Count Folke Bernadotte, the head of the Swedish Red Cross. Bernadotte was shot and killed just before the two were to leave the Middle East to meet in Paris, and Bunche became the acting mediator through 1948 and 1949, finally achieving a peaceful settlement. In 1950, he received the Nobel Peace Prize for his peacemaking success in the Middle East. In 1957 he again successfully negotiated a peaceful settlement between Egypt and Israel.

In 1960, Bunche was a special representative of the secretary general of the United Nations in peacemaking efforts in the Congo. Dag Hammarskjöld had planned to take Bunche back to the Congo with him on the last trip he made, which ended in a fatal plane crash, but had decided against it at the last minute. The new secretary general of the United Nations, U Thant, appointed Bunche deputy secretary general, making him the highest-ranking American to serve under three secretary generals of the United Nations. He resolved the dispute between Prime Minister Cyrille Adoula of the Congo Republic and President Moïse Tshombe of the Katanga province. He was sent to Yemen in 1963 to help contain another civil war. In 1964, he was sent to Cyprus to mediate Greek-Turkish hostilities, and, partially as a result of his efforts, peace was preserved there for another ten years until the Turks invaded in 1974.

In 1965, Bunche turned his attention once again to racial problems at home. In the 1930's and 1940's, he had been much involved in efforts to improve the racial situation in the United States. He served on the national executive board of the National Association for the Advancement of Colored People (NAACP), helped organize a National Committee Against Discrimination in Housing, helped organize the National Negro Congress in 1935, and served as a member of President Franklin D. Roosevelt's "Black Cabinet" of advisers. When he joined the Security Council of the United Nations, he had taken an oath, as an international civil servant, to refrain from activity in domestic problems. Nevertheless, he joined the march led by Martin Luther King, Jr., in Selma, Alabama, in 1965 and addressed the crowd of thirty-five thousand Americans gathered there, remarking that his wife's father had made civil rights speeches in that same city at the turn of the century and apologizing to the crowd for having to speak from the capitol steps, where Dixie's flag still waved.

By that time, Bunche's health was beginning to fail. In 1951, he discovered that he suffered from diabetes. When he returned home from Selma, he had hepatitis, but he continued to work until he developed heart failure in 1970. He recovered from a heart attack and pneumonia, only to suffer a fall at home and die the following year on December 9, 1971. He was buried in Woodlawn Cemetery, Bronx, New York, next to his daughter Jane, who had preceded him in death.

During his lifetime, Bunche received thirty-nine honorary degrees, the Nobel Peace Prize in 1950, the Presidential Medal of Freedom in 1963, and other honors too numerous to mention. He remained a modest man, finding more pleasure in work than in fame and firm in his commitment to build a more truly democratic society.

Significance

Bunche presents both a model and a challenge to all Americans. Facing poverty, discrimination, and a family broken through death in his early life, he became highly educated. He used that education to serve his people and his nation, to sound the alarm about the state of democracy in the United States, forcing others to deal with the contradiction between racial discrimination and democracy. He demonstrated the potential for peace in the world when intelligence and perseverance are applied to achieve it. Through his work with the United Nations, he helped to contain several disputes, any one of which could have escalated into a third world war.

—*Betty Balanoff*

FURTHER READING

Bunche, Ralph J. *The Political Status of the Negro in the Age of FDR*. Edited by Dewey W. Grantham. Chicago: University of Chicago Press, 1973. Consists of the notes Bunche made for the Carnegie-Myrdal report. Gives a good sketch of Bunche's life and career.

Franklin, John Hope, and August Meier, eds. *Black Leaders of the Twentieth Century*. Urbana: University of Illinois Press, 1982. Contains a brief sketch of Bunche.

Haskins, James. *Ralph Bunche: A Most Reluctant Hero*. New York: Hawthorn Books, 1974. Small, compact biography written by a black scholar. Includes information on Los Angeles's black community support for Bunche in his youth.

Henry, Charles P. *Ralph Bunche: Model Negro or American Other?* New York: New York University Press, 1999. An analysis of Bunche's work and life, focusing on how race affected his view of himself and the way he was viewed by other Americans.

Holloway, Jonathan Scott. *Confronting the Veil: Abraham Harris, Jr., E. Franklin Frazier, and Ralph Bunche, 1919-1941*. Chapel Hill: University of North Carolina Press, 2002. A social and intellectual history that examines the early lives and careers of Bunche, sociologist Frazier, and economist Harris, three black scholars who taught at Howard University in the 1930's. Describes how the three were in the vanguard of young blacks who sought more radical solutions to America's racial problems.

Johnson, Ann Donegan. *The Value of Responsibility: The Story of Ralph Bunche*. San Diego, Calif.: Value Communications, 1978. A good biography for young readers. Emphasis is on character building.

Keppel, Ben. *The Work of Democracy: Ralph Bunche, Kenneth B. Clark, Lorraine Hansberry, and the Cultural Politics of Race*. Cambridge, Mass.: Harvard University Press, 1995. Keppel examines how mainstream media and the academy have appropriated the lives of these icons of the Civil Rights movement to soften their antiracist positions, turning Bunche, for example, into a representative of the American Dream while ignoring his stand against McCarthyism.

Kugelmass, Joseph Alvin. *Ralph J. Bunche: Fighter for Peace*. New York: Julian Messner, 1952. The first biography of Bunche, written for advanced preteens and for teenagers. Well-balanced coverage of his life.

Mann, Peggy. *Ralph Bunche: U.N. Peacemaker*. New York: Coward, McCann and Geoghegan, 1975. An excellent, and accurate, biography. The Bunche family, Roy Wilkins, and United Nations coworkers assisted the author. Major emphasis is on Bunche's work at the United Nations.

Urquhart, Brian. *Ralph Bunche: An American Life*. New York: W. W. Norton, 1993. Written by Bunche's former assistant, this substantive biography focuses primarily on Bunche's illustrious career. Illustrated with maps and photos, and indexed.

Richard Byrd

> *A static hero is a public liability. Progress grows out of motion.*

Aviator and explorer

Byrd played a central role in the development of naval aviation and was a major figure in Arctic and Antarctic exploration.

Born: October 25, 1888; Winchester, Virginia
Died: March 11, 1957; Boston, Massachusetts
Also known as: Richard Evelyn Byrd (full name)
Areas of achievement: Exploration; aviation

Early Life

Richard Byrd (burd) was the son of Richard Evelyn Byrd, a lawyer, and Eleanor Bolling Flood. The families of both his parents were active in Virginia politics, and Richard's brother, Harry, became an influential U.S. senator. Small and slender, Richard was nevertheless strong and athletic. Playing war games with his brothers Harry and Tom and exploring the woods and hills near Winchester increased Richard's desire for adventure. When he was twelve, he was invited to visit a family friend who was serving as United States circuit court judge in the Philippines. Richard had his parents' permission to go to Manila by himself. He remained a year, writing about his experiences for a Winchester newspaper. He then completed his journey around the world alone. It was about this time that he wrote in his diary that he wanted to be the first person to reach the North Pole.

Three years at the Shenandoah Valley Military Academy prepared him for admission to Virginia Military Institute, where he studied from 1904 to 1907, before transferring to the University of Virginia for a year. In 1908, he was appointed to the U.S. Naval Academy at Annapolis, from which he was graduated in 1912, sixty-second in a class of 155. As a midshipman, he played tennis and football, wrestled in the 135-pound class, and specialized in the rings in gymnastics. While engaging in these sports, he suffered injuries that would later cause him to terminate his active duty with the Navy. He broke bones in his ankle playing football and broke them again in a fall during a gymnastics routine. Shortly after receiving his commission, he fell down a hatchway on the USS *Wyoming*, reinjuring his right foot and causing him to walk with a slight limp. Despite this setback, he served with distinction in the Caribbean, twice saving men from drowning. It was at this time, in the summer of 1914, that he took his first airplane ride.

In 1915, Byrd married his childhood sweetheart, Marie D. Ames. Secretary of the Navy Josephus Daniels asked Byrd to serve as his aide on the USS *Dolphin*, but after a few months Byrd asked to be retired on a medical disability because his injured foot prevented him from performing regular naval duties. The political influence of his family enabled him to be promoted to lieutenant jg (junior grade) and assigned as administrator of the naval militia of the state of Rhode Island on his retirement. As a retired officer on active duty, he served in various posts for the next forty years.

LIFE'S WORK

During World War I, Byrd persuaded the Navy to allow him to enter flight training at the naval air station in Pensacola, Florida. He received his pilot's wings on April 7, 1917, and began making plans to be the first person to fly across the Atlantic. Wartime duties took him to Nova Scotia, where he helped to establish naval air stations. When the Navy was slow in supporting his plan for a transatlantic flight, he turned to his friend Walter Camp, the popular football coach at Yale University. With Camp's help, Byrd convinced the Navy to create the Transatlantic Flight Section of the Bureau of Aeronautics. Navy regulations prohibited Byrd from accompanying the flight he had organized, so he failed to share the glory of the crew of the NC-4 flying boat when it reached Lisbon, Portugal, on May 27, 1919. Undaunted, Byrd began planning a solo flight across the Atlantic. Navy orders again thwarted his dream when he was sent to England to assist in navigating a British-built dirigible to the United States. He was fortunate, however, when he missed a trial flight that ended in a fatal crash.

Byrd spent the next three years on aviation duty with the Bureau of Navigation. In 1925, he commanded a naval unit on an expedition to northern Greenland. Encouraged by his success in using airplanes in the Arctic, Byrd decided to enter the aerial race for

Richard Byrd.
(Library of Congress)

Byrd, Richard

the North Pole. Norwegian explorer Roald Amundsen and the American aviator Lincoln Ellsworth flew to within a few hundred miles of the pole during the summer in which Byrd was in Greenland. Knowing that Amundsen, Ellsworth, and the Italian adventurer Umberto Nobile all had plans to fly to the pole, Byrd moved quickly. After being released from active duty with the Navy, he secured financial backing from Edsel Ford, organized a team of pilots and mechanics, and sailed for Spitzbergen Island. On May 9, 1926, he and Floyd Bennett flew north in a Fokker monoplane named *Josephine Ford* in honor of Edsel's daughter. Fifteen hours later, they returned with the news that they had flown over the pole. Although their claim would later be disputed, Byrd and Bennett returned to the United States as heroes. Both were awarded the Congressional Medal of Honor. In his book *Skyward* (1928), Byrd explains that they were considered heroes because "in us youth saw ambition realized."

In June, 1927, less than a month after Charles A. Lindbergh's transatlantic flight, Byrd finally flew across the Atlantic. Flying with Bert Acosta, Bernt Balchen, and George Noville in a Fokker trimotor, Byrd demonstrated that regular commercial transatlantic flights were practical, despite the fact that his plane was forced to crash-land on the French coast because of heavy fog in Paris. The energetic and ambitious Byrd now turned his attention to the South Pole. Receiving financial support from Ford, the Rockefellers, the Guggenheims, and others, Byrd sailed with forty-one men, ninety-four dogs, a Ford snowmobile, and three airplanes on two ships, the *City of New York* and the *Eleanor Bolling*.

On January 1, 1929, the party began building a base camp, Little America, on the ice shelf at the Bay of Whales. Eleven months later, on November 28 and 29, Byrd, Balchen, Harold June, and Ashley McKinley flew their Ford trimotor to the South Pole and back. In addition to the historic flight, the expedition mapped and photographed a large section of the unexplored continent; made geological, meteorological, and zoological observations; and proved the feasibility of a permanent base in Antarctica. Byrd again returned home to a hero's welcome, and Congress promoted him to the rank of rear admiral.

Three years later, in the depths of the Depression, Byrd organized a second Antarctic expedition, this time with fifty-five men, three airplanes, an autogyro (a forerunner of the helicopter), and several snowmobiles. After reestablishing Little America, Byrd sent a small party to build an advance base more than one hundred miles south, where he planned to station three men to make weather observations through the winter (April through August) of 1934. When storms prevented the planes and sledges from transporting enough supplies, Byrd decided to remain at Bolling Advance Base alone. Although he nearly died from inhaling carbon monoxide leaking from his stove, Byrd made most of his daily observations. The scientific achievements of the second expedition surpassed the first in many ways: The thickness of the ice was measured in several places, the outline of the continent was mapped more accurately, new astronomical and meteorological observations were made, and oceanographic data were collected.

The four-and-a-half-month struggle for survival at Advance Base left Byrd exhausted mentally and physically, and his career after 1935 was less spectacular than it had been. On the eve of World War II, President Franklin D. Roosevelt recalled Byrd to active duty and put him in command of the first government-sponsored Antarctic expedition since the voyage of Charles Wilkes in 1838-1842. During the war, Byrd helped find new air routes in the Pacific. In 1946, he returned to Antarctica with Operation Highjump, a naval exercise involving four thousand men, the largest expedition ever sent to that area. In 1955, he visited Antarctica for the fifth and last time during the International Geophysical Year (IGY) activities involving thirteen nations. He died two years later, secure in the knowledge that he had contributed significantly to America's awareness of the importance of Antarctica and the need for international cooperation in scientific exploration.

SIGNIFICANCE

Byrd was a complex and controversial person. His drive and success aroused strong feelings, and he was never without his critics. In a sense, Edwin Hoyt was correct in calling him "the last explorer" of the generation of Amundsen, Robert Scott, and Robert Edwin Peary, a person driven by the desire to be the first to stand on uncharted ground and to survive incredible hardships. Certainly his failure to be the first to fly the Atlantic and the little accidents that plagued his early naval career drove him to seek recognition in Antarctic exploration, but there is also a mystical side to Byrd's character. He confesses in *Alone* (1938) that he chose to remain at Bolling Advance Base by himself less for science than "for the sake of experience." He compared himself to Henry David Thoreau at Walden and to Robinson Crusoe. Ultimately he found a harmony with the universe in the freezing Antarctic night.

Byrd's plans for the first two Antarctic expeditions were as much an experiment in social organization as in natural science. There was a traditional American utopianism in the "constitution" he drew up for the government of Little America. "We have no class distinctions as in civilization," he wrote in *Alone*. "He who may have failed back there has his chance to make good here; and he will not be judged by the position he holds so much as by the way he plays the game and does his job, however humble it may be. . . ." Byrd played the game of life in the context of the social and economic upheavals of World War I and the Depression. The failures of the old world made the exploration of a new one all the more urgent. Utilizing the advances in airplane technology, aerial photography, and meteorological instruments, Byrd may also be called the "first explorer of the modern age."

—*Bernard Mergen*

FURTHER READING

Bertrand, Kenneth J. *Americans in Antarctica, 1775-1948*. New York: American Geographical Society, 1971. A scholarly history that places Byrd's expeditions in a larger context. Excellent bibliography.

Bryant, John H., and Harold N. Cones. *Dangerous Crossings: The First Modern Polar Exploration, 1925*. Anapolis, Md.: Naval Institute Press, 2000. Before he went to Antarctica, Byrd was part of an American naval contingent that explored the area north of Canada. This was the first polar expedition to use both aircraft and shortwave radio in its explorations, and the book focuses on the technology that Byrd and others employed during their expedition.

Byrd, Richard E. *Alone*. New York: G. P. Putnam's Sons, 1938. Reprint. Los Angeles:

Byrd, Richard

    Jeremy P. Tarcher, 1986. The most interesting of Byrd's books because it is the most personal. Byrd describes his struggle to survive alone for four and a half months in Antarctica. More than a diary, this book is a discussion of the reasons for seeking extreme hardships. Obviously written to establish the author's reputation as a literary adventurer, it bears comparison to Charles Lindbergh's *We* (1927) and Joshua Slocum's *Sailing Alone Around the World* (1900).

    ———. *Discovery: The Story of the Second Byrd Antarctic Expedition.* New York: G. P. Putnam's Sons, 1935. Reprint. Detroit, Mich.: Tower Books, 1971. Detailed history of the expedition of 1933-1935, omitting discussion of the solitary four and a half months at Advance Base. Good on equipment-testing and life in Little America.

    ———. *Little America: Aerial Exploration in the Antarctic, the Flight to the South Pole.* New York: G. P. Putnam's Sons, 1930. Details of the first Byrd expedition, 1928-1930, and the building of the base Little America.

    ———. *Skyward: Man's Mastery of the Air as Shown by the Brilliant Flights of America's Leading Air Explorer: His Life, His Thrilling Adventures, His North Pole and Trans-Atlantic Flights, Together with His Plans for Conquering the Antarctic by Air.* 1928. Reprint. Chicago: Lakeside Books, 1981. Hastily written first book; the subtitle shows how Putnam promoted Byrd. Portions of this book had already appeared in magazines.

Hoyt, Edwin P. *The Last Explorer.* New York: John Day, 1968. Written without access to Byrd's private papers, but still a complete account of the great explorer's life.

Parfit, Michael. *South Light: A Journey to the Last Continent.* New York: Macmillan, 1985. Updates Bertrand and describes conditions in Antarctica in the late twentieth century. Good discussion of the 1956 treaty under which more than a dozen nations maintain dozens of year-round scientific stations without relying on territorial claims.

Rose, Lisle A. *Assault on Eternity: Richard E. Byrd and the Exploration of Antarctica, 1946-47.* Annapolis, Md.: Naval Institute Press, 1980. Detailed account of Operation Highjump, a naval training and scientific mission in which Byrd was marginally involved.

FRANCES XAVIER CABRINI

> ❝ *We must pray without tiring, for the salvation of mankind does not depend on material success; nor on sciences that cloud the intellect.* ❞

Religious leader

The first American citizen to be canonized a saint in the Roman Catholic Church, Mother Cabrini was the founder of a religious community dedicated to helping the poor. She contributed to missions among Italian immigrants to America, eventually establishing convents, schools, and charitable orphanages all over the world.

Born: July 15, 1850; Sant' Angelo Lodigiano, Lombardy (now in Italy)
Died: December 22, 1917; Chicago, Illinois
Also known as: Mother Cabrini; Saint Frances Xavier Cabrini
Areas of achievement: Religion and theology; evangelism; social reform; education

EARLY LIFE

The last of thirteen children born of Augustino and Stella (Oldini) Cabrini, Frances Xavier Cabrini (FRAN-sihs ZA-vyur kah-BREE-nee) was baptized Maria Francesca, at which time miraculous evidence of her piety was said to have appeared in the form of white doves that flitted about the house on that day. Her family was well-known for its dedication to the Roman Catholic Church, and one of her uncles, Luigi Oldini, was a priest and foreign missionary. Luigi taught her games associated with missionary work that helped to mold young Frances into a surprisingly serious and pious young girl.

By the time Frances was twelve, she began taking an annual oath of virginity, which she declared permanent at the age of eighteen. She attended a private normal school under the direction of the Daughters of the Sacred Heart of Arluno, where her sister Rosa was preceptress. Frances graduated in 1870. In September of that same year, the united kingdom of Italy was established after the Papal States capitulated and acknowledged the sovereignty of Savoyard forces. The birth of a united Italy resulted in a severe curb on the traditional authority of the Roman Catholic Church over schools, hospitals, and charitable enterprises.

In 1872, Frances fell victim to a smallpox epidemic while caring for the sick. While she was still recovering, she began teaching at the school of Vidardo, where she found her ability to teach Christian doctrine firmly repressed by secularizing laws. Unsatisfied with her limited opportunities to serve the Roman Catholic Church in this role, she petitioned in 1874 to become one of the Daughters of the Sacred Heart. Her petition was denied on the basis of her fragile health, but her zeal was noted by Father Antonio Serrati, who appointed her to supervise an orphanage in Codogno.

Three years later, in 1877, Frances founded a new convent, called the Institute of the Missionary Sisters of the Sacred Heart. Her foundation grew rapidly; in 1888, her society received an official decree of commendation. Mother Frances Xavier, as she

Cabrini, Frances Xavier

then became known, led the sisters in founding orphanages and schools all over Italy. Pope Leo XIII commended her work and called her "a woman of marvelous intuition and of great sanctity."

LIFE'S WORK

Mother Frances Cabrini also expressed a strong desire to begin a foreign mission, preferably in China. Pope Leo XIII instead decided to send her to the United States, an area that was becoming a great concern among Vatican leaders. More than one million Italian immigrants were flooding into the United States between 1880 and 1902. These new arrivals crowded into makeshift tenements located in teeming neighborhoods in large American cities. They worked long and grueling hours for pitiful wages under the control of Italian padrones (agents who organized labor gangs to work in exchange for paying for their passage across the Atlantic) and American sweatshop owners. Practically all of these Italian émigrés considered themselves to be Roman Catholics, but their religious practices, if they engaged in any at all, consisted of an informal jumbling of local traditions from back home and family superstitions that bore little resemblance to official Catholic teachings.

By the 1880's, the Vatican was beginning to take an intense interest in the plight of Italian Americans. With the support of Pope Leo XIII, Giovanni Battista Scalabrini began a concentrated endeavor to minister to the spiritual and physical needs of these uprooted people. A Scalabrinian mission was sent to New York. As part of this ministerial program, the Catholic Church would encourage female religious orders to assist Italian American communities by providing staff for local orphanages and schools.

Cabrini was sent to New York to fulfill plans for an Italian orphanage for girls proposed by Countess Mary Reid DiCesnola. The countess's proposal to fund a Catholic charity was common in a day when the intellectual and social elite were expected to engage in at least a token attempt to alleviate the suffering of the illiterate and unwashed masses. Consequently, the countess designed an orphanage to provide young girls with basic schooling as well as training in fine needlework and fine laundrywork, all skills that would be useful to the countess's society friends, where the girls were expected to practice their crafts.

When Scalabrini and the pope suggested that Mother Cabrini go to New York, Cabrini was given the impression that her charitable work would be performed under the supervision of Archbishop Michael Corrigan of New York and that preparations had already been made for the arrival of the sisters. Cabrini arrived in New York on March 31, 1889, only to find that her superiors in Italy had been gravely misinformed. No accommodations for the sisters had been secured; in fact, Corrigan had written to Cabrini shortly before her departure from Italy suggesting that she delay her journey, but the letter had arrived too late.

Corrigan greeted Cabrini coolly and suggested that the sisters return to Italy immediately. Cabrini stoutly refused. Corrigan finally agreed to allow the nuns to stay if they would establish an Italian school on the lower East Side of the city. He quickly came to loggerheads with the countess over this issue. The countess wanted the sisters to serve as inexpensive labor for her orphanage and suggested that they support themselves by seeking outside employment. In the end, the countess was forced to yield to the archbishop and turn control of the orphanage, along with all money previously collected, over to Mother Cabrini. The orphanage opened on April 21, 1889.

Growing tension between the countess and the archbishop convinced Cabrini of the necessity of acquiring another site for the orphanage. By June, 1890, she had raised sufficient funds to purchase a Jesuit novitiate that became the new site of Sacred Heart Orphan Asylum and a novitiate for the Missionary Sisters of the Sacred Heart. Cabrini also became more closely involved in the projects begun by the Scalabrinian missionaries in New York, including a proposal to build an Italian hospital, for which Cabrini and her sisters solicited the funds. Columbus Hospital was incorporated on May 18, 1891.

Not content to rest on her laurels, the dynamic Mother Cabrini left her New York projects in the hands of other sisters and traveled to Nicaragua in September, 1891, where she founded a house and school. From there she opened a school for Italian children in New Orleans, where she remained until recalled to New York to settle a dispute between the Scalabrinian priests and her nuns.

Cabrini returned to New York in April of 1892, where she found the Columbus Hospital in dire financial straits. The leader of the Scalabrinian mission, the Reverend Felice Morelli, had pushed the mission deeply into debt by borrowing money at exorbitant interest to purchase buildings and land. Morelli was unable to pay the debt on the hospital, which was threatened with public auction to satisfy his creditors. In Mother Cabrini's absence, Morelli had attempted to shift the debt onto the shoulders of the sisters. Cabrini decided to disassociate her order from the original hospital, and, with a grant of $550 from Archbishop Corrigan and some wealthy Italians, she opened a new Columbus Hospital in two rented apartments. The new hospital was expanded in 1894.

The work of the Missionary Sisters of the Sacred Heart continued to grow after Corrigan's death in 1902 to include more schools and orphanages. The sisters also visited hospitals and almshouses, tombs and prisons. Quietly but persistently, the small and frail Frances Cabrini cultivated the support of bishop after bishop throughout the United States and around the world. She founded orphanages and schools in Denver, Los Angeles, Chicago, Seattle, and Philadelphia, as well as in such far-off locations as Buenos Aires, Paris, Madrid, London, and Brazil. She also founded several modern charitable hospitals in New York, Chicago, and Seattle.

Following a brief illness, Mother Cabrini died on December 22, 1917, at Columbus Hospital in Chicago. At her death, she was mother-general to some four thousand nuns and had founded seventy charitable institutions the world over. Her funeral was officiated by Archbishop (later Cardinal) Mundelein, and her remains were laid to rest in New York. Soon after her death, her associates, led by Cardinal Mundelein, promoted her cause before the pope and the archdioceses of New York and Chicago. She was beatified by the Roman Catholic Church on November 13, 1938, after the rule that required fifty years to elapse before the beatification process could be initiated was waived for her case. She became the first American to achieve this honor.

Significance

Frances Xavier Cabrini brought increased unity to the Italian community in New York through her charitable efforts. Her highest goal in her mission work was to strengthen the ties between the Italian immigrants and the Roman Catholic Church. Although she

Cabrini, Frances Xavier

was often frustrated in her failure to wipe out "the worldly spirit" that she felt all around her, she contributed greatly to the growth of popular faith in the Italian community in New York City and in cities throughout the United States. Her worldwide missions also established charitable organizations to help those living in less affluent parts of the world.

Mother Cabrini achieved a worldwide reputation for her religious zeal, her diplomatic skill, and her talents as a businesswoman. She fought valiantly to create a role for Catholic women in foreign missionary work. When reminded by a male colleague that missionaries historically had always been men, Cabrini is said to have replied, "If the mission of announcing the Lord's resurrection to his apostles had been entrusted to Mary Magdalene, it would seem a very good thing to confide to other women an evangelizing mission." Contemporaries often referred to her as "a great man" or "a statesman" for want of a better term. Pope Pius XI considered her name "equal to a poem—a poem of activity, a poem of intelligence, a poem above all of wonderful charity." Through her zeal and her intrepid determination, Mother Cabrini helped to establish a vital role for Catholic women in the area of foreign missions and to increase their visibility within the Roman Catholic Church.

—*Kimberly K. Estep*

FURTHER READING

Border, Lucille Papin. *Francesca Cabrini: Without Staff or Script*. New York: Macmillan, 1945. An older biography meant for popular audiences, this work is extremely sympathetic to Cabrini and focuses primarily on her role as head of the Missionary Sisters of the Sacred Heart.

Di Donato, Pietro. *Immigrant Saint: The Life of Mother Cabrini*. Reprint. New York: St. Martin's Press, 1991. Originally published in 1960, this modern, scholarly biography of Cabrini gives the best background information on the period in which she lived. It uses archives of the Vatican opened to the public in 1978, as well as materials from the Congregation of Propaganda File that have been opened recently by Pope John Paul II.

DiGiovanni, Stephen Michael. "Mother Cabrini: Early Years in New York." *Catholic Historical Review* 77, no. 1 (January 1, 1991): 56-77. This is the most comprehensive account of the circumstances that led to Mother Cabrini's dispatch to New York and of her early work with the Italian population there. DiGiovanni sets Cabrini's work in the context of political developments within the Roman Catholic leadership both in Rome and in New York during the 1880's.

Martindale, Cyril C. *Life of Mother Francesca Saverio Cabrini*. New York: Burns, 1931. Based on biographical materials collected by the Institute of the Missionary Sisters of the Sacred Heart, this brief treatment of Mother Cabrini was compiled as part of the campaign by her colleagues and friends to convene a hearing for Cabrini's beatification.

Maynard, Theodore. *Too Small a World: The Life of Francesca Cabrini*. Milwaukee, Wis.: Bruce Publishing, 1945. An uncritical and simple biography, this book concentrates on Mother Cabrini's role as a worldwide ambassador for the Roman Catholic Church. It is the best source for study of Cabrini's work outside the United States.

Sullivan, Mary Louise. *Mother Cabrini: "Italian Immigrant of the Century."* New York: Center for Migration Studies of New York, 1992. Biography placing Cabrini within the framework of the Italian immigrant experience.

Sultan, Timothy, and Alex Heard. "Cabrini at 50." *New York Times Magazine* 145, no. 50481 (July 7, 1996): 8. Brief history of Cabrini's canonization, including the miracles she performed and the display of her remains in New York City.

RACHEL CARSON

❝ *No witchcraft, no enemy action had silenced the rebirth of new life in this stricken world. The people had done it themselves.* ❞

Biologist and writer

A marine biologist and gifted expositor, Carson wrote many articles as well as three lilting, lyrical books about the sea. She is most remembered, however, for her fourth book, Silent Spring *(1962), an exhaustively researched exposé that sparked a national furor over the unchecked, life-altering, and deadly use of pesticides in the United States.*

Born: May 27, 1907; Springdale, Pennsylvania
Died: April 14, 1964; Silver Spring, Maryland
Also known as: Rachel Louise Carson (full name)
Areas of achievement: Environmentalism; biology

EARLY LIFE

Rachel Carson (KAR-suhn) was born in Springdale, Pennsylvania, approximately eighteen miles from Pittsburgh. Her father, Robert Warden Carson, had purchased close to sixty-five acres of land, intending to sell house lots, but the failure of this plan ensured that the young Rachel would be brought up in a fairly rural setting. Her mother, Maria McLean Carson, was the daughter of a Presbyterian minister and instilled her love of language, music, and nature in her three children. Rachel's long walks with her mother in the nearby orchards and woods awakened in her an awe for and joy in the natural world that lasted her entire life.

Carson soon conceived the goal of becoming a writer and proceeded toward that goal with alacrity: Her story "A Battle in the Clouds," which won a $10 prize, was published in *St. Nicholas*, a children's magazine, when she was only ten years old. Throughout her teenage years, she continued to write, and in 1925, at the age of eighteen, she entered the Pennsylvania College for Women (later Chatham College) as an English major. During her first two years there, Rachel contributed many works to the literary supplement of the school newspaper.

Despite her success as a budding writer, Carson changed her major from English to biology midway through her college career. Years later, she was to say that biology

Carson, Rachel

Rachel Carson.
(Library of Congress)

gave her something to write about. One of Carson's mentors, a dynamic biology instructor named Mary Skinker who was returning to the doctoral program at Johns Hopkins University, encouraged Carson to think about graduate school. Carson applied for admission to graduate school at Johns Hopkins for the fall of 1929 and was accepted. Following her graduation from Pennsylvania College for Women in the spring of 1929, Carson studied under a scholarship at the Marine Biological Laboratory at Woods Hole on Cape Cod. That summer, Carson saw the ocean for the first time. Henceforth, the sea remained an integral part of her life.

The following year saw many changes in Carson's life; her parents moved to Baltimore to live with her, and she received a teaching assistantship at Johns Hopkins Summer School. Carson completed her master's degree in marine zoology in 1932, although she continued to teach until 1936.

In 1935, Carson's father died. Under pressure to support her family, she went to work part-time at the Bureau of Fisheries (which later became the U.S. Fish and Wildlife Service), writing and editing radio scripts. While working there, she noticed an announcement of an opening for an assistant biologist at the bureau. She took the civil service examination (earning the highest score that year) and accepted the full-time appointment. Carson continued her work for the bureau for the next sixteen years, eventually rising in rank to become editor in chief of the publications department.

LIFE'S WORK

Oddly enough (considering the Department of Agriculture's subsequent vigorous opposition to her most famous book, *Silent Spring*, 1962), it was Carson's government work that led to her first article on the ocean. Carson had been asked, as she later said, to "produce something of a general sort about the sea. I set to work, but somehow the material rather took charge of the situation and turned into something that was, perhaps, unusual as a broadcast for the Commissioner of Fisheries." Her supervisor found the article unsuitable and suggested that she submit it to *The Atlantic Monthly* magazine. The article, "Undersea," was published in 1937.

As lyrical as it was informative, "Undersea" soon attracted the attention of an editor from the publishing house of Simon & Schuster, who encouraged Carson to write a book. After nearly four years of working in the evenings, during the weekends, and whenever her government job permitted, Carson published *Under the Sea-Wind* (1941). Although the book received excellent reviews, its publication was rather lost in the outrage over the bombing of Pearl Harbor and the entrance of the United States into World War II. Despite its dampening effect on the sales of her first book, the war effort not only provided Carson with a wealth of new information about the ocean but also provided the nation with many new pesticides that were developed as part of the research into chemical warfare.

As early as 1942, when she unsuccessfully proposed an article on the effects of the pesticide dichloro-diphenyl-trichloroethane (DDT) to *Reader's Digest* magazine, Carson was interested in the issues involving the use of untested pesticides. At this time in her life, however, she could not bring herself to believe that human-made chemicals could fundamentally affect what she called the "stream of life" on the land, in the skies, or in the oceans. Thus, she returned to her first love—the sea—writing the lyrical and technically informative book *The Sea Around Us*, published in 1951. One chapter, "The Birth of An Island," was published in 1950 in *The Yale Review* and won the George Westinghouse Science Writing Award. The book was enormously popular, winning the National Book Award in 1951 and the John Burroughs Medal in 1952 and remaining on the best-seller lists for more than a year. She was awarded a Guggenheim Fellowship but returned the money after receiving substantial royalties from her best-selling book. Carson's resulting financial independence allowed her to resign from her government post and devote herself to her writing.

Just before the publication of *The Sea Around Us*, Carson had begun work on what originally was to be a field guide to the Atlantic shore but later became *The Edge of the Sea* (1955), a careful, poetical portrayal of "the marginal world" between ocean and land. This book also became a best seller and added to Carson's financial security as well as to her reputation as an author. These first three books contain themes that pervaded Carson's entire life: her belief that nothing in nature exists alone (for example, that all living things are interconnected by air and water) and her sense of what Albert Schweitzer called a "reverence for life," a phrase she quoted often. These characteristics, together with her technical training and her expository gifts, made Carson the perfect person to write *Silent Spring*. Initially, Carson intended to write only an article on the effects of pesticides. The more studies she read, however, the more horrifying the picture became, finally driving her to relinquish her belief in the inviolability of the natural world. The widespread spraying of toxic chemicals (such as DDT) led to disastrous effects on wildlife and possible links with human diseases (such as cancer) that had not been thoroughly studied. These facts, together with the incomplete information from the chemical industry about its products and the ignorance of the American public about the effects of pesticides, convinced Carson that a book explaining these issues needed to be written.

In *Silent Spring*, Carson suggested that studies on long-term effects of pesticides needed to be conducted. She revealed documented evidence that showed a pattern of increasing concentrations of pesticides in animals. She conservatively combined the results of more than a thousand technical reports to form an unassailable foundation of documentation to support her alarming conclusions. At the same time, she beautifully encouraged love and respect for life in all of its forms. This feature of *Silent Spring*, together with her constructive suggestions for alleviating the damage already done, turned what could have been a doomsaying book into a hopeful guide to "the other road" (one of her chapter titles).

The publication of *Silent Spring* led to a national debate over the use of pesticides. Unable to discredit the scientific precision of the book, her opponents frequently misrepresented her positions, then attacked those misrepresentations as well as the author's scientific ability. Despite these attacks, the public outcry over *Silent Spring* led President John F. Kennedy to appoint a special commission charged with studying the pesticide controversy. This Science Advisory Committee eventually supported most of Carson's conclusions and duplicated many of her suggestions. Carson's work and her testimony before the U.S. Senate formed a large part of the impetus behind the formation of the Environmental Protection Agency (EPA) in 1970. Carson died of cancer and heart disease in 1964, approximately six years before the EPA opened its doors.

Significance

As the beloved author of three well-researched and beautifully written books about the sea, Carson was able to draw a large reading audience for her final book, *Silent Spring*; as a well-trained scientist who was able to consult with specialists in many fields, Carson was able to write with precision and confidence about the technical issues surrounding the use of pesticides; and as a gifted expositor, she was able to hold the audience's attention through understandable explanations and suggestions written in a graceful, impassioned style. Carson's well-documented book incited a national debate over the cavalier use of pesticides, leading to the growth of the American environmental movement and the formation of the Environmental Protection Agency. Despite the passage of three decades, Carson's books are as readable today as they were in the 1950's and 1960's because of her meticulous writing, which distinguished hypotheses and theories from demonstrated facts. The impact of Carson's *Silent Spring* on government, on industry, on everyday citizens, and, thus, on the natural world is unequaled in American history.

—*Katherine Socha*

FURTHER READING

Brooks, Paul. *The House of Life: Rachel Carson at Work.* 2d ed. Boston: Houghton Mifflin, 1989. This biography of Rachel Carson and a survey of her work was written by her editor. Based on Carson's private papers, Brooks's account is primarily made up of many wonderful samples of her writings, both public and private.

Freeman, Martha, ed. *Always, Rachel: The Letters of Rachel Carson and Dorothy Freeman, 1952-1964.* Boston: Beacon Press, 1995. An intimate collection of some 750 letters between friends—and, possibly, lovers—Rachel Carson and Dorothy Freeman that spans a twelve-year period. The book is edited by Freeman's daughter and includes illustrations, a bibliography, and an index.

Gartner, Carol B. *Rachel Carson.* New York: Frederick Ungar, 1983. This readable discussion of Carson carefully blends her personal and public lives and provides a good bibliography for further reading.

Graham, Frank, Jr. *Since "Silent Spring."* Boston: Houghton Mifflin, 1970. This book provides an account of Carson's career and how she came to devote most of her energy during her final years to *Silent Spring*. The author also traces the progress of the pesticide controversy through the 1960's.

Hynes, H. Patricia. *The Recurring Silent Spring.* New York: Pergamon Press, 1989. This work focuses on *Silent Spring*, providing a brief but informative biography of Carson (elegantly refuting the "lonely spinster" stereotype) before discussing the impact and legacy of *Silent Spring* and the state of the American physical and social environment from Carson's time through the 1980's. A detailed bibliography is included.

Lytle, Mark Hamilton. *The Gentle Subversive: Rachel Carson, Silent Spring, and the Rise of the Environmental Movement.* New York: Oxford University Press, 2007. An updated examination of Carson's profound influence in sparking the environmental movement. Book sections are broken down into "seasons"; the final chapter is titled "The Poison Book and the Dark Season of Vindication."

McCay, Mary A. *Rachel Carson.* New York: Twayne, 1993. This excellent biography of Carson puts her major writings in the context of her personal development as a naturalist and analyzes her work as a part of the American naturalist tradition.

Marco, Gino J., Robert M. Hollingworth, and William Durham, eds. *Silent Spring Revisited.* Washington, D.C.: American Chemical Society, 1987. This collection of essays includes a summary of *Silent Spring*, as well as an essay about Carson's motives and the reaction to her book by a personal friend of Carson, in addition to eleven essays that explore the scientific, political, and environmental issues surrounding the use of pesticides.

Murphy, Priscilla Coit. *What a Book Can Do: The Publication and Reception of Silent Spring.* Amherst: University of Massachusetts Press, 2005. Examines the significance of *Silent Spring*. Describes Carson's approach to the book and the response of her opponents, the media, and the public.

Quaratiello, Arlene R. *Rachel Carson: A Biography.* Westport, Conn.: Greenwood Press, 2004. A concise but good overview of Carson's life and legacy. Ideal for high school students and general readers.

Carter, Jimmy

JIMMY CARTER

> *America did not invent human rights. In a very real sense, it is the other way round. Human rights invented America.*

President of the United States (1977-1981)

Carter was a conservative in some policies and a liberal in others. On one hand, he attacked government bureaucracy, moved away from détente with the Soviet Union, and increased military spending. On the other hand, he supported racial equality, took seriously the problems of underdeveloped countries, and pressured repressive regimes to respect human rights. He was awarded the Nobel Peace Prize in 2002.

Born: October 1, 1924; Plains, Georgia
Also known as: James Earl Carter, Jr. (full name)
Areas of achievement: Government and politics; diplomacy; philanthropy

EARLY LIFE

Jimmy Carter was born in Plains, Georgia, a town of 550 residents in Sumter County. He was the first child of James Earl Carter, Sr., an up-and-coming farmer and rural businessman, and Lillian Gordy Carter, a registered nurse. Along with his sisters Gloria and Ruth and his brother William (Billy), he grew up on the family farm three miles from Plains. After graduating from Plains High School in 1941, Carter briefly attended Georgia Southwestern College and Georgia Institute of Technology. He was appointed to the United States Naval Academy in 1943 and graduated three years later with a bachelor's degree in physics, standing fifty-ninth in a class of 820. On July 7, 1946, he married Rosalynn Smith, a friend of his sister Gloria. They had four children: John William (Jack), James Earl III (Chip), Jeffrey (Jeff), and Amy.

After two years' work on battleships, Carter transferred to the Navy submarine service in 1948 and then to the nuclear submarine program in 1951. Subsequently he served on the precommission crew of the nuclear submarine *Seawolf* and rose to the rank of lieutenant commander. Following his father's death in 1953, Carter returned to Plains, took charge of the family businesses, and quickly became a local leader. Between 1955 and 1962, he chaired the Sumter County Board of Education. In 1962, he was elected to the Georgia senate. During two terms, he advocated governmental efficiency, regional planning, and better schools. In 1966 he lost the Democratic nomination for governor but ran a strong third in a field of six.

Carter's defeat produced a mild depression that led in turn to an important though undramatic religious experience. He had been reared a Baptist, conducted Bible classes in the Navy, and taught Sunday school at the Plains Baptist Church. Following his primary loss, however, Carter began to feel insufficiently devout. Guided by his sister, evangelist Ruth Carter Stapleton, he was "born again" and vowed to live a more godly life.

This religious conversion caused no basic change in his personality. On the contrary, Carter's determination to be a better Christian fitted into his long-standing habit of placing high demands on himself. He worked systematically, sometimes taking special courses to improve his memory, reading speed, and knowledge of art, music, and Spanish. He disciplined his body as well as his mind.

A cross-country runner at the Naval Academy in Annapolis, Maryland, Carter continued to jog into middle age to keep fit. In his late forties, Carter stood five feet ten inches tall and weighed a trim 160 pounds. His stern commander in the nuclear submarine program, Admiral Hyman G. Rickover, reinforced his perfectionism. Carter set high standards for his family and subordinates. Anyone who fell short risked "the look," as Carter's staff called a piercing stare from his hazel eyes.

Nor did spiritual rebirth dampen Carter's political ambition. Between 1967 and 1970, he visited Northern cities as a missionary and prepared for his next gubernatorial campaign. In 1970, he defeated former governor Carl Sanders in the Democratic primary and easily won the governorship.

LIFE'S WORK

Governor Carter's inaugural address in January, 1971, attracted national attention when he declared that the "time for racial discrimination is over." Although Carter sometimes courted segregationist voters, he had remained personally moderate on civil rights issues. Now moving in a more liberal direction, he appointed blacks to state office and displayed a portrait of Martin Luther King, Jr., in the executive mansion. As governor, Carter worked hardest to streamline state agencies, but discrediting prejudice as a political issue was his greatest accomplishment. In 1972 he was mentioned as a dark-horse contender for the Democratic vice presidential nomination. However, ineligible for reelection and more conservative than leading Democrats, he was not a major figure in party or national affairs.

Four years later, Carter used his image as an outsider to win the presidency of a nation unsettled by the Vietnam War, the Watergate scandal, the cultural upheaval of the late 1960's, and the energy crisis of the early 1970's. Carter's book *Why Not the Best?* (1975) announced the central theme of his campaign: Government with effective leadership could be open, compassionate, and competent. Furthermore, claiming a governor's managerial skill, a nuclear engineer's technological expertise, and a born-again farmer's sound morality, Carter presented himself as uniquely qualified to lead. In addition, he blamed President Gerald R. Ford for high unemployment and Machiavellian foreign policy. Despite the wide appeal of these themes, Carter probably would have lost the Democratic nomination if liberal rivals had coalesced against him, and he might have lost the general election if the economy had not been facing rising unemployment and inflation. Carter beat Ford by 1.7 million votes.

Although Carter won a narrow victory, the country greeted the start of his term with enthusiasm. By the end of 1977, however, his legislative program had bogged down in Congress and, according to polls, fewer than half of all Americans approved of his leadership. With some justification, Carter attributed these problems to prejudice against a rural southerner in the White House, but other factors were more significant. While continuing to think of himself as an outsider, the president presented a legislative agenda that would have taxed the skill of an old Washington hand. Moreover, impatient with loose ends, Carter offered what he liked to call "comprehensive" programs. In 1977, he backed bills to reorganize the civil service, restructure the welfare system, lift regulations on major industries, create two new cabinet departments, and end price controls on natural gas. Furthermore, Carter and his aides initially underestimated the need to cultivate powerful senators and House representatives. More important than these considerations of style, temperament, and tactics was Carter's ideological position to the right of most congressional Democrats. Unmoved by his rhetoric of efficiency, they resented his disinclination to promote national health insurance, full employment, and comparable liberal measures.

Conflicting aspirations, great expectations, and tactical errors also marked Carter's first efforts in international affairs. The president's chief foreign policy advisers symbolized his (as well as the country's) ambivalence about the Soviet Union: Secretary of State Cyrus Vance wanted to continue détente while National Security Council Chair Zbigniew Brzezinski took a tough anticommunist line. Giving mixed signals himself in 1977, Carter decided against building a new intercontinental bomber and reneged on campaign promises to reduce military spending, while both repudiating the "inordinate fear of Communism" and condemning Soviet suppression of freedom. This criticism of the Soviets may have hindered progress on a strategic arms limitation treaty to succeed the limited accord (SALT I) signed by President Richard Nixon. A more decisive factor was Carter's presentation of a typically comprehensive disarmament plan. Suspicious Soviet officials rejected it, accusing the United States of reopening issues seemingly settled with President Ford.

From the outset, President Carter showed unprecedented concern about human rights abroad. Regimes sanctioning harassment, imprisonment, or murder of dissenters risked White House censure and loss of American aid. Realpolitik, congressional pressure, and bureaucratic maneuvering rendered Carter's human rights policy less "absolute" than he had promised in his inaugural address. Nevertheless, there were notable successes. Carter's intervention saved lives in Argentina, Brazil, Chile, and other nations ruled by military juntas. His ambassador to the United Nations, Andrew Young, who was black, cultivated delegates from the developing world, and, in April, 1978, Carter became the first U.S. president to visit Africa. Also in April, 1978, he secured Senate ratification of treaties that would end American control of the Panama Canal in 1999. Carter's human rights campaign and empathy for the developing world, however, were less popular at home than abroad. By late 1977, Republican and Democratic cold warriors charged that his soft and self-righteous policies damaged American interests.

Despite growing criticism from both the Left and the Right, Carter secured impressive victories between mid-1978 and mid-1979. Congress revised the civil service system, eased regulations on airlines, and enacted decontrol of natural-gas prices. After grueling negotiations at Camp David, Maryland, Carter persuaded Egyptian president Anwar el-Sadat and Israeli prime minister Menachem Begin to accept the so-called Framework for Peace in the Middle East. In December, 1978, he established full diplomatic relations with the People's Republic of China. At the Vienna summit conference in June, 1979, Carter and Soviet president Leonid Brezhnev finally signed a strategic arms limitation treaty (SALT II). However, none of Carter's successes was unmixed. Liberals complained that decontrol of natural-gas prices enriched big business. Conservatives condemned the recognition of China and viewed SALT II as a needless con-

Carter, Jimmy

cession to the Soviets. Perhaps most disappointing to Carter, though he brokered an Egyptian-Israeli peace treaty in March, 1979, the Camp David accords inspired no other Middle East settlements.

During the summer of 1979, Carter faced a faltering economy, oil shortages, and an angry nation. "Stagflation," the combination of rising unemployment and inflation, reappeared after two years in remission. Furthermore, when a revolution that deposed the shah of Iran in January, 1978, also disrupted Iranian oil exports, the Organization of Petroleum Exporting Countries (OPEC) limited production and doubled prices. As American motorists clamored for scarce gasoline, Carter's bills promoting energy conservation and synthetic fuels stalled in Congress. On July 15, Carter attempted to rally the country against what he called a "crisis of the American spirit." This speech temporarily improved his standing in the polls and on Capitol Hill. His subsequent decision, however, to remove several cabinet secretaries and fight inflation instead of unemployment cut short this resurgence. By the early fall, Democratic senator Edward M. Kennedy had decided to contest the president's renomination.

In October, Carter made the most important decision of his presidency, allowing the exiled shah of Iran to enter the United States for medical treatment. On November 4, Iranian revolutionaries seized the United States embassy in Tehran; fifty-two of the original sixty-six Americans stationed there (fourteen were released after a few weeks) remained captive for 444 days. The Middle East situation deteriorated further when Soviet forces invaded Afghanistan in December. Carter responded by withdrawing SALT II from Senate consideration, halting grain sales to the Soviet Union, urging a boycott of the 1980 Olympic Games in Moscow, and asking for a large increase in military spending. According to the Carter Doctrine announced in January, 1980, attempts by outside forces to control the Persian Gulf would be "repelled by any means necessary, including military force." The president's rhetoric masked relative American weakness in the region. Indeed, a military mission to rescue the hostages failed in April when American helicopters collided far from Tehran.

Although Carter turned back Kennedy's challenge to win renomination, his inability to free the hostages combined with the faltering economy cost him the presidency. On November 4, 1980, Republican nominee Ronald Reagan defeated Carter by 8.4 million votes. During his last months in office, Carter, now a convinced cold warrior, stopped aid to the leftist Sandinista government in Nicaragua. Negotiations to free the hostages remained his chief concern. They were released minutes after Reagan took office on January 20, 1981, and former president Carter flew to greet them at an American base in Germany.

Carter resettled in Plains, but secular and religious interests often pulled him away from home, and he maintained a high public profile. He acted as the official representative of the United States in several capacities, such as at the funeral of Sadat in Cairo in 1981. In 1982 he founded the Carter Center at Emory University in Atlanta, where he also joined the faculty as a Distinguished University Professor. Through the Carter Center, he continued to support human rights. In programs ranging throughout the world, the center helped boost grain production, combat disease, and increase treatment of mental illnesses. In one signal example, its Global 2000 program drastically reduced the incidence of river blindness caused by guinea worm in Africa.

Furthermore, Carter became a leading member of Habitat for Humanity International in 1984, an organization that builds housing for the poor. The Jimmy Carter Work Project sponsored new housing in cities in the United States, Mexico, India, eighteen African nations, and the Philippines, projects in which Carter himself frequently worked alongside other volunteer construction workers.

Carter also has monitored elections in more than twenty countries and mediated internal and international conflicts in such trouble spots as Haiti, Bosnia, North Korea, and Sudan. In 1994 he helped negotiate an agreement between U.S. president Bill Clinton and North Korean president Kim Il Sung to stop North Korea's production of weapons-grade nuclear materials in exchange for oil and modern electricity-generating nuclear reactors.

In 2007, Carter toured the Darfur region of Sudan with South African bishop Desmond Tutu as members of the Elders, an international organization of elder statesmen dedicated to fostering peace and human rights. The two condemned the genocidal civil war there and called for greater international involvement. For his untiring efforts to find peaceful solutions to conflict, improve economic conditions, and safeguard human rights, Carter was awarded the 2002 Nobel Peace Prize.

While his dedication is universally acknowledged, Carter nonetheless drew criticism for some of his post-presidency diplomacy and political pronouncements. His independent missions sometimes departed from the policy goals of his successors. He annoyed the administration of George W. Bush, for instance, by traveling to Cuba in 2002, shaking hands with Fidel Castro, long an adversary of the United States, and delivering a speech (in Spanish) on Cuban national television. In 2004 he observed a referendum in Venezuela to recall its president, Hugo Chávez, and declared the results, in Chávez's favor, to be accurate; other analysts disputed that judgment, a controversy that proved a further annoyance to the U.S. government. Carter later criticized President Bush and British prime minister Tony Blair for the 2003 invasion of Iraq and ignited controversy with the publication of *Palestine: Peace Not Apartheid* (2006), in which he argues that Israel established a segregated society that deprives Palestinians of basic human rights.

Carter is a prolific author, publishing in a variety of genres. His works include analyses such as *The Blood of Abraham* (1985), a well-informed study of the Arab-Israeli conflict, in which he rebukes President Reagan for failing to pursue the peace process begun at Camp David; several books of memoirs; a spiritual autobiography, *Living Faith* (1996); social criticism, such as *Our Endangered Values: American's Moral Crisis* (2005); a book of poems, *Always a Reckoning, and Other Poems* (1995); and historical fiction, with *The Hornet's Nest* (2003), a novel about the Revolutionary War. In 2007 he published a retrospective on his post-presidential career, *Beyond the White House: Waging Peace, Fighting Disease, Building Hope*.

In addition to the Nobel Prize, Carter has won many honors for his humanitarian work. Among these are honorary doctorates; awards such as the Albert Schweitzer Prize of Humanitarianism (1987), the W. Averell Harriman Democracy Award (1992), and the United Nations Human Rights Award (1998); a Grammy Award in 2007 for the audio version of *Endangered Values*; and a nuclear submarine christened in his honor, the USS *Jimmy Carter*.

Carter, Jimmy

SIGNIFICANCE

Carter was a more significant—and much better—president than his overwhelming defeat in 1980 suggests. Ironically, part of his significance lay in legitimating themes, such as the need to shrink the federal government, that Reagan used against him during the campaign. Similarly, by lifting regulations on major industries, moving away from détente, and increasing military spending, Carter initiated policies later continued by Reagan. Notwithstanding these unintended contributions to American conservatism, Carter's most important accomplishments derived from his liberal side. In the White House, as in the Georgia state house, Carter, a white southern supporter of racial equality, discredited racial prejudice as a political issue. His presidential appointments included many women and Latinos as well as blacks. In foreign policy, Carter encouraged Egyptian-Israeli peace by accepting an evenhanded approach to the Middle East, paid respectful attention to underdeveloped countries, and placed human rights on the international agenda. Because he continued to champion human rights and initiated programs to battle disease and poverty when out of the White House, many consider him America's greatest former president.

—*Leo P. Ribuffo*

FURTHER READING

Biven, W. Carl. *Jimmy Carter's Economy: Policy in an Age of Limits*. Chapel Hill: University of North Carolina Press, 2002. Analyzes how the Carter administration responded to the massive inflation, oil crisis, and other economic problems that plagued his presidency.

Carroll, Peter. *It Seemed Like Nothing Happened: The Tragedy and Promise of America in the 1970's*. New York: Holt, Rinehart and Winston, 1982. A lively history of the decade, especially perceptive on cultural trends and the social development of minorities. Places Carter in context and views him as a conservative Democrat.

Carter, Jimmy. *Keeping Faith: Memoirs of a President*. New York: Bantam Books, 1982. This defensive memoir shows Carter and liberal Democrats talking past one another. Contains comprehensive accounts of the Camp David negotiations and the Iran hostage crisis.

———. *Palestine: Peace Not Apartheid*. New York: Simon & Schuster, 2006. A controversial book in which Carter continues to hold out hope for a peaceful solution to the Middle East conflict. However, he maintains that the peace process failed because of what he defines as Israel's forced segregation and oppression of Palestinians on the West Bank.

———. *Why Not the Best?* Nashville, Tenn.: Broadman Press, 1975. This combination memoir and campaign tract contains Carter's fullest account of his childhood, naval service, and governorship. Especially useful for understanding his evolving position on civil rights.

Carter, Rosalynn. *First Lady from Plains*. Boston: Houghton Mifflin, 1984. A much more candid book than either of Jimmy Carter's memoirs. Although Carter discusses her own experiences as a mental health reformer, the book is especially valuable for the portrait of her husband.

Glad, Betty. *Jimmy Carter: In Search of the Great White House*. New York: W. W.

Norton, 1980. Glad presents the most detailed scholarly interpretation of Carter's youth, early career, religious beliefs, and 1976 campaign strategy. Relatively little on his presidency, however.

Kaufman, Burton I., and Scott Kaufman. *The Presidency of James Earl Carter, Jr.* 2d ed. Lawrence: University Press of Kansas, 2006. In their assessment of Carter's presidency, the authors conclude that he was a mediocre chief executive who was "long on good intentions but short on knowledge."

Lynn, Laurence E., Jr., and David Whitman. *The President as Policymaker: Jimmy Carter and Welfare Reform.* Philadelphia: Temple University Press, 1981. This thorough account of Carter's unsuccessful attempt to restructure the welfare system effectively uses interviews with cabinet members, senators, representatives, and civil servants. Reveals Carter's strengths and weaknesses as a policymaker along with the institutional constraints he encountered.

Smith, Gaddis. *Morality, Reason, and Power: American Diplomacy During the Carter Years.* New York: Hill & Wang, 1985. An excellent analysis of Carter's foreign policy. Smith places the Carter administration in broad historical context, applauds Carter's human rights record, and regrets his abandonment of détente.

GEORGE WASHINGTON CARVER

" When you do the common things in life in an uncommon way, you will command the attention of the world. "

Botanist and agriculturalist

Through his work with plant diseases, soil analysis, and crop management, Carver enabled many southern farmers to have greater crop yield and profits. He also developed hundreds of products from peanuts, sweet potatoes, and other plants, including beverages, cosmetics, and dyes and paints. In his role as educator and friend, he motivated hundreds of blacks to improve their lives and inspired white friends to work toward racial equality.

Born: July 12, 1861?; near Diamond Grove, Missouri
Died: January 5, 1943; Tuskegee, Alabama
Also known as: George Carver (birth name); George W. Carver
Areas of achievement: Agriculture; botany; education; social reform

EARLY LIFE

George Washington Carver (KAR-vur) was born a slave near Diamond Grove, Missouri. According to an unconfirmed but plausible story, George and his mother, Mary, were kidnapped by slave raiders shortly after George's birth. Mary's owner, Moses Carver, hired a neighbor to search for them. Unable to find Mary, the neighbor returned with George and received a racehorse as payment. George was reared by Moses and Susan Carver. Slaves were given only first names at birth, so George took the

Carver name as his own. Later he added the initial "W" to distinguish himself from another George Carver. The "W" came to stand for Washington.

A sickly child, George became Susan's helper in the house. He proved adept at household tasks, and he displayed keen interest and ability in growing plants. Intelligent and curious, Carver was frustrated that he could not attend the white school in Diamond Grove. About 1877, Carver moved to neighboring Neosho so that he could go to school there. He lived with a black couple and did household chores for his room and board, a situation that was repeated often in his quest for education.

After attending schools throughout Kansas, Carver applied to a small Presbyterian college in Highland, Kansas, in 1884. He was accepted by mail, but when the school learned that he was black, he was denied admission. After homesteading in Beeler, Kansas, Carver moved to Winterset, Iowa. In 1890, he entered Simpson College in Indianola, Iowa. The only black on campus, he soon won the respect and affection of the other students. He supported himself by doing laundry, but students anonymously gave him concert tickets and extra money.

Carver enrolled in Simpson to study art, but he doubted that he could make a living as a black artist. When his art teacher learned of his skill with plants, she suggested that he attend Iowa State, the agricultural college at Ames, Iowa. Believing that he could help his people as a trained agriculturist, he enrolled at Iowa State in 1891. While at Ames, Carver met three future United States secretaries of agriculture: James Wilson, Henry C. Wallace, and Henry A. Wallace. The latter influenced his training in agriculture and helped him later in his work at Tuskegee.

In 1894, Carver received his bachelor of science degree and began graduate work. He was appointed to the faculty as an assistant in botany and was given charge of the greenhouse. Doing graduate work with L. H. Pammel, a noted authority on mycology, Carver developed his expertise in the study of fungi and plant diseases. Before Carver finished his graduate work, Booker T. Washington asked him to head a new agricultural school at Tuskegee Institute in Alabama. Carver accepted the position, believing that it was the mission God had prepared him to undertake.

LIFE'S WORK

In the fall of 1896, Carver completed requirements for his master's of agriculture degree and arrived at Tuskegee to head the agricultural department and direct a new experiment station. In addition to teaching, conducting research, and working with the Tuskegee extension program, Carver was assigned administrative and caretaking duties.

Small in build and high-pitched in voice, Carver already was unorthodox in appearance and habits. He wore the same clothes for years, simply adding more patches, but he always had a fresh flower in his lapel. Somewhat of a loner, he made few close friends on campus, although he welcomed visitors who were interested in his work. Most of his close friends were white, and he sustained many friendships through correspondence.

Because Carver wanted to assist the poorest farmers, he conducted soil-building experiments and research on crop diversification. He also studied plant diseases and how to prevent or control them. For the homemaker, he investigated methods of food dehydration and preservation. He also developed color washes from the clay soil that the farmers could use to beautify their homes. His findings were written in layperson's language, printed in bulletins, and distributed freely.

Before Carver arrived at Tuskegee, Washington was holding yearly farmers' conferences that were attended by farmers and interested whites. The two-day conference gave information and motivated farmers to work for economic independence. Carver expanded conference activities and gave tours of the station grounds, during which he explained the institute's experiments. He obtained free garden seed from the U.S. Department of Agriculture (USDA) to distribute to the farmers. Although conferences helped, Carver wanted to educate the farmers on how to improve their land. As a result, in 1897 he organized monthly farmers' institutes. Members received specific advice on what fertilizers to use, how to improve soil, and when and what crops to plant.

The next step was to inaugurate farm demonstration work and a "movable school." Carver designed the Jesup Wagon, which carried supplies and opened up for displays. The movable school began operations in 1906 and reached more than six thousand people that summer. All farm extension work was limited by a lack of funds, but the program succeeded in helping farmers improve their farms and living conditions.

As Carver became more aware of the nutritional deficiencies of the southern diet, he looked for a source of protein that could easily be grown and would enrich the soil. The three main crops that met these requirements were cowpeas, sweet potatoes, and peanuts. He developed recipes using them and eventually displayed more than 100 products from the sweet potato and about 325 products made from the peanut. In 1923, he was given the coveted Spingarn Medal of the National Association for the Advancement of Colored People (NAACP) for his achievements in agricultural chemistry.

His first experiments with the peanut were simply intended to help southerners improve their diets. Eventually, though, he sought to establish industries to manufacture his products and improve the economic outlook for the South. His plans for commercialization never materialized.

In 1921, his testimony, showmanship, and exhibit of peanut products before the House Ways and Means Committee led Congress to write the highest tariff peanuts had ever had. His success brought him immediate fame. From 1924 to 1938, he served as an industry consultant, speaker, and writer for publications.

In the early 1930's, peanut growers had a problem with peanuts rotting and failing to mature. USDA officials concluded that the problem was not disease and refused to help. Two employees from the Tom Huston Company processing plant disagreed and turned to Carver. After he visited infected fields, Carver agreed that fungi were the cause. His report on peanut diseases and their prevention was circulated, and USDA officials were moved to conduct further research.

Paul Miller, a mycologist with the USDA, was assigned to investigate the problem. Impressed with Carver's ability to locate and identify fungi, Miller persuaded the USDA to make Carver a collaborator who would collect specimens for them. This work brought him appreciation and recognition from specialists. Carver continued to provide technical advice to the Tom Huston Company, and his publicity for the peanut benefited the entire industry. His peanut and sweet potato exhibit won the award for best exhibit at the Southern Exposition at New York in May, 1925. This success established Carver as an influence in the New South movement and the peanut industry.

In the 1920's and 1930's, Carver spoke to various groups all over the country, including diverse black and white civic clubs, churches, colleges, and camps. In these speeches he urged racial harmony and shared his vision for a better world. His life and talks inspired people to respect all races, work toward brotherhood, and strive to improve the world they shared.

Before his death, on January 5, 1943, Carver established the George Washington Carver Foundation and Museum and donated his life savings to it. He personally directed the museum displays of his work and paintings. The foundation provided laboratory facilities for the school and set up a fund for research fellowships.

SIGNIFICANCE

Carver's farm institutes, movable school, and readable bulletins were important contributions to agricultural education. His research and teaching on soil conservation, crop diversification, and nutrition helped raise the standard of living for the families he reached.

The peanut industry greatly benefited from Carver's publicity and research. His work helped peanuts become a leading crop of the South. Carver's primary research was undertaken to find ways of improving life for poor farmers. He also interpreted his own and others' research to laypersons. Farmers could benefit from science because Carver showed them how to apply it in their own lives.

George Washington Carver.
(National Archives)

Carver, George Washington

Carver was a symbol of personal triumph over poverty and racial discrimination. At the University of Iowa he displayed great talent and skill in science, but he sacrificed a career in research to serve blacks in the South. His religious faith gave him a missionary zeal to improve the lives of the oppressed. One of Carver's greatest achievements was the impact he had on individuals. He gave youth, especially, a vision of what the world could be, and he encouraged them to work toward love and understanding of all races.

The publicity attending Carver's achievements prompted contributions to the Carver Foundation, and its establishment may be Carver's greatest legacy. Foundation grants continue to encourage students to study and use their education to benefit humankind.

—Elaine Mathiasen

FURTHER READING

Coulter, Ellis Merton. *The South During Reconstruction: 1865-1877*. Baton Rouge: Louisiana State University Press, 1947. Portrays the South and its people—black and white—during the Reconstruction years. Discusses the Freedmen's Bureau, postslavery labor, Southern economics, and agricultural changes.

Gates, Henry Louis, Jr., and Cornel West. *The African-American Century: How Black Americans Shaped Our Country*. New York: Touchstone, 2002. Carver is one of the African Americans whose biography is included in this book.

Harlan, Lois R. *Booker T. Washington: The Making of a Black Leader*. New York: Oxford University Press, 1972. As head of Tuskegee Institute, Washington recruited Carver to teach there and was Carver's supervisor until the former's death in 1915. This biography gives another perspective on the policies and happenings at Tuskegee.

Hersey, Mark. "Hints and Suggestions to Farmers: George Washington Carver and Rural Conservation in the South." *Environmental History* 11, no. 2 (April, 2006). A corrective interpretation of Carver's lifelong work and passions, including his work in promoting conservation and environmental awareness and in encouraging awareness of how humans are part of, not separate from, the natural world. Hersey also argues that Carver has been nearly forgotten in the annals of environmental history.

Holt, Rackham. *George Washington Carver: An American Biography*. Rev. ed. Garden City, N.Y.: Doubleday, 1963. Laudatory and somewhat inaccurate, this interesting story of Carver's life includes many anecdotes not found in other biographies. It pictures Carver as humble and misunderstood, a brilliant scientist, an able educator, and an inspiration to all who knew him.

Hudson, Wade, ed. *Powerful Words: More than Two Hundred Years of Extraordinary Writing by African Americans*. Illustrated by Sean Qualls. New York: Scholastic Nonfiction, 2004. This important collection includes an excerpt from a 1939 book about Carver, *The Man Who Talks with the Flowers*. Includes a foreword by social reformer Marian Wright Edelman.

Kluger, Richard. *Simple Justice*. New York: Alfred A. Knopf, 1975. Traces the practice of segregation in America from its beginnings in slavery to the 1954 Supreme

Court decision to end legal segregation in public schools. Detailed and scholarly history of the people and organizations involved in the struggle for human dignity and equality.

McMurry, Linda O. *George Washington Carver: Scientist and Symbol.* New York: Oxford University Press, 1981. Well-documented biography; disproves the myths surrounding Carver and describes his most significant accomplishments. Examines his contributions to agriculture, science, race relations, and education.

Mary Ann Shadd Cary

" Self-reliance is the fine road to independence. "

Abolitionist and journalist

A pioneering educator and lifelong advocate of equality for African Americans, Cary wrote and lectured widely in support of abolition and black immigration to Canada, and after emancipation was achieved, she participated in the woman suffrage and temperance movements. She was also the first African American woman newspaper publisher and the first black woman to enter Howard University Law School.

Born: October 9, 1823; Wilmington, Delaware
Died: June 5, 1893; Washington, D.C.
Also known as: Mary Ann Shadd (birth name)
Areas of achievement: Education; social reform; women's rights; journalism

Early Life
Mary Ann Shadd Cary (KA-ree) was born Mary Ann Shadd, the first of thirteen children of Harriet Parnell, a mulatto woman born in North Carolina, and Abraham Shadd, a shoemaker descended from a German soldier named Hans Schad and a free black Pennsylvania woman named Elizabeth Jackson, who married in 1756. Like her father and paternal grandfather, Mary Ann was born free. The fact that her grandfather and great grandfather had been butchers by trade secured the status of the Shadd family within the black middle class of Wilmington, Delaware, where she grew up. However, their comparative material prosperity did not spare free blacks, such as the Shadds, from the black codes that Delaware enacted during the 1830's to restrict the freedoms of former slaves.

At an early age, Mary Ann was exposed to the movements to abolish slavery and achieve political and social equality for free African Americans. Her father was active in local and national social protests throughout his life. He offered his homes in Wilmington and later in West Chester, Pennsylvania, as stations on the Underground Railroad, which was used by people escaping from southern slavery. He also solicited subscriptions for abolitionist newspapers such as William Lloyd Garrison's *Liberator*. In 1831, Abraham Shadd was one of three authors and signatories of a statement condemning the American Colonization Society, which worked to ship freed slaves to Africa. He was also among the first five African Americans on the board of managers of the American Anti-Slavery Society when that organization began in 1833.

During 1833, the Shadd family escaped from the increasing harshness of Delaware's black codes by moving to nearby West Chester, Pennsylvania. There, Mary Ann received six years of private instruction provided by local Quakers, under whom she studied Latin, French, literature, and mathematics. In 1840, when she was seventeen and her schooling was completed, she returned to Wilmington and opened a school for African American children. Throughout the 1840's, she taught not only in Wilmington but also in West Chester and Norristown, Pennsylvania, and in Trenton, New Jersey, where she failed in an effort to establish another school for African Americans in 1844.

LIFE'S WORK

In 1849, Mary Ann Shadd entered the public debate on obtaining black equality. During that year, she published a letter in Frederick Douglass's newspaper, *The North Star*, and also published a pamphlet, *Hints to the Colored People of the North*, in which she stressed education, morality, and economic self-help as the means through which African Americans could integrate themselves into American society. Passage of the Fugitive Slave Act by the U.S. Congress in 1850 permitted federal marshals to reclaim runaway slaves even after they reached free states. That law added new urgency to Mary Ann's emerging activism.

After attending an antislavery convention in Toronto, Canada, in September, 1851, Mary Ann decided to join the thousands of free and slave-born African Americans who were immigrating to Great Britain's Canadian colonies. After giving up her teaching job in New York City, she settled in the town of Windsor (now in Ontario). There she opened a school with the support of the American Missionary Association and became that organization's only black missionary in Canada West. In 1852, Mary Ann published *Notes of Canada West*, an essay extolling the benefits of life in Canada to potential African American migrants. By the end of the decade, Mary Ann's parents as well as several siblings had also moved to Canada.

Mary Ann's advocacy of Canadian immigration and racial uplift challenged the established leadership of Henry Bibb, another immigrant who had established the newspaper *Voice of the Fugitive* in 1851. The friction between Mary Ann and Bibb came to a head in 1853, when the American Missionary Association responded to Bibb's criticisms of Mary Ann by withdrawing its support of her school. On March 24, 1853, the day after her Windsor school closed, Mary Ann began publishing and editing her own newspaper, the *Provincial Freeman*, in Toronto. She was the first African American woman to do so, even though the conventions of the time required her to list a man as the newspaper's editor on its masthead.

The *Provincial Freeman* provided Mary Ann with a public voice with which to articulate her support of black immigration to Canada and racial integration and to critique other abolitionists. The newspaper also published letters and articles debating woman suffrage and women's participation in the public sphere. Mary Ann spread her message further and solicited subscriptions for her newspaper by lecturing in the United States. She was one of only a few black women who spoke publicly during that period. In 1855, she moved her newspaper from Toronto to Chatham.

On January 3, 1856, Mary Ann married Thomas Cary, a free-born African American and barber who relocated to Toronto during the early 1850's and had three children from an earlier marriage. Mary Ann's marriage to Cary was unusual, in that she and her husband traveled back and forth between the separate homes they maintained in Chatham and Toronto. They had two children together: Sara Elizabeth, born in 1857, and Linton, born in 1860.

Mary Ann continued editing the *Provincial Freeman* until it folded in 1860 because of insufficient funds. After her husband's death later that same year, Mary Ann taught briefly in Michigan, opened another school in Chatham with her sister, and continued to publish articles in the abolitionist press. At the urging of the black nationalist leader Martin Delaney, Mary Ann traveled throughout the United States in 1863 to encourage African American men to join the Union army during the Civil War. After the war ended, the promise of Reconstruction and diminishing employment opportunities for African Americans in Canada prompted Mary Ann's permanent return to the United States in 1867. She worked as a teacher in Detroit before moving to Washington, D.C., in 1869.

As Mary Ann settled into life as a teacher, and later as a school principal, in Washington, D.C., she began to pay more attention to women's issues in her social activism. She attended the yearly meetings of the National Women's Suffrage Association during the early part of the decade and wrote frequently for Frederick Douglass's newspaper *New National Era* in support of woman suffrage, a position that diverged from the African American community's primary goal of obtaining the vote for black men. After ratification of the Fifteenth Amendment gave black men the vote in 1870, Mary Ann herself attempted to register to vote several times. In 1880, she established the short-lived Colored Women's Progressive Franchise Association. She also advocated temperance as a means of promoting black self-sufficiency.

Meanwhile, Mary Ann became the first black woman to enter Howard University Law School. She began her legal studies there in 1869 and combined being a law student with being a teacher and school principal until she received her degree in 1883. Throughout the 1880's, she practiced law in Washington and continued to lecture and write on strategies of racial uplift. She died of stomach cancer in Washington, D.C., on June 5, 1893, during her seventieth year.

Significance

Mary Ann Shadd Cary is remarkable not only for her notable firsts in the fields of journalism and law but also for the space that she carved out for herself as a woman activist during the long African American struggle to obtain racial equality. She defied the mainstream social convention that a woman's rightful place was in the home by inserting herself into public debate, first on the issue of abolition of slavery and extension of civil rights to free blacks and later in her advocacy of woman suffrage. She also defied the assumptions of other African American activists who asserted that gender equality should be subordinate to racial uplift. Her career as an educator, lecturer, and newspaperwoman—which did not cease with marriage and motherhood—was its own protest against the twin sets of limitations that she faced as an African American and as a woman.

—*Francesca Gamber*

Catt, Carrie Chapman

FURTHER READING

Cimbala, Paul A. "Mary Ann Shadd Cary and Black Abolitionism." In *Against the Tide: Women Reformers and American Society*, edited by Paul A. Cimbala and Randall M. Miller. Westport, Conn.: Praeger, 1997. This essay places Mary Ann Shadd Cary within the broader community of African American abolitionists and in relation to the particular concerns of black women activists.

Ferris, Jeri. *Demanding Justice: A Story About Mary Ann Shadd Cary*. Minneapolis: Carolrhoda Books, 2003. Illustrated children's book about Shadd Cary.

Rhodes, Jane. *Mary Ann Shadd Cary: The Black Press and Protest in the Nineteenth Century*. Bloomington: Indiana University Press, 1998. A thorough treatment of Shadd Cary's life, this book pays special attention to her years as a newspaper editor and publisher and the role she played in the antebellum black press.

Silverman, Jason H. *Unwelcome Guests: Canada West's Response to American Fugitive Slaves, 1800-1865*. Millwood, N.Y.: Associated Faculty Press, 1985. Contests the view that Canada provided a safe haven for African Americans by describing the obstacles and racism that immigrants such as the Shadds faced there.

CARRIE CHAPMAN CATT

" *There are two kinds of restrictions upon human liberty—the restraint of law and that of custom. No written law has ever been more binding than unwritten custom supported by public opinion.* "

Social reformer and feminist

Recognized as one of the ablest leaders and organizers of the woman suffrage movement, Catt brought new life to a faltering National American Woman Suffrage Association and designed the campaign that won the federal vote for women in 1920.

Born: January 9, 1859; Ripon, Wisconsin
Died: March 9, 1947; New Rochelle, New York
Also known as: Carrie Lane (birth name); Carrie Chapman
Areas of achievement: Women's rights; social reform; civil rights

EARLY LIFE

Carrie Chapman Catt, the second of three children, was born Carrie Lane in Ripon, Wisconsin. Her parents, Maria Clinton and Lucius Lane, originally from the state of New York, had come west to live as farmers. In 1866, lured farther west by the Gold Rush, the family moved to Charles City, Iowa, where they remained throughout Catt's adolescence.

Maria Clinton Lane had attended a women's school, Oread Collegiate Institute, in Massachusetts. She encouraged her daughter to continue her studies beyond high school. Catt entered Iowa State Agricultural College in March, 1877, and graduated in November, 1880, the only woman in her graduating class. During her college career, she supported herself by teaching, washing dishes, and working in the school library. After college, Catt worked first as a law clerk and then as a schoolteacher in Mason City, Iowa. In 1883, she was appointed superintendent of schools, a post that she resigned in 1885 to marry Leo Chapman, editor of the *Mason City Republican*.

Like Catt, Leo Chapman was highly interested in political reform and used his position at the paper to push for social change. When a local Republican candidate sued him for libel, Chapman went to California to look for new employment opportunities. In 1886, Catt was notified that Chapman was ill with typhoid fever. She left Iowa to go to him, but while she was en route to California, she was notified that he had died.

Catt decided to settle in San Francisco, where she earned a barely adequate living through freelance journalism. The following year, she encountered George Catt, a fellow student at Iowa State. He encouraged her to become a public lecturer. She returned home to Charles City in 1887, working as a professional lecturer and the temporary editor of the *Floyd County Advocate*.

LIFE'S WORK

On returning to Iowa, Catt joined the Women's Christian Temperance Union (WCTU), the antialcohol, pro-suffrage organization run by Frances Willard. The issue of woman suffrage increasingly interested Catt; in 1889, she was elected secretary of the Iowa Woman Suffrage Association. In 1890, she spoke at the convention of the newly merged National American Woman Suffrage Association (NAWSA), held in Washington, D.C. In June of that year, she moved to Seattle, Washington, to marry George Catt.

A few months later, Carrie Chapman Catt went to South Dakota to work for a state referendum for woman suffrage, traveling throughout the eastern part of the state to speak. Although the campaign was unsuccessful, she gained valuable experience and began to be touted as a leading figure in the suffrage movement.

In 1892, Catt again attended the NAWSA convention in Washington, D.C., where Susan B. Anthony asked her to speak before Congress on the proposed suffrage amendment. After she and her husband moved to Bensonhurst, New York, Catt became more active and worked more closely with Anthony and other leaders of the suffrage movement. At the World Columbian Exposition in Chicago in 1893, Catt was approached about campaigning in support of a state suffrage amendment in Colorado. Initially reluctant, she agreed and was instrumental in making Colorado the second state to allow women to vote, on November 7, 1893.

Throughout the next decade, Catt used her superlative organizational skills to establish political equality clubs, make speeches, and raise money for the suffrage movement. She headed the organizational committee within the NAWSA, which worked to coordinate suffrage campaigns throughout the United States and to educate women about suffrage.

When Anthony stepped down as president of the NAWSA in 1900, she chose Catt as her successor, citing her ingenuity and political sagacity. Catt served as president of

Catt, Carrie Chapman

Carrie Chapman Catt.
(Library of Congress)

the NAWSA for the next four years. During her tenure, she worked to raise money, increase enrollment, and establish links between the NAWSA and the International Council of Women, as well as the International Woman Suffrage Alliance. In 1904, she resigned her NAWSA presidency to care for her ailing husband. She became vice president at large under the organization's new president, Anna Howard Shaw.

On October 8, 1905, George Catt died of a perforated duodenal ulcer. The death of Anthony in February, 1906, further shattered the grief-stricken Catt. Concerned for her health, Catt's friends and doctor urged her to travel, and she spent much of her time for the following nine years abroad, working with the International Woman Suffrage Alliance to promote woman suffrage around the globe.

Catt's international efforts helped make her even more well known at home, and she became recognized as a world leader in the suffrage movement. In 1914, she turned her attention to New York State, believing that if it passed a suffrage amendment, other states would soon follow suit. She toured the state, making numerous speeches and appearances. That same year, Mrs. Leslie, a publisher's widow, died and left an estate worth more than $900,000 to Catt to use as she saw fit to promote woman suffrage. Because of legal difficulties arising from suits filed by Leslie's relatives, who hotly contested the will, Catt did not receive the legacy until 1917, when she used it to set up the Leslie Woman Suffrage Commission.

In 1915, Shaw announced her resignation as president of the NAWSA. The organization's members turned to Catt, asking her to resume the presidency. She resisted their request until she was promised a free hand in governing the organization. Then she accepted the presidency and proceeded to make the NAWSA the most powerful woman's organization in the history of the United States.

Following Anthony's example, Catt refused to allow the NAWSA to work on any cause other than suffrage, realizing that a single goal would unify the organization and allow it to use its energy and resources more effectively. Her "Winning Plan," put before the NAWSA in 1916, was to push for congressional passage of the suffrage amendment to the U.S. Constitution rather than work on the slow process of getting the vote state by state. She proposed a campaign that would encompass every state, saying that each organization must run "a red-hot, never-ceasing campaign."

Catt's plan was hindered by divisions within the suffrage movement. Some of the movement's more radical members broke off to form the Congressional Union (later known as the National Woman's Party), headed by Alice Paul. Catt believed that the radical tactics adopted by such groups alienated the public and harmed the suffrage cause far more than they helped it. Another impediment to her goal was the inevitable involvement of the United States in World War I. Some suffragists, including Catt, were open advocates of peace, an unpopular premise in a country gearing itself for military action. Nevertheless, when diplomatic relations were broken with Germany in 1917, Catt and the NAWSA drafted a letter saying they would stand by the government in case of war. This act drew more criticism of Catt than anything else she had ever done. Despite her personal inclinations as a pacifist, Catt believed that getting women the vote must take precedence, and she would not let the peace activists stand in its way.

In designing her strategy, Catt took the Republican and Democratic parties as her model, knowing that the NAWSA could challenge these institutions only if it worked along the same principles. She wanted to establish a well-organized network that could affect public opinion in every state. Under her guidance, the NAWSA worked tirelessly to set up such a network and to educate the public about the importance of woman suffrage by distributing pamphlets, buttons, flyers, leaflets, posters, and even playing cards. The NAWSA purchased the popular suffrage newspaper *Woman's Journal*, renamed it *Woman Citizen*, and used it to spread even more information.

On January 10, 1918, the House of Representatives passed the suffrage amendment. Jubilant suffragists sang on their way out of the Capitol, and the Congressional Union threw down their picket signs. The Senate delayed its vote on the suffrage amendment for ten months, eventually voting it down on October 1. Catt and her supporters refused to give up hope, insisting that votes for women were just around the corner. Rallying her organization, Catt plunged into another year of intensive campaigning.

In 1919, both the House and the Senate passed the Nineteenth Amendment, paving the way for state ratification. Catt sent telegrams to the state governors, urging them to call immediate special sessions for ratification of the amendment. She also notified the women's organizations in each state to prepare themselves for the last desperate push. That fall, she went west on her "Wake up America" tour to drum up support for the amendment. On August 20, 1920, Secretary of State Bainbridge Colby signed the

Catt, Carrie Chapman

proclamation declaring the Nineteenth Amendment officially part of the United States Constitution.

After the ratification of the suffrage amendment, Catt stepped down from the presidency of the NAWSA and was succeeded by Maud Wood Park. She continued to work with the International Woman Suffrage Alliance and founded the new League of Women Voters. Her main focus, however, was world peace; she stated "war is to me my greatest woe." Catt spoke across the country on behalf of the Versailles Treaty and the League of Nations, insisting that the United States must accept internationalism. In 1925, she founded the Committee on the Cause and Cure of War, whose purpose was to educate the public on peace issues and to pressure the U.S. government to work toward world peace. She was an influential political figure who worked for Prohibition and endorsed Herbert Hoover for the presidency in 1928, approving of his strong Prohibitionist views.

When the Nazis came to power in Germany in the 1930's, Catt worked to help Jewish victims of Nazism and was instrumental in the formation of the Protest Committee of Non-Jewish Women Against the Persecution of Jews in Germany in 1933. She helped organize the Women's Centennial Congress in 1940, and during World War II, she served as the honorary chair of the Women's Action Committee for Victory and Lasting Peace. Her last public appearance was in 1941, when she was presented with the Chi Omega Achievement Award, at a formal dinner at the White House. She retired to New Rochelle, New York, where she died on March 9, 1947, of heart failure following a gallstone operation.

Significance

A pragmatic, shrewd politician, Catt designed and implemented the plan of action that brought about the passage of the suffrage amendment at a time when its passage seemed doubtful. She worked tirelessly for the suffrage cause, giving literally thousands of speeches across the country and around the world. In her speeches, she stressed woman suffrage before suffrage for immigrants and American Indians, views that alienated some of her adherents. She would not have called herself a racist, however, since she saw herself as simply assessing realities. Her focus was always on voting rights for women; all other matters took second place.

Unlike some other suffragists, Catt did not believe the suffrage she worked so hard to establish would automatically change women's status, nor was she surprised that American politics were not transformed by the events of 1920. She believed that women's achievement of economic power, through their entrance into the workplace, would prove to be the key to improving women's lives, and she stressed the importance of women supporting other women in the workplace.

—*Catherine Francis*

Further Reading

Baker, Jean H., ed. *Votes for Women: The Struggle for Suffrage Revisited*. New York: Oxford University Press, 2002. This revisionist look at the woman suffrage movement includes an essay on Catt and the last years of the long struggle for suffrage.

Campbell, Karlyn Kohrs, ed. *Women Public Speakers in the United States, 1800-*

1925: A Bio-Critical Sourcebook. Westport, Conn.: Greenwood Press, 1993. This collection includes an article on Catt by David S. Birdsell focusing on her use of rhetoric and her persuasive powers as a speaker. Contains a chronology of Catt's speeches.

Catt, Carrie Chapman, and Nettie Rogers Shuler. *Woman Suffrage and Politics: The Inner Story of the Suffrage Movement*. 1923. Reprint. Seattle: University of Washington Press, 1969. Catt's book gives her own account of the events leading up to the passage of the suffrage amendment and provides insight into her brilliant and reasoned political strategies.

Evans, Sara M. *Born for Liberty: A History of Women in America*. New York: Free Press, 1989. While not focusing specifically on Catt, Evans provides a thoughtful overview of the woman suffrage movement in the United States and the events leading up to women's achievement of the right to vote.

Faderman, Lillian. *To Believe in Women: What Lesbians Have Done for America—A History*. Boston: Houghton Mifflin, 1999. Faderman presents profiles of early civil rights activists, including Catt, who were woman-identified and were likely lesbians.

Fowler, Robert Booth. *Carrie Catt: Feminist Politician*. Boston: Northeastern University Press, 1986. Primarily interested in Catt's ability and vision as a leader, Fowler focuses for the most part on her political career, although he does provide a brief account of her early life.

Peck, Mary Gray. *Carrie Chapman Catt: A Biography*. 1944. Reprint. New York: Octagon Books, 1975. Written by one of Catt's friends, who also worked in the suffrage movement, this first biography is the most detailed of the various accounts of Catt's life. Nevertheless, in her attempts to write an impersonal account of which Catt would approve, Peck ignores most of Catt's private life.

Van Voris, Jacqueline. *Carrie Chapman Catt: A Public Life*. New York: Feminist Press at the City University of New York, 1987. A straightforward account of Catt's life, focusing on her suffrage activism.

WILT CHAMBERLAIN

❝ *Everybody pulls for David, nobody roots for Goliath.* **❞**

Basketball player

Chamberlain revolutionized the game of basketball not only because of his height and skills but also because he was an African American in a game of white men. He was inducted into the Basketball Hall of Fame in 1978 and was chosen as one of the fifty greatest players in the history of the National Basketball Association.

Born: August 21, 1936; Philadelphia, Pennsylvania
Died: October 12, 1999; Bel-Air, California
Also known as: Wilton Norman Chamberlain (full name); Goliath; Big Dipper; Wilt the Stilt
Area of achievement: Sports

EARLY LIFE

Little has been written about the early life of Wilt Chamberlain (CHAYM-bur-layn). He was one of nine children and was a talented athlete even as a youngster. His early love was track and field, and he excelled at the long jump, shot put, and the broad jump. Chamberlain did not play his first organized game of basketball until he was in the seventh grade. At six feet eleven inches when he started Overbrook High School in west Philadelphia, he quickly found that he was built for the game. His size was unusual in the early 1950's; indeed, it was unusual for any time period.

Chamberlain became one of the most dominating high school players in Philadelphia. He broke scoring records, had a high school career total of 2,252 points, and had individual game performances of 90, 74, and 71 points. It was during high school that Chamberlain earned three nicknames that would follow him the rest of his life: Goliath, Big Dipper, and Wilt the Stilt. Wilt the Stilt was the one nickname he hated the most; his favorite was Big Dipper. Many have said that he gained this favorite nickname because he had to dip his head before entering or existing doorways.

Chamberlain was recruited by some of the best colleges and universities around the United States. He chose to enhance his talent for basketball by learning from one of the greatest coaches of the game, Forrest "Phog" Allen of the University of Kansas. (Allen had also coached Dean Smith and Adolph Rupp, who would become legendary coaches in their own right.) At the time of Chamberlain's recruitment, the university had just completed construction of its fifteen-thousand-seat Allen Field House.

LIFE'S WORK

Chamberlain led the Kansas Jayhawks through the Big Seven Conference in the 1956-1957 season. It was a tough year for Chamberlain, who endured racial taunts from fans, players, and people in general, especially when the team traveled to the South. In the 1957 Midwest Regional championship, Kansas had to defeat SMU (Southern Methodist University) in Dallas, Texas. One Jayhawks player recalled that Chamberlain was spat upon, pelted with debris, and subjected to vile racial epithets. Officials did little to maintain order. There were so many outrageous, uncalled fouls that Cham-

Chamberlain, Wilt

berlain's teammates feared that he risked serious injury simply by staying in the game. Despite the uncivil actions by opposing players and referees, Chamberlain responded by playing some his best basketball, leading Kansas to a 73-65 victory over SMU.

Kansas would go on to compete for the national title in 1957 against North Carolina in Kansas City, Missouri. The game was one of the great basketball classics of all time. Chamberlain was guarded by two players, and sometimes three, during most of the game. The championship game went into triple overtime and was decided by a pair of North Carolina free throws with only a couple of seconds on the game clock. It was a heart-wrenching loss for Kansas players and fans but also for Chamberlain personally, who would carry the stigma of the game for the rest of his college and most of his professional career. Chamberlain had failed to win the "Big Game." For many years, he considered that loss his most devastating, even though he was named the tournament's Most Valuable Player.

Chamberlain returned for his junior year but suffered a midseason injury from which he never fully recovered. The Jayhawks were not able to advance to the Big Seven league title and, ultimately, the National Collegiate Athletic Association (NCAA) tournament. Even though he earned All-American honors and averaged a record-breaking 30.1 points per game in twenty-one contests, Chamberlain left college and joined the exhibition team the Harlem Globetrotters. He was not allowed immediate entry into the National Basketball Association (NBA) because it had a rule against signing college players who left college early to play in the NBA. Chamberlain was part of the 1959 Globetrotters team that toured to sold-out crowds in the Soviet Union. Years later, Chamberlain reflected on his time as a Globetrotter with fondness, stating that it was a time he was not jeered at for being black or asked to break records. He could just be "one of the guys."

Chamberlain entered the 1959 NBA draft and made an immediate impact on the game. As a rookie with the Philadelphia Warriors (now the 76ers), he averaged an amazing 37.6 points and 27 rebounds during the regular season, while taking the NBA's Most Valuable Player (MVP) and Rookie of the Year awards. During the postseason, Chamberlain ran into his nemesis and future Hall-of-Fame player, Bill Russell of the Boston Celtics, beginning one of the greatest rivalries the NBA would ever see. While he flirted with retirement after his first season because of harsh treatment by fans, media, and other players around the league, Chamberlain decided to come back for another year.

Luckily for the Warriors Chamberlain returned. His second and third seasons in the league were even greater than his first. By the end of the 1962 season, he had averaged more than 50 points and 25 rebounds per game. He had also become the first player to break the 4,000-point barrier in a single season. Michael Jordan remains the only player to have come close to that record with 3,041 points during the 1986-1987 season. Other records that Chamberlain added to his impressive NBA résumé include his 100-point game against the New York Knicks as well as an NBA record eleven seasons as the league's rebounding leader.

Chamberlain played with several NBA teams. The Warriors moved to San Francisco in 1962, but Chamberlain was traded back to Philadelphia in 1965. As a 76er, he would earn three straight MVP awards. He also won his first championship with the 76ers in 1967. However, that feat did not keep the owners of the team happy, so they traded

Chamberlain, Wilt

Chamberlain to the Los Angeles Lakers in 1968 after the 76ers failed to maintain a 3-1 game lead against Boston in the Eastern Conference finals of that year. With the Lakers, Chamberlain would help lead the team to an impressive 69-13 record in the 1971-1972 season, a feat topped only by the Chicago Bulls in 1995-1996 (72-10), and a second NBA championship. Chamberlain would retire from the Lakers and the NBA in 1973.

SIGNIFICANCE

After retiring as a player, Chamberlain tried coaching basketball and playing volleyball. He also wrote several books, opened a nightclub in New York, invested in the stock market, and invested in horses. He also became an actor, performing in the film *Conan the Destroyer* (1984) with Arnold Schwarzenegger and singer-actor Grace Jones. Chamberlain also was a major sponsor of many highly competitive women's track, basketball, volleyball, and softball teams. He wanted to expand the popularity of women's sports. In 1978, Chamberlain was elected into the NBA Hall of Fame, holding basketball records that may never be equaled or broken.

Those persons who new Chamberlain best—teammates, coaches, and later NBA stars such as Jordan—considered Chamberlain one of the greatest players in the history of the sport. He has been called a freak of nature by some and a gentle giant by others. Regardless, Chamberlain was larger than life. His immense height and stature and his tremendous athletic abilities changed forever the way basketball would be played.

—*Karen L. Hayslett-McCall*

FURTHER READING

Bjarkman, Peter C. *The Biographical History of Basketball*. Chicago: Masters Press, 2000. This biographical history compares Chamberlain with NBA greats Michael Jordan, Bill Russell, and Oscar Robertson.

Chamberlain, Wilt, with David Shaw. *Wilt: Just Like Any Other Seven-Foot Black Millionaire Who Lives Next Door*. New York: Macmillan, 1973. This book discusses the trials and tribulations of the basketball star during the 1960's and 1970's. The book deals with the racism faced by Chamberlain as well as criticisms leveled against him because his college team failed to win the "Big Game."

Cherry, Robert. *Wilt: Larger than Life*. Chicago: Triumph Books, 2004. A fact-filled book that details the life and times of Chamberlain. Includes discussion of his feelings during big games to his behind-the-scenes activities with the many women he claims to have slept with.

Pomerantz, Gary M. *Wilt, 1962: The Night of 100 Points and the Dawn of a New Era*. New York: Crown, 2005. More like a film than a book, this publication not only focuses on the biggest game of Chamberlain's career but also uses "flashbacks" to allow readers to connect with his past. Also discusses the state of the NBA in the early 1960's and how that style of play helped change the way the game would come to be played and promoted.

Taylor, John. *The Rivalry: Bill Russell, Wilt Chamberlain, and the Golden Age of Basketball*. New York: Random House, 2005. A finely crafted historical chronicle of one of the great rivalries in the NBA's early years. Includes biographies of not only Chamberlain and Russell but also other players of the period.

César Chávez

> *If you stand on a man's head and push it into the dirt, he may not even see the heel of your boot. But if his whole face is already above ground, he can see your heel and he can see freedom ahead.*

Labor leader and social reformer

Founder of the United Farm Workers, Chávez was one of the earliest and most influential advocates of immigrant farmworkers and Latinos in U.S. history. He worked to improve conditions for farm laborers by organizing the California farmworkers' movement through events such as the Delano strike of 1965, thereby engineering the passage of the nation's first farm labor law in the late 1970's.

Born: March 31, 1927; near Yuma, Arizona
Died: April 23, 1993; San Luis, Arizona
Also known as: César Estrada Chávez (full name)
Areas of achievement: Labor movement; civil rights; social reform

EARLY LIFE

César Chávez (SEH-sahr CHAH-vehs) was born on an Arizona farm that his grandfather first cultivated during the 1880's. Hit hard by the economic chaos created by the Great Depression, the Chávez family lost the farm and a small grocery store by 1937. The young Chávez and his family joined the ranks of migrant farmworkers, traveling throughout the southwestern United States in search of work. From 1944 to 1946, Chávez served in the U.S. Navy, returning to work in the agricultural fields around Delano, California, upon his discharge. He married Helen Fabela in 1948. Chávez's direction in life changed dramatically after he met Fred Ross in 1952.

LIFE'S WORK

Ross, an organizer for the Community Service Organization (CSO), was affiliated with Saul Alinsky, founder of the Chicago-based Industrial Areas Foundation, and successfully recruited Chávez to work with his organization. Chávez's involvement with the CSO during the 1950's laid the groundwork for his founding of the United Farm Workers union.

Driven by his desire to improve conditions for farmworkers, Chávez left the CSO in 1962. He devoted all of his efforts to organizing farm laborers, founding the Farm Workers Association. Chávez recruited CSO colleague Dolores Huerta to his fledgling organization. By 1964, the National Farm Workers Association (NFWA) had one thousand members in fifty areas, mostly in California. A black eagle on a red background and the words "Viva la causa" (long live the cause) became the emblem and motto of the union. Chávez embraced the concept of nonviolence, incorporating the philosophies of Martin Luther King, Jr., and Mohandas Gandhi into his work.

Chávez, who had been organizing farmworkers to protest low wages and rent increases in the migrant labor camps, joined with other organizations in 1965 to support a strike against grape growers in Delano. Organized by the Filipino workers of the Ag-

Chávez, César

César Chávez.
(Library of Congress)

ricultural Workers Organizing Committee (AWOC), the strike was also supported by the Student Nonviolent Coordinating Committee (SNCC) and the Congress of Racial Equality (CORE). This action led to a successful five-year effort that combined the strike with a boycott of table grapes and lettuce that eventually won international support.

The grape strike helped focus national attention on the conditions endured by migrant farm laborers. In 1966, Senator Robert F. Kennedy of New York conducted Senate hearings in Delano about the agricultural industry's treatment of farmworkers. Chávez assembled a coalition of supporters that included labor unions, religious and minority groups, students, and consumers. The NFWA merged with AWOC to become the United Farm Workers (UFW), affiliated with the AFL- CIO (American Federation of Labor-Congress of Industrial Organizations). The UFW membership pledged to adhere to the principles of nonviolence, seeking peaceful methods of protest and social action such as marches, rallies, and demonstrations. In 1968, Chávez demonstrated his personal commitment to nonviolence by fasting for nearly a month when fights broke out on UFW picket lines. By 1970, most table grape growers, tired of the successful boycott, had signed contracts with the UFW.

Although Chávez gained enormous respect for his commitment to social justice and nonviolence, the agricultural industry quickly turned to the Teamsters Union in the early 1970's to negotiate more favorable contracts. Chávez called for a worldwide grape boycott. Public opinion polls indicated that by 1975, seventeen million Americans supported this effort. California, under the leadership of Governor Jerry Brown, enacted the first law governing farm labor organizing, which established the Agricultural Labor Relations Board.

In the early 1980's, UFW health clinics began to see a rise in the number of pesticide poisonings among farmworkers. Calling attention to the harmful effects of pesticide residue on produce, Chávez and the UFW embarked on a new grape boycott in 1984. In addition to marches and demonstrations, the UFW produced a film entitled *The Wrath of Grapes*, which graphically depicted the effects of pesticide poisoning. Chávez also held another hunger fast protesting the use of pesticides by the agricultural industry.

Chávez, still serving as president of the UFW, died of natural causes in 1993 at the age of sixty-six.

SIGNIFICANCE

César Chávez was not only a charismatic leader whose quiet dignity inspired the social activists of the 1960's and beyond. He also understood, from having lived in poverty, the meaning of being poor and being an immigrant in the American Southwest. He was one of the most influential Latino leaders in American history. Working conditions for farm laborers improved immeasurably because of his efforts, and he successfully engineered the passage of the nation's first farm labor law in the late 1970's.

—*Cecilia M. Garcia*

FURTHER READING

Acuña, Rodolfo. *Occupied America: A History of Chicanos*. 5th ed. New York: Pearson Longman, 2004. A general history of Chicanos, now a classic. Detailed sections on Chicano agricultural labor organizing, tracing Chicano labor struggles to the turn of the century. Also details labor struggles in other sectors of the economy. Well referenced, with an excellent index.

Ferriss, Susan, and Ricardo Sandoval. *The Fight in the Fields: César Chávez and the Farmworkers Movement*. Edited by Diana Hembree. San Diego, Calif.: Harcourt Brace, 1997. Based on the PBS documentary of the same name, this work is full of photographs and text that trace Chávez's life from his Arizona boyhood through the harsh years of drought during the Great Depression to his devotion to farmworkers' rights. Includes bibliography, index, and a map.

Griswold del Castillo, Richard, and Richard A. Garcia. *César Chávez: A Triumph of Spirit*. Norman: University of Oklahoma Press, 1995. A concise (203-page), illustrated biography for general readers, including bibliographical references and an index.

LaBotz, Dan. *César Chávez and La Causa*. New York: Pearson Longman, 2006. A concise (210-page) biography suitable for students. Starting with Chávez's childhood, the text quickly moves to experiences that shaped him as a community organizer and labor leader, focusing both on Chávez's actions and on his ideas. Includes a list of acronyms, a glossary, and notes.

Levy, Jacques E. *César Chávez: Autobiography of La Causa*. Foreword by Fred Ross, Jr. Minneapolis: University of Minnesota Press, 2007. A close history of the farmworkers' movement and Chávez's key role, from meetings at all-night cafés to days on the strike lines—a definitive, six-hundred-page history of both the movement and the man. The term "autobiography" is appropriate here because Levy had unprecedented access to Chávez and the UFW in writing this work, and his intimate portrayal has been called the closest to what Chávez himself would have written. Illustrations, index.

McGregor, Ann, and Cindy Wathen, eds. *Remembering César: The Legacy of César Chávez*. Clovis, Calif.: Quill Driver Books, 2000. A collection of accounts of this complex yet humble leader by forty-five contributors who knew him well, including Henry Cisneros, Edward James Olmos, Martin Sheen, Coretta Scott King, and Jerry Brown. Includes black-and-white photographs by George Elfie Ballis, who documented the farmworkers' movement beginning in the 1950's.

SHIRLEY CHISHOLM

" *At present, our country needs women's idealism and determination, perhaps more in politics than anywhere else.* **"**

U.S. congresswoman (1969-1983) and social activist

Chisholm was the first African American woman elected to the U.S. Congress and the first to run as a candidate for the presidency. She also was an advocate for women, children, and ethnic minorities.

Born: November 30, 1924; Brooklyn, New York
Died: January 1, 2005; Ormond Beach, Florida
Also known as: Shirley Anita St. Hill (birth name)
Area of achievement: Government and politics; civil rights; social reform

EARLY LIFE

Shirley Chisholm (CHIHZ-holm) was born Shirley Anita St. Hill in the Bedford-Stuyvesant section of Brooklyn. Her parents were West Indian emigrants. Charles Christopher St. Hill, her father, was born in British Guiana, and her mother, Ruby Seale St. Hill, was born in Barbados. Seeking relief from the 1920 famine that besieged their homeland of Barbados, both parents immigrated to New York City. Unable to save enough money from her work as a seamstress in the garment district or his work as an unskilled laborer in a burlap bag factory, the St. Hills sent three-year-old Shirley, along with her two younger sisters, Muriel and Odessa, to Barbados to live on a farm with their maternal grandmother, Emmeline Seale.

The next seven years under the stern, disciplined eye of Grandma Seale, a towering woman who was more than six feet tall, shaped Shirley's compassion and concern for the well-being of others and further strengthened her understanding that commitment to one's principles, while rewarding, could be a lonely existence. The foundation of Shirley's future academic success would be based on the structured academic environment of the British-style schools of Barbados.

The transition back into American life in 1934 at the height of the Depression was difficult for eleven-year-old Shirley. The meager resources of the St. Hill family were further divided with the arrival of baby sister Selma. The stark contrast between the warm, balmy climate of Barbados and the harsh, cold reality of New York winters made the adjustment even more painful.

The family moved from the predominantly Jewish neighborhood of Brownsville to the more ethnically diverse community of Bedford-Stuyvesant in Brooklyn. This neighborhood, which was 50 percent black, would help sharpen Shirley's developing political awareness, especially as the economic conditions of the neighborhood worsened.

Shirley's fertile teenage mind was challenged by the daily lectures and discussions with her father, who was largely self-educated. Charles St. Hill was a voracious reader who devoured several publications a day. Like many working-class blacks, he was an avid follower of the charismatic Pan-Africanist leader Marcus Garvey. Garvey's Universal Negro Improvement Association (UNIA), which promoted racial pride and encouraged self-sufficiency, was one of the most important black political and cultural movements during the early part of the twentieth century in the United States.

Upon returning to the New York school system, Shirley was held back in a lower grade because of her lack of knowledge about U.S. civic history. After receiving tutored lessons, she was promoted to her appropriate grade level and quickly surpassed the efforts of many of her classmates. Chisholm would always retain one trait from her years in the Caribbean—a slight, melodious West Indian accent. A petite young woman, Chisholm soon learned that her size tended to disguise her surprisingly forceful, straightforward manner.

Upon graduation from high school in 1942, Chisholm received offers to attend college at Vassar and Oberlin. Because of her family's limited economic resources and her own desire to remain close to home, however, she accepted a scholarship to study sociology at Brooklyn College. She involved herself in several campus organizations, notably a social club that she started after an existing club denied her membership because she was black. She also was on the debating team. These activities caught the attention of one Brooklyn College professor, who encouraged her to pursue a political career. In the end, Chisholm chose to become a teacher, a more realistic career choice for African American women of her day.

In 1946, Chisholm graduated cum laude from Brooklyn College with a degree in social work. She immediately began work on a master's degree in elementary education at Columbia University's night school. During the day, she was employed at a local nursery school. At about this time, she met a recent Jamaican transplant, Conrad Chisholm, who was working as a waiter. They were married on October 8, 1950, and settled in Brooklyn. Conrad returned to school and then became an investigator for the New York City Department of Hospital Services.

Chisholm, Shirley

For the next several years, Chisholm worked for a number of schools, including Friends Day Nursery in Brownsville and the Mount Calvary Child Care Center in Harlem. From 1953 to 1959, she served as director of the Hamilton-Madison Child Care Center in Lower Manhattan. She further distinguished herself as a bilingual educator because of her ability to communicate fluently in Spanish. Gradually, her reputation as a leading early-childhood specialist spread, resulting in increased demands for her services as a consultant to such organizations as the New York City Bureau of Child Welfare.

LIFE'S WORK

Chisholm's growing interest in politics began in the mid-1950's when she stepped up her involvement in several organizations, including the Bedford-Stuyvesant Political League, the National Association for the Advancement of Colored People (NAACP), the Democratic Women's Workshop, and the League of Women Voters. The organization that most directly sparked Chisholm's activism was the Seventeenth Assembly District Democratic Club. She became active in the district's party politics after meeting an old college associate, Wesley Holder. Holder had carved out a reputation for getting black candidates elected while still remaining loyal to the white-dominated Democratic Party agenda. Chisholm's distaste for such blind allegiance to the party machine, however, soon found her at odds with Holder and outside the club's inner circle. This situation rendered Chisholm politically inactive for a number of years.

Chisholm reentered politics in 1960 when she helped form the Unity Democratic Club with the goal of destroying the grip the party held over her district. The club specialized in mobilizing African American and Latino voters. In 1964, Chisholm succeeded in winning a seat to the New York State assembly for the Fifty-fifth District as the first black woman from Brooklyn to serve in the state legislature. During her four years in Albany, New York, she was the only woman and one of only eight black representatives in the state assembly. As a state representative, Chisholm spearheaded the passage of a bill for unemployment insurance for domestic workers and also developed a program known as Search for Elevation, Education and Knowledge (SEEK), which was designed to increase higher-education opportunities for disadvantaged youth.

Having cut her political teeth at the state level, Chisholm beat James L. Farmer, Jr., former leader of the Congress of Racial Equality (CORE), in the 1968 race for the newly created Twelfth Congressional District of Brooklyn. (Farmer was running as a Republican candidate.) This new congressional district included Chisholm's old Bedford-Stuyvesant neighborhood, a community comprising 70 percent black and Puerto Rican residents by the late 1960's. Her victory made her the first African American woman to win a seat to the U.S. Congress.

Hiring an all-woman staff, Chisholm immediately saw it as her task to be a champion for the underdog and a passionate critic of the Vietnam War. She proclaimed: "Women in the country must become revolutionaries. We must refuse to accept the old, the traditional roles and stereotypes." At the same time, she was pragmatic. She made it clear, for instance, that she would always align herself with the most able candidate. Accordingly, in 1969 she crossed party lines when she supported Republican candidate John Lindsay in his successful New York City mayoral bid.

Shirley Chisholm.
(Library of Congress)

During her fourteen years on Capitol Hill, Chisholm served on a number of congressional committees. She was originally appointed to the agricultural committee, but she aggressively lobbied to be removed from this committee because it did not serve the direct interests of her urban constituents. While on the education and labor committee, Chisholm worked diligently to increase the minimum wage standard and increase federal subsidies for day-care centers. Her proposed bill, however, was later vetoed by President Gerald R. Ford. Other noteworthy but unsuccessful legislation introduced by Chisholm called for increasing the level of federal reimbursement of state welfare programs to 70 percent and the establishment of a Department of Consumer Affairs as a cabinet-level position. In 1969 she became a founding member of the Congressional Black Caucus.

Always active in the women's movement, Chisholm was involved in the early years of the National Organization for Women. She was a founding member of the National Women's Political Caucus, was a spokeswoman for the National Abortion Rights Action League, and served as a guiding force in the formation of the National Political Congress of Black Women. From 1972 to 1976, Chisholm served on the Democratic National Committee.

Chisholm, Shirley

Convinced that the status quo power structure of American politics needed to be changed, Chisholm decided in 1972 to run for the presidency. Returning to her old campaign slogan, Unbought and Unbossed, Chisholm waged an uphill battle against the reigning power oligarchy and many old prejudices. Despite her lack of strong financial backing, Chisholm succeeded in mounting a groundbreaking campaign, assembling a coalition of blacks, feminists, and other ethnic minorities. Nevertheless, she failed to gain the largely symbolic yet influential support of the members of the Congressional Black Caucus. Moreover, never flinching at controversy, she ignored the stir that she caused when in May she visited fellow candidate George Wallace at the hospital soon after he was shot, and she accepted the endorsement of the Black Panthers despite party disapproval. (Wallace later showed his appreciation for her gesture by gathering key political support for a bill requiring minimum wage for domestic servants.)

Losing support of even many liberal Democrats, she faced many kinds of resistance. She had to file a complaint with the Federal Communications Commission to join Senator George McGovern and former vice president Hubert H. Humphrey in a televised debate for the candidates. She arrived at the 1972 Democratic National Convention with only twenty-four delegate votes; later, she received an additional 151 votes released to her by Humphrey.

Although Chisholm never expected to win, the campaign, more than any other venture, left a bitter taste, as she came to grips with the unexpected opposition she encountered from two previously supportive sectors: women's groups and black civil rights organizations. Nevertheless, Chisholm remained convinced that her nascent journey had opened the door for future generations of women as full-fledged candidates, not simply as symbols of causes. She later said that she ran for president to inspire others to question the status quo: "I ran because somebody had to do it first. In this country everybody is supposed to be able to run for president, but that has never really been true."

The year 1977 was a momentous time in Chisholm's life, highlighted by her appointment to the powerful House Rules Committee. This political success was nearly overshadowed by the dissolution of her marriage to Conrad Chisholm. After her divorce became final in 1978, she married Arthur Hardwick, Jr., a black businessman and an old acquaintance from her days in the New York state assembly. In 1979, Hardwick was involved in a serious car accident, sustaining injuries that necessitated a long recovery. This personal burden combined with the pressures of a changing political atmosphere in Washington, D.C., to place Chisholm at a challenging crossroad in her career. She retired from the House of Representatives in 1983, surrendering her seat to fellow Democrat Major Owens.

After her retirement, Chisholm essentially remained out of the political arena, limiting her involvement to endorsing and advising Jesse Jackson in his 1984 and 1988 presidential campaigns. Chisholm accepted an appointment as the Purington Professor at Mount Holyoke College, in Massachusetts, teaching classes in women's studies and political science from 1983 to 1987, and she was popular on the lecture circuit as an advocate for women's rights and for measures to relieve poverty. Her husband died from cancer in 1986. Although her outspoken nature created a stormy relationship with the Democratic Party during the 1990's, she was nominated to serve as U.S. ambassador to Jamaica by President Bill Clinton in 1993. Ill health forced her to resign soon after taking the position.

Chisholm moved to Ormond Beach, Florida, in 1991. It was there that she died on January 1, 2005, after a series of strokes. She is buried at Forest Lawn Cemetery in Buffalo, New York. In addition to her work in politics, she wrote two memoirs, *Unbought and Unbossed* (1970) and *The Good Fight* (1973), and remained a popular commentator on topics relating to equality and social justice. She received several honorary doctorates and in 1993 was inducted into the National Women's Hall of Fame.

SIGNIFICANCE

As an outspoken and charismatic maverick, Chisholm enjoyed a lengthy political career that witnessed many firsts. Her trailblazing journey inspired others to overcome seemingly insurmountable hurdles. Chisholm served as a voice for many who could not speak for themselves. Her political agenda included the introduction of legislation that improved conditions for women and their children and created employment opportunities for city residents. Undaunted and confident in her ability to wage "the good fight," Chisholm continued to pursue an independent course and was proud to remain unaccountable to either a party agenda or the narrow goals of special interests. After fourteen years on Capitol Hill, Chisholm succeeded in altering and realigning portions of the Democratic Party platform to reflect her own political beliefs. Even so, she was unable to placate some interest groups and often clashed with environmentalists, whose causes sometimes placed obstacles in the way of her efforts to secure much-needed jobs for her constituents.

Chisholm's public career inspired other women to pursue careers in politics, and her achievements helped shape and influence an entire generation of African American political leaders, most notably California congresswomen Maxine Waters and Barbara Lee and presidential candidate Jesse Jackson. In spite of the obstacles and petty feuds she faced throughout her political career, and particularly during her unconventional run for the presidency, Chisholm could look back on nearly forty years of public service as a dedicated American who had followed the advice of one of her own heroes, Eleanor Roosevelt: Never let anyone get in your way. In announcing her candidacy for the presidency on January 25, 1972, Chisholm said, "I am not the candidate of black America, although I am black and proud. I am not the candidate of the women's movement of this country, although I am a woman and equally proud of that. I am not the candidate of the political bosses or special interests. I am the candidate of the people."

—Donna Mungen

FURTHER READING

Barron, James. "Shirley Chisholm Dead at Eighty; 'Unbossed' Pioneer in Congress." *The New York Times*, January 3, 2005. Obituary for Chisholm, providing an overview of her life and accomplishments as the first black woman to serve in Congress and the first woman to seek the nomination of a major political party.

Brownmiller, Susan. *Shirley Chisholm: A Biography*. Garden City, N.Y.: Doubleday,

Chisholm, Shirley

1970. A short biography for young readers covering Chisholm's life from her return to New York City through her successful bid for a congressional seat.

Chisholm, Shirley. *The Good Fight.* New York: Harper & Row, 1973. This memoir provides Chisholm's own perspective on the prejudices and obstacles she encountered in her unsuccessful 1972 bid for the American presidency.

———. *Unbought and Unbossed.* Boston: Houghton Mifflin, 1970. Chisholm's first autobiography profiles her early life through her election to the U.S. House of Representatives for New York's Twelfth Congressional District in 1968.

Drotning, Philip T., and Wesley W. South. *Up from the Ghetto.* New York: Cowles, 1970. An entire chapter of this book is devoted to Chisholm's effort to succeed against all odds. Places her struggle within the context of efforts by other African Americans to carve out productive careers in the face of racial prejudice and discrimination.

Duffy, Susan, comp. *Shirley Chisholm: A Bibliography of Writings By and About Her.* Metuchen, N.J.: Scarecrow Press, 1988. A useful source for locating writings by Chisholm, this work also serves as a good starting point for surveying the variety of sources of biographical information on Chisholm.

Gutgold, Nichola D. *Paving the Way for Madam President.* Lanham, Md.: Lexington Books, 2006. A brief study of women presidential candidates, including Chisholm, Margaret Chase Smith, Elizabeth Dole, Carol Moseley Braun, and others.

Pinkney, Andrea Davis. *Let It Shine: Stories of Black Women Freedom Fighters.* San Diego, Calif.: Harcourt, 2000. A brief presentation of the history of African American women who fought for civil rights in the United States. Includes a chapter on Chisholm and her career as a political and social activist.

Scheader, Catherine. *Shirley Chisholm: Teacher and Congresswoman.* Hillsdale, N.J.: Enslow, 1990. A well-organized biography aimed at a juvenile audience, this work provides a straightforward overview of Chisholm's career and accomplishments and includes some discussion of her activities after leaving Congress.

Steinem, Gloria. "Shirley Chisholm: Front-Runner." *New York*, January 17, 2005. A tribute to Chisholm written by noted feminist and writer Gloria Steinem.

HILLARY RODHAM CLINTON

❝ *We must stop thinking of the individual and start thinking about what is best for society.* **❞**

U.S. presidential candidate

Clinton became the first former First Lady also to go on to a seat in the U.S. Senate and the presidential candidacy, basing her campaign on years of advocacy for children, human rights, national health care, and experience in both the executive and legislative branches of government.

Born: October 26, 1947; Chicago, Illinois
Also known as: Hillary Diane Rodham (birth name); Hillary Clinton
Area of achievement: Government and politics

EARLY LIFE

Hillary Rodham Clinton (HIHL-lah-ree RAWD-uhm KLIHN-tuhn) was born in Chicago, Illinois, to Hugh Rodham, a small-business owner, and Dorothy Howell Rodham, a homemaker. While growing up in the Chicago suburbs, Clinton was raised as a Republican and faithfully attended Sunday school at a local Methodist church. After graduating from high school in 1965, she attended Wellesley College in Massachusetts, where she majored in political science. Clinton graduated with honors on May 31, 1969, and was the first student of Wellesley to deliver a commencement address, for which she received a seven-minute standing ovation.

Clinton then attended Yale Law School and worked on the journal *Yale Review of Law and Social Action* and for the Yale Child Study Center. It was at Yale in the spring of 1971 where she met fellow law student and future U.S. president Bill Clinton. Clinton said she was drawn to his strong intellect. "He can astonish me with the connections he weaves between ideas and words and how it makes it all sound like music." After attending the 1968 Republican National Convention, Clinton decided that she could no longer be a Republican. With the nomination of Richard M. Nixon for president, the Republican Party had become too conservative.

LIFE'S WORK

After receiving her law degree in 1973, Clinton served as a staff attorney for the Children's Defense Fund. In 1974 she joined the staff House Committee on the Judiciary and advised that body on the historical and constitutional grounds for impeachment. The committee had been investigating President Nixon's involvement in the Watergate scandal.

In late 1974, Clinton joined her soon-to-be husband by moving to Little Rock, Arkansas, a decision that did not come easily for her. They both began to teach at the Fayetteville School of Law at the University of Arkansas, and they married in the living room of their Fayetteville home on October 11, 1975.

Marriage did not stop Clinton from working. In 1978, U.S. president Jimmy Carter appointed her to the board of directors of the Legal Services Corporation, and she became chair of the board in 1980. By the time her tenure ended in 1981, she had over-

Clinton, Hillary Rodham

Hillary Rodham Clinton. (AP/Wide World Photos)

seen the expansion of the corporation's funding from $90 to $300 million. In 1979 Clinton was made a partner at the Rose Law Firm in Little Rock. That same year her husband was elected governor of Arkansas. The couple moved into the governor's mansion in January, 1980.

Beginning a pattern that would continue through her husband's political career, even into the U.S. presidency, Clinton began working in state and federal government. With Bill as governor, she was appointed to the Rural Health Advisory Committee. She became an advocate for health care for the poor, and she secured federal funding for medical facilities in rural Arkansas. On February 27, 1980, Clinton gave birth to the couple's only daughter, Chelsea Victoria Clinton. After some time on maternity leave, Clinton continued working full-time for the Rose Law Firm, earning a salary larger than that of her husband, until he became president.

Clinton's husband announced his candidacy for president in late 1991. She became an active campaigner and adviser. Indeed, during the campaign, Bill had promised voters that they would get "two for the price of one" if he were elected, but the campaign started on a bad note. Allegations of past adultery by Bill had surfaced, and, during a television interview with Hillary sitting next to him, he confessed to causing "pain" in his marriage. Nevertheless, he became president in January, 1993.

Hillary Clinton promised to be a different kind of First Lady, and indeed she was. She was determined to be more than simply host to official White House functions, as First Ladies were expected to do; she would play an active role in policy making. To that end, she had an office in the West Wing of the White House, close to the Oval Office, making her the first First Lady to have her own official work space in the White House. In September, 1993, President Clinton appointed Clinton chair of the Health Care Task Force, which had been assigned the job of developing a plan for universal health care in the United States. The plan would have mandated employers to provide health care through health maintenance organizations (HMOs) and was quickly dubbed "Hillarycare" by those opposed to the plan. After harsh attacks by insurance companies and congressional Republicans, the plan failed.

During a major scandal of 1998, in which the president was accused of having a sexual relationship with White House intern Monica Lewinsky, Hillary staunchly defended her husband. She went on NBC's *Today Show* and blamed a "vast right-wing conspiracy" for the allegations against her husband. In late 1998, Bill confessed to having had an "inappropriate" relationship with Lewinsky and was impeached by Congress but not removed from office.

Also in 1998, Democratic senator Daniel Patrick Moynihan of New York announced his retirement, leading Clinton to consider running for his soon-to-be-open congressional seat. She decided to run after purchasing a home in Chappaqua, New York, to establish residence in the state. She went on to win with 55 percent of the vote, making her the first First Lady to be elected to office.

Once in the Senate, Clinton joined the Armed Services Committee and advocated the purchase of updated weaponry and personal protection for U.S. troops. She was quick to voice her support for rescue workers in New York City after the terrorist attacks of September 11, 2001. Upon returning to Washington, D.C., she became one of the first legislators to raise concerns about the health effects of the poor air quality at Ground Zero. Her work led to the awarding of compensation to first responders and their families by Congress. Clinton also worked with Republicans on such issues as veterans' health care and other benefits. She was criticized, however, for voting in October, 2002, for a resolution later used by President George W. Bush to justify the invasion of Iraq in 2003.

Significance

Clinton's popularity led to her reelection to the Senate with 67 percent of the vote in November, 2006, and she announced her candidacy for the presidency in late January, 2007. Throughout 2007 and into 2008, she was a leader in national polls on the presidential race, and she won the New Hampshire primary—the first woman to do so. By the end of January, however, it became clear that Clinton's chief contender for the Democratic nomination would be Illinois senator Barack Obama, who won South Carolina's primary on January 26. On February 5, the results of twenty-six more state primaries made it clear that the Clinton campaign's expectation that Clinton would become the frontrunner by the end of February would not be met. The fight for the nomination did not end until the last primaries, on June 3. By then, Obama had succeeded in winning enough delegates to secure his nomination.

On June 7, Clinton delivered her concession speech to a crowd of loyal supporters dismayed by her defeat. She thanked them and urged that the party come together to support Obama's candidacy. Finally, she noted the significance of the prolonged Democratic contests:

Could a woman really serve as Commander-in-Chief? Well, I think we answered that one. And could an African American really be our President? Senator Obama has answered that one. Together Senator Obama and I achieved milestones essential to our progress as a nation, part of our perpetual duty to form a more perfect union.... I ran as a daughter who benefited from opportunities my mother never dreamed of. I ran as a mother who worries about my daughter's future and a mother who wants to lead all children to brighter tomorrows. To build that future I see, we must make sure that women and men alike understand the struggles of their grandmothers and mothers, and that women enjoy equal opportunities, equal pay, and equal respect.... You can be so proud that, from now on, it will be unremarkable for a woman to win primary state victories, unremarkable to have a woman in a close race to be our nominee, unremarkable to think that a woman can be the President of the United States. And that is truly remarkable.... Although we weren't able to shatter that highest, hardest glass ceiling this time, thanks to you, it's got about 18 million cracks in it. And the light is shining through like never before, filling us all with the hope and the sure knowledge that the path will be a little easier next time. That has always been the history of progress in America.

—*David Murphy*

Further Reading

Clinton, Hillary Rodham. *An Invitation to the White House*. New York: Simon & Schuster, 2000. Clinton, in her role as traditional First Lady, details the planning and implementing of official White House functions, from formal state dinners to the annual White House Easter Egg Roll. Includes behind-the-scenes photographs.

———. *It Takes a Village*. New York: Simon & Schuster, 2006. A reprint—the tenth anniversary edition—of Clinton's 1996 book detailing her policy ideas on how to provide a better life for the children of the world.

———. *Living History*. New York: Simon & Schuster, 2003. Clinton's official memoirs of her life from birth until her election to the Senate.

Estrich, Susan. *The Case for Hillary Clinton*. New York: Regan Books, 2005. Estrich, a political analyst who worked for President Clinton and other Democrats, argues that Hillary Clinton is well qualified for the presidency.

Ty Cobb

> **❝** *Baseball is . . . no pink tea, and mollycoddles had better stay out. It's a struggle for supremacy, a survival of the fittest.* **❞**

Baseball player

Cobb's aggressive and inventive style of play in baseball enabled him to set records in every phase of the game. Many believe that he is the greatest player in the history of baseball.

Born: December 18, 1886; Narrows, Georgia
Died: July 17, 1961; Atlanta, Georgia
Also known as: Tyrus Raymond Cobb (full name)
Area of achievement: Sports

Early Life

Ty Cobb (ti kawb), born in Narrows, Georgia, was proud of his southern heritage and his family. His father was a teacher and a landowner, and an ancestor had been a Civil War general who died at the Battle of Fredricksburg. Cobb even claimed George Washington as a distant ancestor. As he was born only twenty years after the defeat of the Confederacy, however, Cobb's proud claim to southern gentility was mocked by the reduced circumstances and opportunities of the area. Cobb's father wanted him to attend college or, perhaps, to win an appointment to West Point, but the young Cobb was determined to be a baseball player. He saw baseball as a career in which he might excel, while he could not hope to compete with his father's record in academic studies. Baseball players were not, however, socially accepted at the time; even some of the greatest ballplayers were not admitted to many hotels or restaurants. Cobb, however, had a burning desire to try this career, so his father gave him six fifteen-dollar checks and sent him off to join the minor-league team in Augusta.

Cobb played for Augusta for only a few games before he was released because a veteran had returned to the team. Cobb did, however, manage to catch on with the Anniston, Alabama, club, and he performed so well that he was sent back to Augusta. His batting average was only .237 for Augusta that year, but he impressed everyone with his aggressive style of play. He was given a contract for the next year for $125 a month; finally, he was a professional baseball player.

Cobb began to become the Ty Cobb known to history while at Augusta. His new manager, George Leidy, worked with him every day on his hitting, running, and fielding. Cobb was not a natural ballplayer as Babe Ruth and Shoeless Joe Jackson were; he had to learn to hit and to take advantage of the weaknesses of others on the base paths or in the batter's box. In addition, he was not very tall or heavy; he stood only five feet ten inches tall and weighed about 155 pounds at the time, but he compensated for his size with desire for excellence and dedication to the game.

Cobb, Ty

LIFE'S WORK

Cobb had a mediocre rookie year in the major leagues; he played centerfield with the Detroit Tigers for forty-two games and batted a meager .240. In addition, he had a serious conflict with many of the established veterans on the Tigers. Some of those involved later called the treatment Cobb received normal rookie hazing, but Cobb took it personally. He thought there was a clique of players who wanted to drive him off the team. In his typical fashion, Cobb fought back against the veterans—and, in so doing, may have made the problem worse. He challenged any or all of the contentious veterans to a fight and almost got himself traded because of the dissension on the team. Apparently, Cobb never spoke to Wahoo Sam Crawford even though he played next to him for a number of years.

Cobb claimed that he benefited from his trouble with the veterans; since he was isolated, he did not have an opportunity to waste his time at shows or pool halls but could use that time improving his base-running and hitting skills. He hit .320 and stole twenty-three bases in his second year, 1906.

The season of 1907 was even more successful for Cobb and the Tigers. He hit .350 to lead the league in batting average for the first time, and the Tigers won their first pennant. The Tigers lost the World Series to the Chicago Cubs in four straight games, however, and Cobb only hit .200. On the other hand, the feud between him and the veterans ended, although Cobb was never popular with the players on his team and was hated by the players and fans in other American League cities, especially Philadelphia. The reasons for this conflict and dislike are easy to find. Cobb tried to take advantage of every situation with which he was confronted, whether it was a catcher's arm, a pitcher's attention, an infielder's position, or a sportswriter's influence. This aggressiveness and combativeness carried over to his relationships with his teammates and opponents. He was not pleasant or sociable but a loner with an obsession to excel and to take advantage of less dedicated players. Most of Cobb's autobiography is a defense of his side of the many fights and quarrels he got into. He never gave an inch and retaliated when he thought he had been wronged, and it did not take much to make him believe that someone had wronged him.

In 1908, Cobb held out for a salary of $5,000; this was the first of many holdouts for Cobb. He did not trust his owner and tried to get whatever he could out of the recalcitrant boss. Cobb was determined that no one was going to get the best of him on the field or off it. He did win his second straight batting championship that year, although his average was twenty-five points lower; the Tigers also won the pennant again, but they lost the World Series once more to the Chicago Cubs. Cobb had his best series and batted .368.

Cobb won his third straight batting title in 1909, and the Tigers won their third straight pennant. In the World Series with the Pittsburgh Pirates, it was rumored that Cobb had a personal duel with the great shortstop of the Pirates, Honus Wagner. Cobb was quoted as saying "I'll show that Kraut," and some said he threatened to "spike" Wagner (injure him with his cleated shoes) when he came down to steal. Cobb denied making such threats, but the public both expected and believed that Cobb would spike the popular Wagner. Cobb batted only .231, however, and the Tigers lost again. Cobb was never to play on a winning World Series team and would not be on another pennant winner for the rest of his career.

Cobb's performance continued to be superior over the next fifteen years. He won nine straight batting championships from 1907 to 1915 with a personal high of .420 in 1911. He stole a record high of ninety-six bases in 1915. These records remained individual achievements, however, since the Tigers could not win another pennant. Meanwhile, controversy continued to follow Cobb. He was accused of spiking the very popular Frank "Home Run" Baker, thus unleashing the wrath of the Philadelphia fans. He beat up Buck Herzog in a fight in his hotel room and got into a brawl with an umpire, Billy Evans, under the stands. Cobb claimed that he was merely acting in self-defense, but his playing style and attitude seemed to invite trouble. Anyone who played as savagely as he did was bound to spend his life with controversy.

Cobb hit .371 in 1915, but he lost the batting title to Tris Speaker. He did come back to win the next three batting championships for a record total of twelve championships. In 1921, after a dismal finish for the Tigers, Cobb was offered the position of player-manager. Cobb accepted, although he claimed that the job was forced on him. Cobb certainly was an unlikely candidate for the manager's job since he was baseball's supreme example of a loner who seemed more interested in individual than team records. One reason Cobb was offered the job was the sudden popularity of Babe Ruth as a home-run hitter. Apparently, the Detroit management hoped to increase the fans' interest by making Cobb more visible and more powerful. Cobb spent four years as manager of the Tigers, but under his tenure the team never won a pennant. In his autobiography, Cobb claimed that the reason the Tigers did not win was that the management refused to buy or trade for the players he believed were needed. Cobb does seem to be very defensive in this book; his problems or failures were always attributable to someone else, while his victories were results of his efforts alone.

In 1926, Cobb was suddenly released by the Tigers because of a betting scandal. The charge was that Cobb and Speaker, who was also released by Cleveland, conspired to fix a game between the Tigers and Indians and then bet on it. Cobb claimed that it was only a rumor started by a player he had released from the team and the charges were never proved, but Cobb was himself released and then joined the Philadelphia A's for his last two years as a baseball player.

Once Cobb ended his career as a ballplayer, he never had another job in organized baseball. He was, by this time, wealthy from his investments, especially those he made in Coca-Cola. He was married twice but divorced twice, and he was not very close to his children. The fierce loner on the field became an angry loner off the field. Cobb's collaborator on his autobiography, Al Stump, has written of Cobb's last years, and Stump's picture of the once-great ballplayer reduced to near madness is terrifying.

Significance

There is little doubt that Cobb was one of the greatest baseball players of all time, a judgment certified by his selection as the first man inducted into the Baseball Hall of Fame. He set records for base-stealing and batting that seem unlikely to be broken. Many of them, such as the record for having made the most hits, and another for having stolen the most bases, in a single season and in a career, have been broken, but it is doubtful that anyone will match his nine consecutive batting championships or his lifetime batting average of .367.

Cobb, Ty

However, admittedly, Cobb was most successful as a player. It has been suggested that Cobb's fearsome, alienating personality was the result of an intense desire to win, at any cost, the approval of his father, who had died when Cobb was young. In the course of achieving greatness, however, he did not evoke among fans and colleagues the love that Babe Ruth inspired or the admiration that Joe DiMaggio received, but only fear and loathing.

—*James Sullivan*

FURTHER READING

Alexander, Charles C. *Ty Cobb*. New York: Oxford University Press, 1984. A highly critical scholarly biography. The author, a historian, drew heavily on newspapers and secondary sources for this detailed account of Cobb's life and career. Well documented, generally fair-minded, but not engagingly written. Includes bibliography.

Appel, Marin, and Burt Goldblatt. *Baseball's Best: The Hall of Fame Gallery*. New York: McGraw-Hill, 1977. A good, brief summary of Cobb's career.

Bak, Richard. *Peach: Ty Cobb in His Time and Ours*. Ann Arbor, Mich.: Sports Media Group, 2005. An account of Cobb's life on and off the baseball field, illustrated with 150 photos. Focuses on the treatment of Cobb in popular culture and on public memory.

Cobb, Ty, with Al Stump. *My Life in Baseball: The True Record*. Garden City, N.Y.: Doubleday, 1961. Cobb's view of the important events in his career; he is scathing about his enemies and scornful of modern baseball.

Holmes, Dan. *Ty Cobb: A Biography*. Westport, Conn.: Greenwood Press, 2004. Provides an overview of Cobb's life and career, as well as a time line, a bibliography, and a chapter about the evolution of Cobb's baseball legacy.

Ritter, Lawrence S. *The Glory of Their Times*. New York: Collier Books, 1966. Ritter interviewed a number of players from Cobb's era, including Wahoo Sam Crawford; they are quite critical of Cobb's ferocity, but none disputes his greatness. This is one of the finest books ever written on baseball.

Stump, Al. "Ty Cobb's Wild Ten-Month Fight to Live." In *The Baseball Reader*, edited by Charles Einstein. New York: Thomas Y. Crowell, 1980. A revealing portrait of Cobb's demanding and difficult personality by the person who helped Cobb write his autobiography.

BESSIE COLEMAN

" *The air is the only place free from prejudices.* "

Aviator

Coleman was the first female African American pilot, performing stunts and aerial acrobatics before audiences in the United States and Europe. Facing explicit racism and ridicule from critics, she still earned a living with her skills as a flamboyant barnstorming flyer. She inspired many to pursue aviation as a career at a time when that career was almost unthinkable for blacks, and for women. Her career preceded by several years that of aviator Amelia Earhart.

Born: January 26, 1893; Atlanta, Texas
Died: April 30, 1926; Jacksonville, Florida
Also known as: Queen Bess
Area of achievement: Aviation

EARLY LIFE

Bessie Coleman (KOHL-muhn) was born to farm laborers George Coleman and Susan Coleman in Atlanta, Texas, near the Arkansas border. Three of her paternal great grandparents were American Indian. When Coleman was two years old, her parents constructed a home in Waxahachie, Texas, south of Dallas. The racism the family faced because of their African and American Indian ancestry led George to move the family north to Indian Territory (now Oklahoma). Although George emphasized that the family would experience better socioeconomic conditions in Indian Territory, Susan stayed in Texas with several of her youngest children, including Coleman.

Intrigued by mathematics, Coleman walked several miles to the closest school for African American children when she did not have to pick cotton to earn wages for her family. Because her mother was illiterate, she read the Bible aloud to her family. Her mother encouraged literacy by subscribing to a bookmobile so her children had access to books. Coleman preferred biographies of notable African Americans such as Harriet Tubman. After completing eight grades, Coleman wanted an advanced education. By 1910, she enrolled in the Oklahoma Colored Agricultural and Normal University (now Langston University). Unprepared for college curricula, however, Coleman had to take basic courses. For a writing class, she read news accounts of pioneer male and female pilots.

Coleman returned to Texas in 1911 because she could not afford additional tuition. She started working as a housekeeper and launderer. The next year, she read a newspaper report that aviator Harriet Quimby (whom she admired), the first licensed U.S. female pilot and the first woman to fly across the English Channel, had died in an airplane crash.

LIFE'S WORK

In 1915, Coleman traveled by train to Chicago. Frustrated with her monotonous life in Texas, Coleman had written to her brothers, who were living in Chicago, about her plans to move there. She started working as a manicurist in a barbershop, tending to

Coleman, Bessie

customers including Robert Abbott, publisher of the *Chicago Defender*, an African American newspaper. (Abbott would later support her financially.) While reading news articles, she learned about white female pilots who flew locally. She also read about African American World War I pilot Eugene Bullard. Coleman's brother, John, who had served in France during World War I, told her he had seen women aviators in that country. Aspiring to learn to fly, Coleman applied to flight schools in the United States but was refused admission because of her gender and race. Aware of Coleman's ambition, Abbott urged her to travel to France, where racism and sexism would not be as much of a hindrance, offering to assist her financially. Preparing to travel overseas, Coleman took French language courses.

In November, 1920, Coleman sailed to France and went to Le Crotoy to study with Gaston Caudron and René Caudron at École d'Aviation des Frères Caudron (aviation school of the Caudron brothers). Although Coleman saw a fatal crash soon after she started instruction, she decided she would risk such hazards. In ground school, she learned mechanics and other basic skills before taking flying lessons in a Nieuport biplane. On June 15, 1921, the French Fédération Aéronautique Internationale granted Coleman license #18310, the first license presented by the agency to an American woman. Moreover, she became the first African American woman to earn a pilot li-

Bessie Coleman. (NASA)

cense anywhere. Coleman took additional lessons at Le Bourget Field in Paris until September, when she returned to the United States. Soon, the African American press was reporting her accomplishments on its front pages.

Coleman hoped for a career as a barnstormer, popular entertainment in the 1920's, needing to raise enough money to establish an aviation school for African Americans in the United States. Because stunt flying was so popular, Coleman sailed again to Europe in February, 1922, to learn aerobatics. She flew for six months in France, Germany, and Holland. Newsreels of her flights impressed American audiences and captured the attention of *The New York Times*, which published a brief article about her stunt flying in its August 14, 1922, edition. She had just arrived in New York to prepare for her first public flights in the United States.

On September 3, Coleman debuted at the Curtiss Field air show on Long Island, New York. Her next performance was held October 15 at Chicago's Checkerboard Airdrome, where her family watched. Later, Coleman offered to let people fly with her for five dollars. Also, she agreed to drop advertisements while she flew for the Coast Tire and Rubber Company, visiting executives in Oakland, California. After a visit to Los Angeles to examine military surplus aircraft, she purchased a Curtiss JN-4 biplane, flown during World War I.

On February 4, 1923, Coleman's engine in her recently acquired aircraft malfunctioned, causing her to crash in Santa Monica, California. While her fractured bones healed for three months, she continued her plans for what would be called the Coleman School of Aeronautics, placing advertisements in newspapers. After Coleman recovered, she barnstormed in Texas, including her hometown, and other cities in the South, Midwest, and New England. She spoke and showed films of her flights and emphasized that aviation was a possible career for African Americans, especially women. Furthermore, she refused to fly at a show if its ticket sales and stands were segregated by race.

Coleman prepared a media release that re-created her history, hoping to garner more media attention. African American newspapers published articles featuring Coleman, but other media often mocked her and her flying, if they mentioned her at all. Her stylish French flight clothing and showmanship attracted crowds who were astonished to see an African American aviator. To further her publicity, she permitted African American preachers to fly with her without cost, shrewdly realizing they would publicize her flights to their congregations.

In contrast to most pioneering female pilots, who were white and had money, Coleman had to seek sponsors and borrow or purchase used planes, which sometimes had technical problems. In early 1926, John Betsch, representing the Jacksonville, Florida, Negro Welfare League, invited Coleman to fly at a May festival. She also spoke at African American schools in Jacksonville, urging children to pursue their goals. Because Coleman was unable to lease a plane because of her race, a Florida patron provided her funds to buy and transport a plane from Texas. Mechanic William D. Wills flew the airplane to Jacksonville, commenting that he had experienced some glitches in the air. Although aware of dangers, Coleman decided that performing to raise money merited the risks.

On Friday, April 30, Coleman and Wills took off from Paxon Field for a morning

Coleman, Bessie

practice flight, during which Coleman surveyed the area for parachute landing sites while Wills piloted. Attaining an altitude of three thousand feet, the airplane jolted into an unstoppable nosedive. Coleman, who had not fastened her safety belt, was ejected from the plane and fell approximately fifteen hundred feet to her death. The airplane plunged to the ground, killing Wills. Mourners in Florida and Chicago attended funerals for Coleman, who was buried in Chicago's Lincoln Cemetery.

SIGNIFICANCE

In the face of racism and sexism, Coleman's perseverance inspired generations of pilots, including Willa Brown, the first African American woman to earn a commercial pilot license and who started a Chicago flight school, and Mae Jemison, the first African American female astronaut. Determined to fly, Coleman exulted in knowing that Jim Crow laws were not applicable in the air. Her efforts to educate and encourage African Americans about aviation led many to pursue careers as pilots or as professionals in other areas of aviation.

People began preserving Coleman's legacy soon after her death. In 1929, William J. Powell, a World War I veteran, started the Bessie Coleman Aero Club, a school in Los Angeles to teach flying. Bessie Coleman Aero Clubs soon formed around the country to promote African American aviation and stage air shows solely with African American pilots. Powell began distributing the *Bessie Coleman Aero News* in May, 1930. The Lambert-St. Louis International Airport depicted Coleman in its mural, *Black Americans in Flight*. On April 27, 1994, the U.S. Postal Service issued a stamp that featured Coleman.

—*Elizabeth D. Schafer*

FURTHER READING

Freydberg, Elizabeth, and Amelia Hadley. *Bessie Coleman: The Brownskin Lady Bird*. New York: Garland, 1994. Based on the author's doctoral dissertation. Discusses contemporary women pilots, African American efforts to integrate flight, and popular culture and entertainment. Examines the importance of France to Coleman's training and career. Includes facsimiles of advertisements and correspondence.

Hardesty, Von, and Dominic Pisano. *Black Wings: The American Black in Aviation*. Washington, D.C.: Smithsonian Institution Press, 1987. Chronicles a 1984 National Air and Space Museum exhibition on black aviators. Includes a photograph of Coleman, a discussion of her significance as a pioneer African American pilot, and an examination of her influence on other minority aviators.

Lebow, Eileen F. *Before Amelia: Women Pilots in the Early Days of Aviation*. Washington, D.C.: Brassey's, 2002. Profiles pioneering European and U.S. female flyers, describing situations that Coleman and her contemporaries experienced regarding training and earning licenses, promoting barnstorming, enduring negative public opinion, and risking accidents and death. Illustrations, bibliographical essay, and an appendix that provides license information.

Rich, Doris L. *Queen Bess: Daredevil Aviator*. Afterword by Mae Jemison. Washington, D.C.: Smithsonian Institution Press, 1993. Thoroughly researched account of

Coleman's life and endeavors based on primary sources. Corrects errors perpetuated in other biographical accounts. Illustrations from Coleman's family, newspapers, and letters complement the text.

Walker, Mike. *Powder Puff Derby: Petticoat Flyers and Flying Flappers*. Chichester, England: John Wiley & Sons, 2003. Discusses Coleman in a chapter also examining the life of German test pilot Hanna Reitsch. Emphasizes their struggles and challenges and how Coleman overcame racial and gender discrimination.

BILL COSBY

" Decide that you want it more than you are afraid of it. "

Entertainer and actor

Following his time as a touring stand-up comedian, Cosby turned to television to star in the 1960's action series I Spy *and other shows, bringing with him controversy over representations of race on television. He is best known for his role as the family patriarch in the hit television series* The Cosby Show.

Born: July 12, 1937; Philadelphia, Pennsylvania
Also known as: William Henry Cosby, Jr. (full name)
Areas of achievement: Theater and entertainment; education; social reform

EARLY LIFE

Bill Cosby (KAWZ-bee) grew up in Philadelphia, Pennsylvania, and attended Mary Channing Wister Elementary School, Fitz-Simmons Junior High School, and Central High School. Long before becoming one of the most beloved American comedians turned actor-producer-author, his interests were in athletics, specifically track, baseball, basketball, and football. In tenth grade, he transferred to Germantown High School, though a poor report card inspired him to join the U.S. Navy, leading to assignments at military bases in Quantico, Virginia, and Bethesda Naval Hospital in Maryland. During his time in the service, Cosby also became more serious about school and earned his high school diploma through correspondence classes.

In 1961, Cosby entered Philadelphia's Temple University on a track scholarship and picked up a bartending job at a local club, The Cellar, where he began incorporating humor into his service routines. Eventually he took his comedy to the venue's stage. His performances continued with a warm reception throughout the next year. By his sophomore year in college, the athlete turned stand-up star left the university and moved to New York City, developing his routine at the Big Apple's Gaslight Café (a Greenwich Village staple) in 1962.

After being showered with adulation back home, Cosby began booking dates throughout 1962 in other cities, eventually capturing the attention of NBC's *The Tonight Show*. He appeared on the late-night television hit show in 1963 and released his comedy album *Bill Cosby Is a Very Funny Fellow, Right!* with Warner Bros. Records,

Cosby, Bill

paving the way for a series of other audio projects and his eventual transition from the stage to the screen. Cosby also married his longtime girlfriend Camille Hanks in 1964, with whom he had five children.

LIFE'S WORK
Cosby's big break came in 1965 when he secured a role on NBC's *I Spy*. He was an African American newcomer starring alongside an established white actor, Robert Culp. Aside from making television history, *I Spy* was incredibly popular because of its James Bond-style format. However, the program was not without controversy. Cosby's role was criticized for being "equal" to that of Culp to the exclusion of the tension-filled race relations between such colleagues of the time period.

Following the show's demise in 1968, Cosby became a recurring guest host on *The Tonight Show*, returned to the touring world, and prepared for his very own series. He starred in the comedic sitcom *The Bill Cosby Show* for NBC in 1969, which got off to a strong ratings start but was cut from the schedule in 1971 following mixed critical reviews. Cosby then returned to college and earned a doctorate in education from the University of Massachusetts in 1972. However, his yearning for performing on television soon returned, prompting the 1972 revival of *The New Bill Cosby Show*; it was canceled after one year.

Cosby professionally regrouped with the Saturday morning CBS cartoon series *Fat Albert and the Cosby Kids*, which he hosted and based, partly, on his own experiences growing up as a child. The show ran from 1972 to 1977 initially and was "rebranded" as *The New Fat Albert Show* (running from 1979 to 1984). Though the animated program was incredibly successful, the actor's programs for adults, including the short-lived ABC variety show *Cos* in 1976 and a few barely noticed films, floundered.

Good fortune, though, came with Cosby's comedy concert and subsequent video *Himself* in 1983, which explored his life as an adult growing up and as a family man. The project proved to be so popular that he took many of those same ideas and presented them to NBC for a television series. NBC bought the concept and even agreed to let Cosby star in and produce his own program. *The Cosby Show* first aired in 1984 with the creator playing Cliff Huxtable (a medical doctor), who, along with his wife, Claire, a lawyer (played by Phylicia Rashad), raise five children. Each episode not only focused on the characters' trials and triumphs but also showcased an African American family as an educated and successful unit that addressed and broke racial stereotypes. *The Cosby Show* aired through the 1992 season, becoming one of the world's most beloved and critically acclaimed television programs of all time.

Though Cosby continued throughout the 1990's into the twenty-first century with a variety of projects, these projects never matched his peak period with *The Cosby Show*. From 1992 to 1993, he hosted the game show *You Bet Your Life*, starred in several additional films, and launched the short-lived *The Cosby Mysteries* in 1994 (a television show that combined the suspense of his *I Spy* days with his signature comedic spark). Two years later, he reunited with Rashad on CBS for *Cosby* (which cast the pair as seniors). This series lasted only four years and proved to be incomparable to the hit *The Cosby Show*.

During that program, Cosby also made headlines because of a series of personal

Bill Cosby.
(AP/Wide World Photos)

tragedies, including the murder of his son, Ennis William, in 1997 in Los Angeles. The death of his son was followed by allegations by Autumn Jackson that Cosby was her father (an allegation found to be false). The twenty-two-year-old Jackson was sent to prison on extortion charges. In 2006, Cosby faced a lawsuit from a woman accusing him of sexual assault, but the accusation did not lead to criminal charges. Undaunted by these incidents, the multifaceted entertainer remains active on the road, regularly touring theaters and colleges and universities, often speaking boldly about racial and family topics (in particular, he addresses issues faced by African Americans). He also celebrated the release of the film *Fat Albert* in 2004, along with the DVD release of several television programs (including *The Bill Cosby Show* and *The Cosby Show*).

SIGNIFICANCE

In addition to his achievements as an entertainer and actor, Cosby has succeeded as a positive role model for African Americans and as a spokesperson for ending racial stereotyping and race discrimination. He has earned his fair share of controversy, however, by focusing his acting career around the breaking down of racial stereotypes as a way to encourage African Americans to raise the bar for themselves. In doing so, he has sent a message of empowerment to people of all races, colors, and creeds.

As an entertainer Cosby has provided countless hours of not only laughter-filled shows but also programs with messages of social reform for viewers across the globe. Additionally, his original programming had a mixture of artistry and ingenuity that continues to influence comedians, actors, producers, and authors who have tried to reproduce his type of work.

—Andy Argyrakis

FURTHER READING

Cosby, Bill. *Childhood*. New York: Putnam, 1991. An insightful and humorous look at raising children, told through Cosby's role as a parent. Includes general observations that occasionally popped up in *The Cosby Show* plots.

———. *Cosbyology: Essays and Observations from the Doctor of Comedy*. New York: Hyperion, 2001. Cosby provides a look back on his lengthy career and personal life spanning the subjects of school, sports, and work. Provides hopeful words on aging and comedic elixirs against worrying.

———. *Fatherhood*. New York: Dolphin/Doubleday, 1986. The comic tells a series of personal and fictional tales about raising children and settling into the role of becoming a father. Many of these stories surfaced in his television programs.

———. *I Am What I Ate . . . and I'm Frightened!!! And Other Digressions from the Doctor of Comedy*. New York: HarperCollins, 2003. A twist on his more traditional topics, Cosby dabbles in the world of dietary practices, citing several of his worst vices, including the hoagies he would eat during *The Cosby Show*.

———. *Love and Marriage*. New York: Doubleday, 1989. Dedicated with the inscription "For Camille Forever," this text simultaneously addresses Cosby's love life and advice for other couples.

———. *Time Flies*. New York: Dolphin/Doubleday, 1987. Cosby reflects on his life and family. Includes assessments of society's progression with regard to race relations.

Coutreyer, Keith. *Bill Cosby Ain't Crazy*. Bloomington, Ind.: AuthorHouse, 2006. A quick look at the issues discussed by Cosby over the years, particularly the need to raise children with proper parenting and a nurturing environment.

Dyson, Michael Eric. *Is Bill Cosby Right? Or Has the Black Middle Class Lost Its Mind?* New York: Perseus Books, 2006. An independent critical assessment of the racial commentaries offered by Cosby both on and off screen. Though not particularly flattering toward Cosby, the text also explores some of the most relevant issues in black culture.

Haskins, James. *Bill Cosby: America's Most Famous Father*. New York: Walker, 1988. A straightforward, biographical-style book chronicling Cosby's rise to fame in all aspects of the entertainment industry.

CRAZY HORSE

" *One does not sell the earth on which the people walk.* **"**

Native American war leader

The greatest of the Lakota (Sioux) war chiefs, Crazy Horse led his people in a valiant but futile struggle against domination by the white Americans and white culture. He fought to the last to hold his native land for the Indian people.

Born: 1842?; Black Hills (now in South Dakota)
Died: September 5, 1877; Fort Robinson, Nebraska
Also known as: Curly; His Horse Looking; Tashunca-uitko (birth name)
Area of achievement: Native American affairs

EARLY LIFE

Crazy Horse's Lakota name was Tashunca-uitko. Little is known of his early life; even the date of his birth and the identity of his mother are uncertain. He was probably born in a Lakota camp along Rapid Creek in the Black Hills during the winter of 1841-1842. Most scholars believe that his mother was a Brule Lakota, the sister of Spotted Tail, a famous Brule chief. His father, also called Crazy Horse, was a highly respected Oglala Lakota holy man. Tashunca-uitko was apparently a curious and solitary child. His hair and his complexion were so fair that he was often mistaken for a captive white child by soldiers and settlers. He was first known as "Light-Haired Boy" and also as "Curly." At the age of ten, he became the protégé of Hump, a young Minneconjou Lakota warrior.

When he was about twelve years old, Curly killed his first buffalo and rode a newly captured wild horse; to honor his exploits, his people renamed him "His Horse Looking." One event in Crazy Horse's youth seems to have had a particularly powerful impact on the course of his life. When he was about fourteen, His Horse Looking witnessed the senseless murder of Chief Conquering Bear by the troops of Second Lieutenant J. L. Grattan and the subsequent slaughter of Gratton's command by the Lakota. Troubled by what he had seen, His Horse Looking went out alone, hobbled his horse, and lay down on a high hill to await a vision. On the third day, weakened by hunger, thirst, and exposure, the boy had a powerful mystical experience that revealed to him that the world in which men lived was only a shadow of the real world.

To enter the real world, one had to dream. When Curly was in that world, everything seemed to dance or float—his horse danced as if it were wild or crazy. In this first crucial vision, His Horse Looking had seen a warrior mounted on his (His Horse Looking's) horse; the warrior had no scalps, wore no paint, and was naked except for a breech cloth; he had a small smooth stone behind one ear. Bullets and arrows could not touch him; the rider's own people crowded around him, trying to stop his dancing horse, but he rode on. The people were lost in a storm; the rider became a part of the storm with a lightning bolt on his cheek and hail spots on his body. The storm faded, and a small red-tailed hawk flew close over the rider; again the people tried to hold the rider back, but still he rode on. By the time he revealed this vision a few years later, His Horse Looking had already gained a reputation for great bravery and daring. His father

Crazy Horse

and Chips, another holy man, made him a medicine bundle and gave him a red-tailed hawk feather and a smooth stone to wear.

When Curly went into battle thereafter, he wore a small lightning streak on his cheek, hail spots on his body, a breech cloth, a small stone, and a single feather; he did not take scalps. He was never seriously wounded in battle. His Horse Looking's father, in order to honor his son's achievements, bestowed his own name, Crazy Horse, upon the young man (he then took the name Worm) and asserted to his people that the Lakota had a new Crazy Horse, a great warrior with powerful medicine.

The Grattan debacle had one immediate effect other than the vision: It resulted in brutal reprisals by the Bluecoats. On September 3, 1855, shortly after Crazy Horse had experienced the vision, General W. S. Harney attacked the Brule camp in which Crazy Horse was living with Spotted Tail's people. The soldiers killed more than one hundred Indians (most of them women and children), took many prisoners, and captured most of the Lakota horses. Crazy Horse escaped injury and capture but was left with an abiding hatred of the whites. Because the major white invasion of the West did not begin until after the Civil War, Crazy Horse spent his youth living in the traditional ways: moving with the seasons, hunting, and warring with the other Plains Indians.

LIFE'S WORK

The solitary boy grew into a strange man who, according to Black Elk,

> would go about the village without noticing people or saying anything. . . . All the Lakotas (Sioux) liked to dance and sing; but he never joined a dance, and they say nobody heard him sing. . . . He was a small man among the Lakotas and he was slender and had a thin face and his eyes looked through things and he always seemed to be thinking hard about something. He never wanted many things for himself, and did not have many ponies like a chief. They say that when game was scarce and the people were hungry, he would not eat at all. He was a queer man. Maybe he was always part way into that world of his vision.

Crazy Horse and the Oglala north of the Platte River lived in relative freedom from the white man's interference until 1864. From the early 1860's, however, there was ever-increasing pressure from white settlers and traders on the U.S. government to guarantee the safety of people moving along the Oregon and Santa Fe trails and to open the Bozeman Road that ran through the Lakota country.

The military began preparations early in 1865 to invade the Powder River Indian country; General Patrick E. Connor announced that the Indians north of the Platte "must be hunted like wolves." Thus began what came to be known as Red Cloud's War, named for the Lakota chief who led the Lakota and Cheyenne warriors. General Connor's punitive expedition in 1865 was a failure, as were subsequent efforts to force the free Indians to sign a treaty. In 1866, General Henry B. Carrington fortified and opened the Bozeman Road through Lakota territory. By 1868, having been outsmarted, frustrated, and beaten again and again by Red Cloud's warriors, the United States forces conceded defeat, abandoned the forts, closed the Bozeman Road, and granted the Black Hills and the Powder River country to the Indians forever.

Crazy Horse rose to prominence as a daring and astute leader during the years of

Crazy Horse

Red Cloud's War. He was chosen by the Oglala chiefs to be a "shirt-wearer," or protector of the people. All the other young men chosen were the sons of chiefs; he alone was selected solely on the basis of his accomplishments. Crazy Horse played a central role in the most famous encounter of this war. On December 21, 1866, exposing himself repeatedly to great danger, he decoyed a troop of eighty-one of Colonel Carrington's men, commanded by Captain William J. Fetterman, into a trap outside Fort Phil Kearny. All the soldiers were killed.

Red Cloud's War ended in November, 1868, when the chief signed a treaty that acknowledged that the Powder River and Big Horn country were Indian land into which the white man could not come without permission. The treaty also indicated that the Indians were to live on a reservation on the west side of the Missouri River. Red Cloud and his followers moved onto a reservation, but Crazy Horse and many others refused to sign or to leave their lands for a reservation; Crazy Horse never signed a treaty.

As early as 1870, many whites who were driven by reports of gold in the Black Hills began to venture illegally into Indian territory. Surveyors for the Northern Pacific Railroad protected by United States troops also invaded the Black Hills in order to chart the course of their railway through Indian land. Crazy Horse, who became the war chief of the Oglala after Red Cloud moved onto the reservation, led numerous successful raids against the survey parties and finally drove them from his lands. The surveyors returned in 1873; this time they were protected by a formidable body of troops commanded by Lieutenant Colonel George A. Custer.

In spite of a series of sharp attacks, Crazy Horse was unable to defeat Custer, and the surveyors finished their task. In 1874, Custer was back in Indian territory; he led an expedition of twelve hundred men purportedly to gather military and scientific information. He reported that the hills were filled with gold "from the roots on down"; the fate of the Indians and their sacred hills was sealed. Not even the military genius of their war chief, their skill and bravery, and their clear title to the land could save them from the greed and power of the white men.

During the years between the signing of the 1868 treaty and the full-scale invasion of Indian lands in 1876, Crazy Horse apparently fell in love with a Lakota woman named Black Buffalo Woman, but she was taken from him through deceit and married another man, No Water. Crazy Horse and Black Buffalo Woman maintained their attachment to each other over a period of years, causing some divisiveness among the Lakota and resulting in the near-fatal shooting of Crazy Horse by No Water. Crazy Horse eventually married an Oglala named Tasina Sapewin (Black Shawl) who bore him a daughter. He named the child They Are Afraid of Her, and when she died a few years later, he was stricken with grief.

Because of the reports concerning the great mineral wealth of the Black Hills, the U.S. government began to try to force all the Indians to move onto reservations. On February 7, 1876, the War Department ordered General Philip Sheridan to commence operations against the Lakota living off of reservations. The first conflict in this deadly campaign occurred March 17, when General George Crook's advance column under Colonel Joseph J. Reynolds attacked a peaceful camp of Northern Cheyennes and Oglala Lakota who were on their way from the Red Cloud Agency to their hunting grounds. The survivors fled to Crazy Horse's camp.

Crazy Horse

Crazy Horse took them in, gave them food and shelter, and promised them that "we are going to fight the white man again." Crazy Horse's chance came in June, when a Cheyenne hunting party sighted a column of Bluecoats camped in the valley of the Rosebud River. Crazy Horse had studied the soldiers' ways of fighting for years, and he was prepared for this battle. General Crook and his pony soldiers were no match for the Lakota and Cheyenne guided by Crazy Horse. Crook retreated under cover of darkness to his base camp on Goose Creek.

After the Battle of Rosebud (June 17), the Indians moved west to the valley of the Greasy Grass (Little Bighorn) River. Blackfoot, Hunkpapa, Sans Arc, Minneconjous, Brule, and Oglala Lakota were there, as well as the Cheyenne—perhaps as many as fifteen thousand Indians, including five thousand warriors. The soldiers had originally planned a three-pronged campaign to ensnare and destroy the Indians. Crook's withdrawal, however, forced General Alfred Terry to revise the plan. On June 22, he ordered Colonel John Gibbon to go back to the Bighorn River and to march south along it to the Little Bighorn River. Custer and the Seventh Cavalry were to go along the Rosebud parallel to Gibbon and catch the Indians in between. General Terry, with the remaining forces, would trail them and provide whatever support was necessary. General Terry expected that Gibbon and Custer would converge and engage the enemy on June 26.

General Custer and his troops arrived on June 25, and Custer elected to attack the Indian encampment without waiting for Gibbon's column. His rash decision was fatal to him and to the Seventh Cavalry. The Lakota and Cheyenne, led by Crazy Horse and Gall, Sitting Bull's lieutenant, crushed Custer; more than 250 soldiers died. Perhaps Crazy Horse and Gall could have defeated the troops of Gibbon and Terry as well, but they were not committed to an all-out war, as were the whites, and they had had enough killing, so they moved on, leaving the soldiers to bury their dead.

The Battle of the Little Bighorn is recognized as a great moment in the history of the Lakota nation, but it also proved to be a sad one, for it confirmed the U.S. government's conviction that in spite of the Treaty of 1868, the free Indians must be either confined to a reservation or annihilated. In the brutal days that were to follow, Crazy Horse clearly emerged as the single most important spiritual and military leader of the Lakota.

The federal government's response was swift: On August 15, Congress enacted a new law that required the Indians to give up all rights to the Powder River country and the Black Hills. Red Cloud and Spotted Tail succumbed to what they took to be inevitable and signed documents acknowledging that they accepted the new law. Sitting Bull and Gall fought against the forces of General Crook and Colonel Nelson Miles during the remainder of 1876 but decided to take their people to Canada in the spring of 1877. Crazy Horse alone resolved to stay on his own lands in the sacred Black Hills.

General Crook led an enormous army of infantry, cavalry, and artillery from the south through the Powder River country in pursuit of Crazy Horse, and Colonel Miles led his army from the north, looking for the Oglala war chief. Crazy Horse was forced to move his village from one place to another in order to avoid the Bluecoats. He had little ammunition or food, the winter was bitterly cold, and his people were weary. In December, he approached Colonel Miles's outpost and sent a small party of chiefs and warriors with a flag of truce to find out what the colonel's intentions were. The party was attacked as it approached the outpost; only three Lakota survived. Miles's brutal intentions were made quite clear, and Crazy Horse was forced to flee again.

Colonel Miles caught up with the Lakota on January 8, 1877, at Battle Butte; in spite of his lack of ammunition and the weakened condition of his warriors, Crazy Horse was able, through bravery and superior tactics, to defeat Miles. Crazy Horse and his band escaped through the Wolf Mountains to the familiar country of the Little Powder River. The soldiers decided to cease their military operations until spring, but they redoubled their efforts to persuade the Indians to surrender. Numerous emissaries were sent throughout the northern lands with pack trains of food and gifts to tempt the suffering Lakota and Cheyenne into coming in to the security of the agencies.

Many small bands yielded to these entreaties, but Crazy Horse only listened politely and sent the messengers home. His fame and his symbolic value to the Indians grew daily; the longer he resisted, the more important he became to the thousands of Indians now confined to reservations. When Spotted Tail himself came to entice them to give up, Crazy Horse went off alone into the deep snows of the mountains in order to give his people the freedom to decide their own fate. Most chose to stay with their leader, but Spotted Tail did persuade Big Foot to bring his Minneconjous in when spring came.

In April, General Crook sent Red Cloud to plead with Crazy Horse and to promise him that, if he surrendered, the Lakota would be given a reservation in the Powder River country, where they could live and hunt in peace. At last, Crazy Horse gave in; the suffering of his people was so great, the prospects of renewed conflict with Crook and Miles so grim, and the promise of a Powder River reservation so tempting that he led his band to the Red Cloud Agency, arriving in an almost triumphal procession witnessed by thousands on May 5, 1877.

Predictably, Crazy Horse did not like living at the agency, and General Crook did not make good on his promise of a Powder River reservation. Black Shawl died, and Crazy Horse married Nellie Larrabee, the daughter of a trader. The more restive Crazy Horse became, the more concerned the government became, and the more vulnerable the chief was to the plots of his enemies. Wild rumors that Crazy Horse planned to escape or to murder General Crook circulated.

The government officials decided that it would be best to arrest and confine the war chief. On September 4, 1877, eight companies of cavalry and four hundred Indians, led by Red Cloud, left Fort Robinson to arrest Crazy Horse and deliver him to the fort. Crazy Horse attempted to flee but was overtaken and agreed to go and talk with Crook. When it became clear to him that he was not being taken to a conference but to prison, Crazy Horse drew his knife and tried to escape. He was restrained by Little Big Man and other followers of Red Cloud, and Private William Gentles bayoneted him. He died during the early hours of September 5; his father, Worm, was at his side. Crazy Horse's parents were allowed to take the body; they rode into the hills and buried their son in a place known only to them.

Later that fall, the Lakota were forced to begin a journey eastward to the Missouri River and a new reservation/prison. Among the thousands of Indians were Crazy Horse's Oglala. After approximately seventy-five miles of travel, the Oglala, two

Crazy Horse

thousand strong, broke from the line and raced for Canada and freedom. The small cavalry contingent could only watch as these Lakota fled to join Sitting Bull—manifesting, in their refusal to submit to the white man, the spirit of Crazy Horse.

SIGNIFICANCE

Crazy Horse, like numerous other Indian patriots, was a martyr to the westward expansion of the United States, to the unity and technological superiority of the white culture, to its assumed racial and cultural superiority, and to the greed of white Americans. He also seems to have been a truly exceptional and admirable man; he was the greatest warrior and general of a people to whom war was a way of life. He provided a powerful example of integrity and independence for the Indians during a very difficult period of their history; he never attended a peace council with the whites, never signed a treaty, never even considered giving up his lands: "One does not sell the earth upon which the people walk." Furthermore, he seems to have been a basically selfless man who was genuinely devoted to the greater good of his people, to protecting his native land and his traditional way of life. To quote Black Elk:

> He was brave and good and wise. He never wanted anything but to save his people, and he fought the Wasichus (the whites) only when they came to kill us in our own country.... They could not kill him in battle. They had to lie to him and kill him that way.

When Crazy Horse was born, the Lakota were a strong, proud, and free people; they were skilled horsemen and masters of war and hunting. The rhythms of their lives were the rhythms of the seasons and of the game they hunted. They venerated nature and cherished individual freedom and achievement. When Crazy Horse died, the Lakota were still proud, but they were no longer truly strong or free. Freedom, independence, and cultural integrity were realities for Crazy Horse in his youth, but particularly after the tragic battle at Wounded Knee in December, 1890, freedom and independence and integrity as a people have only been dreams for the Lakota—dreams in which the legend and spirit of Crazy Horse, fierce, intelligent, indomitable, continue to play a vital part, as is evidenced by Peter Matthiessen's choice of a title for his angry and eloquent 1983 study of the contemporary struggles of the Lakota: *In the Spirit of Crazy Horse*.

—*Hal Holladay*

FURTHER READING

Ambrose, Stephen E. *Crazy Horse and Custer: The Parallel Lives of Two American Warriors*. New York: Anchor Books, 1996. Ambrose, a historian who has written several popular biographies and military histories, examines the similarities between Crazy Horse and Custer.

Andrist, Ralph K. *The Long Death: The Last Days of the Plains Indians*. New York: Macmillan, 1964. The story of the military conquest of the Plains Indians, the Lakota as well as others. A vivid, meticulous, and well-written survey. Excellent maps.

Brown, Dee. *Bury My Heart at Wounded Knee: An Indian History of the American West*. New York: Holt, Rinehart and Winston, 1971. A revisionist history of the

West from 1860 to 1890 told from an Indian point of view. Crucial to a full understanding of American history and the destruction of the culture and civilization of the American Indian. Crazy Horse's story is one of many.

Connell, Evan S. *Son of the Morning Star: Custer and the Little Bighorn.* San Francisco: North Point Press, 1984. An intelligent and thorough reconstruction of what might have happened and why at the Little Bighorn on June 25, 1876. A fascinating study of the major participants in that historic battle, focusing on Custer.

Hinman, Eleanor. "Oglala Sources on the Life of Crazy Horse." *Nebraska History* 57, no. 1 (1976). Interviews with Oglala Indians who witnessed various events in the life of Crazy Horse. Provides particularly interesting insights into his conduct in battle, his feud with No Water, and his death.

Josephy, Alvin M., Jr. *The Patriot Chiefs: A Chronicle of American Indian Resistance.* New York: Viking Press, 1958. The life stories of outstanding Indian leaders, including Crazy Horse, Tecumseh, and Chief Joseph. A good brief biography. Places Crazy Horse's struggle in the context of the heroic and tragic resistance of Indians to the white man throughout North America.

Marshall, Joseph, III. *The Journey of Crazy Horse: A Lakota History.* New York: Viking Press, 2004. Marshall, a Lakota who was raised on the Rosebud Sioux Reservation, drew on the recollections of his grandfather and other oral histories to produce this biography.

Neihardt, John G. *Black Elk Speaks.* Lincoln: University of Nebraska Press, 1961. A fascinating document that contains the life story of an Oglala holy man as told by himself. Black Elk was a member of Crazy Horse's tribe and was present at the Little Bighorn, as well as at Fort Robinson when Crazy Horse was killed. Invaluable insights into the Lakota culture and way of life.

Olson, James C. *Red Cloud and the Sioux Problem.* Lincoln: University of Nebraska Press, 1965. Well-documented appraisal of Indian affairs in the Western plains during the 1860's and the 1870's. Thorough account of relations between the Lakota and the federal government. Judicious treatment of contending leaders.

Sajna, Mike. *Crazy Horse: The Life Behind the Legend.* New York: John Wiley & Sons, 2000. Detailed biography, offering new perspectives on Crazy Horse's role in the battle at the Little Bighorn and his eventual surrender and murder.

Sandoz, Mari. *Crazy Horse: The Strange Man of the Oglalas.* New York: Alfred A. Knopf, 1941. A comprehensive and authoritative biography in which the author attempts to tell not only the chief's story but also that of his people and culture. Told from Crazy Horse's point of view.

Vaughn, Jesse W. *Indian Fights: New Facts on Seven Encounters.* Norman: University of Oklahoma Press, 1966. A flawed study of seven significant battles that occurred between 1864 and 1877 in Wyoming and Montana. Vaughn's accounts of the Fetterman Massacre and Major Reno's part in the Battle of the Little Bighorn are quite useful.

Crockett, David

David Crockett

❝ *Be always sure you are right; then, go ahead.* **❞**

Frontiersman and politician

As a congressman from western Tennessee and the author of a best-selling autobiography, Crockett became the most celebrated backwoodsman in the United States. His heroic death at the Battle of the Alamo transformed him into a legendary frontier hero.

Born: August 17, 1786; Greene County, Tennessee
Died: March 6, 1836; The Alamo, San Antonio, Texas
Also known as: Davy Crockett
Areas of achievement: Exploration; government and politics; military

Early Life

David Crockett (KRAW-kiht) grew up in the poverty-stricken frontier regions of eastern Tennessee, where his father operated a tavern. His formal education was limited to a six-month period during which he worked two days per week for the village schoolmaster in return for board and four days of schooling. Crockett's manuscript letters prove that he learned basic literacy in the one hundred or so days he attended school, although his spelling was always erratic and his grasp of grammatical rules was uncertain. On August 14, 1806, shortly before his twentieth birthday, he married Mary Finley, with whom he had three children. Crockett moved to central and then western Tennessee in search of better land, supporting his family through subsistence farming and his skill as a hunter.

When the Creek Indian War broke out in 1813, Crockett enlisted and served as a scout until March of 1815, during which time he was promoted to sergeant. Crockett's duties took him south into Alabama and eventually to Pensacola, Florida. The army was poorly supplied and constantly short of food; Crockett spent much time hunting to help feed his companions. He observed with some bitterness the effect of his lack of social rank when the commander of his regiment ignored his warning that an Indian attack was imminent but acted immediately when an officer reported the same information the next day.

Shortly after Crockett's return from the war, his first wife died. Within one year he had remarried. His new wife, Elizabeth Patton, was a widow with two young children of her own, as well as a substantial inheritance of cash and slaves. Her funds enabled Crockett to move to Lawrence County and set up a gristmill and a distillery in the spring of 1817. For a while he seemed to prosper, but his businesses did not succeed. In 1831 he had to sell some slaves in order to reduce his debts. Crockett was appointed a justice of the peace by the state of Tennessee in November, 1817. The next year his neighbors elected him colonel of the fifty-seventh regiment of militia in Lawrence County. In 1821 he was elected to the state legislature and was reelected in 1823. He failed to win his bid for Congress in 1825, but in 1827 he went to Washington, D.C., for the first of his three terms in the House of Representatives.

Life's Work

Crockett's tall tales and backwoods humor entertained and attracted the press, which covered his activities, real or imaginary, in detail and spread his fame across the country. Many of the reports were intentional exaggerations, such as claiming that his reputation as a hunter had spread so wide among the animals that when he aimed his rifle at a treed raccoon the animal meekly climbed down and surrendered, or that while traveling to the 1829 session of Congress he had waded into the Ohio River and towed a disabled steamboat back to shore. He was reputed to have shot forty-seven bears in one month and was said to ride alligators for exercise. When Crockett supported President Andrew Jackson, the Whig papers sneered at him as an example of an uncivilized westerner and alleged that he drank the water from his finger bowl at a White House dinner. After Crockett broke with Jackson, the Whig papers began to compliment him while the Jacksonian press, which had praised his rustic wisdom and virtue, began to attack him.

As much as he enjoyed his celebrity status and was willing to perform the part of the ignorant but shrewd backwoodsman, Crockett took seriously his work as a congressman. He was frustrated by his lack of success in advancing the interests of his subsistence farming constituents. In the state legislature, he had championed the cause of the western Tennessee squatters against the eastern Tennessee landholding aristocrats. In Congress he broke with the Jackson forces when they failed to support his Tennessee Vacant Land Bill, which would have allowed those living on and improving federal lands in western Tennessee to secure title to the land. When Crockett opposed Jackson's Indian Removal Bill in 1830 and also proposed using federal funds to aid poor American Indians living in his district, the break with Jackson was complete. Jacksonian opposition led to Crockett's loss in the 1831 election; however, he succeeded in winning a third term in 1833.

After his break with the Jacksonians, Crockett wrote an autobiography with the assistance of Thomas Chilton, a Kentucky congressman who lived in the same Washington, D.C., boardinghouse as Crockett. Crockett freely acknowledged Chilton's help and informed his publisher that Chilton was entitled to half the royalties from the work. The book was a campaign autobiography intended to help Crockett's bid for reelection. Like Benjamin Franklin's autobiography, a copy of which Crockett owned, the work described the rise of a self-made man who overcame hardships to achieve greatness.

Crockett's own voice and language dominated the book, which was a fairly accurate account of his life, apart from some exaggerations about his military career in the Creek Indian War and his prowess as a hunter. Crockett described several battles during which he was not present. The work portrayed a humorous braggart and backwoods trickster who rose to national prominence as a congressman. The language of the autobiography faithfully reproduced southwestern frontier idioms, and the book included some of the first printed examples of frontier humor. For example, when Crockett returned from an extended hunting trip to discover that his companions had reported him dead, he remarked, "I know'd this was a whapper of a lie, as soon as I heard it."

Narrative of the Life of David Crockett of the State of Tennessee appeared in 1834 and was an immediate success. Within one year, it went through seven editions, including one in London, England, and twelve new printings were released in 1835. Encouraged by the success of the autobiography, Crockett permitted the Whigs to publish, under his name, two books attacking the Jacksonians. *An Account of Colonel Crockett's Tour to the North and Down East* (1835) described the reception of Crockett's speeches attacking Jackson during his tour of Whig cities in the North. *The Life of Martin Van Buren* (1835) was a vitriolic satire of the Jacksonian candidate for president in 1836. Crockett wrote neither book, and they failed to attract the public.

The autobiography's success as a literary work did little to advance Crockett's political career. He reacted bitterly when he lost a hotly contested election for his House seat in August, 1835. He told his constituents that they could go to hell and that he was going to Texas. On November 1, Crockett and several of his friends left for Texas, where American settlers had revolted against Mexico. He hoped to find fertile land where he and his family could rebuild their fortunes and perhaps revive his political career in the new republic. Crockett was welcomed wherever he went in Texas, and in January, 1836, he took an oath of allegiance to the provisional government of Texas that entitled him to vote and run for office during the pending constitutional convention. He then joined the rebel army and moved south to San Antonio in early February.

The president of Mexico, General Antonio López de Santa Anna, determined to crush the Texan rebellion, arrived at San Antonio with some 2,400 troops. The Texan defenders, numbering 183, barricaded themselves in an old mission building, the Alamo, where they held out from February 23 to March 6. Santa Anna had ordered his men to take no prisoners, and none of the defenders survived. Crockett's active role and bravery during the siege is attested in all authentic accounts. However, the legendary scene in which Crockett, out of ammunition and using his broken rifle as a club, dies surrounded by the bodies of a dozen Mexicans he has shot is mythical. Documentary evidence shows that Crockett, along with a half-dozen other defenders, was captured after resistance ceased and brought before Santa Anna, who angrily ordered him executed.

SIGNIFICANCE

The process of turning David Crockett, eccentric backwoods congressman, into Davy Crockett, legendary superhero, began while Crockett was still alive. His colorful personality had made him one of the best-known politicians of the 1830's. Even before his death, exaggerated stories about him, some based on tall tales he loved to tell to amused Washington reporters and congressmen, had begun to circulate. Many were included in a work that Crockett repudiated, although it was published under his name: *Sketches and Eccentricities of Colonel David Crockett of West Tennessee* (1833). The work contained incidents that appeared to be based on Crockett's anecdotes.

Crockett's heroic death elevated him to almost mythic status. Crockett's publisher immediately commissioned Richard Penn Smith to write a fictional diary of Crockett's activities in Texas called *Col. Crockett's Exploits and Adventures in Texas, Written by Himself* (1836). Only the first two chapters, which were based on letters Crockett wrote to his publishers, are authentic. The fifty Crockett almanacs printed between 1835 and 1856 completed the transformation of Crockett into an American legend. These pamphlets, along with the usual calendars, weather predictions, domestic hints, and farming suggestions, included improbable Crockett hunting stories and endowed him with superhuman powers. Crockett is credited with saving the earth one winter when the entire planet froze: Crockett thawed the earth's axis with hot bear grease and kicked it loose again. Another tale claimed that he deflected Halley's comet from a collision course by climbing the Allegheny Mountains and twisting the tail off the comet.

Davy Crockett also figured as a fantastically successful hunter in six nineteenth century dime novels. A play that ran for over two thousand performances between 1874 and 1896 portrayed him as a handsome frontiersman whose gentlemanly conduct won the love of a wealthy neighbor's daughter. The most influential presentation of the legendary figure was Walt Disney's 1955 television production and film, *Davy Crockett, King of the Wild Frontier*, which used many of the legends that had grown up over the years to portray him as an ideal frontiersman and martyr of the Alamo. The production set off an enormous fad: Every young boy seemed to need a coonskin hat and fringed Crockett-style jacket so he could copy his hero. Crockett had become an icon of American heroism, and historians who wrote about the factual Crockett were assailed for subverting the image of this truly American hero.

—*Milton Berman*

FURTHER READING

Crockett, David. *Narrative of the Life of David Crockett of the State of Tennessee*. Knoxville: University of Tennessee Press, 1973. A facsimile edition with annotations and an introduction by James A. Shackford and Stanley J. Folmsbee. The insightful annotations make this the most useful version of Crockett's autobiography.

Davis, William C. *Three Roads to the Alamo: The Lives and Fortunes of David Crockett, James Bowie, and William Barret Travis*. New York: HarperCollins, 1998. Davis examines the lives of these three disparate men, describing what brought them to Texas and how they died there.

Derr, Mark. *The Frontiersman: The Real Life and the Many Legends of Davy Crockett*. New York: William Morrow, 1993. Derr supplies an informative and entertaining narrative of Crockett's life.

Hauck, Richard Boyd. *Crockett: A Bio-Bibliography*. Westport, Conn.: Greenwood Press, 1982. This book contains an excellent biography of Crockett and an analysis of the style and content of his writings.

Kilgore, Dan. *How Did Davy Die?* College Station: Texas A&M University Press, 1978. Kilgore provides a careful analysis of the evidence concerning the way Crockett died.

Lalire, Gregory J. "David Crockett." *American History* 38, no. 6 (February, 2004): 16. A modern tribute to Crockett, the politician and soldier.

Lofaro, Michael A., ed. *Davy Crockett: The Man, The Legend, The Legacy, 1786-1986*. Knoxville: University of Tennessee Press, 1985. This volume deals mostly with the legends about Crockett, from the early almanacs through Disney's television series of the 1950's.

Lofaro, Michael A., and Joe Cummings, eds. *Crockett at Two Hundred: New Perspectives on the Man and the Myth*. Knoxville: University of Tennessee Press, 1989. This book contains ten scholarly articles on Crockett's life, death, and writings, along with an extensive bibliography.

Shackford, James Atkins. *David Crockett: The Man and the Legend.* Edited by John B. Shackford. Chapel Hill: University of North Carolina Press, 1956. This is the definitive scholarly biography of Crockett, although it needs to be brought up to date by Kilgore's book on Crockett's death.

WALTER CRONKITE

❝ *And that's the way it is....* **❞**

Broadcast journalist

Cronkite, a television journalist and anchor for, most famously, CBS Evening News with Walter Cronkite *from 1962 to 1981, earned the title "the most trusted man in America" from his viewing audience for his objective and judicious coverage.*

Born: November 4, 1916; St. Joseph, Missouri
Also known as: Walter Leland Cronkite, Jr. (full name)
Area of achievement: Journalism

EARLY LIFE

Walter Cronkite (KRON-kit) was born in St. Joseph, Missouri, to Walter Cronkite and Helen Fritsche Cronkite. His paternal forebears were Dutch, descending from Hercks Seiboutzen Krankheidt. Cronkite grew up in Houston, Texas, where his family had moved when he was ten years old. As a student at San Jacinto High School, he worked on the school's newspaper, *Campus Club*, and won a Texas Interscholastic Press Association newswriting contest. The young Cronkite worked hard to earn his own spending money by selling newspapers and *Liberty* magazines. He was influenced by *American Boy* magazine, leading him to pursue a career in journalism.

Cronkite enrolled at the University of Texas at Austin (1933-1935) and worked on the *Daily Texan* (the university's newspaper). He also worked as a cub (novice) reporter for major newspapers in their respective capital bureaus during the Depression. His mentors, such as Gordon Kent Shearer, bureau chief for United Press (now United Press International, or UPI) in Austin, influenced Cronkite to be accurate and fair. Cronkite accepted a full-time position with the *Houston Press* in 1935, then moved to the *Houston Post*. He became a newswriter and editor for Scripps-Howard and UPI in Houston, Kansas City, Dallas, Austin, El Paso, and New York. He worked in radio broadcasting in Oklahoma City for an affiliate of NBC (station WKY), covering football games, then joined the United Press in 1937 and earned a good reputation as a World War II correspondent covering military action in North Africa and Europe from 1942 to 1945.

Cronkite also assisted in reopening the United Press news bureaus in postwar Amsterdam and Brussels as a foreign correspondent, and went to Nuremberg, Germany, as chief correspondent to report on the Nazi war crimes trials. He then worked in Moscow as the UP bureau manager from 1946 to 1948 and was a lecturer and magazine contributor in 1948 and 1949. In 1940 he had married Mary Elizabeth Maxwell (who died in 2005), and he had three children with her—Nancy Elizabeth, Mary Kathleen, and Walter Leland III.

LIFE'S WORK

Cronkite became a national network correspondent in 1950 with CBS News in Washington, D.C. His program, *CBS Evening News with Walter Cronkite*, was a well-respected broadcast that ran from 1962 to 1981 and was headquartered in New York. Cronkite also hosted the *CBS Morning Show*. His reputation as a respected journalist was sealed because of his coverage of the major news events of the 1950's and 1960's: the Korean War; the 1952 presidential election; summit meetings in Vienna, Paris, and Moscow; the Cuban Missile Crisis; the Vietnam War; the assassination of President John F. Kennedy; the Medgar Evers story; the assassination of Robert F. Kennedy; Martin Luther King's assassination and the Civil Rights movement and struggle; the Apollo 11 landing on the Moon; the Watergate scandal and trial; and the anniversary of D day, which he had covered originally as a UP war correspondent in 1945.

Cronkite traveled the globe to get his stories. He journeyed to war theaters in Vietnam and returned after the Tet Offensive convinced that the United States should negotiate an end to the Vietnam War. Soon after Cronkite's return, and after his news report on Vietnam, President Lyndon B. Johnson decided not to run for reelection and attempted to end the war.

Cronkite also narrated the historical documentary television series *You Are There* (1953-1957), *Twentieth Century* (1957-1967), and *Eyewitness to History* (1961-1962). As anchor of the *CBS Evening News* in 1962, Cronkite competed with the NBC team of Chet Huntley and David Brinkley, but by the late 1960's he surpassed them in television ratings and viewer numbers. He had become an icon with a reputation for truthfulness and honesty, came to be known as Uncle Walter, and ended each evening's program with the now-iconic phrase "and that's the way it is." His calm, firm, and assured baritone voice informed his viewers of national and world news.

During many news-making moments, Cronkite often reported nonstop. One example was his twenty-seven-hour coverage of the Moon landing of Neil Armstrong and Buzz Aldrin. He believed the Moon landing to be one of the biggest stories of the twentieth century and the one event that would be remembered five hundred years later. Cronkite traveled to the Middle East and was instrumental in bringing Egypt's Anwar el-Sadat and Israel's Menachem Begin together to negotiate a peace agreement.

Cronkite hosted several television specials, including *Vietnam: A War That Is Finished* (1975); *The President in China* (1975); *In Celebration of US* (1976); *Our Happiest Birthday* (1977); *Why the World* (1981) for the Public Broadcasting Service (PBS); *Universe* (1982) for CBS; *Solzhenitsyn: 1984 Revisited* (1984); *Dinosaur* (1991); and *The Holocaust: In Memory of Millions* (1993) for the Discovery Channel. He received the Peabody Award in 1962 and won several Emmy Awards. He received the William A. White Award for journalistic merit in 1969 and the George Polk Journalism Award in 1971. He won the Gold Medal from the Radio and TV Society in 1974, and the Alfred I. Dupont-Columbia University Award in broadcast journalism

Cronkite, Walter

in 1978. He was awarded the Presidential Medal of Freedom by Jimmy Carter in 1981.

Following his retirement as anchor for CBS on March 6, 1981, he wrote a news column through King Features Syndicate. He took on special assignments, such as anchoring news coverage of the second spaceflight of John Glenn in 1998 (as he had of Glenn's first flight), and returned periodically as a special correspondent for CBS and for Cable News Network (CNN). He broadcast a series of commentaries for National Public Radio (NPR) on historic events such as Dwight D. Eisenhower's role in the D day campaign, as well as the Gulf of Tonkin incident, the 1968 Democratic Convention, the Vietnam War, and the terrorist skyjacking in 1970.

Cronkite believed journalists held a great responsibility because they reported what was to become "history"—a nation's collective memory. His news commentary, too, was deeply meaningful to his audience. On March 9, 2004, Cronkite broadcast a reflective commentary on NPR that recalled an earlier CBS television show produced by Fred Friendly and Edward R. Murrow that questioned the bullying tactics of Senator Joseph R. McCarthy, who engineered a campaign of terror against alleged communists in government and in the entertainment industry. Cronkite applauded his news colleagues' refusal to be politically intimidated, and he praised their justice-seeking reportage. His professional ethics and his own pursuit of the truth set the standard for the type of news reporting he described in his 2004 NPR commentary.

After retiring from CBS as anchor, Cronkite served on the board of directors of CBS and continued to work for several networks as a news correspondent. He even performed the voice of Benjamin Franklin for the children's animated series *Liberty's Kids*. He also created a series of historical videotapes, CDs and DVDs for *The Vietnam War with Walter Cronkite* (1985-1987), *Walter Cronkite Remembers the Twentieth Century* (1997-1998), *All You Want to Know About the United States Constitution* (1998), and *You Are There* (2004). Cronkite received the Harry S. Truman Good Neighbor Award for his "truth in broadcasting" in 2004.

Among Cronkite's many books are *Vietnam Perspective: CBS News Special* (1965), *The Challenge of Change* (1971), *Eye on the World* (1971), *A Reporter's Life* (1996), and *Around America* (2001). He wrote the commentary to CBS photographer Irving Haberman's *Eyes on an Era* (1995) and contributed book forewords to *The Rise of the Computer State* (1983), *Places of Power* (2000), *The Heart of Success* (2000), and *Architects of Peace* (2002), as well as the forewords to several children's books on U.S. presidents. The Walter Cronkite School of Journalism and Mass Communication was established at Arizona State University in recognition of Cronkite's life achievements as a journalist, critic, and author.

Significance

Cronkite pioneered television news, elevated broadcast journalism to the highest levels of honesty and integrity, and increased the popularity of broadcast news among television viewers during the turbulent 1960's and 1970's and into the early 1980's. His voice was one of reason, recording some of the twentieth century's most memorable events. His stature and style provided a strong role model for future commentators—in print and on radio and television.

Cronkite also was an excellent researcher who checked his facts. He was an affable and photogenic television personality, and his broadcasts were clear, genuine, authoritative, and accurate. He deftly worked within the time constraints of television, which broadcasted his image around the world. He strived to maintain objectivity, and he shunned bias in reporting.

—*Barbara Bennett Peterson*

FURTHER READING
Aaseng, Nathan. *Walter Cronkite*. Minneapolis, Minn.: Lerner, 1981. A praising, well-written, yet factual biography.
Cronkite, Walter. *Eye on the World*. New York: Cowles, 1971. Cronkite surveyed the previous decades' major historical events at home and abroad, selecting certain events for comment.
_____. *A Reporter's Life*. New York: Alfred A. Knopf, 1996. A most valuable autobiographical source, giving anecdotes from Cronkite's personal life and professional career and revealing the friends who contributed to his success.
_____. *Vietnam Perspective: CBS News Special Report*. New York: Pocket Books, 1965. Cronkite's name will forever be linked to reporting the Vietnam War, which he accomplished with informed analysis and historical clarity in this small primer.
Westman, Paul. *Walter Cronkite: The Most Trusted Man in America*. Minneapolis, Minn.: Dillon Press, 1980. This work discusses Cronkite's credibility and his career with CBS.

CLARENCE DARROW

" *I am an agnostic; I do not pretend to know what many ignorant men are sure of.* **"**

Attorney

The most renowned defense attorney of his time, Darrow won a number of significant verdicts in difficult cases, including the Scopes trial, while espousing unpopular causes.

Born: April 18, 1857; Kinsman, Ohio
Died: March 13, 1938; Chicago, Illinois
Also known as: Clarence Seward Darrow (full name)
Area of achievement: Law and jurisprudence

EARLY LIFE
The fifth of eight children (one of whom died in infancy), Clarence Darrow (DAYR-roh) was born in Kinsman, a small town in northeastern Ohio. His father, Amirus Darrow, was a carpenter who increasingly supplemented his income by working as an undertaker; he was also an avid reader who scattered books on all subjects throughout the house. In addition to his own commitment to reading and self-instruction, young Darrow

owed some of his later outlook to his father's unorthodoxy and skepticism toward revealed religion. His mother, Emily Eddy Darrow, bestowed much attention on him and, until her death when he was fifteen, had great hopes for his success. He was educated at a local school and spent his summers playing baseball or working on a farm. At the age of sixteen, Darrow enrolled at Allegheny College, in Meadville, Pennsylvania; he gave up his studies there after a year and for a time was employed as a schoolteacher. In 1877, he spent a year at the University of Michigan's law school. Apparently, Darrow grew weary of formal education, and he spent a further year working and studying at a law office in Youngstown, Ohio. After a brief and apparently perfunctory oral examination, Darrow was admitted to the Ohio bar, at the age of twenty-one.

With his career now fairly started, Darrow took a fancy to Jessie Ohl, the daughter of a prosperous mill keeper, and after an involved courtship they were married in 1880; their son Paul was born three years later. Darrow opened law offices in Andover and then in Ashtabula, Ohio; although few cases came his way, in 1884 he was elected borough solicitor, or prosecutor. Darrow had already campaigned actively for the national Democratic Party. He chafed at a small-town existence and thought it likely that his legal career would advance further in a large city. Accordingly, in 1887, he moved with his family to Chicago, where social and political strife had already given the city some notoriety.

Life's Work
For a time, Darrow served on the legal staff of the city of Chicago, and he also obtained a position as corporation counsel for the Chicago and North Western Railway. Increasingly disaffected with the venality and easy ethics of his employer, he took another job with a law firm and began to specialize in cases with social implications. After the mayor of Chicago was shot to death, Darrow tried unsuccessfully, in an appeal, to save the assassin from the gallows. In 1894, widespread disorders accompanied a massive strike of the Pullman Company's railroads; Darrow offered his services but was unsuccessful in his efforts to defend Eugene V. Debs from charges of criminal conspiracy. Darrow also attempted a sortie into national politics but was defeated when he ran for the U.S. Congress as a Democrat in 1896. As his professional commitments mounted, Darrow became estranged from his wife, Jessie, and they were quietly divorced in 1897. For a time, Darrow considered a literary career; he produced works that dealt with crime and social ills, as well as *Farmington* (1904), a semiautobiographical novel.

In 1898, Darrow took up another criminal conspiracy case, brought against Thomas I. Kidd and other leaders of a woodworkers' union in Wisconsin; he persuaded a jury that Kidd could not be held responsible for incidental acts of union violence that the leaders had neither foreseen nor encouraged. Elected to the Illinois legislature in 1902, Darrow continued to take labor cases, and he served as counsel for the United Mine Workers at United States Anthracite Coal Arbitration Commission hearings in Scranton, Pennsylvania. His remarriage, to Ruby Hamerstrom in 1903, seemed to put his personal life on a firmer footing. Social concerns continued to attract him; in 1907, he won acquittal for William D. Haywood, of the Western Federation of Miners, who had been charged with complicity in the bombing death of a former governor of Idaho.

Darrow, Clarence

Clarence Darrow.
(Library of Congress)

In 1911, in another case involving union violence, Darrow defended James B. and John J. McNamara, who had planted dynamite in the *Los Angeles Times* building; the resulting explosion had killed twenty-one people. Pleading his clients guilty and pointing out that they had not intended to cause any loss of life, Darrow prevailed on a jury to spare the lives of the defendants; one was sentenced to life imprisonment and the other received fifteen years in prison. After this trial, Darrow himself was charged with jury bribery, and he assisted in his own defense. During the proceedings, the testimony of detectives and police informants was discredited, and he retained his freedom.

Darrow often gave the impression of studied casualness; he was tall, large boned, with prominent cheekbones, a sharp beaklike nose, and an overhanging forehead. He had light-blue eyes that, according to his contemporaries, could be animated by kindness or contracted in anger and outrage. In his gait, he seemed to slump forward; frequently during arguments, an unruly shock of hair would fall over his eyes. His clothes, though well tailored, seemed invariably unpressed, and Darrow claimed that he usually slept in them. His voice was deep, resonant, and slightly rasping. He was a born debater, skilled at the parry and thrust of cross-examination. His summations were moving and masterfully devised treatises on morality and the law, which frequently attracted overflow audiences into the courtroom.

Darrow, Clarence

Darrow was a confirmed skeptic, whose views were tempered by humanity and an instinctive sympathy for the downtrodden. He inveighed against the death penalty, which he considered a barbaric relic of more intolerant ages. An openly avowed agnostic, he sometimes contended that life had no meaning. Frequently, he took controversial cases for the sake of defendants and ideas that were out of public favor. Much of his success derived neither from factual expertise nor from technical mastery of the law; rather, he was determined and generally able to sway juries and judges with deeply felt moral appeals.

As word of his prowess spread, Darrow attracted numerous clients. Many times, he took their cases simply because he did not have the heart to turn them away. About certain issues he felt deeply; in 1920, he invoked the guarantee of freedom of speech in his unsuccessful defense of twenty Chicago communists. Abhorrence of the death penalty prompted him, in 1924, to defend Nathan F. Leopold, Jr., and Richard Loeb, who had carried out the wanton and senseless murder of a fourteen-year-old boy. Darrow pleaded his clients guilty, and in a lengthy, heartfelt plea, he kept them from execution. To protest the rising tide of fundamentalism, in 1925 he took the case of John T. Scopes, who was charged with violation of a Tennessee statute against teaching evolution in the public schools. Although ultimately the defendant was fined, Darrow arranged a dramatic courtroom confrontation by examining counsel for the prosecution, William Jennings Bryan; in the process, Darrow pointed up the inconsistencies that resulted when biblical literalism was applied to the problems of science. For many years, Darrow had been outraged by racial inequality; by his own account his most satisfying case came with his defense, in 1926, of a black family in Detroit. While defending their house against an angry, rampaging mob, Dr. Ossian Sweet and his sons had fired on their assailants, killing one man and wounding another. By evoking the atmosphere of extreme prejudice against them and demonstrating the severe provocation that beset the Sweets, Darrow obtained a verdict of self-defense. In 1927, he won acquittal for two antifascist Italian émigrés who had killed two of their political opponents during a quarrel in New York.

Darrow read widely and had an abiding interest in science, literature, and social thought; he also propounded his views readily and augmented his income by taking part in platform debates. Against some of the well-known figures of his day, Darrow defended agnosticism, condemned Prohibition and capital punishment, and morbidly contended that life was not worth living. He also considered retirement from the practice of law. By this time, his son Paul had established a career in business and was in no sense inclined to emulate his famous father's professional pursuits. For nine months in 1929 and 1930, Darrow and his wife traveled extensively on a vacation in Europe.

Darrow's last major case, which he claimed he took because he wanted to visit Hawaii, was a defense of Lieutenant Thomas Massie and three others in 1932. They had killed one of the men who had allegedly raped Massie's wife. At length, verdicts of manslaughter were returned against the defendants; in an agreement with the prosecution, Darrow and his colleagues obtained executive clemency for their clients in return for dismissals of the indictments still pending in the rape cases. In 1934, Darrow was called to Washington and made chair of the National Recovery Administration Review Board. Decidedly uncomfortable in this position, he contended that the government was acting as much to sanction as to control the growth of combinations in business. After a year, he resigned. Failing health was accompanied by increasing despondency; Darrow made few public appearances, and some of those close to him felt that his death, when it came on March 13, 1938, must also have brought relief.

SIGNIFICANCE
During his lifetime, Darrow served as defense attorney in nearly two thousand cases; more than one hundred of them were for charges of murder. At one time, Darrow estimated that he had represented one-third of his clients without payment; many other cases were taken to protest what he regarded as cruelty and injustice. His most celebrated cases have become a permanent part of the nation's legal lore, and his summations have been taken as models of expository speaking.

In important respects, Darrow was unique, and he spoke for the unpopular and the outcast during an age before legal consensus had delineated the rights of the accused. Some of his abiding concerns, such as opposition to the death penalty, are still warmly debated. Although he did little to advance the technical growth of the law, his stance of strident advocacy is still cited in recalling some of the most memorable courtroom confrontations in American legal practice.

—*J. R. Broadus*

FURTHER READING
Darrow, Clarence. *Closing Arguments: Clarence Darrow on Religion, Law, and Society*. Edited by S. T. Joshi. Athens: Ohio University Press, 2005. A collection of Darrow's writings on philosophy and religion, law and crime, and politics and society.

_____. *Crime, Its Cause and Treatment*. New York: Thomas Y. Crowell, 1922. This work constitutes the most extensive single statement of Darrow's views on crime and penology. He argues that heredity and environment create most criminals; crime would be reduced by improving social conditions. Darrow maintains that, for the most part, punishment is meant not to deter criminal acts, but to satisfy society's primal longings for vengeance.

_____. *The Story of My Life*. New York: Grosset and Dunlap, 1932. Brash, irreverent retelling of Darrow's life in law, which becomes markedly world-weary toward the end. Interspersed among accounts of his famous cases are excursions into science, religion, and criminology. This work is valuable not so much for its discussion of particular clients or trials—some are dealt with rather sketchily—as for its evocation of the issues and concerns that moved Darrow.

Leopold, Nathan F., Jr. *Life Plus Ninety-Nine Years*. Garden City, N.Y.: Doubleday, 1958. The memoirs of one of Darrow's most celebrated clients, this work deals largely with the author's trials and imprisonment. Early in the book, Leopold writes admiringly of Darrow's work during his Chicago murder trial of 1924; he also mentions Darrow's visits and continuing concern during his incarceration.

Ravitz, Abe C. *Clarence Darrow and the American Literary Tradition*. Cleveland, Ohio: Press of Western Reserve University, 1962. Early in Darrow's career, literature was a sometime avocation for him, and this study points to the relationship between Darrow's legal theories and his ventures into fiction and literary criticism. Many of his early writings dealt with crime and industrial accidents; the themes of these now nearly forgotten productions foreshadowed concerns he also voiced in the courtroom and in his later, nonfiction works.

Scopes, John T., and James Presley. *Center of the Storm.* New York: Holt, Rinehart and Winston, 1967. The defendant during the famous Tennessee trial of 1925, Scopes discusses his beliefs on evolution, science, and religion. He describes Darrow as the second most influential person in his life, after his father, and depicts at length the unusual but incisive defense his attorney offered.

Stone, Irving. *Clarence Darrow for the Defense.* 1941. New ed. New York: New American Library, 1971. A popular biography on a broad canvas, this work is dated in some ways but was also written close to the events it describes. It is sufficiently thorough and still detailed enough to warrant consultation. Darrow's major trials and triumphs are set forth at length, at times projecting a heroic image. Darrow's personal papers, published materials available at the time, and interviews with nearly two hundred contemporaries and associates of the great advocate were used in the preparation of this work.

Tierney, Kevin. *Darrow: A Biography.* New York: Thomas Y. Crowell, 1979. A sober and clear study that assesses Darrow's limitations as well as his strengths. Factual problems in some of Darrow's cases, and also his inconsistencies as a thinker, are presented along with his many achievements. While in no way disparaging, this closely argued and well-documented work delineates the one-sided qualities that indeed contributed so much to Darrow's greatness.

Vine, Phyllis. *One Man's Castle: Clarence Darrow in Defense of the American Dream.* New York: Amistad, 2004. Vine recounts the murder trial of Ossian Sweet, an African American physician who purchased a home in a white area of Detroit in the 1920's.

Weinberg, Arthur, and Lila Weinberg. *Clarence Darrow: A Sentimental Rebel.* New York: G. P. Putnam's Sons, 1980. A thorough and well-rounded though somewhat uncritical modern biography. Darrow's own trial for jury bribery is treated at some length. The relationship between his great cases and his manner of thinking is developed through each stage of his career; along the way, tribute is paid to his espousal of unpopular causes. This work draws extensively on court records, Darrow's own writings, and unpublished papers of Darrow and several of his associates.

DOROTHY DAY

> " *Don't call me a saint. I don't want to be dismissed so easily.* "

Social reformer and journalist

Cofounder of a radical Roman Catholic social movement, the Catholic Worker, and editor and publisher of its paper, Day linked traditional piety to immediate relief for the needy and to nonviolent direct action to end injustice and warfare.

Born: November 8, 1897; Brooklyn, New York
Died: November 29, 1980; New York, New York
Areas of achievement: Social reform; religion and theology; journalism

EARLY LIFE

The third of the five children of John I. Day and Grace Satterlee, Dorothy Day was born in Brooklyn, New York, into a comfortable home. At the time of Dorothy's birth, John Day, the ambitious son of an impoverished Confederate surgeon, was a clerk but advanced to sports editor, columnist, and partner in the Hialeah Racetrack venture later in life. During prosperous periods, the family employed a domestic servant. Reared in Protestant churches, the Days were not regular churchgoers when their children were growing up. On her own initiative, Dorothy was baptized into the Episcopal church as a teenager.

Shortly after Dorothy started school, the family moved across the continent to the San Francisco Bay Area, where John accepted a position as sports editor at one of the city's major papers. The 1906 earthquake devastated the family's home and ruined John's employer. Resettled in Chicago, the Days experienced unaccustomed poverty. The family rented a grim tenement apartment above a saloon, and Grace assumed the duties once performed by the maid.

Parental protectiveness failed to shield the children from social reality and radicalism. Their seedy neighborhood provided an observant child such as Day with an education about injustice. A precocious reader, she devoured the writings of muckrakers and socialists, whose lurid realism inspired progressive reform during the early twentieth century. She enjoyed writing and performed well enough in high school to win a coveted Hearst scholarship to the University of Illinois. As an undergraduate, Day nurtured her talent in the Scribblers' Club and reinforced her radical leanings by joining a socialist group, experiencing student poverty, and reading whatever interested her. In 1916, after two years of mediocre academic performance, she quit the university and joined her family in New York, where her father had assumed a promising position after the failure of still another of his employers.

LIFE'S WORK

At age eighteen, armed with a thin portfolio of writings from small-town newspapers, Day became a reporter, despite her father's edict that women belonged at home. Hired as a lowly features writer by a New York-based socialist daily, the *Call*, Day wrote vividly about women workers, a series much admired by the reform-minded Russell

Day, Dorothy

Dorothy Day.
(Library of Congress)

Sage Foundation. Soon the *Call* sent Day to cover strikes, riots, birth control activists, and the peace movement. Perhaps the rookie reporter's greatest coup was an interview of Russian revolutionist Leon Trotsky weeks before the czar was overthrown.

Day's career was boosted when Floyd Dell hired her to assist him with the editing of *The Masses*, Greenwich Village's chic radical monthly. Within a few months, wartime censorship shut down the magazine, leaving Day without regular work. At the urging of a friend, she traveled to Washington and picketed for woman suffrage in front of the White House. The pair was arrested a few times and jailed, along with members of the militant National Woman's Party. At the notorious Occoquan Workhouse Day, the women engaged in a hunger strike, and Day scuffled with guards over inmate conditions. Ironically, Day never voted in a national election on principle. Throughout her life, she preferred direct action, especially picketing, to the debates and deals of politicians. She joined in this demonstration out of boredom and a desire to address the treatment of political prisoners in American penal institutions.

Between 1918 and 1924, a period of drift, Day fell in and out of love, was married and divorced, and traveled throughout Europe and the United States. She published a novel of disillusionment, *The Eleventh Virgin* (1924), patterned on her life, and entered into a common-law marriage with Forster Batterham, a biologist with whom she had a daughter, Tamar. Her search for self-purpose led her into the Roman Catholic Church in 1927, which precipitated a break with Batterham, whose commitments to anarchism and atheism made him hostile to organized religion. Day tried to maintain her friendships with radicals and for a few years sought work within the radical movement. Before 1931, she wrote a few articles for the *New Masses*, a communist literary magazine, and was a propagandist for a communist front group.

Accepting a contract to write dialogue in Hollywood, Day moved with Tamar to California. Uncomfortable in this bourgeois setting, she left for Mexico. On their return to the United States, Day wrote for Catholic magazines but felt unfulfilled. A radical at heart and a Catholic convert with a social conscience, Day wanted to help change the social order that created injustice. Writing about it was not enough, especially when she saw the human suffering caused by the Depression.

In 1932, she met the person who helped her to resolve her vocational crisis. Peter Maurin, twenty years Day's senior and a French immigrant, was a devout Catholic, well read in Catholic and social issues, and committed to nonviolent revolution. Encouraged by her platonic friend, Day founded *The Catholic Worker*, a tabloid edited, published, and at first largely written by her. Within five years, the paper reached nearly 200,000 readers each month. Lively writing about work and social injustice and a sense of urgency attracted readers, many of whom wanted to put radical Catholic social ideals into practice. The bold works of art that graced its pages, as well as its trademark penny cover price, added to the paper's appeal.

The Catholic Worker movement started with the paper, the feeding of the hungry, and later the establishment of houses of hospitality, where homeless people could find shelter without the annoying difficulties of welfare bureaucracies and the condescension of do-gooders. A clothing room outfitted the tattered. All were to be treated with dignity, each person an ambassador of Christ. Peaceful protests aroused social consciences. Catholic Workers picketed with striking workers, taught black children in Harlem how to draw, and spoke at the U.S. Capitol against the military draft. The movement spread to other American cities, including Boston, St. Louis, Washington, and Seattle. By 1941, twenty-seven cities had Catholic Worker houses.

Like her contemporaries in the radical movement, Day predicted that the Depression of the 1930's was evidence that American capitalism was dying from its own structural weaknesses. To replace it, she envisioned Christian community: voluntary, cooperative, nonviolent, egalitarian, and distributist, based on production for need and not for profit. A just society would help to prevent evil. In the meantime, Day and the Catholic Worker movement supported stopgap measures: the right of workers to unionize, earn fair wages, and improve industrial safety. Maurin's "green revolution," an alternative to industrialism and urbanization, was translated into Catholic Worker farming communes, the first of which was founded within a few years. On the communes, Catholic Worker families, volunteers, and guests theoretically would live in rural simplicity and produce food for their own use. The contrasts between theory and reality posed some of the more problematic aspects of the Catholic Worker movement. Intellectuals, unemployed industrial workers, and the frail were rarely equipped to run a farm.

A socialist opponent of World War I, Day was predisposed to Christian pacifism. Clinging to the belief that the possession of arms leads to war, the Catholic convert believed that human life was sacred and must be protected. Since she understood violence to be an ever-escalating condition, each conflict breeding greater violence to counter it, Day found no moral justification for war. To critics who scoffed at nonviolence, she replied that spiritual weapons—prayer, penance, and fasting—were the best defense against evil. During World War II, however, the novelty of Catholic pacifism divided the Catholic Worker movement. Dissenting volunteers claimed that war was a lesser evil than fascism.

Day put pacifism into practice in several ways. She opposed the military draft and supported the right of conscientious objection. Urging noncooperation with the war effort, Day suggested that workers should not take jobs in defense plants, and she refused to pay war taxes. When Japanese Americans were sent to armed detention camps for the duration of the war, she was one of a handful who criticized the federal government order. The use of the atomic bomb on civilian targets likewise sparked her outrage. In the Cold War era, Day promoted peace through nonviolence and was arrested for challenging compulsory Civil Defense air raid drills. The nuclear arms race and its potential for global holocaust emboldened Day to educate the bishops of the Catholic Church about pacifism when they gathered in Rome for the Second Vatican Council (1962-1965). During the Vietnam War, she supported new Catholic peace groups and was widely credited for building the foundation of modern Catholic pacifism.

Weakened by heart trouble for more than a decade and barely able to write her monthly column, Day died in 1980 at the age of eighty-three.

Significance

Day revitalized American Catholicism. She found ways for volunteers to work for a nonviolent revolution within the church and to care for the immediate needs of the poor and oppressed. Her inclusive understanding of Christian community led to the establishment of the first true Catholic pacifist movement in the United States. Her steady leadership for nearly fifty years made the Catholic Worker one of the most durable of American alternative movements. Her deep faith and good judgment preserved Catholic Worker religious orthodoxy and prevented church officials from silencing her or dismantling the controversial movement.

Day's powerful writing attracted volunteers and introduced pacifism and nonviolent direct action to Catholics. During the Second Vatican Council, Day was among those who moved the Catholic Church toward pacifism. She was justly celebrated for her contributions to nonviolent change by the American bishops in a 1983 pastoral statement on peace.

Since 1933, the Catholic Worker movement has challenged many injustices: poverty, war, and racism. In death, Day lives through her writings, the work of her followers, and in the memories of all who have been touched by her deep faith in Christian radicalism. *The Catholic Worker*, still sold for a penny, and Catholic Workers throughout the United States, England, Canada, Australia, and Mexico bring Day's message of nonviolent revolution to a new generation.

—*Anne Klejment*

FURTHER READING

Coles, Robert. *Dorothy Day: A Radical Devotion.* Reading, Mass.: Addison-Wesley, 1987. Psychiatrist Coles's brief study features excerpts from taped interviews with Day but offers surprisingly little psychological analysis.

Day, Dorothy. *Dorothy Day, Selected Writings: By Little and by Little.* Edited by Robert Ellsberg. Maryknoll, N.Y.: Orbis Books, 1992. A wide-ranging anthology of Day's writings on social and spiritual issues drawn from published works. Ellsberg's well-crafted biographical introduction is based on a personal relationship with Day and careful scholarship.

———. *The Long Loneliness.* New York: Harper & Row, 1952. An autobiography written primarily to explain her conversion and the work of the Catholic Worker movement especially relating to the poor, the labor movement, gospel pacifism, and nonviolent social revolution. Weak on the period from 1918 through 1924.

Klejment, Anne, and Alice Klejment. *Dorothy Day and "The Catholic Worker": A Bibliography and Index.* New York: Garland, 1986. Helpful for researchers. Lists all known publications by Day, indexes *The Catholic Worker* from 1933 through 1983, and comments on selected titles.

McNeal, Patricia. *Harder than War: Catholic Peacemaking in Twentieth-Century America.* New Brunswick, N.J.: Rutgers University Press, 1992. Examines leading American Catholic peace organizations and peace advocates with emphasis on the formative role played by Day and her movement in the emergence of Catholic pacifism.

Miller, William D. *A Harsh and Dreadful Love: Dorothy Day and the Catholic Worker Movement.* New York: Liveright, 1973. Dated, but an interesting history of the Catholic Worker movement with portraits of many key figures and quotations from volunteers.

O'Connor, June. *The Moral Vision of Dorothy Day: A Feminist Perspective.* New York: Crossroad, 1991. Views Day as a writer, convert, radical, and moralist and presents her as an occasionally antifeminist feminist.

Piehl, Mel. *Breaking Bread: The Catholic Worker and the Origin of Catholic Radicalism in America.* Philadelphia: Temple University Press, 1982. A demanding but rewarding work that explains the religious context of the movement. Roughly covers events to 1965.

Roberts, Nancy L. *Dorothy Day and the Catholic Worker.* Albany, N.Y.: State University of New York Press, 1984. One of the most readable accounts of Day's life at *The Catholic Worker*, with a focus on Day the advocacy journalist.

Zwick, Mark, and Louise Zwick. *The Catholic Worker Movement: Intellectual and Spiritual Origins.* New York: Paulist Press, 2005. Examines the intellectual and spiritual influences that led Day and Peter Maurin to organize the Catholic Worker movement.

Debs, Eugene V.

EUGENE V. DEBS

" *The most heroic word in all languages is revolution.* "

Labor leader and social reformer

Debs's work in the organization of labor and the adoption of social welfare legislation had a significant impact on the American economy and government. He campaigned several times for the presidency of the United States as a representative of the Socialist Party.

Born: November 5, 1855; Terre Haute, Indiana
Died: October 20, 1926; Elmhurst, Illinois
Also known as: Eugene Victor Debs (full name)
Areas of achievement: Labor movement; social reform; government and politics

EARLY LIFE

Eugene V. Debs (dehbz) was the third child of six who survived to adulthood and the first son of Jean Daniel Debs and Marguerite Marie Bettrich Debs. His parents had emigrated in 1849 from Alsace, lived briefly in New York City and Cincinnati, and settled in Terre Haute, opening a grocery store that provided the family with a modest but sustaining income.

In his reading of Victor Hugo's *Les Misérables* (1862)—he was named by his father after Hugo and Hugo's compatriot and fellow novelist, Eugène Sue—Debs early became aware of the wretchedness of poverty and the dream of its eradication. His formal education was perhaps less influential; in 1871, against his parents' wishes, he left high school, worked for the Terre Haute and Indianapolis Railroad, and in December, 1871, was promoted to the position of fireman.

Debs was employed as a railroad man for two years. In 1873, as a result of the financial panic and the subsequent economic depression, he lost his job, moved to East St. Louis, and at first hand witnessed the realities of urban beggary and desperation. After his return to Terre Haute the next year, he secured employment in a wholesale grocery company and participated in the cultural and civic institutions of the small midwestern city. He established, along with others, the Occidental Literary Club, served as its president, and provided a platform for such national figures as the atheist propagandist and orator Robert Ingersoll; the former abolitionist Wendell Phillips, who had embraced the cause of labor; and the poet James Whitcomb Riley. The visit to Terre Haute of Susan B. Anthony, and the refusal of the literary club to sponsor her speech, brought him into contact with the cause of women's rights and the hostility that the intrepid suffragist constantly encountered.

LIFE'S WORK

In February, 1875, although no longer involved in the industry, Debs became a member of the newly established Vigo Lodge of the Brotherhood of Locomotive Firemen, rose rapidly to prominence in union circles, and with labor support was elected first as Terre Haute city clerk and then, in 1884, as a representative to the lower house of the Indiana General Assembly. His legislative record reveals a dedication to labor issues, the sponsoring of railroad workers' safety and employers' liability bills, and the abortive support of a law extending the ballot to Indiana women.

The year 1885 was a momentous one in Debs's life and career. A photograph taken sometime later shows him clean-shaven, with a receding hairline, and smart clothes. On June 9, 1885, he married Katherine Metzel, the stepdaughter of a Terre Haute druggist. He was grand secretary of the Brotherhood of Locomotive Firemen and editor of its magazine; before the year's end, he left his positions in the grocery warehouse and as state legislator and devoted himself fully to the cause of labor organization.

In the pages of the union's official publication, Debs frequently commented on labor strategies and the structure of unionization. He was opposed to strikes except as a last resort. He believed that the use of boycott was a terrible example of economic coercion. He dissociated himself from any project that would effect an "amalgamation" of labor organizations and the dissolution of the independent craft unions.

The 1888 strike against the Chicago, Burlington and Quincy Railroad, which concluded in defeat for the union, had an important impact on Debs and modified his attitude toward labor organization. If not yet advocating the establishment of an industrial union, he urged that the railway unions develop a federation similar to the American Federation of Labor and, by numbers and a united front, win concessions on wages and other terms and conditions of employment. His efforts and those of other railroad labor leaders reached a brief fruition in 1889, in the establishment of a Supreme Council of

Eugene V. Debs.
(Library of Congress)

Debs, Eugene V.

the United Orders of Railroad Employees, combining in a federation firemen, brakemen, and switchmen. The organization was too weak, however, to resolve disputes among its members and caused bitterness and estrangement among the railroad unions; thus, at its 1892 annual convention, Debs reluctantly sponsored a successful resolution dissolving this experiment in labor federation.

Disillusioned by the impotency of the Supreme Council of the United Orders of Railroad Employees, believing that a federation of craft unions would not prove effective in ameliorating labor conditions, Debs turned to the creation of an industrial railroad union. The American Railway Union (ARU) founded in Chicago in June, 1893, with Debs serving as president, represented a threat not only to railroad corporations but also to the railroad unions of craftsmen and to the American Federation of Labor. It proposed to organize all railroad workers, coal miners, and longshoremen employed in the industry, irrespective of their skills. Reflecting the racism of the 1890's, it barred black Americans from membership. (Debs, however, opposed such exclusionary language in its constitution.)

The year 1893 was an unpropitious time to form a new labor organization. There was another financial panic and another depression; the ranks of the unemployed swelled, and the breadlines in the cities grew longer. On the other hand, the depression caused railroad men to desert the unions; before a year was over, the ARU had become the largest single labor union in the United States, with a membership of more than 150,000. In April, 1894, it won a brilliant victory and a wage increase after an eighteen-day strike against the Great Northern Railroad. Yet its triumph was transitory: A month later began the strike and lockout at the Pullman Palace Car Company outside Chicago. The employee-inhabitants of Pullman town had long been resentful of the unwillingness of the company to sell them the houses in which they lived, to accord them political rights in the selection of town officials, and to lower rents as wages were reduced in September, 1893. Against the advice of Debs and other ARU officers, in May, 1894, they struck and, the next month, sent their delegates to the first annual convention of the industrial union that by coincidence was meeting in Chicago. Their accounts of exploitation and deprivation swayed the convention to support a boycott of all railroad companies with Chicago terminals unless they refused to link Pullman cars to their passenger trains.

The Pullman Strike of 1894 pitted the ARU against the General Managers Association, a trade organization of twenty-four railroad companies with terminals in Chicago. Allied with management were the judges of the federal courts, the Democratic administration of Grover Cleveland, and particularly Attorney General Richard Olney. Olney was determined to crush the railroad workers and to destroy their union. He attained both objectives. Borrowed from the Chicago, Milwaukee, and St. Paul Railroad, appointed as special district attorney, Edwin Walker successfully petitioned the federal court in Chicago to grant an injunction that prohibited the ARU, its president, and other officials from any further supervision of the strike. They could not speak, write instructions, or use telegraph or telephone lines to support ARU members who had paralyzed railroad traffic, not only in and out of Chicago but also in twenty-seven Western states and territories. Unemployed railroad workers were transported from the East to replace striking employees, and on July 4, 1894, federal troops appeared in Chicago by Cleveland's order. Labor had suffered one of the most devastating defeats in its history. The ARU was wrecked, its members blacklisted, and the Pullman workers were forced to return to their jobs under the old conditions. Debs was sentenced to six months' imprisonment in Woodstock Jail for violating the federal court's injunction.

The failure of the ARU and the subsequent incarceration converted Debs to socialism as a preferable economic system. Within two years after his release, he joined the Social Democratic Party (in 1901, it became the Socialist Party of America), served on its executive board, and, in 1900, ran for president of the United States. It was the first of five campaigns. Debs used his candidacies as forums for education, attracting large crowds, arguing that socialism and democracy were compatible, standing on party platforms that advocated, among other things, woman suffrage, industrial safety legislation, shorter workdays, and the abolition of child labor. He received 96,978 votes in the 1900 election, 402,406 in 1904, and eight years later, a climactic vote of 897,011, representing 6 percent of the electorate.

World War I and the entry of the United States in April, 1917, marked the end of the socialist electoral momentum. In June, 1917, Congress passed the Espionage Act (amended the next year to include nine new federal criminal offenses) to enforce the Selective Service Act and to suppress verbal opposition to the war. Debs was angered by the imprisonment of many of his socialist colleagues under the congressional legislation. On June 15, 1918, in Canton, Ohio, he addressed the Ohio Socialist Party Convention. In a long and sometimes eloquent speech, he expressed sympathy for his incarcerated socialist comrades, excoriated the United States Supreme Court, and criticized conscription and the United States' participation in the European conflagration. He did not directly counsel draft resistance or illegal action in the military forces or say anything to promote the success of the German army. Nevertheless, he was arrested, indicted, and, in September of 1918, tried in a Cleveland courtroom, convicted, and sentenced to ten years' imprisonment. His appeal to the United States Supreme Court, his attorneys arguing that the Espionage Act violated the First Amendment guarantee of freedom of speech, was concluded in March, 1919, by Justice Oliver Wendell Holmes, Jr.'s opinion affirming the conviction.

Debs, sixty-three years old, confronted a decade of imprisonment. Depressed at times by his confinement in Atlanta Penitentiary, elated at others by the steady flow of sympathetic letters and visitors, in 1920 he ran once more for president, the only candidate ever to have done so while in prison.

Ironically it was Republican President Warren G. Harding who ordered Debs's release on Christmas Day, 1921. The socialist leader was not able to unite his party, which had been torn by dissension over the war and by the emergence of two communist political organizations. His personal popularity, however, had not waned. He spoke out against violent revolution, criticized the Soviet government, and worked to revise Socialist Party fortunes. Hampered by failing health, he nevertheless continued his speaking tours throughout the country, edited the *American Appeal*, and, in a last pamphlet, pleaded the case of Nicola Sacco and Bartolomeo Vanzetti. He died on October 20, 1926, in Lindlahr Sanatorium in a Chicago suburb and was buried in his hometown of Terre Haute.

Debs, Eugene V.

Significance

Although the ARU failed and the Socialist Party declined in influence during his lifetime, Debs left behind him important legacies in the currents of twentieth century American history. The ARU served as a model of the industrial organization of labor, emulated by the establishment of the more enduring Congress of Industrial Organizations. The Socialist Party of America, under his leadership, impelled the major political parties of Democrats and Republicans to co-opt reformist elements in their rival's platform. The abolition of child labor, maximum hour and minimum wage legislation, the protection of employees in the workplace, woman suffrage, and the graduated income tax became part of state and federal legal codes or amendments to the U.S. Constitution.

Debs's conviction and incarceration under the Espionage Act educated the American public and the Supreme Court about the dangers of suppressing dissent and the crucial relationship between the free speech guarantee and the preservation of democratic institutions. Perhaps most important, his dedication to the alleviation of poverty, to social justice, and to peace has inspired other Americans in later generations and has contributed to the richness of American political life.

—*David L. Sterling*

Further Reading

Chace, James. *1912: Wilson, Roosevelt, Taft, and Debs: The Election That Changed the Country*. New York: Simon & Schuster, 2004. Relates the events of the 1912 presidential election, including Debs's campaign on the Socialist Party ticket.

Debs, Eugene Victor. *Writings and Speeches of Eugene V. Debs*. New York: Hermitage Press, 1948. A collection of Debs's works, with an introduction by Arthur M. Schlesinger, Jr., including an abridged version of the Canton speech for which the socialist leader was convicted and imprisoned for violation of the Espionage Act. The book further exhibits the quality of Debs's rhetorical skills.

Ginger, Ray. *The Bending Cross: A Biography of Eugene Victor Debs*. New Brunswick, N.J.: Rutgers University Press, 1949. The most colorful and readable study of Debs's life, narrative in form, but perpetuating a mythic portrait of the socialist leader.

Lindsey, Almont. *The Pullman Strike*. Chicago: University of Chicago Press, 1942. The only systematic account of the conflict between the Pullman workers and the ARU on one side and the railroad corporations and the Cleveland administration on the other. The author emphasizes employee grievances relative to conditions in Pullman, Illinois, and, along with a careful analysis of the course of the strike, presents the reactions and recommendations of the United States Strike Commission in its aftermath.

Morgan, H. Wayne. *Eugene V. Debs: Socialist for President*. Syracuse, N.Y.: Syracuse University Press, 1952. Focuses on the five presidential campaigns as well as on the history of the party between 1900 and 1925.

Peterson, J. C., and Gilbert C. Fite. *Opponents of War: 1917-1918*. Madison: University of Wisconsin Press, 1957. One of many such studies, a wide panorama of the suppression of dissent during World War I, the closing of German-language and socialist newspapers, the prosecutions under the Espionage Act, and the antilibertarian record of the Woodrow Wilson administration.

Salvatore, Nick. *Eugene V. Debs: Citizen and Socialist*. 2d ed. Urbana: University of Illinois Press, 2007. The best and most analytic biography to date. The author argues that Debs's career can be viewed in an American tradition of radical reformism rather than as an attempt to implant into American politics an alien European ideology.

Shannon, David A. *The Socialist Party of America: A History*. New York: Macmillan, 1955. An overview of the fortunes of the Socialist Party from its origins in 1901 to the early 1950's, placing Debs in a context of intraparty factionalism.

Stephen Decatur

> *Our country! In her intercourse with foreign nations, may she always be in the right; but our country, right or wrong.*

Naval commander

The most colorful and successful open-sea naval commander of his time, Decatur was a national hero of the Barbary Wars and the War of 1812.

Born: January 5, 1779; Sinepuxent, Maryland
Died: March 22, 1820; Bladensburg, Maryland
Area of achievement: Military

Early Life

Stephen Decatur (deh-KAY-tur) was the son of a seafaring man who earned his living as a merchant ship captain and, during the American Revolution, as a privateer. Decatur was a sickly child during his early years. At the age of eight, suffering from a prolonged and severe cough, he accompanied his father on a voyage to the French port of Bordeaux. His malady, probably whooping cough, disappeared.

Because his father was at sea much of the time, Decatur was raised in Philadelphia, Pennsylvania, by his mother, Ann, who sent him to the Episcopal Academy and later to the University of Pennsylvania in the hope that he would become either a clergyman or a scholar. However, despite his health problems and his mother's wishes, Decatur craved the active over the contemplative life. As a young man, he was five feet ten inches in height, possessed a muscular build, and had a handsome countenance with an aquiline nose.

Decatur first worked as a clerk in 1796 for Gurney and Smith, a Philadelphia shipping company, but after the United States Navy was established on April 30, 1798, and a naval war had commenced with France, Decatur, through his father's influence, secured a midshipman place on the newly constructed ship, the *United States*. Built in Philadelphia, this forty-four gun frigate was familiar to Decatur. Its captain, John

Decatur, Stephen

Barry, was both a friend and professional colleague of Decatur's father.

The reasons for Decatur's determination to join the Navy are unclear. Perhaps it was the lure of adventure presented by the new United States Navy and the war with France, or perhaps he wanted to follow his father's nautical footsteps. A more murky reason was the apparent result of Decatur's attack upon a prostitute who had solicited him. He struck her with a blow that was powerful enough to kill her. To avoid a prison sentence for their client, Decatur's lawyers assured the court that Decatur would join the Navy.

LIFE'S WORK

Decatur's first real taste of glory occurred in 1804 during the Barbary Wars, when, as captain of the schooner *Enterprise* in Commodore Edward Preble's Mediterranean squadron, he captured a Barbary slave ship, the *Mastico*. Renamed the *Intrepid*, it was sixty feet in length with a twelve-foot beam. A scheme was devised to burn the former U.S. frigate *Philadelphia*, which had run aground and been captured by the Tripolitans. Decatur chose a crew of seventy-four volunteers who would sail the *Intrepid* into Tripoli Harbor under the guise of a Barbary ship seeking repairs from a recent storm. The Americans were to board, burn, and escape, leaving the *Philadelphia* in ashes. It was a daring plan well suited to Decatur's adventuresome temperament.

Although delayed for one week because of severe weather, the attack, when executed at dusk on February 16, 1804, was a huge success. Decatur's crew sailed within a few yards of the *Philadelphia* before they were found out. They quickly overcame the defenders, many of whom feared for their lives and jumped overboard. During the next thirty minutes, twenty Tripolitans were killed, combustibles were laid and ignited, the attackers returned to the *Intrepid*, and the *Philadelphia* was engulfed in flames. During all of this, only one of Decatur's sailors was wounded. Burning the *Philadelphia* assured Decatur's role as a hero. He was promoted to captain at the age of twenty-five, the youngest American naval officer to attain that rank. Lord Horatio Nelson called the attack "the most bold and daring act of the age." President Thomas Jefferson presented Decatur with a sword and words of praise.

Later that same year, Decatur's brother, James, was killed by the commander of a Tripolitan gunboat, who shot James when he was boarding the already surrendered vessel. Along with ten others, Decatur tracked down the commander and killed him after some brutal hand-to-hand fighting. During the melee, Decatur's life was saved by a sailor who intentionally absorbed a blow that would have killed Decatur.

At the conclusion of the Tripolitan phase of the Barbary Wars, Decatur returned home, where he broke with his former fiancé and met and married Susan Wheeler, the daughter of the mayor of Norfolk, Virginia. She was a popular and beautiful young woman who had already rejected advances made by Vice President Aaron Burr and Jerome Bonaparte.

Decatur served in various naval positions during the six years from 1806 to 1812. In 1807 he served on the court-martial panel that suspended Captain James Barron, Decatur's erstwhile friend and former tutor, from the Navy for five years because of his behavior as captain of the *Chesapeake*. Barron was found guilty for failing to adequately prepare his ship for action against the British ship the *Leopard* and thereby humiliating the United States Navy by demonstrating its inability to prevent the seizure of four British Royal Navy deserters, three of whom were Americans impressed earlier by the British. Another more personal reason for the deterioration and ultimately fatal culmination of Decatur and Barron's relationship was the latter's implied criticism of Decatur's attraction to Susan Wheeler when Decatur already had a fiancé in Philadelphia. Decatur thought that it was none of Barron's concern.

When Britain and the United States went to war in 1812, the still young United States Navy consisted of just sixteen warships. Decatur was captain of one of them, the familiar *United States*. Sailing alone between the Azores and Madeira, he sighted the *Macedonian*, a British frigate. The U.S. ship was larger and now carried fifty-four 24-pound guns, compared to the *Macedonian*'s forty-nine 18 pounders. Ironically, this very encounter had been discussed prior to the war by Decatur and Captain John Carden, commander of the *Macedonian*. Despite the heavier gun advantage of the *United States*, Carden had argued that his ship would prevail because its crew was more experienced and because the *Macedonian* was a more maneuverable vessel.

As it turned out, even though Carden had the wind advantage, he failed to recognize the *United States* and instead assumed it was a smaller frigate with guns of lesser range and shot than his own. Carden's tactics played into Decatur's hands by allowing Decatur to press his advantage of more guns and greater destructive shot. Carden surrendered the *Macedonian* after losing one-third of his three-hundred-man crew in a two-hour fight, while seven were killed and five wounded aboard the *United States*. Decatur's reputation as a hero reached its summit. The government also awarded him thirty thousand dollars in prize money. Decatur's achievements during the remainder of the war were a good deal less dramatic, although his status as a genuine American hero remained high.

By tightening their blockade along the Atlantic coast, the British were able to prevent most ships from entering and sailing from U.S. ports. On January 14-15, 1815, unaware that the war had ended three weeks earlier, Decatur attempted to liberate his ship, the *President*, by escaping from New York Harbor. Heavy winds caused the ship to run aground for two hours and compelled Decatur to make a fifty-mile run along the Long Island coast. Four British warships chased him, and, although the frigate *Endymion* had to retire because of battle damage, the remaining British ships forced his surrender. British losses were less than half of the twenty-four Americans killed and the fifty-five who were wounded. Despite the defeat, Decatur maintained his status as a hero. A naval court of inquiry not only exonerated him but also determined that the surrender of the *President* was an American victory.

Two months after the Treaty of Ghent, which ended the War of 1812, the United States was at war again, this time with Algiers. Decatur, now a commodore (at that time the highest rank in the United States Navy), assembled a squadron of ten ships, including three frigates, one of which was the *Macedonian*. After capturing the Algerine flagship and killing the grand admiral of the Algerine fleet, Decatur's entire squadron sailed into Algiers Harbor. A treaty favorable to the United States was the result. Additional concessions were later made by Tunis as well. Decatur was the principal negotiator in both cases.

After returning home, Decatur was appointed to the three-member Board of Naval

Decatur, Stephen

Commissioners. The Decaturs (they had no children) moved to Washington, D.C., where Decatur continued to contribute to naval affairs.

Decatur died as he had lived: defending his honor. The cashiered Barron returned to the United States from Denmark in 1818 and unsuccessfully applied for reinstatement in the U.S. Navy. Barron blamed the Board of Naval Commissioners and Decatur in particular. He initiated a correspondence with Decatur that ended when Barron challenged Decatur to a duel. They met at Bladensburg, Maryland, on March 22, 1820. Although Decatur, an excellent pistol marksman, aimed to wound his opponent, Barron aimed to kill—and succeeded. Shot in the groin, Decatur died twelve hours later. Congress adjourned to attend Decatur's funeral, naval officers wore crepe for thirty days, guns on ships at Washington and Norfolk fired at thirty-minute intervals, and numerous eulogies were presented by people of all ranks and classes. President James Monroe and his cabinet marched in the funeral procession.

Barron was finally reinstated in 1824. He was given command of the Philadelphia Navy Yard and later the Norfolk Navy Yard. He died in 1851 at the age of eighty-three.

Significance

Decatur's contributions to the United States were revered a great deal more during his lifetime than by subsequent generations of Americans. Although no naval history of the post-Revolutionary War period would be complete without devoting considerable attention to Decatur, his heroic accomplishments, impressive as they were, made a limited impact on naval policy and strategy. Early nineteenth century Americans needed a hero to help represent and justify their nation's brief history and its full membership among contemporary nations. Decatur was the right person at the right place at the right time. Perhaps his dedication to his country was best expressed by a toast he made at a dinner held in his honor in 1816: "Our Country! In her intercourse with foreign nations, may she always be in the right; but our country, right or wrong."

—*John Quinn Imholte*

Further Reading

Anthony, Irvin. *Decatur*. New York: Charles Scribner's Sons, 1931. Anthony's book is subjective but remains one of the few book-length biographies of Decatur. Includes much personal detail.

Blassingame, Wyatt. *Stephen Decatur: Fighting Sailor*. Champaign, Ill.: Garrard, 1964. This volume is suitable for early elementary students.

De Kay, James Tertius. *A Rage for Glory: The Life of Commodore Stephen Decatur, U.S.N.* New York: Free Press, 2004. A comprehensive, popular biography. De Kay, a naval historian, recounts the origins of Decatur's fierce patriotism and provides new details about his death.

Guttridge, Leonard F., and Jay D. Smith. *The Commodores*. New York: Harper & Row, 1969. This volume includes pithy accounts of Decatur and Barron, along with other high-ranking naval officers. Especially valuable for the Bladensburg duel.

Lewis, Charles Lee. *The Romantic Decatur*. Philadelphia: University of Pennsylvania Press, 1937. This is the standard book-length biography of Decatur. For the most part, Lewis remains objective throughout the book.

Schroeder, John H. "Stephen Decatur: Heroic Ideal of the Young Navy." In *Command Under Sail: Makers of the American Naval Tradition*, edited by James C. Bradford. Annapolis, Md.: Naval Institute Press, 1985. Most of this overview of Decatur's naval career is supported by primary sources.

Tucher, Glenn. *Dawn Like Thunder: The Barbary Wars and the Birth of the U.S. Navy*. Indianapolis: Bobbs-Merrill, 1963. Tucher details Decatur's participation in the Barbary Wars.

Tucker, Spencer. *Stephen Decatur: A Life Most Bold and Daring*. Annapolis, Md.: Naval Institute Press, 2005. A biography, in which Tucker relates Decatur's military achievements to the rise of the United States Navy in the nineteenth century. In his description of Decatur's raid at Tripoli Harbor, Tucker explains how Decatur's heroism set a new standard of courage for future naval officers.

JACK DEMPSEY

" *A champion is someone who gets up when he can't.* "

Boxer

Dempsey was one of the greatest sports personalities of the so-called Golden Age of Sports (the 1920's) and the first boxer to make major contributions to sporting life in the United States.

Born: June 24, 1895; Manassa, Colorado
Died: May 31, 1983; New York, New York
Also known as: William Harrison Dempsey (birth name); the Manassa Mauler, Jack the Giant Killer
Area of achievement: Sports

EARLY LIFE

Jack Dempsey (DEHMP-see), one of eleven children, was of Indian, Irish, and Scottish ancestry. The son of Hyrum Dempsey and Celia Dempsey, he became accustomed to a nomadic existence early in life, a primary requisite for a boxing career. Hyrum had converted to the Church of Jesus Christ of Latter-day Saints and had moved to Manassa in 1880 because it was a center of Mormon life. Hyrum, however, never was a successful businessman and was regarded as somewhat of a dreamer. The family began a succession of moves from Manassa when Jack was four or five years old; the longest stay was at a ranch near Montrose, Colorado, for two years.

Jack permanently left his family in 1911, when they were living in Lakeview, Utah, and he was sixteen years old. He had already been attracted to the sport that made him famous, for he had begun to fight at about ten years of age, and it had become a way of life. This was a type of boxing in which there were no holds barred, and the biggest and toughest competitors usually won. As a preventive against cuts (which might interfere with his vision and hence his ability to hit and block blows), the budding boxer bathed his face and hands in beef brine. Cuts were lessened this way, and his hands were toughened as well.

Dempsey was never large, especially if compared to boxers of the late twentieth century. In his prime as an adult, Dempsey stood six feet one-and-one-half inches tall and weighed between 180 and 187 pounds; in his earlier years, he often weighed less than 150. From 1911 to 1916, Dempsey led the life of what one could legitimately call a hobo, though a hobo who worked and would accept any gainful employment. During this time he also fought and sharpened his skills and techniques. His was a rather brutal existence, an existence that forced Dempsey to remain aloof from most other hoboes because of his fear of homosexual attack from older, stronger individuals or groups. This in itself was good training for a boxer; once he is in the ring, a boxer is completely on his own, simply one individual who is pitted against another.

Dempsey was not the only man of his family to box. At one time, his older brother Bernie was fighting under the name of Jack Dempsey. This Jack was one of the more popular earlier middleweights and was known as "The Non-pareil." One night, William Harrison substituted for his older brother in the ring and used the name Jack Dempsey. This fight in Denver gave him his permanent professional name.

Dempsey needed two more ingredients for a really successful boxing career. Most successful boxing careers are shaped, if not made, by a manager, and an astute boxing promoter of matches can make or break a career. Dempsey's fights in the West gave him these, for he was introduced to the men who would be the two most important figures in his professional life. John Leo McKernan, or Jack Kearns, was the epitome of the fight manager: a master storyteller whom Nat Fleischer, editor of *The Ring*, credited with having invented the art of "ballyhoo." The promoter was George L. "Tex" Rickard, who was to develop boxing's first million-dollar gates, with Dempsey as the prime attraction.

Kearns was the most successful manager in the history of boxing, until the 1970's, for producing revenue for his boxers and himself. He managed six world champions, four of whom have been elected to *The Ring*'s Hall of Fame. Dempsey, Kearns, and Rickard were also lucky: They were at the right place at the right time. Boxing had only recently been legalized in the state of New York, opening the largest populated area of the country to mass spectator sports. For the first time, boxing was being taken from small, seedy arenas that housed only a few hundred or a thousand seats, to the sporting meccas of America.

Dempsey's first two managers were Jack Price and John "the Barber" Reisler. It was not until 1917, when he was twenty-two, that Dempsey met Kearns and began his rise to fame. By the time he met Kearns, he had knocked out practically every opponent he had faced, but without recognition and the good paydays that went with that accomplishment. By the time he won the heavyweight championship of the world in 1919 from Jess Willard, he had knocked out twenty-one opponents in the first round, and newspapers had begun calling him the "Manassa Mauler" and "Jack the Giant Killer." From 1917 until 1919, he suffered only one defeat, and by 1919 he had won more than eighty victories.

Dempsey had also married by this time. His first wife, Maxine Gates, was a saloon piano player whom he had met during his early days in the West. He then married Estelle Taylor, an actor, who he had met after becoming heavyweight champion. They

Jack Dempsey.
(Library of Congress)

were later divorced and Dempsey married a singer, Hannah Williams. They had two daughters, Joan in 1934 and Barbara in 1936, but again he was divorced, in 1943. Dempsey was given custody of the children. He was married for the fourth time in 1958, to Deanna Piatelli, who survived him. Dempsey also adopted his fourth wife's daughter from a previous marriage, who took the name Barbara Piatelli Dempsey. She later helped him to write his 1977 autobiography, *Dempsey*.

LIFE'S WORK

Dempsey's status as a serious contender was established when he knocked out Fireman Jim Flynn in one round. In July, 1918, he knocked out Fred Fulton in twenty-three seconds of the first round. Dempsey threw the only punch, a right. This got him a title fight with Jess Willard, who had won the title in 1915 but who had defended it only once since then, in a no-decision match with Frank Moran in 1916.

The championship bout with Willard, on July 4, in Toledo, Ohio, made Dempsey a national hero. Willard was five inches taller and seventy pounds heavier and was the overwhelming favorite. The fight was held in a specially made outdoor arena constructed of rough-hewn planks, a Rickard trademark. Although the ring was set up on the shores of Maumee Bay, it was blisteringly hot. Dempsey began to stalk Willard; he had

Dempsey, Jack

to stand on his tiptoes to reach the champion. Reach the champion he did, however, for Dempsey knocked him down seven times in the first round, breaking Willard's jaw in twelve places. Both Dempsey and Kearns left the ring at the end of the first round, believing the fight won. Dempsey had to reenter the ring, but at the end of the fourth round Willard retired, after taking a frightful beating. Dempsey was now champion.

What is not generally known about Dempsey, however, is that this time of his life was not a particularly happy one. He was not immediately accepted by the public as a champion; indeed, he did not become a real hero until he lost the crown to Gene Tunney. A large part of this lack of acclaim was because of questions concerning his role in the war effort during World War I. Supposedly doing essential work in a Philadelphia shipyard, he had posed for a news photograph while holding a riveting gun and wearing overalls. He was also, however, wearing patent-leather dress shoes. The photograph convinced many that he had evaded fighting, and the sobriquet "draft dodger" was hung on him. Partly as a result of this unfavorable publicity, Rickard matched Dempsey with Georges Carpentier, the light-heavyweight champion. Carpentier was advertised as the archetypal hero; he had been decorated while serving in the French armed forces during the war. Rickard shrewdly surmised that many fans would buy tickets hoping to see Dempsey lose. Rickard built one of his stark wooden arenas in an area of Jersey City known as Boyle's Thirty Acres. A crowd of 80,183 paid $1,789,238 to see the fight—it was the first of the legendary million-dollar gates. Carpentier, however, did not stand a chance. He was knocked out in the fourth round.

There were some unpleasantries associated even with the Willard fight. Dempsey maintained that he never received any funds from the proceeds of his share of the fight. Kearns reportedly bet ten thousand dollars on Dempsey to win in a first-round knockout. When Dempsey had to return to the ring, he lost the bet. The rest of the money supposedly went for training expenses. This was the first intimation that all was not well between Dempsey and Kearns. Kearns later claimed that Dempsey's pounding of Willard was a result of his wrapping of Dempsey's hands with plaster of paris the previous night, actually a common ploy then used by fighters, especially those employed by circuses and traveling carnivals, who regularly took on all comers. Generally, if the challenger lasted three rounds, he was declared the winner. Most did not, thanks to such ploys.

Dempsey's next fight after Carpentier was held in Shelby, Montana. This fight is still cited as an example of what small-town promoters should *not* do: hock the family jewels for a bit of national recognition. Kearns had received a guarantee of $250,000 for Dempsey to fight Tommy Gibbons in Shelby. The fight was held in the oil-rich town, but very few people came to witness Dempsey's victory in a five-round decision. Nevertheless, Kearns collected the entire guarantee; one of the most fabled stories of sports and gambling concerns Kearns's foresight in hiring a locomotive and caboose to whisk the Dempsey entourage out of town.

Dempsey actually fought only six fights defending the championship. During this period, there were no boxing commissions or organizations mandating that champions defend their title at least twice a year. He won the title in 1919, then in 1920 defeated, for the second time, Billy Wiske and Bill Brennan, before meeting Carpentier in 1921. It had taken Dempsey twelve rounds to dispose of Brennan by knockout. He did not defend the title in 1922. In 1923, he defeated Gibbons and then fought the famous bat-

Dempsey, Jack

tle with Luis Angel Firpo of Argentina in New York City. This short fight probably contained more action than any other heavyweight championship bout. Early in the first round, Dempsey was stopped by a right to the jaw, but he was able to knock Firpo down four times. Firpo then knocked Dempsey into the press row. Reporters broke his fall and helped push him back into the ring. Dempsey then knocked Firpo down for the fifth time—and all this happened in the first round. The second round was all Dempsey's, and he finished Firpo off by knocking him down twice.

Dempsey did not fight again for three years. Then came his two losses to Gene Tunney. Tunney, a former marine, won the title from Dempsey on September 23, 1926. More than 100,000 spectators witnessed the bout. Dempsey lost by a ten-round decision. By this time, Kearns was no longer Dempsey's manager and was suing Dempsey for his share of the Tunney purse. A year later, Dempsey challenged Tunney for the title. Dempsey was soundly outboxed, except for the long-count seventh round. Dempsey knocked Tunney down but refused to go to a neutral corner as newer rules mandated. Dempsey stood over the fallen Tunney for at least four seconds before moving to a neutral corner. Only after Dempsey had done so did the referee begin his count. Tunney recovered, and any hope that Dempsey would win was lost.

Dempsey made a comeback in August of 1931, but a loss to Kingfish Levinsky in August of 1932 convinced him to retire again. In 1940, he returned to the ring once again, but only to knock out three stiffs.

During his career, Dempsey fought sixty-nine professional bouts. He won forty-seven by knockout, seven by decision, and one by foul; in five of his fights there was no decision, and four were declared a draw; he lost four by decision and was knocked out once.

While champion, Dempsey had been attracted to the glamour and charisma of the stage and screen. His featured role in a Broadway play was, to say the least, not outstanding. The female lead was played by his second wife, Estelle Taylor, a star of silent films whom he had met while in Hollywood. His Hollywood career was a disaster, however, as was the film *Manhattan Madness* (1925), in which he appeared.

After the Tunney bouts, Dempsey refereed bouts and tended to his business interests. During World War II, he was unable to enlist in the U.S. Army but joined the Coast Guard as director of its physical fitness program. He held the rank of commander, ending his service in November, 1945.

Dempsey was the first winner of the New York Boxing Writers Association's Edward J. Weil Memorial Plaque in 1938 and was elected to the Boxing Hall of Fame in 1954. By this time, his popularity was at an all-time high, and he was generally regarded as the best boxer in history until the postwar period. Probably the most important reason for this public acclaim was Dempsey's mellowing personality. His successful restaurant on Broadway in New York City kept him in the public eye, for he was always willing to greet a customer and have his picture taken with him or her. He died on May 31, 1983, in New York City.

SIGNIFICANCE

Dempsey is a sports legend, along with such epic American sports heroes as Harold "Red" Grange and the Four Horsemen of Notre Dame, of football fame, and the other

Dempsey, Jack

greats of sports' Golden Age. Although his record in the ring is possibly overrated, his fights were marked by a ferocity seldom encountered elsewhere in boxing. His long life enabled him to become a genial host in the most populous city in the United States, a position that continued to keep him in the national limelight. The champ thus came to personify much that was good in American life.

—Henry S. Marks

FURTHER READING

Bromberg, Lester. *Boxing's Unforgettable Fights*. New York: Ronald Press, 1962. Bromberg graphically depicts the fights with Willard, when Dempsey won the championship, the Carpentier and Firpo fights, and the two Tunney fights. Interesting reading.

Cavanaugh, Jack. "The Long Count Is a Long Memory." *The New York Times*, September 22, 2002, sec. 8, p. 9. Recounts the 1927 boxing match between Dempsey and Gene Tunney, in which Tunney was knocked out in the seventh round but eventually won the fight.

Dempsey, Jack, with Barbara Piatelli Dempsey. *Dempsey*. New York: Harper & Row, 1977. The official autobiography by Dempsey, who was assisted by his adopted daughter. Should be read with care and compared to other sources.

Fleischer, Nathaniel S. *Fifty Years at Ringside*. New York: Fleet, 1958. Fleischer, editor and publisher of *The Ring* in its heyday, was considered "Mr. Boxing" after World War II. Provides an excellent evaluation of Dempsey, compared to other ring greats such as Jack Johnson and Joe Louis. Fleischer always considered Johnson to be the greatest champion.

———. *The Heavyweight Championship*. New York: G. P. Putnam's Sons, 1949. Includes excellent comparisons between Dempsey and Tunney and captures the reasons for which Dempsey was so popular with the public after his defeats by Tunney.

Heimer, Mel. *The Long Count*. New York: Atheneum, 1969. Focuses on the long-count knockdown in the second Dempsey-Tunney bout; provides good insights into the private life as well as the career of Dempsey.

Kahn, Roger. *A Flame of Pure Fire: Jack Dempsey and the Roaring '20's*. New York: Harcourt Brace, 1999. A biography placing Dempsey in the context of his times. Kahn describes Dempsey as a "wild and raucous champion of the wild and raucous 1920's."

Kearns, Jack, with Oscar Fraley. *The Million Dollar Gate*. New York: Macmillan, 1966. An "as-told-to" autobiography providing Kearns's version of his life with Dempsey. Anti-Dempsey, it should be read in conjunction with Dempsey's own autobiography.

Roberts, Randy. *Jack Dempsey: The Manassa Mauler*. Baton Rouge: Louisiana State University Press, 1979. The best source for beginning to understand Dempsey's problems both inside and outside the ring.

Smith, Red. "Jack Dempsey Is Dead." *The New York Times*, June 1, 1983, sec. 2, p. 4. In-depth obituary of Dempsey, prepared by Smith, who was a noted sports columnist for the *Times*.

Joe DiMaggio

> *If you keep thinking about what you want to do or what you hope will happen, you don't do it, and it won't happen.*

Baseball player

DiMaggio was one of the greatest players in major-league baseball history. In addition to generating impressive career batting and fielding statistics and leading the New York Yankees to ten American League pennants during his thirteen-year career, DiMaggio played with a verve, grace, and style that have made him a symbol of excellence on the baseball diamond as well as an American cultural icon. He was the first baseball player to earn a six-figure annual salary when he signed a contract in 1949 for $100,000.

Born: November 25, 1914; Martinez, California
Died: March 8, 1999; Hollywood, Florida
Also known as: Joseph Paul DiMaggio, Jr. (full name); the Yankee Clipper (nickname)
Area of achievement: Sports

Early Life

Joe DiMaggio (dih-MAJ-ee-oh) was the eighth of nine children born to Giuseppe DiMaggio and Rosalia DiMaggio, Italian immigrants who migrated to California around the beginning of the twentieth century. Giuseppe, who made his living as a crab fisherman, moved his family to San Francisco the year after Joseph's birth. As youngsters, the DiMaggio boys worked with their father, attended local public schools, and played sandlot baseball, a sport for which they seemed to possess a natural gift. Two of Joseph's brothers, Vincent and Dominic, also had major-league baseball careers, though their older brother Tom, who followed Giuseppe into crab fishing, was said to be the family's most proficient baseball player.

Joe DiMaggio left school during his sophomore year of high school and searched for work, which was difficult to obtain during the Great Depression year of 1931. At the time, however, his older brother Vincent was playing baseball for the San Francisco Seals of the highly competitive Pacific Coast League. Vincent secured a place on the team for Joe for the final three games of the 1932 season. By this time, DiMaggio's baseball playing abilities were well known around San Francisco. As a teenager, he had excelled on the sandlots and in the local Boys' Club league, and he had already been recruited by the San Francisco Missions, the Seals' local rival.

DiMaggio became a star outfielder for the Seals during the season of 1933. He batted .340 and at midseason secured a hit in sixty-one consecutive games, a minor-league record that still stands. DiMaggio's extraordinary achievements during that maiden professional season attracted the attention of several major-league baseball scouts. The next year, the New York Yankees purchased DiMaggio from the Seals for $25,000, but they allowed him to play one more season in San Francisco to gain addi-

DiMaggio, Joe

Joe DiMaggio.
(Library of Congress)

tional playing experience. During that final season with the Seals, DiMaggio batted .398, hit thirty-four home runs, and was voted the Pacific Coast League's most valuable player.

LIFE'S WORK
DiMaggio broke into the major league with a big season. In 1936, playing for the Yankees, DiMaggio logged a .323 batting average, hit 29 home runs, and recorded 125 runs batted in (RBIs) and 132 runs scored. He helped the Yankees win their first American League pennant since 1932 and batted .346 in his team's World Series victory over the New York Giants.

By age twenty-two, DiMaggio had grown to six feet two inches tall, and his slender adolescent frame had filled out to 200 pounds. He had developed rugged good looks, and after beginning to draw a major-league baseball salary, he started to collect a wardrobe that would perennially place him on the lists of America's best-dressed men. In the batter's box, DiMaggio assumed a very wide stance and generated power from a classic sweeping swing of the bat. He possessed extremely strong wrists and forearms that enabled him to drive the bat across the plate with enormous speed and power.

DiMaggio followed his outstanding rookie performance with perhaps the best season of his baseball career. In 1937, DiMaggio batted .346, led the American League with 46 home runs, scored 151 runs, and batted in another 167. Again the Yankees won the American League pennant and bested the New York Giants in the World Series. During the next five seasons, DiMaggio established himself as the American League's most feared hitter. He led the league with a .381 batting average in 1939 and a .352 average in 1940. In 1941, he recorded the single most noteworthy achievement of his baseball career when he secured a hit in fifty-six consecutive games (which smashed the previous mark of forty-four games). In every Yankees game played between May 15 and July 16 of that season, DiMaggio recorded at least one hit. Twice, in 1939 and 1941, he was voted the American League's most valuable player. Each year he was named to the American League's all-star team.

DiMaggio was more than a skilled batsman; he excelled in every phase of the game. He developed into a splendid outfielder who effectively covered the large centerfield area of Yankee Stadium. At the crack of the bat, DiMaggio seemed to have a sense of where the ball would land, and he gracefully dashed to the far reaches of the outfield to snag long drives hit by opposing batters. His smooth and fluid running stride earned him the nickname the Yankee Clipper. Until he developed a sore shoulder late in his career, DiMaggio also possessed a strong throwing arm; he was frequently among the league leaders in outfield assists. Although DiMaggio was not blessed with incredible speed, he was an outstanding base runner as well, and he was rarely thrown out trying to take an extra base.

DiMaggio missed three full seasons, 1943 through 1945, to serve in the armed forces during World War II. As a twenty-eight-year-old married man—he had married Dorothy Arnold, an actor and singer, in 1939—DiMaggio was exempted from military service, but he joined the Air Force cadets and served in California and Hawaii during the war, though he never engaged in combat.

DiMaggio was less effective on the baseball diamond after the war. In 1946, his batting average dropped below .300 for the first time in his career, and the Yankees failed to win the American League pennant. At this point in his career, DiMaggio began to feel the effects of several chronic injuries and physical ailments. He suffered foot and shoulder injuries, and he developed ulcers. These impairments often forced DiMaggio out of the Yankees lineup and reduced his effectiveness when he was able to play. Nonetheless, he earned the respect of both teammates and opponents for often playing in severe pain.

In 1948, however, DiMaggio was healthy, missing only one game, and he led the American League in home runs with 39 and in runs scored with 155. On the basis of that excellent performance, DiMaggio convinced the Yankees to offer him a contract for $100,000 for the season of 1949, making DiMaggio the first baseball player to earn a six-figure annual salary.

The next season, however, DiMaggio was troubled by bone spurs in his heel that required surgery for removal. He missed the opening months of the 1949 season and remained disabled through late June, watching the Yankees battle the Boston Red Sox for first place in the American League. On June 28, DiMaggio felt well enough to play, and he was in the Yankee lineup for a big game against Boston that evening at Fenway Park. Having missed the entire spring exhibition season and the team's first sixty-nine games, DiMaggio felt rusty, but in his first at-bat of the game he hit a single. In his second plate appearance, he hit a home run. The Yankees won the game 5-4. The next day,

DiMaggio, Joe

DiMaggio hit two home runs in another Yankee victory. In the final game of the series, DiMaggio hit another home run that propelled the Yankees to victory. After not having played a game in almost nine months, DiMaggio had returned to the lineup to record four home runs and nine RBIs in a three-game series against the first-place Red Sox— an exhibition of hitting noted as one of the highlights of DiMaggio's baseball career.

By that time, however, DiMaggio was clearly nearing the end of his brilliant career. He played two more years and retired after the 1951 season with a .325 lifetime batting average and 361 home runs. In 1955, DiMaggio was inducted into the Baseball Hall of Fame, and, in 1969, he was voted baseball's greatest living player. After his retirement, DiMaggio's name remained in the headlines. Having divorced his wife Dorothy, DiMaggio commenced a romance with Marilyn Monroe. They married on January 14, 1954. The marriage never worked out, however, and the couple divorced in October of that same year, though they continued to see each other on occasion until Monroe's death in 1962.

For ten years after his retirement, DiMaggio separated himself from major-league baseball. He devoted his time to charities and worked in public relations for several businesses. In 1961, he returned to the Yankees as a spring training coach, a post that he held for several seasons. In 1969, the Oakland Athletics hired DiMaggio as a vice president and coach, but that arrangement lasted only a few seasons. DiMaggio continued to make himself present on special baseball occasions such as opening day and Old Timers' Day at Yankee Stadium and at the annual Baseball Hall of Fame induction ceremony until his death in 1999.

Significance

DiMaggio was unquestionably one of the greatest players in baseball history, but his legacy on the baseball diamond cannot be summarized effectively by statistics alone. Having played with great ability as well as grace and style, DiMaggio developed into a symbol of athletic excellence and an authentic American hero, the child of immigrants who gained fame and fortune through great skill and determination. In retirement, DiMaggio became an American cultural hero, noted in story and song as a symbol of great skill, courage, and dignity. Santiago, the old Cuban fisherman of Ernest Hemingway's novel *The Old Man and the Sea* (1952), invokes DiMaggio's name to sustain his courage while he battles a huge marlin. In his hit song "Mrs. Robinson" (1968), Paul Simon laments the loss of genuine American heroes with the words, "Where have you gone, Joe DiMaggio?/ A nation turns its lonely eyes to you./ What's that you say, Mrs. Robinson?/ Joltin' Joe has left and gone away."

Baseball fans born decades after the conclusion of DiMaggio's great career know DiMaggio's achievements on the baseball diamond and respect his professionalism. When he appeared at baseball stadiums, DiMaggio was wildly applauded by young fans who never saw him play, and he was recognized on the street by people who knew little about the game of baseball. He received numerous awards and accolades, including honorary degrees from American universities. DiMaggio is among a small group of American athletes—Babe Ruth, Jackie Robinson, Mickey Mantle, Arnold Palmer, Muhammad Ali—whose names and legacies carry far beyond the field of sports.

—*James Tackach*

Further Reading

Allen, Maury. *Where Have You Gone, Joe DiMaggio: The Story of America's Last Hero.* New York: E. P. Dutton, 1975. Contains first-person reminiscences from a score of DiMaggio's teammates, coaches, opponents, friends, and family members.

Cramer, Richard Ben. *Joe DiMaggio: The Hero's Life.* New York: Simon & Schuster, 2000. Cramer's biography debunks the mythology surrounding DiMaggio, revealing that the great ballplayer was a troubled and self-centered person.

Creamer, Robert W. *Baseball in '41.* New York: Viking Penguin, 1991. Re-creates the baseball season of 1941, the year of DiMaggio's fifty-six-game hitting streak.

DiMaggio, Joe. *Lucky to Be a Yankee.* New York: Grosset & Dunlap, 1951. DiMaggio's autobiography, covering his childhood and professional baseball career.

Durso, Joseph. *DiMaggio: The Last American Knight.* Boston: Little, Brown, 1995. A detailed biography of DiMaggio covering his life from childhood through his retirement years.

Halberstam, David. *The Summer of '49.* New York: William Morrow, 1989. Re-creates the great pennant race between the New York Yankees and the Boston Red Sox during the baseball season of 1949.

Moore, Jack. *Joe DiMaggio: A Bio-Bibliography.* Westport, Conn.: Greenwood Press, 1986. Contains a biography of DiMaggio, a review of the literature about him, interviews with three of his baseball contemporaries, a detailed statistical summary of his career, and an extensive bibliography of books and articles.

Sultans of Swat: The Four Great Sluggers of the New York Yankees. New York: St. Martin's Press, 2006. As originally reported by *The New York Times*, this collection examines the careers of DiMaggio and Babe Ruth, Mickey Mantle, and Lou Gehrig.

Walt Disney

" *If you can dream it, you can do it.* "

Businessman and film producer

Disney was an innovator in the entertainment industry—including television, film, and theme parks—a chance-taker responsible for what he termed "imagineering," leading the way in amusements for children as well as adults.

Born: December 5, 1901; Chicago, Illinois
Died: December 15, 1966; Burbank, California
Also known as: Walter Elias Disney (full name)
Areas of achievement: Theater and entertainment; business; film

Early Life

Walt Disney (DIHZ-nee) was born in Chicago, Illinois. His mother, née Flora Call, was German-American; his father, Elias Disney, was Irish-Canadian. Both parents had farming backgrounds. Walt Disney was the youngest of four sons by eight years

Disney, Walt

but was older than his only sister, Ruth. With little doubt, the strongest influence on Walt during his childhood was his father. The older Disney was a religious fundamentalist and stern taskmaster who was always ready to beat his children with his belt. The beatings finally led to a showdown in Walt's teen years, when he physically prevented his father from beating him, marking a turning point in their relationship.

The Disney children were denied a typical childhood environment, their father refusing to provide toys, games, and sporting equipment. Added to this were the frequent job changes of their father, who sought success in such areas as farming, railway shops, carpentry and contracting work, newspaper distributing, and factory owning. The disruption of moves from Chicago to Marceline, Missouri, to Kansas City, Missouri, and back to Chicago in the space of eleven years principally accounted for Walt never getting past the ninth grade.

Disney's favorite childhood memories were of Marceline, where he lived from the age of four to eight. The Disneys worked a forty-eight-acre farm, a life Disney loved. It also provided him with his first acquaintance with a variety of animals, contact that his closest brother, Roy, stressed was the start of a sensitive, lifelong consideration. Marceline was also a railroad hub, and Disney was ever after captivated by trains.

Following the collapse of the farm, the Disneys rode in a boxcar to Kansas City, where Elias bought a newspaper delivery route. Seven days a week, Walt Disney delivered early morning newspapers over a sprawling route, sometimes falling asleep in warm buildings and then waking in panic to find himself behind schedule. Nightmares of that panic affected him for the rest of his life. Tardiness at school regularly resulted, and post-school hours were occupied by afternoon paper deliveries. Paid nothing for this work, Disney had a job in a candy store at noontime to earn spending money.

In his teen years, Disney participated in vaudeville amateur nights, doing a prizewinning Charles Chaplin act, and took some beginning art lessons. When Elias sold his business to move back to Chicago to take over a jelly factory, the fifteen-year-old Disney stayed in Kansas City. He tutored the new owner of the newspaper distributorship and became a vendor on the Santa Fe Railroad through the summer.

Rejoining his parents in Chicago, Disney became a school newspaper cartoonist, pursued photography, worked at the jelly factory, took odd jobs, and joined an art class at the Chicago Academy of Fine Arts. When he finished the ninth grade, he worked for the post office through the summer and decided to enlist in the military. The United States had recently entered World War I. Disney, eager to serve and to wear a uniform to impress the girls, was rejected by every recruiter; he was too young. With his mother's cooperation, Disney obtained forged documents that enabled him to be accepted as a driver in the Red Cross Ambulance Corps. The war ended just before Disney went overseas, but his experiences in France made an indelible mark on him. Though not yet eighteen when he returned to Chicago, he knew that he could not return to school. Disney had reached his full height (five feet ten inches) and weighed a solid 165 pounds. He was ready to strike out on his own.

LIFE'S WORK

Moving to Kansas City, Disney went through an assortment of jobs as a commercial artist and cartoonist, his work leading to an enthusiastic interest in filmed cartoons. He also met, and even tried a business partnership with, Ub Iwerks, a young man his own age who was a more gifted artist than Disney. Thus started a long and interesting, often troubling, relationship between the consummate artist Iwerks and the consummate organizer and visionary Disney.

During this period, Disney combined a live performer with cartoon figures in *Alice's Wonderland* (1923), which led to a popular *Alice in Cartoonland* (1923-1926) series after Disney had moved to Hollywood, California. Over three years, Disney produced fifty-six *Alice in Cartoonland* comedies.

Disney returned to a straight cartoon format with the *Oswald the Rabbit* (1927) series, producing twenty-six cartoons in the series in less than two years before losing the rights to Oswald in a New York contract dispute with Charlie Mintz and Universal Pictures. Oswald was tremendously popular, and Disney knew that he had to have a dynamic, new character.

Disney had by then married Lillian Bounds (July 13, 1925), an original employee in the first Disney Brothers Studio. She had accompanied Disney to New York and now faced with him the important trip back to California. Referring to a series of Iwerks sketches and reminiscing with Lilly about past experiences, Disney settled on a cartoon mouse as his next star. Disney first called his character Mortimer, but Lilly thought that pompous and suggested Mickey. Soon after, Disney—with Iwerks get-

Walt Disney.
(Library of Congress)

Disney, Walt

ting prominent credit as the major cartoonist—finished two Mickey Mouse cartoons, *Plane Crazy* (1928), based on the exploits of Charles A. Lindbergh, and *Gallopin' Gaucho* (1928), with Mickey emulating Douglas Fairbanks. Prior to their release, however, Disney saw the first feature talkie, *The Jazz Singer* (1927), and realized that the future of films was in sound. He immediately worked on a third Mickey Mouse cartoon, *Steamboat Willie*, incorporating sound and thus revolutionizing the film cartoon industry. Its premiere on November 18, 1928, stands as a hallowed date in Disney annals. After its success, sound was added to the first pair of Mickey Mouse cartoons, and they were released.

Within three years, Mickey Mouse had captured audiences throughout the United States, and by 1936 it was said in all seriousness that the famous mouse was the most widely recognized figure in the world. Disney himself was acclaimed as one of the two top geniuses in filmmaking; Chaplin was the other. Sales of Mickey Mouse watches and windup handcars literally saved the Ingersoll Watch Company and the Lionel Corporation from bankruptcy during the Depression. Figures such as songwriter Cole Porter, conductor Arturo Toscanini, and King George VI of England were dedicated Mickey Mouse fans, while famed Russian film director Sergei Eisenstein pronounced Mickey Mouse to be America's most original cultural contribution.

Most intriguing of all was the symbolic tying together of Mickey Mouse and his creator. Mickey's voice, on all sound tracks until 1946, was Disney's own. During that period, Mickey, along with the other featured characters (Donald Duck and Pluto are prime examples), had progressed from a Depression barnyard to comfortable middle-class suburbia. Mickey Mouse had ventured into dozens of occupations, from airplane pilot to polo player to orchestra conductor, and had ended as an entrepreneur. Some claimed that Disney had used Mickey to grope for his own niche—and the entrepreneur won in the end.

In 1931, Disney had suffered a nervous breakdown. Fully recovered, he launched into the rest of the decade with enormous energy. He earned plaudits for innovative moves and won a string of Academy Awards. In 1932, he was the first in animated cartooning to use the Technicolor process. His Academy Award-winning *Three Little Pigs* (1933) had uplifted American morale during the Depression by supplying a theme, "Who's Afraid of the Big Bad Wolf?" *Snow White and the Seven Dwarfs* (1937), the first feature-length cartoon in history, also took an Oscar and paved the way for many later classics. Academy Awards were also won by *The Tortoise and the Hare* (1935), *The Old Mill* (1937), and *The Ugly Duckling* (1939), among other films. To Disney, the most important development of the 1930's was the growth of the studio. From a handful of employees and a garage studio had emerged many hundreds of workers in a huge complex.

The 1940's were quite different. Disney actually could have gone bankrupt. World War II gravely affected the studio's overseas market, and American entry into the war came on the heels of two box-office disasters: *Fantasia* (1940) and *The Reluctant Dragon* (1941). *Fantasia* was not to be seen as a masterpiece until the 1960's. A traumatic labor union strike (1941) devastated Disney, whose belief that he headed one big, happy family was shattered when roughly half the cartoonists picketed. An irony through this episode was that the conservatively Republican, strongly anticommunist

Disney, who blamed the strike on communists, had come full spectrum from his father, who had been an active labor unionist supporter of oft-defeated socialist presidential candidate Eugene V. Debs. The strike so affected Disney that, appearing close to a second breakdown, he agreed to tour Latin America for the State Department. In his absence, the strike was settled.

The surprising success of *Dumbo* (1941), the shortest feature Disney ever made, and *Bambi* (1942), as well as a United States government contract to produce training films, barely kept Disney in business. The goodwill tour of Latin America inspired *Saludos Amigos* (1943) and *The Three Caballeros* (1945), but Disney's finances had to wait for the war's end before significant recovery.

Disney's first postwar feature was *Make Mine Music* (1946), which was later cut into ten short cartoons, another innovation by Disney and one he followed with later omnibus features. *Song of the South* (1946) followed, combining live action and cartoon animation, and gaining an Academy Award for its song "Zip-a-dee Doo-dah." The National Association for the Advancement of Colored People (NAACP) and the National Urban League, however, criticized the work for perpetuating racial stereotyping.

Two years later, Disney produced one of his favorite films, *So Dear to My Heart*, entirely live-action. Though animated features immediately followed—*The Adventures of Ichabod and Mr. Toad* (1949) and the extremely profitable *Cinderella* (1950)—the 1950's, and especially the 1960's, saw Disney shifting emphasis to live-action films.

Disney practically took over the field of nature documentaries in the 1950's with his *True-Life Adventure* series, winning three Oscars and several international awards. The decade also witnessed Disney's entry into television, starting innocently with consecutive Christmas specials in 1950-1951, proceeding to a weekly *Disneyland* series in 1954 (during which a *Davy Crockett* serial led to a surprise multimillion-dollar bonanza) and a daily *Mickey Mouse Club* show in 1955. Thereafter, Disney virtually wrote his own ticket in television.

Disney's most important accomplishment of the 1950's, however, was Disneyland, which opened in Anaheim, California, on July 13, 1955, the Disneys' thirtieth wedding anniversary. When taking his daughters, Sharon (adopted) and Diane, to amusement parks, Disney had been constantly disappointed and had determined to create a far superior park. He insisted that Disneyland was not an amusement park, though he claimed that it was his own private amusement area. The fantastic success of Disneyland and the later Walt Disney World (1971) in Florida stood as final testimony to Disney's courage and vision. He had stood virtually alone against other Disney executives, willing to risk frightening losses against a dream, something he had done fairly often before. Controversial in this regard is what happened to his EPCOT (Experimental Prototype Community of Tomorrow) idea at Disney World. Disney's intention was to have an actual live-in community of thousands of people, under an all-weather dome, with its own schools, shopping and entertainment areas, and innovative technology placing them a minimum of twenty-five years into the future. Those thoughts died when Disney died. EPCOT, as exciting as many of its projects are, and as Disney-like as its practices are, falls far short of Disney's own concept.

Disney, Walt

By the 1960's, Disney was wealthy and in full command of a respected, diversified empire. Despite the tremendous expansion of Disney holdings, he remained in dictatorial control, as he had since the 1920's. Yet, in the 1960's, critics suggested that Disney had lost his spirit, pointing to the lack of any outstanding films. His answer was the supercalifragilisticexpialidocious *Mary Poppins* (1964). The biggest financial hit in Disney's life, the film was nominated for thirteen Academy Awards and garnered five. Though more projects followed, *Mary Poppins* proved to be his last hurrah. Disney, a heavy smoker through his career, was hospitalized for lung cancer in 1966, appeared to have recovered from major surgery, but suffered a relapse, dying on December 15, 1966, in a hospital room that overlooked his Burbank studio. An entire world mourned the loss of a person who had come to seem like a favorite uncle.

SIGNIFICANCE

Disney was said to have the facility of seeing things no others saw, from chairs being reshaped into acrobatic animals to swamps converted into paradises. More important, he was willing to express his ideas openly, despite the risk of ridicule. Had Disney been an outstanding artist himself, it is entirely possible, even probable, that his success would have been much more limited, given the tens of thousands of talented artists who do not achieve fame. Disney learned early, however, that his own drawing skills were limited. Thus, he became the organizer, the "idea man," and exercised absolute control of his own, and hence his corporation's, destiny. Disney's attention to the most minute detail, his insistence on perfection, his enormous drive, and his need to be boss caused him to be both loved and hated by his employees. The finished product, be it feature film, cartoon short, comic book, or Disneyland ride, bore his unmistakable stamp, however, whether employees were happy or not: That was the Disney way. Disney always assumed that others were as fiercely devoted to each project as he, an assumption that often misled him into thinking that others shared his joy as well.

Disney, born in the big city and spending most of his life in major cities, nevertheless loved small-town and country life, often painting the contrast between urban ugliness and rural beauty. Indeed, his works created a Disney America, and the effects of these Disney impressions on American culture are inestimable. Presented through his films, television productions, comic and story books, and theme parks, Disney's America may well represent the nation's image to most Americans, especially given that children learn with Disney products at an early age.

The probability is that Disney never intended to create a substitute America. Instead, Disney in many ways was Everyperson. He did not cater as much to a mass public as to his own taste, which was clearly reflective of conservative American ideals. When he aimed to please the public, his objective was to entertain, to amuse, to bring smiles to his consumers, rather than to propagandize. He was his own best audience. By suiting himself—almost as if he were giving himself a childhood he had never had fulfilled—he innately satisfied the public. Certainly creative, he also accumulated wealth that could have made him a snob. However, Disney never lost the common touch.

Disney's place in the American panorama is secure. His classic works are regularly reissued in cinemas, a Disney Channel and other television productions keep his name prominently in the limelight, copyrighted Disney materials are marketed abundantly every day, and the California and Florida amusement parks easily exceed any others in attendance. Indeed, it has been suggested that Disneyland and Walt Disney World constitute America's Mecca, shrines that most Americans visit at least once in their lives.

Disney seized opportunities as they presented themselves and, though hating failure, never feared it. The greatest key to Disney's stunning success was probably his willingness to be selfish enough not only to be himself but also to risk his own and others' bankrolls to prove that his ideas worked.

—*John E. DiMeglio*

FURTHER READING

Apple, Max. "Uncle Walt." *Esquire*, December, 1983. A quick and frank look at Disney and his accomplishments in a readable magazine format.

Barrier, Michael. *The Animated Man: A Life of Walt Disney*. Berkeley: University of California Press, 2007. Barrier, a noted animation historian, presents a detailed examination of Disney's life and work and an analysis of his impact on American culture.

Culhane, John. *Walt Disney's "Fantasia."* New York: Harry N. Abrams, 1983. A rich, sensitive study by one of Disney's most valued employees, concentrating on a film classic that caused Disney more than a few headaches. An excellent source.

Davidson, Bill. "The Fantastic Walt Disney." *The Saturday Evening Post*, November 7, 1964. An interesting look into a Disney who had ventured into his varied nooks and crannies. Poignant in that Disney had little more than two years to live at the time of its publication.

Finch, Christopher. *The Art of Walt Disney*. New York: Harry N. Abrams, 1973. Probably the best work done on Disney. Rich with illustrations, it also contains important biographical data, as well as a number of extremely challenging premises, not the least being a defense of Disney as a great artist.

Gabler, Neal. *Walt Disney: The Triumph of the American Imagination*. New York: Knopf, 2006. A thorough examination of Disney's life and work, especially good for its in-depth description of the early years of the Disney studio and how the studio created its groundbreaking animation.

Jackson, Kathy Merlock, ed. *Walt Disney: Conversations*. Jackson: University Press of Mississippi, 2006. A collection of newspaper and magazine interviews and speeches from 1929 through 1966 that provide an overview of Disney's ideas, work, and personality.

Maltin, Leonard. *The Disney Films*. New York: Bonanza Books, 1973. An excellent source by one of the best film historians. The book is compartmented into such matters as features and shorts so that a sense of continuity is somewhat missing, but the book remains one of the best sources on Disney films.

Mosely, Leonard. *Disney's World*. New York: Stein and Day, 1985. This study reveals some data never before published. For example, the author contends with the question of whether Disney's corpse is in a cryogenic state and reaches no definite conclusions.

Munsey, Cecil. *Disneyana: Walt Disney Collectibles.* New York: Hawthorn Books, 1974. A fascinating work that seems to cover every marketed product from Disney's long career. The book's lone drawback is that, since its publication, the collector's market has experienced tremendous inflation.

Schickel, Richard. *The Disney Version.* New York: Touchstone Books, 1985. A strong, challenging study, loaded with provocative side trips. Probably the most stimulating of the biographical studies, this latest edition is superior to the earlier works by the same author.

Thomas, Bob. *Walt Disney.* New York: Simon & Schuster, 1976. The warmest Disney biography, without being sugarcoated. The author is a dependable, fair-minded, noted biographer, and his work served greatly to aid the later Leonard Mosely work.

Wallace, Kevin. "Onward and Upward with the Arts: The Engineering of Ease." *The New Yorker,* September 7, 1963. A well-written, witty, informative, and thought-provoking treatment, typical of *The New Yorker.*

DOROTHEA DIX

" In a world where there is so much to be done, I felt strongly impressed that there must be something for me to do. "

Educator and social reformer

A crusader for the rights of the mentally ill, Dix devoted her life to establishing psychiatric hospitals to provide proper care for those with mental and emotional problems and set the stage for worldwide reforms in the care and treatment of people with mental disabilities.

Born: April 4, 1802; Hampden, District of Maine, Massachusetts (now in Maine)
Died: July 17, 1887; Trenton, New Jersey
Also known as: Dorothea Lynde Dix (full name)
Areas of achievement: Mental health; social reform

EARLY LIFE

Dorothea Lynde Dix (dihks) had a difficult childhood. By his family's standards, her father married below his station. Because married students were not accepted at Harvard, where he was studying at the time, he was sent to manage family holdings in Maine—nothing less than the frontier during the early nineteenth century. Never a financial success, he did win some notice as a traveling Methodist preacher and a writer of tracts. Thus, Dorothea was often without her father, and unfortunately her mother was often too ill to give her the attention that young children require.

Dorothea's happiest memories of her solitary childhood revolved around visits to her paternal grandparents in Boston. Her grandfather, a successful if curmudgeonly physician, and grandmother provided a warm welcome. Dorothea's first exposure to public service came from watching her grandfather practice medicine. She had few playmates her own age and was four years older than her nearest sibling. At least one biographer believes that isolation from children and involvement with adults led to a high degree of self-interest and blocked the development of personal emotional commitment. In any case, she never married, and most, though not all, of her friendships were with people involved in her charitable endeavors.

When Dix was around the age of twelve and unhappy at home, she began to live permanently with her then-widowed grandmother. To her dismay, her grandmother insisted on both academic and social discipline, and Dorothea's sense of rejection was actually worsened. After two years, she was sent off to live with a great-aunt, where she finally found a congenial home. Although still a teenager, she was allowed to open a school for small children, which she ran successfully for three years before returning to Boston. Two years later, in 1821, she opened a school for girls. Education for women was unusual—public schools accepted girls only for the few months when many boys were out for agricultural labor—and even more unusual was Dix's insistence on including natural science in the curriculum. Dorothea Dix proved to be a gifted teacher, and she seemed to have found her life's work. In a gesture that was a harbinger of her future, she added a program for poor girls who otherwise had no opportunity for schooling.

Ill health—apparently tuberculosis—and the collapse of a romance with her cousin resulted in a new direction for Dix. While recovering her strength during the mid-1820's, she became interested in Unitarianism and the ideas of William Ellery Channing. This Christian sect's emphasis on the goodness of humanity and the obligation to serve it would inspire her for the rest of her life. A new attempt to run a school, however, led to her complete collapse in 1836 and her doctor's orders never to teach again.

Life's Work

While recuperating, Dorothea Dix visited England. During her two-year stay with the William Rathbone family, she met a variety of intellectuals and reformers. When she returned to the United States, she found that the deaths of her mother and grandmother had left her financially independent. She spent several years seeking some focus for her life. Then, in 1841, she was asked to teach Sunday School for women at the East Cambridge Jail. She found the innocent and guilty, young and old, sane and insane crowded into the same miserable, unheated facility. Those regarded as insane were often chained or otherwise restrained. Her discussions with humanitarians such as George Emerson, who would become a longtime friend, led her to understand that conditions in East Cambridge Jail were, if anything, better than those in most jails. There was virtually no distinction made between mental illness and impairment, and in the entire country there were only about 2,500 beds specifically for those with emotional problems. Dix quickly had a sense that she had come upon something important that needed doing.

Dix's first move was to demand and get heat for the insane in the East Cambridge Jail. Then, after talking with other reformers, including Samuel Gridley Howe and Charles Sumner (later a radical Republican leader during Reconstruction), she began a

Dix, Dorothea

survey of facilities for the insane in Massachusetts. Although the McLean Psychiatric Hospital was relatively progressive, most of the mentally ill were kept in local poorhouses, workhouses, and jails. She visited every one. Conditions were horrendous. Patients were often locked in dirty stalls, sometimes for years, and many were chained to the floor. Many were virtually naked, and physical restraint was virtually universal. She also found time to discuss treatment with the best doctors, finding that much more humane treatment was being successfully used in leading hospitals in Europe and a few in the United States. More common in the United States were strong sedatives to induce quiescence and the application of shocks, such as surprise dousings with ice water, to bring individuals back to reality.

After eighteen months, Dix prepared a petition to the Massachusetts legislature. The petition stated that psychiatric facilities should provide for physical health and comfort (she would later expand this to prisons) and seek, with kindness and support, to cure diseased minds. When it was published, this document at first produced embarrassment and denial and then attacks upon the author. Her friends—Howe, Sumner, and others—rushed to defend her. She had her first victory when a bill providing for more and better accommodations for the mentally ill was passed. Her career was beginning to take shape.

Dix's initial investigations had occasionally taken her outside Massachusetts, where she found conditions to be generally worse than in her home state. From the mid-1840's to the mid-1850's, she traveled many thousands of miles around the United States and Canada, finding and exposing the suffering of the indigent insane. Although she did not travel to the far West (she did work in Texas), Dix visited almost every one of the thirty-one states of that era.

Dix developed an investigative technique in which, by means of simple persistence and will, she forced her way into every facility where the insane were kept. There followed dramatic revelations of suffering and abuse that shamed all but the most hardened and/or fiscally conservative. Finally, she launched a petition to the legislature for the necessary funds and regulations to ensure improved care. She found the inevitable compromises necessary in any political campaign frustrating, but she settled for whatever state legislatures would fund and began again.

Results varied. New Jersey and Pennsylvania established state psychiatric hospitals as a result of Dix's efforts. New York, however, rejected her call for six hospitals and only expanded the beds available in an existing facility. In 1845, with the help of Horace Mann and George Emerson, Dix expanded her efforts to prison reform and published a manual on that subject. Proper care for the mentally ill, however, remained her main focus.

From 1845 to 1846, Dix worked in Kentucky, Tennessee, Louisiana, Alabama, Georgia, and Arkansas, and she was working her way up the Mississippi when, in September, she collapsed in Columbus, Ohio. By December, she was sufficiently recovered to resume traveling, and in January, 1847, she presented a petition to the Illinois legislature, which resulted in the passage of a bill creating a psychiatric hospital. Later that year and in the following year, she had similar successes in Tennessee and North Carolina. Her fame was growing enormously, as were the respect and love with which Americans regarded her. One of the greatest marks of the latter came in 1863, when

Dix, Dorothea

Confederate troops invading Pennsylvania stopped a train on which Dix was riding. A North Carolina officer recognized her, and the train was released to continue on its way. Not even the passions of Civil War could change people's feelings about Dorothea Dix.

Despite local successes—between 1844 and 1854 Dix persuaded eleven states to open hospitals—Dix recognized by the late 1840's that only a national effort would resolve the problems of the insane. No more than one-fourth of those needing care got it. She began to push for a federal effort, suggesting that five million acres of public land be committed to set up a fund to provide care for insane, epileptic, and mentally impaired Americans. A bill to this effect was introduced in Congress in 1848. Dix was provided with a small office in Washington from which to lobby. Questions about cost and constitutionality blocked the various versions of the bill until 1854, when, to her joy, it passed both houses. Her exultation was brief, however, for President Franklin Pierce vetoed the bill on the grounds that Congress had no authority to make such grants outside the District of Columbia. It was the final blow—the effort was abandoned.

Exhausted and ill, Dix planned to renew efforts in individual states, but friends and doctors persuaded her to rest. She visited friends in England, and within two weeks she was involved in efforts to reform psychiatric care there. She went so far as to go personally to the home secretary, Sir George Grey, to argue for improvements in Scotland. Before she left, a Royal Commission to investigate the problem was in the works. She also helped to sustain a reform effort in the Channel Islands before touring the Continent, where she visited hospitals, asylums, and jails, exposing problems and demanding change. The force of her personality seems to have made her irresistible; even Pope Pius IX was forced to initiate improvements in the Vatican's handling of the mentally ill.

Dix's return to the United States in 1856 brought a large number of requests for aid. She was soon traveling again, seeking various reforms and funding. In the winter of 1859 alone, she asked state legislatures for a third of a million dollars, and in 1860, she got large appropriations for hospitals in South Carolina and Tennessee. The outbreak of the Civil War brought reform work to a halt, and Dix promptly volunteered her services.

After being appointed superintendent of U.S. Army nurses, Dix spent four years of very hard work developing the Medical Bureau from a service set up for an army of ten thousand to one that could handle more than that many casualties from one battle. Unfortunately, she was too straitlaced at the age of sixty to cope with the rough-and-tumble style of the military. Her New England Puritanism showed in her tendency to think that an army doctor who had had a few drinks should be dishonorably discharged. Although her work in ensuring the provision of nurses and medical supplies at the beginning of the war was of great importance, in 1863 her authority was quietly reduced, to her bitter disappointment. After the war, Dix spent another fifteen years traveling as the advocate of the insane. Worn out in 1881, she retired to the hospital (the first created by her efforts) in Trenton, New Jersey, where she lived until her death in 1887.

Significance

Dorothea Dix's importance can be seen from simple statistics. In 1843, the United States had thirteen institutions for the mentally ill; in 1880, it had 123. Of the latter, 75

Dix, Dorothea

were state-owned, and Dix had been a key factor in the founding of 32 of them. She had also been able to get a number of training schools for the mentally impaired established, and specialized training for psychiatric nurses had begun.

More important, the lives of many unfortunate people had been made easier thanks to Dix's efforts. The idea that the insane, even if poor, deserved humane care and treatment intended to help them recover had been established in the United States. Dix's efforts began a process that has continued throughout the twentieth century and has left the United States a world leader in the treatment of mental illness.

—*Fred R. van Hartesveldt*

FURTHER READING

Brown, Thomas J. *Dorothea Dix: New England Reformer*. Cambridge, Mass.: Harvard University Press, 1998. This study of Dix provides new insight into her passions and methods.

Dain, Norman. *Concepts of Insanity in the United States, 1789-1865*. New Brunswick, N.J.: Rutgers University Press, 1964. A useful description of attitudes and problems that Dix had to confront during her career.

Dix, Dorothea. *Asylum, Prison, and Poorhouse: The Writings and Reform Work of Dorothea Dix in Illinois*. Edited by David L. Lightner. Carbondale: Southern Illinois University Press, 1999. Dix traveled to Illinois in 1846 and 1847 to publicize the need for more humane treatment of prisoners, the insane, and the poor. This book is a collection of her writings during that trip, including a series of newspaper articles about conditions in jails and poorhouses. There also are two memorials she presented to the state legislature: One describes the treatment of inmates at a state penitentiary, and the other urges the establishment of a state insane asylum. Lightner has provided detailed notes and introductions to these documents, and in a concluding essay he assesses the immediate and continuing impact of Dix's work.

_____. *On Behalf of the Insane Poor: Selected Reports*. New York: Arno Press, 1971. A valuable source of Dix's ideas and opinions expressed in her own words. Her eloquence and passion shine through.

Gollaher, David. *A Voice for the Mad: A Life of Dorothea Dix*. New York: Free Press, 1995. A balanced biography highlighting Dix's strengths and weaknesses, her efforts in the area of legislative reform, and her second career as head of the Civil War nurses.

Marshall, Helen. *Dorothea Dix: Forgotten Samaritan*. Chapel Hill: University of North Carolina Press, 1937. Although it is sometimes overly sympathetic to its subject, this is a solid and well-written biography.

Snyder, Charles M., ed. *The Lady and the President: The Letters of Dorothea Dix and Millard Fillmore*. Lexington: University Press of Kentucky, 1975. Provides interesting insights into one period in Dix's life.

Tuke, Daniel. *The Insane in the United States and Canada*. London: M. K. Lewis, 1885. Reprint. New York: Arno Press, 1973. This contemporary description of the problems Dix tried to solve gives a valuable perspective of the situation. It is very useful for modern students trying to achieve an understanding of her work.

Jimmy Doolittle

> *If we should have to fight, we should be prepared to so so from the neck up instead of from the neck down.*

Aviator

Doolittle was a pioneer in American aviation, establishing numerous records and gathering data vital to aviation history. His defining accomplishment as a military pilot was an air raid on Tokyo in 1942 that shocked Japan during World War II. Also, as an aviation researcher, Doolittle combined test-flight information with laboratory data to prove that pilots needed visual aids to know wind and direction information. This was a major contribution to the knowledge of instruments and their use, making flying more precise and less dangerous.

Born: December 14, 1896; Alameda, California
Died: September 27, 1993; Pebble Beach, California
Also known as: James Harold Doolittle (full name); the Lone Pilot (nickname)
Areas of achievement: Aviation; military

Early Life

Jimmy Doolittle (DOO-liht-tuhl) was born in Alameda, California. He was the only child of Frank Doolittle and Rosa Doolittle. While he was still an infant, his father left the family for Alaska in search of gold. After three years, the family was reunited in Nome, Alaska. The next eight years, in the most lawless town in Alaska, taught Doolittle independence and self-defense. A difficult relationship with his father, plus his mother's insistence that her son have better educational opportunities than those offered in Alaska, led to a return to California in 1908. Now eleven years old, Doolittle lived with his mother in Los Angeles.

Reaching college age, Jimmy enrolled in the University of California, Berkeley, as a mine engineering major. His self-defense skills led him to amateur boxing. Although only five feet four inches tall, he became a West Coast bantamweight and middleweight champion. To earn extra money he briefly turned to professional boxing.

Jimmy was a college junior in 1917 when the United States entered World War I. Having already developed a strong interest in aviation, he enlisted in the U.S. Army's Signal Enlisted Reserve Corps as a flying cadet. Quickly earning his pilot's license, he became a second lieutenant in the Army Air Corps. He served in the Air Corps until 1930, leaving as a major.

During these early years, Doolittle served as an instructor pilot and engaged in air aerobatics, with the goal of breaking aviation records. His first record came in 1922 when he crossed the North American continent from Florida to California, becoming the first to do so in less than twenty-four hours. He finished his bachelor's degree at Berkeley the same year.

Life's Work

In 1923, Doolittle, with a two-year leave of absence from the military, enrolled at the Massachusetts Institute of Technology. By 1925 he had earned both a master's degree

Jimmy Doolittle.
(© 2002 National Air
and Space Museum,
Smithsonian Institution/
SI Neg 2001-13008)

and a Ph.D. in aeronautical engineering. His doctoral dissertation, "Wind Velocity Gradient and Its Effect on Flying Characteristics," disproved the assumption that pilots knew instinctively the direction and speed of the wind, as well as the direction in which their plane was flying. Doolittle combined test-flight information with laboratory data to prove that pilots needed visual aids to know wind and direction information. This was a major contribution to the knowledge of instruments and their use, making flying more precise and less dangerous.

Doolittle's daredevil feats reached their peak in the last half of the 1920's. By 1925 he had won all major racing trophies, including the Schneider Trophy for winning a seaplane race and flying his Curtiss Navy seaplane an average of 232 miles per hour. This feat earned Doolittle the nickname Lone Pilot. Taking another leave of absence from the Air Corps in April, 1926, he did demonstration flights in South America. On one occasion, after breaking his ankles in an accident unrelated to flying, he flew with his ankles strapped to the plane's rudders, leaving his parachute behind since he could not have bailed out in an emergency.

In 1927, after recovering from his injuries, Doolittle, at Wright Field in Dayton, Ohio, accomplished a feat previously thought impossible. In what was called an "out-

Doolittle, Jimmy

side loop," he dived in his Curtiss fighter plane from ten thousand feet, reached a speed of 280 miles per hour, bottomed out upside down, then climbed to complete the loop.

Major Doolittle left the Air Corps in 1930 but continued his record-setting exploits as a civilian. Working for Shell Oil Company in 1931, he established a new speed record, flying from Burbank, California, to Cleveland, Ohio. He set a new cross-county record the same year. In 1932 he averaged 252 miles per hour, with a top speed of 406 miles per hour, in winning the Thompson Trophy race in Cleveland.

Doolittle, despite his risky aerobatics, was dedicated to improving aviation safety. Based on the ideas of his doctoral dissertation, he became the first pilot to fly with total reliance on instruments, sometimes called "flying blind."

Following the German invasion of Poland in September, 1939, Doolittle reentered the Army Air Corps. Although the United States was not yet directly involved in the war, it was obvious that the nation would soon need experienced pilots. After the Japanese attack on Pearl Harbor, Doolittle was promoted to lieutenant colonel.

Just nineteen weeks after Pearl Harbor, Doolittle successfully carried out the plan that made his name a household word in the United States. His mission is best summarized by the headline that ran in newspapers across the country, "TOKYO BOMBED! DOOLITTLE DOOD IT!"

Early in 1942, Doolittle was chosen to lead a retaliatory, post-Pearl Harbor raid on Japan. The Seventeenth Bombardment Group was formed and began special and top-secret training. Sixteen specially equipped B-25 bombers, each with a five-person volunteer crew, were soon assigned to the mission. Two aircraft carriers also were involved: The USS *Hornet* was modified to carry and launch the bombers, and the USS *Enterprise* led a task force to provide support. Because of the large distance between the *Hornet* and the island of Japan, the plan was for the bombers, after dropping their bombs, to continue on and land in an area of China unoccupied by Japan instead of returning to the *Hornet* at sea.

On April 18, without the element of surprise because the Japanese unexpectedly sighted the *Enterprise*, the bombers were launched; they hit their military targets. Thirteen bombs were dropped around Tokyo, and three were dropped on as many Japanese cities. Although the physical damage was minimal, the psychological blow to Japan was tremendous. However, the planes failed to reach the safe airfields of China. Most crash-landed in the China Sea or in Japanese-occupied China. One landed in the Soviet Union. Five crew members were killed and eight were captured by the Japanese, who executed three. Another captured crew member died of his injuries. In total, seventy-one of the eighty men involved in the operation, including Doolittle, survived; most were saved by the Chinese, but some returned with life-altering injuries.

Shortly after the raid, Doolittle was promoted to brigadier general, skipping the rank of colonel. In May, 1942, President Franklin D. Roosevelt presented General Doolittle with the Congressional Medal of Honor.

During the remainder of the war, Doolittle commanded the Twelfth Air Force in North Africa and the Eighth Air Force in Europe and in the Pacific. He retired from active duty as a lieutenant general in 1959. He gave up action flying in 1961. Curiosity, however, led him to test-fly several new military aircraft, including the F-100, which was the first supersonic fighter, and the huge B-52 bomber. These were his last flights

Doolittle, Jimmy

as first pilot, and, surprisingly, he said later that he never missed it.

As a civilian, Doolittle was chair of the board of Space Technology Laboratories. He enjoyed his retirement years with Joe, his wife of more than seventy years. The two eventually took a trip to Alaska, a visit Doolittle had promised her long before. He died at the age of ninety-six in 1993.

Significance

The bombing of Tokyo and other cities in Japan caused the Japanese to accelerate their plans of expansion. A premature attack on Midway Island in June, 1942, designed to cripple the U.S. aircraft carrier fleet, ended with the loss of four of their own carriers and none from the U.S. Navy.

Doolittle's accomplishments in early aviation technology alone were enough to rank him as a legend, especially given his innovative idea that instrument flying was safe. His wartime activities led to honors by Great Britain, France, China, Belgium, Poland, and Ecuador.

His military service to his own country, before, during, and after World War II, led to numerous honors. The culmination of those honors came in 1985, when President Ronald Reagan presented him with an honorary promotion to the elite rank of four-star general.

—*Glenn L. Swygart*

Further Reading

Larson, Ted W. *Thirty Seconds over Tokyo*. New York: Random House, 1943. Written by the pilot of plane seven of Doolittle's raid, who lost both of his legs crashing into the China Sea. Provides the most detailed account of the raid and the experiences of the crew after the raid, including those captured by the Japanese.

Murray, Williamson. *War in the Air, 1914-1945*. London: Cassell, Wellington House, 1999. Places Doolittle, the raid, and Doolittle's later World War II leadership in the context of early military aviation history. Reveals his impact on the bombing missions that became a vital part of World War II.

Nelson, Craig. *The First Heroes: The Extraordinary Story of the Doolittle Raid, America's First World War II Victory*. New York: Viking Press, 2002. Based on original accounts of aging survivors. Excellent photos of war leaders and events, including the listing and photos of all crew members of all planes involved in the raid.

Thomas, Lowell, and Edward Jablonski. *Doolittle: A Biography*. Garden City, N.Y.: Doubleday, 1976. Perhaps the best of several biographies of Doolittle, all of which repeat the same basic information, including Doolittle's autobiography *I Could Never Be So Lucky Again*, written with Carroll Glines in 1991.

Wilson, William R. "Jimmy Doolittle Reminisces About World War II." *American History*, August, 1997. Based on comments by Doolittle in about 1980. The author first met Doolittle about six months after the raid. Includes biographical and autobiographical information.

HELEN GAHAGAN DOUGLAS

> *I became active in politics because I saw the possibility, if we all sat back and did nothing, of a world in which there would no longer be any stages for actors to act on.*

U.S. congresswoman (1945-1951) and social reformer

Both personally and as a U.S. representative from California, Douglas advocated for civil liberties and opportunities for oppressed minorities. She became only the third woman elected to Congress from California and the first who did not take her congressional seat from a deceased husband.

Born: November 25, 1900; Boonton, New Jersey
Died: June 28, 1980; New York, New York
Also known as: Helen Mary Gahagan (birth name)
Area of achievement: Government and politics

EARLY LIFE

Helen Gahagan Douglas (geh-HAY-guhn DUH-glihs) was born Helen Mary Gahagan in Boonton, New Jersey, where her parents briefly rented a home so that her father could supervise a construction project nearby. Her twin brothers had been born two years earlier, and a sister and brother would follow in 1902 and 1910. She grew up in Brooklyn, New York, in a comfortable household with strong-willed parents intent on imbuing their children with strong moral and educational ideals. Her father, Walter, was an engineer who founded his own construction company in 1899 and prospered from the outset. A graduate of the Massachusetts Institute of Technology, he read insatiably and filled the Gahagan house with shelves of books. Helen's mother, Lillian, had been reared on the Wisconsin frontier. She was a country schoolteacher before her marriage, and her beauty, optimistic outlook, and exquisite singing voice were inherited by her elder daughter.

Douglas had the benefit of the accoutrements of affluence during her childhood. These included a summer home in Vermont, a family trip to Europe when she was twelve, accompanying her mother to the opera (which, ironically, Douglas disliked intensely), and private schools. The first of these was the Berkeley School for Girls, which was located only a block from the Gahagans' home. It was at this school that her interest in acting blossomed under the direction of her drama teacher, Elizabeth Grimball. Her grades were mediocre in subjects unrelated to performing, but she studied intensely for a college preparatory school. She matriculated at Barnard College in New York to be close to the stage and her drama instructor.

Douglas would spend only two years at Barnard College before her debut into the Broadway theatrical world. Her impressive performances in school productions and an Off-Broadway play led director William A. Brady, Jr., to cast her as the ingenue in *Dreams for Sale* by Owen Davis in 1922. Over the extremely strong protests of her father, who insisted that she complete her education, Douglas accepted.

Douglas quickly became a star. Her generally favorable reviews led to contracts with

Douglas, Helen Gahagan

Brady and other well-known producers and assured her a niche in the roster of leading ladies of the 1920's stage. Practically every new theatrical season brought a new role, and she toured the country in roles she established in New York. She was the subject of much press coverage, not only for her acting talent but also for her great beauty.

Douglas's ambition to perform ultimately led in another direction. During the run of a New York play in 1926, she began to take vocal lessons from a Russian émigré, Madame Sophia Cehanovska. For the next several years, Douglas would devote time, money, and trips to Europe to the pursuit of performing operatic roles with leading companies, a pursuit that was never as successful as her Broadway acting career.

Douglas's performance in the 1930-1931 Broadway production of *Tonight or Never* by Lili Hatvany was important for a number of reasons. The play was her only collaboration with the legendary David Belasco (he would die during its run), her father died during the same run, and she married her costar, Melvyn Douglas. By the end of 1931, she had moved from New York to the West Coast, where Melvyn began his career in motion pictures. Except for some brief performing engagements, Helen would not live in New York again until after her immersion in and forced withdrawal from another career of a very different type.

Life's Work

The first task for Douglas and her husband, on reaching California, was to establish a new way of life in new surroundings. Melvyn had a studio contract with Metro-Goldwyn-Mayer (MGM), and Douglas was busy with singing lessons and performances on the West Coast stage in both acting and singing roles. Although Douglas would have the opportunity to read dozens of film scripts in search of suitable parts, her efforts to find strong roles or to receive reasonable financial offers were stymied. She appeared in only one picture, *She* (1935), a film later considered a "classic" for its overblown production and acting rather than for any positive contributions to the cinematic arts.

The hectic pace of life on the dramatic and sound stages for the couple soon led both to seek a respite. They accomplished this by traveling around the world in 1933. A few months after their return home, Douglas gave birth to their first child, Peter. A daughter, Mary Helen, would follow five years later. Douglas continued her theatrical performances and vocal training, and the family settled into a new home built on three acres in the hills above the Hollywood Bowl.

Two significant events contributed to Douglas's involvement in political causes. The first involved her awakening to conditions in Germany and Austria during a concert tour there in 1937. She ultimately canceled several engagements on the tour after encountering anti-Semitism directed against the pianist who was traveling with her. Although she was not Jewish, her husband Melvyn was, so she regarded these sentiments as a personal affront.

Back in California, Douglas became involved in Democratic Party campaign activities in 1938. Her husband had joined in the statewide gubernatorial and congressional campaign efforts; at first, she merely accompanied him to meetings. After becoming acquainted with social and economic conditions firsthand, however, she began to take the lead in organizing efforts to assist migrant workers. As a result of their activities on

Douglas, Helen Gahagan

behalf of California Democrats, the Douglases were invited to visit President Franklin D. Roosevelt and First Lady Eleanor Roosevelt in the White House in 1939. Douglas was greatly impressed by Eleanor Roosevelt, who became for her something of a political mentor and role model.

Douglas's intelligence and capacity for hard work, as well as her friendship with the First Lady, led to her rapid rise within the leadership of the Democratic Party in California. In 1940, she was selected as the state's Democratic national committeewoman. In that capacity, she attended the party's national convention, where she was an enthusiastic supporter of a third term for Roosevelt. Following Roosevelt's reelection, Douglas was appointed vice chair and head of the Women's Division for the California State Democratic Party. Her efforts for Southern California Democratic candidates in 1942 contributed to party successes there in spite of Republican victories throughout the rest of the state.

Douglas's high visibility in state Democratic politics made her a natural choice for the congressional race in the Fourteenth District in 1944, when popular congressmember Thomas Ford announced his retirement. Although she did not live in the largely working-class district in central Los Angeles, she campaigned thoroughly there and won the nomination in the May primary. Prior to the general election, Douglas delivered a principal address before the Democratic National Convention in Chicago, in which she reviewed the accomplishments of the Roosevelt administration. In the fall campaign, she followed the lead of Democrats nationally in identifying her programs with Roosevelt and the New Deal, a strategy that produced a narrow victory. She became only the third woman elected to Congress from California and the first who did not take over her seat from a deceased husband.

In Washington, D.C., Douglas adhered to the same formula that had produced political success in California. She maintained a grueling schedule, largely eschewed social events, and applied her keen mind to the process of absorbing all available information on issues pending before Congress. Her legislative interests lay in two areas, one involving foreign affairs, the other domestic. She secured an appointment to the House Foreign Affairs Committee, which is usually an unimportant body, since only the Senate ratifies treaties. Nevertheless, with negotiations under way for the postwar international organization that became the United Nations, Douglas believed that the House as well as the Senate would play an integral role in the increased nationwide commitment to internationalism. Membership on the House Foreign Affairs Committee would provide a forum for activities designed to ensure world peace. In domestic affairs, Douglas's natural inclinations were bolstered by the makeup of her congressional district. She lent support throughout the postwar period to legislation benefiting organized labor and African Americans and other minorities.

Through her diligence, her charismatic appeal, and her high visibility in the press, Douglas became a leading figure in California politics. Following her second reelection, in 1948, her congressional seat seemed to be secure; she and her supporters now looked to a greater challenge—the seat in the U.S. Senate held by the conservative Democrat Sheridan Downey. Following the incumbent's withdrawal from the 1950 primary, Douglas won the nomination in spite of vicious attacks on her internationalist position as being procommunist.

Douglas, Helen Gahagan

The smear tactics begun in the Democratic primary intensified in the general election, when Douglas faced Congressman Richard M. Nixon. In an election that has since become famous for the infamous dirty tricks of the Nixon campaign, Douglas was removed from public office. In her autobiography some thirty years later, she wryly remarked that "there's not much to say about the 1950 campaign except that a man ran for the Senate who wanted to get there, and didn't care how."

Douglas's life after politics was spent partly in the public eye, since she continued to speak in favor of causes such as world peace. She campaigned for Democratic presidential candidates Lyndon B. Johnson in 1964 and George McGovern in 1972. During the last three decades before her death from cancer in 1980, she was certainly not forgotten, but neither was she occupying her accustomed place in the limelight.

SIGNIFICANCE

In a number of respects, Douglas had an enviable life and a great deal of good fortune. She became a famous actor almost overnight, not only because of her talent but also because of her great beauty. Capitalizing on her acting fame, she became a force in politics through intelligence and hard work. Although her fame boosted her political career at the outset, it eventually became a liability to Douglas as a politician seriously intent on pursuing an important agenda. She constantly downplayed her glamour in order to be taken seriously.

She was able, in the end, to use the press attention focused on her to advance an international and domestic social program that was liberal, enlightened, and forward-looking. She did not hesitate to challenge bigotry, isolationism, and red-baiting. Although her public service was cut short because of Nixon's malicious campaign against her in 1950, she stood as a symbol for other intelligent, forthright, public-spirited women and men to emulate.

—*Richard G. Frederick*

FURTHER READING

Douglas, Helen Gahagan. *The Eleanor Roosevelt We Remember*. New York: Hill & Wang, 1963. In her autobiography, Douglas clearly indicated that Eleanor Roosevelt was a major influence in her decision to become a political activist. This book, a tribute to Roosevelt, contains photographs from a variety of sources and an admiring text by Douglas.

_____. *A Full Life*. Garden City, N.Y.: Doubleday, 1982. An engaging autobiography in which the author thoroughly discusses her family life, stage experiences, and involvement in political affairs.

Douglas, Melvyn, and Tom Arthur. *See You at the Movies: The Autobiography of Melvyn Douglas*. Lanham, Md.: University Press of America, 1986. A posthumously published autobiography that focuses on the author's acting career and includes occasional anecdotes about his wife's careers and their marriage.

Lowry, Margaret M. S. "Pretty and Therefore 'Pink': Helen Gahagan Douglas and the Rhetorical Constraints of U.S. Political Discourse." *Rhetoric Review* 22, no. 3 (2003): 282. Lowry's feminist and rhetorical analysis examines Douglas's 1946 speech "My Democratic Credo." She concludes that Douglas adapted a "mascu-

line" discourse to create the image of a rational, authoritative representative.
Mitchell, Greg. *Tricky Dick and the Pink Lady: Richard Nixon vs. Helen Gahagan Douglas—Sexual Politics and the Red Scare, 1950.* New York: Random House, 1998. Mitchell examines the California Senate campaign of 1950.
Morris, Roger. *Richard Milhous Nixon: The Rise of an American Politician.* New York: Henry Holt, 1990. Includes the fullest description and analysis of the 1950 Senate campaign in California. Especially valuable for establishing the context of California politics. Morris covers the Douglas and Nixon primary campaigns as well as the general election.
Scobie, Ingrid Winther. *Center Stage: Helen Gahagan Douglas, a Life.* New York: Oxford University Press, 1992. A thorough biography by a professional historian who conducted research in manuscript and oral history collections around the country. Scobie also met with and interviewed the Douglases.

WILLIAM O. DOUGLAS

" *The Constitution is not neutral. It was designed to take the government off the backs of people.* **"**

Associate justice of the United States (1939-1975)

As the longest-serving justice in the history of the U.S. Supreme Court, Douglas was reputed as an outspoken advocate of civil rights and liberties during his thirty-six years on the Court. In particular, he played a critical role in establishing a constitutional right to privacy and developing broad protections for freedom of speech.

Born: October 16, 1898; Maine, Minnesota
Died: January 19, 1980; Washington, D.C.
Also known as: William Orville Douglas (full name)
Area of achievement: Law and jurisprudence

EARLY LIFE
William O. Douglas (DUH-glihs), the son of a minister, was born in the small town of Maine, Minnesota. At the age of three, his family moved to California and two years later to Yakima, Washington, the town where he would grow up. Douglas, just five years old when his father died after stomach surgery, grew up in modest circumstances. His mother struggled to provide for him and his two younger siblings. From an early age, Douglas held many jobs, such as picking fruit and delivering newspapers. His outstanding performance in high school earned for him a scholarship to Whitman College in Walla Walla, Washington. After graduating from college, he taught high school for a brief time before earning his law degree from Columbia University in New York.

After serving as a law professor at Columbia and Yale, Douglas entered government service when Franklin D. Roosevelt became president of the United States in

Douglas, William O.

1933. Roosevelt appointed Douglas to serve as chair of the Securities and Exchange Commission (SEC), the government agency that regulated and investigated corporations' sale of stock. Douglas chaired the agency until March, 1939, when Roosevelt selected the forty-year-old Douglas for the U.S. Supreme Court. Because the U.S. Constitution does not limit the term of service for Supreme Court justices, many justices serve for life. As the youngest appointee in the twentieth century, Douglas was on the Court for thirty-six years and helped decide several thousand cases.

LIFE'S WORK

Associate Justice Douglas helped to initiate a significant shift in the Court's focus during Roosevelt's presidency. Roosevelt's long tenure as president (1933-1945) allowed him to appoint many replacements for justices who retired or died. At the time of Roosevelt's death in 1945, eight of the nine justices on the Court, including Douglas, were his appointees. Douglas joined the other Roosevelt appointees in shifting the Court's focus from cases analyzing the legality of social programs and economic regulation to devoting much of its attention to defining individual rights and liberties. It was during Douglas's tenure as a justice that the Court made many of its most important decisions concerning racial equality, freedom of speech, and the rights of criminal defendants.

Douglas voted consistently in interpreting the Constitution as a document protecting the rights of individuals and limiting the government's authority to control people's lives. Studies of Supreme Court decision making found that Douglas, more frequently than any other justice of the twentieth century, favored individuals in their disputes with the government over civil rights and liberties, especially those cases concerning the First Amendment rights of freedom of speech and religion.

Douglas was a prolific author of judicial opinions. He often wrote the dissenting opinion in those cases in which he disagreed with the Court's decision. He dissented in those cases in which a majority of justices supported government authority over claims of individuals' rights. For example, in *Miller v. California* (1973), he dissented against the Court's efforts to create definitions for permissible obscenity and pornography because he believed that the First Amendment broadly protected people's right to express themselves with words and pictures, even if those expressions were offensive to others. Similarly, he dissented during the 1950's, in cases such as *Dennis v. United States* (1951), when the majority of justices permitted the government to prosecute and imprison people for teaching and advocating a political philosophy of communism. In *Terry v. Ohio* (1968), when the Court permitted police officers to stop and frisk people on the streets after observing suspicious behavior, Douglas was the lone justice to argue that there must be concrete evidence of criminal misconduct—and not mere suspicion—before police can interfere with a person's liberty simply to be on a street.

Justice Douglas also wrote important majority opinions. In *Skinner v. Oklahoma* (1942), for example, Douglas wrote the decision that prohibited states from imposing forced sterilization on persons convicted of crimes. His most famous—and controversial—majority opinion came in *Griswold v. Connecticut* (1965), the case that announced the existence of a constitutional right to privacy. Although the word "privacy" does not appear in the Constitution, Douglas wrote that the right to privacy is older than the Constitution itself and can be recognized by reading between the lines of other provisions concerning search and seizure, freedom of association, and other rights. The reasoning in Douglas's opinion in *Griswold* was later used by the Court to establish rights concerning abortion (*Roe v. Wade*, 1973), the private sexual conduct of gay and lesbian adults (*Lawrence v. Texas*, 2003), and other controversial matters. Many critics claim that Douglas went too far in *Griswold* by inventing a right to privacy that does not exist in constitutional law.

Douglas gained a reputation as a fiercely independent justice who was not afraid to express his political views and conclusions about legal matters. In one memorable episode, lawyers approached him during the Court's summer recess to challenge the legality of President Richard M. Nixon's decision to expand U.S. military action in Cambodia during the Vietnam War. Douglas drafted a temporary order prohibiting Nixon from further bombing in Cambodia, but the other justices quickly communicated with one another and unanimously overruled Douglas, thus preventing a major confrontation between the Court and the president (*Holtzman v. Schlesinger*, 1973).

The books he wrote about freedom, democracy, and American society clearly show Douglas's independence and legal philosophy. His writings were controversial because critics believed that he was encouraging antiwar protesters and civil rights activists to rebel against society during the 1960's. Indeed, his nonjudicial writings were used by Congressmember Gerald R. Ford in 1970 in his unsuccessful bid to persuade federal lawmakers to impeach Douglas and remove him from the Court. The impeachment effort was also fueled by the Nixon administration's desire to seek revenge against political liberals after the U.S. Senate refused to confirm two conservative southern judges whom Nixon had sought to appoint to the Court. Douglas's independence continued even after he retired from the Court in 1975 because of a debilitating stroke. He unsuccessfully sought to initiate a new policy that would permit retired justices to continue to participate in the Court's deliberations in selected cases.

Significance

Douglas contributed significantly to the expansion of constitutional rights for Americans in the middle decades of the twentieth century. As an associate justice from 1939 to 1975, he participated in many of the Court's most famous, and infamous, decisions, including the prohibition on governmental racial discrimination in *Brown v. Board of Education* (1954); the provision of free speech protection for inflammatory, antigovernment speeches in *Brandenburg v. Ohio* (1969); and the requirement that police officers inform suspects of their rights prior to questioning (*Miranda v. Arizona*, 1966). Douglas's own opinion in *Griswold v. Connecticut* (1965) established the constitutional right to privacy and laid the foundation for subsequent Court decisions protecting individuals' personal choices against intrusion by government. Because Douglas was both the Supreme Court's longest-serving justice and its most outspoken advocate of individual liberty and free expression, his influence reached thousands of decisions that shaped, and will shape, the evolving definition of constitutional rights.

—Christopher E. Smith

FURTHER READING
Ball, Howard, and Phillip J. Cooper. *Of Power and Right: Hugo Black, William O. Douglas, and America's Constitutional Revolution*. New York: Oxford University Press, 1992. Analysis of Douglas's contributions to constitutional law and his legacy as a Supreme Court justice. Focuses on specific issues, including racial discrimination, freedom of speech, and freedom of religion.

Douglas, William O. *The Court Years, 1939-1975*. Vol. 2 in *The Autobiography of William O. Douglas*. New York: Random House, 1981. Focuses on Douglas's role in decision making on the Supreme Court.

_____. *Go East Young Man: The Early Years—The Autobiography of William O. Douglas*. New York: Random House, 1974. Contains a first-person account of Douglas's childhood, education, and early career. Later authors have challenged the honesty and accuracy of certain aspects of Douglas's retelling of the details of his early life.

Murphy, Bruce Allen. *Wild Bill: The Legend and Life of William O. Douglas*. New York: Random House, 2003. A comprehensive biography of Douglas. Presents a critical view of Douglas's unfulfilled aspirations for political office and his efforts to shape his public image.

O'Brien, David M. *Storm Center: The Supreme Court in American Politics*. 6th ed. New York: W. W. Norton, 2003. Analysis of the history and internal operations of the Supreme Court. Includes discussion of Douglas's role on the Court and his participation in the Court's decision making.

FREDERICK DOUGLASS

> *" I prefer to be true to myself, even at the hazard of incurring the ridicule of others, rather than to be false, and to incur my own abhorrence. "*

Abolitionist, journalist, and social reformer

The best-known and most influential African American of his time, Douglass had a lifelong concern with freedom and human rights for all people. He articulated these concerns most specifically for black Americans and women.

Born: February, 1817?; Tuckahoe, Talbot County, Maryland
Died: February 20, 1895; Washington, D.C.
Also known as: Frederick Augustus Washington Bailey (birth name)
Areas of achievement: Civil rights; social reform; journalism; oratory

EARLY LIFE
Born a slave, Frederick Douglass (DUH-glihs) was originally named Frederick Augustus Washington Bailey. He was of mixed African, white, and Indian ancestry, but other than that, he knew little of his family background or even his exact date of birth.

Douglass, Frederick

Douglass believed that he was born in February, 1817, yet subsequent research indicates that he may have been born a year later in February, 1818. Douglass never knew his father or anything about him except that he was a white man, possibly his master. Douglass's mother was Harriet Bailey, the daughter of Betsey and Isaac Bailey. Frederick, his mother, and his grandparents were the property of a Captain Aaron Anthony.

In his early years, Frederick experienced many aspects of the institution of slavery. Anthony engaged in the practice of hiring out slaves, and Douglass's mother and her four sisters were among the slaves Anthony hired out to work off the plantation. Consequently, Douglass seldom saw his mother and never really knew her. The first seven years of his life were spent with his grandmother, Betsey Bailey, not because she was his grandmother but because as an elderly woman too old for field work she had been assigned the duty of caring for young children on the plantation.

The boy loved his grandmother very much, and it was extremely painful for him when, at the age of seven, he was forced by his master to move to his main residence, a twelve-mile separation from Betsey. It was there, at Anthony's main residence, that Douglass received his initiation into the realities of slavery. The years with his grandmother had been relatively carefree and filled with love. Soon, he began to witness and to experience personally the brutalities of slavery. In 1825, however, Douglass's personal situation temporarily improved when Anthony sent him to Baltimore as a companion for young Tommy Auld, a family friend. Douglass spent seven years with the Aulds as a houseboy and later as a laborer in the Baltimore shipyards. The death of Anthony caused Douglass to be transferred to the country as a field hand and to the ownership of Anthony's son-in-law. Early in 1834, his new owner hired him out to Edward Covey, a farmer who also acted as a professional slave-breaker. This began the most brutal period of Douglass's life as a slave.

After months of being whipped weekly, Douglass fought a two-hour battle with Covey that ended in a standoff, and the beatings stopped. Douglass's owner next hired him out to a milder planter, but Douglass's victory over Covey had sealed his determination to be free. In 1836, Douglass and five other slaves planned an escape but were detected. Douglass was jailed and expected to be sold out of state, but the Aulds reprieved him and brought him back to Baltimore, where he first served as an apprentice and then worked as a ship caulker. However improved Douglass's situation might be in Baltimore, it was still slavery, and he was determined to be a free man. On September 3, 1838, Douglass borrowed the legal papers and a suit of clothes of a free black sailor and boarded a train for New York.

In New York, he was joined by Anna Murray, a free black woman with whom he had fallen in love in Baltimore. Douglass and Anna were married in New York on September 15, 1838, and almost immediately moved farther north to New Bedford, Massachusetts, where there were fewer slave catchers hunting fugitives such as Douglass. It was also to elude slave catchers that Douglass changed his last name. He had long abandoned his middle names of Augustus Washington; he now dropped the surname Bailey and became Frederick Douglass. The move and the name change proved to be far more than symbolic; unknown to Douglass, he was about to launch on his life's work in a direction he had never anticipated.

Douglass, Frederick

LIFE'S WORK

New Bedford was a shipping town, and Douglass had expected to work as a ship caulker; however, race prejudice prevented his working in the shipyards, and he had to earn a living doing any manual labor available: sawing wood, shoveling coal, sweeping chimneys, and so on. Anna worked as a domestic when she was not caring for their growing family. Anna bore Douglass five children: Rosetta, Lewis, Charles, Frederick, Jr., and Annie. Unexpectedly, the abolitionist movement of the 1830's, 1840's, and 1850's changed both Douglass's immediate situation and his whole future.

Within a few months of his escape to the North, Douglass chanced on a copy of William Lloyd Garrison's abolitionist newspaper, *The Liberator*. *The Liberator* so moved Douglass that, in spite of his poverty, he became a subscriber. Then, on August 9, 1841, less than three years after his escape, Douglass and Garrison met. This and subsequent meetings led to Garrison offering Douglass an annual salary of $450 to lecture for the abolitionist movement. Douglass was so convinced that he would not succeed as a lecturer that he accepted only a three-month appointment. In fact, he had begun his life's work.

Scholars have debated whether Douglass's greatest accomplishments were as an orator or a writer; both his speaking and his writing stemmed from his involvement with the abolition movement, and both were to be his primary activities for the remainder of his life.

From the beginning, Douglass was a powerful, effective orator. He had a deep, powerful voice that could hold his audiences transfixed. Moreover, Douglass was an impressive figure of a man. He had a handsome face, bronze skin, a leonine head, a muscular body, and was more than six feet in height. He stood with dignity and spoke eloquently and distinctly. Indeed, his bearing and speech caused critics to charge that Douglass had never been a slave; he did not conform to the stereotypic view of a slave's demeanor and address.

Even Douglass's allies in the abolition movement urged him to act more as the public expected. Douglass refused; instead, he wrote his autobiography to prove his identity and thus began his career as a writer. *Narrative of the Life of Frederick Douglass: An American Slave* (1845) remains his most famous and widely read book. It was an instant success. However, in the narrative, Douglass had revealed his identity as Frederick Bailey, as well as the identity of his owners, making himself more vulnerable than ever to slave catchers. Anna was legally free, and because of her their children were free also, but Douglass was legally still a slave. To avoid capture, he went to England, where he remained for two years.

In England, Douglass was immensely successful as a lecturer and returned to the United States, in 1847, with enough money to purchase his freedom. By end of the year, he was legally a free man. Also in 1847, Douglass moved to Rochester, New York, and began publication of his own newspaper, *The North Star*. While editing *The North Star*, Douglass continued to lecture and to write. In 1855, he published an expanded autobiography, *My Bondage and My Freedom*; he also published numerous lectures, articles, and even a short story, "The Heroic Slave" in 1853. Much later in life, he published his third, and most complete, autobiography, *Life and Times of Frederick Douglass, Written by Himself* (1881).

In all of his writings and speeches, Douglass's major concerns were civil rights and human freedom. As a person born in slavery, and as a black man living in a racially prejudiced society, Douglass's most immediate and direct concerns were to end slavery, racial prejudice, and discrimination. However, he always insisted that there was little difference between one form of oppression and another. He proved the depth of his convictions in his championing of the women's rights movement at the same time he was immersed in his abolitionist activities. In fact, Douglass was the only man to participate actively in the Seneca Falls Convention that launched the women's rights movement in the United States in 1848. Moreover, his commitment was lasting; on the day of his death, in 1895, Douglass had returned only a few hours earlier from addressing a women's rights meeting in Washington, D.C.

By the 1850's, Douglass was active in politics. He also knew and counseled with John Brown and was sufficiently implicated in Brown's Harpers Ferry raid to leave the country temporarily after Brown's capture and arrest. From the beginning of the Civil War, Douglass urged President Abraham Lincoln not only to save the Union but also to use the war as the means to end slavery. Douglass also urged black men to volunteer and the president to accept them as soldiers in the Union armies.

By the end of the Civil War, Douglass was the most prominent spokesperson for black Americans in the country. With the end of the war and the advent of Reconstruction, Douglass's work seemed to have reached fruition. By 1875, with the passage of the Civil Rights Act of that year, not only had slavery been ended and the Constitution amended but also the laws of the land had guaranteed black Americans their freedom, their citizenship, and the same rights as all other citizens. However, the victories were short-lived. The racism, both of North and of South, that had dominated the antebellum era triumphed again during the 1880's and 1890's. According to the Constitution, black Americans remained equal, but it was a paper equality. In fact, prejudice and discrimination became the order of the day across the whole United States.

For Douglass personally, the years following the Civil War contained a number of successes. He was financially solvent. He served in a number of governmental capacities: secretary of the Santo Domingo Commission, marshal and recorder of deeds in the District of Columbia, and United States minister to Haiti. For twenty-five years, he was a trustee on the board of Howard University. Nevertheless, these personal successes could not alleviate Douglass's bitter disappointment over the turn of public events, and he never ceased to fight. He continued to write, to lecture, and even began another newspaper, *New National Era*.

SIGNIFICANCE

Frederick Douglass's career and his personal life were all the more remarkable when one considers the times in which he lived. His life was an example of the human will triumphing over adversity. Born into slavery, by law a piece of chattel, surrounded by poverty and illiteracy, he became one of the greatest American orators, an accomplished writer and editor, and for more than fifty years the most persistent and articulate voice in the United States speaking for civil rights, freedom, and human dignity regardless of race or sex. Douglass, more than any other individual, insisted that the ideals of the Declaration of Independence must be extended to all Americans.

Douglass, Frederick

Douglass's personal life reflected the principles for which he fought publicly. He always insisted that race should be irrelevant: Humanity was what mattered, not race and not sex. In 1882, Anna Murray Douglass died after more than forty years of marriage to Frederick, and in 1884, Douglass married Helen Pitts, a white woman who had been his secretary. The marriage caused a storm of controversy and criticism from both black and white people and members of Douglass's own family. However, for Douglass there was no issue: It was the irrelevance of race again. His own comment on the criticism was that he had married from his mother's people the first time and his father's, the second.

Douglass is most frequently thought of as a spokesperson for black Americans and sometimes remembered as a champion of women's rights as well. Up to a point, this is accurate enough; Douglass was indeed a spokesman for black Americans and a champion of women's rights, because in his own lifetime these were among the most oppressed American people. Douglass's concern, however, was for all humanity, and his message, for all time.

—*D. Harland Hagler*

FURTHER READING

Chesebrough, David B. *Frederick Douglass: Oratory from Slavery*. Westport, Conn.: Greenwood Press, 1998. Analysis of Douglass's oratory skills and techniques. Beginning with a biographical sketch, the author moves to Douglass's techniques and finally presents three speeches from different periods in his career.

Douglass, Frederick. *Frederick Douglass: The Narrative and Selected Writings*. Edited by Michael Meyer. New York: Vintage Books, 1984. In addition to being a readily accessible, complete edition of *Narrative of the Life of Frederick Douglass*, this book includes excerpts from Douglass's two later autobiographies and twenty selected writings by Douglass on various topics that are not easily obtainable.

_____. *Life and Times of Frederick Douglass*. Hartford, Conn.: Park Publishing, 1881. Reprint. New York: Citadel Press, 1984. First published in 1881 and reissued in 1892. The 1892 edition is the most commonly reproduced and the most complete of the three autobiographies.

_____. *My Bondage and My Freedom*. New York: Miller, Orton and Mulligan, 1855. Reprint. New York: Dover, 1969. Originally published in 1855, this is the least read of Douglass's autobiographies.

_____. *Narrative of the Life of Frederick Douglass: An American Slave*. Boston: Anti-Slavery Office, 1845. Reprint. Garden City, N.Y.: Doubleday, 1963. Originally published in 1845, the work covers Douglass's life up to that time; it was his first book and remains the most widely read of his three autobiographies.

Factor, Robert L. *The Black Response to America: Men, Ideals, and Organization from Frederick Douglass to the NAACP*. Reading, Mass.: Addison-Wesley, 1970. Factor offers an interesting theoretical interpretation of Douglass as a black spokesman and informative comparison of Douglass with other black spokesmen and leaders.

Lawson, Bill E., and Frank M. Kirkland, eds. *Frederick Douglass: A Critical Reader*. Malden, Mass.: Blackwell, 1999. Essays by fifteen leading American philosophers who revisit Douglass and the place his work has in contemporary social and political thought.

Meier, August. *Negro Thought in America: 1880-1915*. Ann Arbor: University of Michigan Press, 1963. Meier offers a good account of the varieties of thought among black Americans for the period covered and suggests an intriguing, plausible thesis regarding shifts of opinion in the black community. Although the book covers only the last fifteen years of Douglass's life, it is still worth reading for insight into Douglass, especially for any comparison or contrast of Douglass with later black spokesmen such as Booker T. Washington and W. E. B. Du Bois.

Quarles, Benjamin. *Frederick Douglass*. Washington, D.C.: Associated Publishers, 1948. Reprint. New York: Atheneum, 1976. Originally published in 1948, this is an easily available, thorough biography.

Stauffer, John. *The Black Hearts of Men: Radical Abolitionists and the Transformation of Race*. Cambridge, Mass.: Harvard University Press, 2002. Describes the interracial alliance of Douglass, James McCune Smith, Gerrit Smith, and John Brown. The four men worked together on temperance and feminist issues as well as on abolition, seeking to achieve what Stauffer describes as a "vision of sacred, sin-free and pluralistic society."

Wu, Jin-Ping. *Frederick Douglass and the Black Liberation Movement: The North Star of American Blacks*. New York: Garland, 2000. Reassesses Douglass's place in the history of the black liberation movement, focusing on his impact on other black leaders and his Legitimate Reform Society.

W. E. B. Du Bois

" *The cost of liberty is less than the price of repression.* **"**

Educator and civil rights leader

One of the principal founders of the National Association for the Advancement of Colored People, or NAACP, and editor of several influential journals, Du Bois was for many years the leading black intellectual in the United States. Through his teaching, writings, and speeches he advocated economic, political, and cultural advancement of blacks not only in the United States but also abroad.

Born: February 23, 1868; Great Barrington, Massachusetts
Died: August 27, 1963; Accra, Ghana
Also known as: William Edward Burghardt Du Bois (full name)
Areas of achievement: Civil rights; education; social reform

Early Life
W. E. B. Du Bois (dew BOYS) was born of mixed African, French Huguenot, and Dutch descent in Massachusetts. His father, Alfred Du Bois, was the son of Alexander Du Bois, a light-skinned man born of a union between a mulatto slave girl in Santo Domingo and a wealthy American of French Huguenot descent. He lost his father

Du Bois, W. E. B.

early and was reared by his mother, Mary Burghardt, whose family traced its roots to a freed slave in the days of the American Revolution. The Burghardts were proud of their long, stable residence in Massachusetts as free farmers, but because they were black they remained outside the social elite.

Du Bois grew up as part of a small black community of about fifty people among some five thousand whites in Great Barrington. Though his childhood was basically happy, he learned early that blacks were not fully accepted as equal, even in New England. Determined to be a leader of his people, Du Bois studied hard and dreamed of getting a degree from Harvard. Books and writing interested young Du Bois more than athletics, although he did enjoy games and socializing with his friends. When he was graduated from high school in 1884 at the age of sixteen, he was the only black in his class of twelve and was already urging blacks to take advantage of their opportunities to advance through education and other forms of self-help.

The death of his mother shortly after his graduation, lack of funds, and his young age forced deferment of his plans to attend Harvard. After working several months and receiving scholarship aid from some interested churches, however, he was able to enter Fisk University in Nashville, Tennessee, in the fall of 1885. Because of his superior academic background, he was admitted at the sophomore level. Fisk was a radically different world from that of Great Barrington, and, significantly, it provided him with the long-sought opportunity to relate to blacks his own age. Now living among the two hundred blacks at Fisk, he felt a stronger sense of identification with his people and continued his instinctive efforts to make his fellow blacks more conscious of what they could accomplish. He also learned more about the deep-rooted racial discrimination of the South after Reconstruction. Summers were spent teaching in small western Tennessee schools, adding to the profound influence of his Fisk years.

Du Bois was graduated from Fisk in 1888 and at last was able to attend Harvard. With financial aid he matriculated that fall at the junior level. In 1890, he earned a second baccalaureate degree, and the next year a master's degree. From 1892 to 1894, he interrupted his Harvard doctoral program to take advantage of a fellowship to study at the University of Berlin. There he came into contact with some of Europe's most prominent scholars, such as sociologist Max Weber, Heinrich von Treitschke, and Rudolf von Gneist. Like George Santayana and the famous psychologist-philosopher William James at Harvard, these seminal thinkers left a deep mark on his formative mind. Again, he used his summers to good advantage by traveling on the Continent. This European experience did not lessen his commitment to uplifting his race, but it did, he recalled, help him emerge "from the extremes of my racial provincialism . . . and to become more human."

Du Bois returned to Harvard in 1894 and completed his dissertation, "The Suppression of the African Slave Trade to the United States" (1896). That it was accepted for publication by Harvard proved to be the beginning of a career in writing and scholarship. When he was graduated in 1895—the first black to earn a Ph.D. at Harvard—he was ready to enter the academic world and become part of what he called the Talented Tenth —the intellectual elite that, he believed, was the key to the advancement of blacks. He was chosen to speak at the commencement ceremonies and was recognized for his oratorical abilities.

Du Bois, W. E. B.

W. E. B. Du Bois.
(Library of Congress)

LIFE'S WORK

Du Bois's first appointment was at Wilberforce College in Ohio as an instructor in classics, a field in which he had excelled both at Fisk and at Harvard. He was not happy there, however, and in 1896 took a position at the University of Pennsylvania in Philadelphia, where his primary responsibility was to undertake a study of black society in the city's Seventh Ward slums. His experience in Philadelphia was another disappointment. His apartment in the slum area brought him close to the worst effects of poverty, and he felt slighted by the university leadership. On the positive side, his year there produced his second major work and the first serious sociological study of American black social life, *The Philadelphia Negro: A Social Study*, which was published in 1899 after he moved to Atlanta.

From 1897 to 1910, Du Bois headed the economics and history program at Atlanta University and for the first time settled into a rewarding job. During that crucial period when black Americans were going through many important changes, Du Bois developed his ideas in *Atlanta University Studies* and wrote for prominent journals such as the *Atlantic Monthly*. In 1903, he compiled his thoughts in his best-known work, *The Souls of Black Folk*. By then he was openly challenging the ideas of Booker T. Washington, head of the Tuskegee Institute in Alabama. Washington had rapidly risen to prominence after his Atlanta Exposition Address of 1895, in which he urged blacks to acquire industrial education, property, and good personal habits rather than push immediately for political rights or social equality.

The Washingtonian approach has been called accommodationism, while Du Bois's strategy emphasized immediate acquisition of rights such as voting, education, and access to public facilities. Known as a "radical" at that time, in contrast to the more conservative Tuskegee mentality, Du Bois became an intense rival of Washington, who nevertheless remained the most influential black spokesman until his death in 1915. In 1905, Du Bois led a group of like-minded people in the formation of an organization to counter the Tuskegee approach. Meeting on the Canadian side of Niagara Falls in July, they established the Niagara Movement, a short-lived group that never attracted much popular support. Its program was in some ways the opposite of Washington's. It emphasized integration of education, voting rights for black men, and more rapid development of blacks' economic resources. Washington had urged blacks: "Cast down your bucket where you are." Du Bois and the Niagara Movement insisted that they must actively protest against inequality and seize every opportunity to move into the mainstream of American life.

The Niagara Movement failed by 1909, but that same year Du Bois worked with Mary White Ovington and other interested whites in formally establishing the National Association for the Advancement of Colored People (NAACP). It grew out of an interracial meeting triggered by the violent racial disturbances in Springfield, Illinois, in 1908. Du Bois left Atlanta University in 1910 to become director of publicity and research for the NAACP. He also established a new journal, *The Crisis*, which became a semiofficial organ of the NAACP and afforded Du Bois larger opportunities than the Niagara Movement's journal, *The Horizon*, to promulgate his ideas on the Talented Tenth, racial solidarity of blacks, and many other issues. *The Crisis* became essentially self-supporting, and Du Bois often argued with other NAACP leaders about its content. Regarding it essentially as his, he felt that *The Crisis* was actually the spearhead of the movement rather than of the parent NAACP organization.

Du Bois's career after 1910 went through many changes that reflected the varying conditions of race relations in the United States. He retained his editorial position until his break with the NAACP in 1934, but he frequently departed from official NAACP positions. Increasingly he advocated black separatism in the economic sphere, a modified version of Marxist socialism, and Pan-Africanism. Du Bois organized the first important Pan-African congress in Paris in 1919 and became a major rival of Marcus Garvey, the famous Jamaican who led the "back to Africa" movement between the world wars. Until the end of his life, Du Bois advocated various versions of Pan-Africanism and became known in Africa for both this and his many involvements in peace organization. A light-skinned, distinguished-looking man with a mustache and goatee, he contrasted physically with most Africans but, nevertheless, identified with them. By the time his book *Black Reconstruction* (1935) was published, he was openly supporting socialism and racial separatism.

A third stage of his career began in 1934 as he returned to teaching at Atlanta University. From then until 1944, he resumed his academic work and added to his growing

Du Bois, W. E. B.

list of publications: *Black Folk: Then and Now* (1939); his autobiographical *Dusk of Dawn: An Essay Toward an Autobiography of a Race Concept* (1940); after returning to an NAACP job in 1944, *Color and Democracy: Colonies and Peace* (1945); and *The World and Africa* (1947).

After World War II, Du Bois continued to change as the history of blacks in the United States and the world evolved. The persistence of colonial rule after the war disturbed him, and he frankly criticized the great powers for not totally freeing their dependencies. While he continued to see the Soviet Union as a model in some respects, he did not refrain from criticizing that country's domination of Eastern Europe and other areas. His displeasure with American foreign policy further alienated him from his own country, and in 1951 he was charged with failing to register as an agent for a foreign power because of his pivotal position in the Peace Information Center. Although he was acquitted, he never felt at home in the United States after that. He was invited by Kwame Nkrumah to the 1957 ceremonies marking the end of British colonial rule in Ghana but was not allowed to go—although Vice President Richard M. Nixon and black leader Martin Luther King, Jr., were present. Eventually, in 1961, he joined the Communist Party and left his native land for Ghana. Du Bois became a citizen of Ghana and died there, at age ninety-five, in 1963.

SIGNIFICANCE

The life of Du Bois was a mirror of the growing independence of black thought. On the surface he embodied many contradictions: capitalism and socialism, separatism and integration, militancy and accommodationism. However, the common thread of his evolving thought was his awareness of the racial question and the necessity to resolve it. "The problem of the Twentieth Century," he wrote in *Souls of Black Folk*, "is the problem of the color-line." To him, it would yield only to determination and information. His commitment to scientific sociological research was so profound that some have said that he relied too much on it.

Du Bois, however, was not merely a social scientist. He took pride in his blackness even as he recognized its complexity. He sensed in himself and all black Americans a dual identity.

> One ever feels his two-ness,—an American, a Negro; two souls, two thoughts, two unreconciled strivings; two warring ideals in one dark body, whose dogged strength alone keeps it from being torn asunder.
>
> The history of the American Negro is the history of this strife,—this longing to attain self-conscious manhood, to merge his double self into a better and truer self.

Thus, science and poetry flowed together in Du Bois's mind as he wrestled with the universal problem of racism and ways to deal with it.

Du Bois anticipated several salient themes of modern black history, including the emphasis on development of capital resources by blacks and cultural identification with Africa. Although he left the United States, he was widely respected among mainstream black reformers for his literary and personal contributions to black liberation. Ironically, his death occurred on August 27, 1963, as more than 200,000 people were

Du Bois, W. E. B.

assembling to march on Washington. They paused to honor Du Bois, and on the next day NAACP head Roy Wilkins paid tribute to him at the Lincoln Memorial, where Martin Luther King, Jr., delivered his historic "I Have a Dream" speech.

—*Thomas R. Peake*

FURTHER READING

Broderick, Francis L. *W. E. B. Du Bois: Negro Leader in a Time of Crisis*. Stanford, Calif.: Stanford University Press, 1959. An older work still valuable for understanding the evolving views of Du Bois. It contains much biographical information and is especially incisive in capturing the troubled spirit of Du Bois through his many difficult transitions. Credits Du Bois with two major accomplishments: emphasis on equal rights for blacks and his service to the morale of black Americans.

Du Bois, W. E. B. *The Autobiography of W. E. B. Du Bois: A Soliloquy on Viewing My Life from the Last Decade of Its First Century*. New York: International, 1968. One of two major autobiographies by Du Bois. Along with his *Dusk of Dawn*, it provides a useful overview of his life, especially his periodic challenges to other points of view about racial advancement.

———. *Dusk of Dawn: An Essay Toward an Autobiography of a Race Concept*. 1940. New ed. New York: Oxford University Press, 2007. The first of Du Bois's autobiographical works, this one first published in 1940, which examines race, science and empire, war and propaganda, education, and more. Includes a foreword by African American scholar K. Anthony Appiah.

———. *The Philadelphia Negro: A Social Study*. 1899. New ed. New York: Schocken Books, 1967. A new edition of the Du Bois classic from 1899, with a useful introduction by E. Digby Baltzell. Established Du Bois as a serious social analyst of racial problems. Historically based and well documented, it remains a valuable examination of what was the oldest and largest northern black community.

———. *The Souls of Black Folk: Essays and Sketches*. 1903. New ed. Edited and introduced by Brent Hayes Edwards. New York: Oxford University Press, 2007. Du Bois's best-known work, partly autobiographical. Gives insight into his views of the dual nature and citizenship of the black American. The economic, social, and psychological conditions of blacks are explored by an insider torn by his own conflicting drives. Each section is preceded by "sorrow songs" showing the painful struggle of blacks for dignity and self-esteem despite the burdens of slavery and lingering discrimination.

Marable, Manning. *W. E. B. Du Bois: Black Radical Democrat*. New ed. Boulder, Colo.: Paradigm, 2005. Examines Du Bois's life and writings, including his founding of the NAACP, his work as a social scientist, and his political involvement. Marable concludes that as a radical Democrat, Du Bois believed that racism was linked to capitalism.

Rampersad, Arnold. *The Art and Imagination of W. E. B. Du Bois*. Cambridge, Mass.: Harvard University Press, 1976. One of the few good treatments of Du Bois's creative genius. Essentially a biography, this work traces Du Bois's life from his New England beginnings to his last years in Ghana. Not so much concerned with controversies and rivalries as with his literary accomplishments, especially his fiction. Du

Bois comes through as a concerned man, not a self-styled propagandist.
Rudwick, Elliott M. *W. E. B. Du Bois: Voice of the Black Protest Movement*. Champaign: University of Illinois Press, 1982. Previously published as *W. E. B. Du Bois: A Study in Minority Group Leadership* (1960), this well-documented study covers the full sweep of Du Bois's career from his youth to his later involvements in Pan-Africanism and peace promotion. Presents Du Bois as both a realist and an idealist, a skilled propagandist, and a devoted believer in equality. Rudwick suggests that although Du Bois erred in predicting socialism as the answer to the needs of black Americans, he accurately forecast the strong African orientation of modern black culture.
Tuttle, William M., ed. *W. E. B. Du Bois*. Englewood Cliffs, N.J.: Prentice-Hall, 1973. The first section offers a good selection of Du Bois's writings and his basic ideas such as the Talented Tenth, Pan-Africanism, and socialism. The second part includes articles by A. Philip Randolph, Kelly Miller, Marcus Garvey, E. Franklin Frazier, and others reacting to Du Bois's ideas and impact. The final section comprises essays by scholars. An outstanding work for viewing Du Bois in his historical context.
Wolters, Raymond. *Du Bois and His Rivals*. Columbia: University of Missouri Press, 2002. A biography that explores Du Bois's disagreements with other African Americans on topics of racial equality and injustice.

AMELIA EARHART

> *Courage is the price that life exacts for granting peace. The soul that knows it not, knows no release from little things....*

Aviator

By being the first woman to fly across the Atlantic and by establishing numerous other flying records, Earhart helped to promote commercial aviation and advance the cause of women in aviation.

Born: July 24, 1897; Atchison, Kansas
Died: July 2?, 1937; near Howland Island in the Pacific Ocean
Also known as: Amelia Mary Earhart (full name); Lady Lindy (nickname); AE
Areas of achievement: Aviation; women's rights

EARLY LIFE
Amelia Earhart (eh-MEEL-yeh EHR-hahrt), the daughter of Amy Otis and Edwin Stanton Earhart, was born in the home of her maternal grandparents in Atchison, Kansas. Her grandfather was Alfred G. Otis, a pioneer Atchison settler who became a prominent lawyer, banker, and federal district court judge. Her father worked for a railroad as an attorney and claims agent.

Earhart, Amelia

Amelia Earhart.
(Library of Congress)

Earhart's early childhood was spent in Kansas City, Kansas, where she and her younger sister learned to ride horseback. When her father accepted a job in Des Moines, Iowa, in 1905, Earhart and her sister remained for a year in Atchison, where she later recalled, "There were regular games and school and mud-ball fights, picnics, and exploring raids up and down the bluffs of the Missouri River." After joining her father in Des Moines, Earhart attended school and began reading the books that further encouraged her spirit of adventure. Sir Walter Scott, Charles Dickens, George Eliot, and William Makepeace Thackeray were her favorite authors, and she and her sister made up imaginary journeys while they played in an abandoned carriage.

When her father went to work for the Great Northern Railroad, the Earharts moved to St. Paul, Minnesota, but Edwin's alcoholism grew worse and her mother took her daughters to Chicago, where Earhart was graduated from Hyde Park High School in June, 1916. She attended the Ogontz School in Rydal, Pennsylvania, then went to Toronto, Canada, where her sister was in school. In Toronto, she saw wounded veterans of World War I and became a Red Cross volunteer. She worked at Spadina Military Hospital, where she came to know and admire the young fliers of the Royal Flying Corps. In 1918, she was ill with pneumonia and went to live with her sister in Northampton, Massachusetts. While her sister was enrolled at Smith College, Earhart took a course in automobile repair. In 1919, she moved to New York City to study medicine at Columbia University but left after a year to join her parents in Los Angeles.

Earhart, Amelia

The aviation industry was just beginning to develop in Southern California, and Earhart was attracted to the air shows and flying demonstrations at local airports. She took her first airplane ride from the Glendale airport and soon convinced her parents to help her take flying lessons with a pioneer woman pilot, Neta Snook. In June, 1921, Earhart made her first solo flight in a Kinner Airster. One year later, she had saved two thousand dollars to buy a three-cylinder Kinner Canary, a plane in which she set a woman's altitude record of fourteen thousand feet. Her career as a pilot was launched.

Life's Work

Even in 1922, however, flying was expensive, and paid employment for women in aviation was limited. When her parents were divorced, Earhart sold her plane and returned to Massachusetts, where she taught English to immigrants and became a social worker at Denison House, a Boston settlement. She was able to combine her interests in social work and aviation, on one occasion flying over Boston and dropping leaflets announcing a Denison House street fair and, on another, judging a model airplane contest for the National Playground Association.

In 1928, she was selected by the publisher George P. Putnam to fly with pilot Wilmer Stutz and mechanic Lou Gordon in a Fokker trimotor across the Atlantic. The plane, named *Friendship*, had been purchased from the explorer Richard Byrd by Amy Phipps Guest, an American flying enthusiast who had married and settled in England. When Guest was unable to make the flight herself, she asked Putnam to find a young woman (he found Earhart) to represent her in the promotion of women in aviation. On June 3, *Friendship* left Boston for Halifax, Nova Scotia, and Trepassy, Newfoundland. Delayed by bad weather for several days, the plane left Trepassy on June 17 and landed the following day at Burry Port, Wales. Earhart was given a hero's welcome on her return to New York.

Because her flight came only a little more than a year after the solo flight by Charles A. Lindbergh, and because of her tall, slender build and short, blond hair, she was nicknamed Lady Lindy, but she preferred to be called "AE." Within a few months Putnam rushed her account of the flight, *Twenty Hours Forty Minutes* (1928), into print. The book is part autobiography, part journal of the flight, and part advocacy of flying in general. It is the third part that is most interesting because of her observations on the future of flying and on the role of women in aviation.

After stating that the remarkable thing about flying is that it is not remarkable, Earhart goes on to discuss the need for more attractive airports, a review of safety regulations, and better weather reporting. Women will have a role to play in all these areas, she asserts, because they have already had a major impact on the automobile industry. The airplane will be used for leisure and recreation, and the growing purchasing power of American women will help to shape the airline industry. Earhart concludes her book with a characteristically honest assessment of the ways in which her life has been changed by her sudden fame.

For the remainder of her life, Earhart campaigned tirelessly for the cause of women in flying. She participated in many cross-country air races, flew an autogyro (a forerunner of the helicopter), and was one of the founders of an organization of licensed women pilots, the Ninety-nine Club. In 1932, she was elected a member of the Society

Earhart, Amelia

of Women Geographers. She also wrote a column on aviation for *Cosmopolitan* magazine. Her advice was sought by many airlines and airplane manufacturers, and she became a model for young women throughout the country.

In 1931, she married Putnam, who had been managing her career. Her second book, *The Fun of It*, was published in 1932. In it Earhart adds details about her childhood and further explains her attraction to flying, especially to unusual aerial maneuvers known as "stunting."

> I had fun trying to do [stunts] . . . so much so, in fact, I have sometimes thought that transport companies would do well to have a "recreation airplane" for their pilots who don't have a chance to play in the big transports or while on duty. If a little stunt ship were available, the men could go up 5000 feet, and "turn it inside out" to relieve the monotony of hours of straight flying.

Her assurance that flying was safe and fun and her example as the first woman to fly the Atlantic alone increased her popularity with the public. Earhart's solo flight from Harbor Grace, Newfoundland, to Culmore, Ireland, May 21-22, 1932, won for her the Distinguished Flying Cross from the Congress of the United States, an award from the French Legion of Honor, and a medal from the National Geographic Society.

In 1935, she became the first person to fly alone from Hawaii to California and the first to fly nonstop from Mexico City to Newark, New Jersey. The trustees of Purdue University purchased a twin-engine Lockheed Electra for her, and she began to plan a round-the-world flight. After several false starts and minor accidents, Earhart and her navigator, Fred Noonan, took off from Miami, Florida, on June 1, 1937. A month of flying brought them across the Atlantic, Africa, and southern Asia to Lae, New Guinea. She and Noonan took off July 2, intending to land and refuel on tiny Howland Island in the middle of the Pacific Ocean. Several hours later, the Coast Guard cutter *Itasca*, anchored off Howland Island, heard a radio message from Earhart that she was lost and running low on fuel. Neither the plane nor its pilot and navigator was ever found.

Because the Japanese claimed many of the islands in the mid-Pacific, rumors grew that Earhart and Noonan had crashed on a Japanese-held island and been captured and killed. After World War II, attempts were made to find the wreckage and confirm the rumors, but no convincing evidence has come to light.

Significance

Earhart was one of the most appealing heroes in an age of American hero worship. Like Lindbergh and Byrd, Earhart pioneered air travel by establishing flying records and opening new routes. Like Babe Didrikson Zaharias the athlete and Louise Arner Boyd the Arctic explorer, Earhart showed that women had a place in fields that were generally restricted to men.

Although she was criticized during her life for using her fame for profit—at various times she promoted Lucky Strike cigarettes, luggage, and sports clothes—Earhart remained essentially a private person. Because her parents believed that girls should have the same opportunities as boys, she was able to learn to fly. Because she believed that she should help others by sharing her experiences, she maintained a hectic schedule of flying and lecturing.

Once she had been given the opportunity to be the first woman to fly across the Atlantic, Earhart dedicated herself to flying. She was able to combine pleasure with business, and she worked hard at both. Success brought her into contact with other notable women from First Lady Eleanor Roosevelt to film star Mary Pickford. Earhart was also a celebrity, and her untimely death at the age of thirty-nine enshrined her in the hearts of her generation.

Earhart was a product of the social changes in the United States between the world wars. In many ways she epitomized her generation's desire to break with the past and to create a better world. She captured something of that spirit in one of her poems, which begins,

> Courage is the price that life exacts for granting peace.
> The soul that knows it not, knows no release
> From little things;
> Knows not the livid loneliness of fear
> Nor mountain heights, where bitter joy can hear
> The sound of wings.

—Bernard Mergen

Further Reading

Backus, Jean L. *Letters from Amelia: 1901-1937*. Boston: Beacon Press, 1982. A candid biography with quotations from letters to family members and friends. Backus was a friend of Earhart's mother and the owner of the house in Berkeley, California, where Earhart lived in 1949. The book supplements the biographies by Earhart's sister, Muriel Earhart Morrissey, and her husband, George P. Putnam.

Earhart, Amelia. *The Fun of It: Random Records of My Own Flying and of Women in Aviation*. 1932. Reprint. Detroit, Mich.: Gale Research, 1975. The most complete autobiographical account of Earhart's life and the most interesting of her books. Earhart depicts herself as a tomboy who loved books.

———. *Last Flight*. 1937. Reprint. Detroit, Mich.: Gale Research, 1975. Earhart's last writings, compiled and annotated by her husband.

———. *Twenty Hours Forty Minutes*. New York: G. P. Putnam's Sons, 1928. Reprint. New York: Arno Press, 1980. Her first book, hastily written after her Atlantic flight, June 17-18, 1928. Interesting details from her log kept during the flight.

Gillespie, Ric. *Finding Amelia: The True Story of the Earhart Disappearance*. Annapolis, Md.: Naval Institute Press, 2006. Gillespie, executive director of the The International Group for Historic Aircraft Recovery (TIGHAR), compiles the information obtained by TIGHAR to present a knowledgeable and comprehensive explanation of Earhart's disappearance.

Loomis, Vincent V. *Amelia Earhart: The Final Story*. New York: Random House, 1985. An attempt to prove that Earhart and Noonan survived the crash of the Electra in 1937. Loomis was a pilot in the South Pacific during World War II and adds many interesting technical details about Earhart's round-the-world flight, but his evidence for Earhart's capture and death in a Japanese prison camp is circumstantial.

Morrissey, Muriel Earhart. *Courage Is the Price.* Wichita, Kans.: McCormick-Armstrong, 1963. A brief biography by Earhart's younger sister.

Pellegreno, Ann Holtgren. *World Flight: The Earhart Trail.* Ames: Iowa State University Press, 1971. The story of the author's successful completion in 1967, using a reconstructed Lockheed Electra, of Earhart's attempted round-the-world flight. Good technical details and a discussion of the mystery of Earhart's disappearance.

Putnam, George Palmer. *Soaring Wings.* New York: Harcourt Brace, 1939. A biography by Earhart's husband. It is good on her attitude toward marriage and women in aviation and business.

Van Pelt, Lori. *Amelia Earhart: The Sky's No Limit.* New York: Forge, 2005. Basic introduction to Earhart's life and career.

MARY BAKER EDDY

" *Health is not a condition of matter, but of Mind.* **"**

Religious leader

A deeply religious thinker, Mary Baker Eddy established the Church of Christ, Scientist—the first church movement to be founded in the United States by a woman.

Born: July 16, 1821; Bow, New Hampshire
Died: December 3, 1910; Chestnut Hill, Massachusetts
Also known as: Mary Morse Baker (birth name)
Areas of achievement: Religion and theology; journalism

EARLY LIFE
The youngest of six children, Mary Morse Baker (BAY-kur) was born on her parents' New Hampshire farm. Her father, Mark Baker, was a respected farmer whose deep interest in theology prompted him to engage in serious religious debates with his neighbors. Mary's mother, Abigail Ambrose Baker, had grown up as the daughter of a prominent deacon of the Congregational church in nearby Pembroke and was known for her tender solicitude toward her family and neighbors. Both parents were devout members of the Congregational church; Mary was nurtured in their Calvinist faith and joined the church herself at the age of twelve.

As a young girl, Mary began her formal education in 1826. An intelligent, highly sensitive child, Mary suffered from ill health that frequently kept her at home. She became a diligent reader and an avid writer of poetry. Mary received individual instruction from her second brother, Albert, who served as a schoolmaster at Mary's school when he was twenty. Her brother's instruction provided Mary with an education well in advance of that commonly available to young women of the period, and she was introduced to the rudiments of Greek, Latin, and Hebrew as well as contemporary works of literature and philosophy.

In December of 1843, Mary Baker was married to Major George Washington Glover, a successful builder with business interests in the Carolinas. The newlyweds eventually settled in Wilmington, North Carolina. By June of 1844, George Glover's investments in building supplies for a project in Haiti were lost, and he was stricken with yellow fever. He died on June 27, forcing his pregnant and impoverished widow to return to her parents' home. Despite her dangerously poor health, Mary gave birth in September to a healthy son, whom she named George in honor of his late father.

When Abigail Baker died in 1849, her daughter's grief and precarious health made further care for the boisterous young George Glover even more difficult. Mark Baker's second marriage less than one year later forced Mary and her son to leave the Baker house. Mary went to stay with her sister Abigail Tilton, but George Glover was placed in the care of Mary's former nurse. Mary was devastated by her separation from her son, but her family insisted that reuniting the two would further strain Mary's tenuous health.

In 1853, Mary was married to Daniel Patterson, a dentist who promised to provide a home for her and her son. That promise was never fulfilled, however, and Patterson's failings as a husband became increasingly evident. Mary's son moved with his foster parents to the West; they later told him that his mother had died. Mary's new husband was often absent in the course of his itinerant practice, and the couple found lodgings in various communities in New Hampshire. In the spring of 1862, while on commission to deliver state funds to Union sympathizers in the South, Patterson was taken prisoner by Confederate forces.

Barely able to care for herself, Mary sought relief from her persistent ill health at an institute in New Hampshire that promoted hydropathy, or the water cure. Finding little improvement during her visit, she traveled to Portland, Maine, to visit Phineas P. Quimby, a clockmaker who had developed a reputation as a magnetic healer and hypnotist. After her first treatment at his office, Mary experienced a marked improvement in her health. In her enthusiasm to learn more about the methods Quimby used, she sought to reconcile Quimby's ideas with the spiritually based biblical healings with which she was so familiar.

Reunited with her husband in December of 1862 after his escape from prison, Mary returned to New Hampshire, where she experienced relapses of ill health. She sought relief by visiting Quimby at various times but could not discover a permanent cure for her illnesses. After Quimby's death in early January of 1866, Mary was seriously injured when she fell on an icy pavement in Lynn, Massachusetts, on February 1.

After being taken to a nearby house, Mary eventually regained consciousness sufficiently to persuade her doctor and friends to move her to her lodgings in nearby Swampscott, where she was given little hope of recovery from the injuries to her head and spine. Visited by a clergyman on the Sunday after her accident, she asked to be left alone with her Bible. Turning to the ninth chapter of Matthew, she read the account of Jesus' healing of the man sick of the palsy (paralysis). Upon reading the story, she felt a profound change come over her and found that she was fully recovered from her injuries. Rising from her bed to dress and then greet the friends who waited outside her

Eddy, Mary Baker

door, Mary astonished them with the rapidity and completeness of her healing, one that she credited to the power of God alone.

LIFE'S WORK

During the decade from 1866 to 1876, Mary Patterson's outward life seemed little improved, yet her conviction that she could discover the source of her healing experience inspired her to continue her study of the Bible. Her husband deserted her soon after her healing; they were divorced in 1873, and she resumed using the surname Glover.

Although her financial situation was precarious and she was still separated from her son, Mary realized that, at the age of forty-five, she was healthier than she had ever been in her entire life. For three years after her recovery, she dedicated herself solely to searching the Bible for answers to her questions regarding spiritual healing, withdrawing from social pursuits and her temperance movement activities in order to record the revelations she was gaining through her studies. She lived frugally in a series of boardinghouses, began sharing her notes and interpretations of Bible passages with individuals who seemed receptive to her new ideas, and occasionally offered instruction in her healing methods in exchange for the cost of her room and board. A group of committed students eventually began to gather around her. In October of 1875, she managed to publish the first edition of her work, entitled *Science and Health*, with the financial assistance of some of her students.

It was in March of 1876 that Asa Gilbert Eddy, a native of Vermont who was ten years her junior and worked in Massachusetts as a salesperson for the Singer Sewing Machine Company, became one of Mary's students. Asa Eddy, better known as Gilbert, became a successful healer. At a time when many of her most talented students were challenging her authority and attempting to undermine her teachings, Mary came to rely on Gilbert Eddy's sound judgment and his steady support of her leadership. The two were married on January 1, 1877.

Around this time, Mary Baker Eddy began revising *Science and Health*, adding five new chapters. This two-volume second edition was so rife with typographical errors that only the second volume was circulated. During this time, Eddy began to lecture weekly at the Baptist Tabernacle in Boston. The success of her public sermons led her to make a motion at a meeting of her students in 1879 that they organize a church; it was called the Church of Christ, Scientist. In Eddy's own words, the purpose of this church was "to commemorate the word and works of our Master, which should reinstate primitive Christianity and its lost element of healing."

The new church was incorporated under a state charter, and Eddy was designated its president and appointed its first pastor. By the winter of 1879, Eddy and her husband had moved to rooms in Boston to be nearer to the growing church. She continued to teach new adult students about Christian Science, and the church established a Sunday school for the instruction of children in 1880. That same year, Eddy published the first of her many pamphlets: a sermon entitled *Christian Healing*. In an effort to give a more solid legal foundation to her classes, Eddy applied for a state charter in order to incorporate the Massachusetts Metaphysical College, a school dedicated to furthering the spread of her healing method by ensuring that students received unadulterated instruction directly from her.

Eddy, Mary Baker

Earlier, Mary Baker Eddy had begun revising and expanding *Science and Health* once again. The third edition of *Science and Health*, which appeared in 1881, was the first accurate edition of her writings to incorporate part of the treatise she used to instruct students in her classes. This publishing enterprise brought Eddy into contact with one of the leading printers of her day: John Wilson of the University Press in Cambridge, Massachusetts. Prospects for selling all one thousand copies of the third edition were not promising, but Wilson was convinced that Eddy would be able to finance the printing of her book through its sales. By 1882, the book had gone back to print for two additional editions of one thousand copies each.

Other publishing activities began. In April of 1883, Eddy published the first issue of *The Journal of Christian Science*. Originally a bimonthly periodical with articles designed to explore issues of interest to both newcomers and longtime students of Eddy's religion, the *Journal* was expanded to become a monthly publication and was one of the first authorized organs of the Christian Science church. A sixth edition of *Science and Health* appeared in 1883; it was the first to contain Eddy's "Key to the Scriptures," a section initially consisting of a glossary with her metaphysical interpretations of biblical terms and concepts. By 1885, nine additional printings were made, bringing the total number of copies in circulation during the book's first ten years to fifteen thousand.

The years following the publication of the sixth edition of *Science and Health* were prosperous ones, with many new students working to spread Christian Science and its healing practice throughout the United States. Nevertheless, several events occurred in the period from 1889 to 1892 that radically altered the structure and direction of the Christian Science church. Schisms among her students and the burdens resulting from those who increasingly relied on her personal leadership in all matters led Eddy to close her college at the height of its popularity and resign her post as pastor of the Boston church. Services continued to be conducted in Christian Science churches, but students voted to adjourn the activities of the National Christian Scientist Association for three years beginning in 1890. Withdrawing to a new home in Concord, New Hampshire, Eddy commenced work on a major revision of *Science and Health* to be published as the fiftieth edition in 1891.

September 23, 1892, marked the establishment of Eddy's newly reorganized church: the First Church of Christ, Scientist, in Boston, Massachusetts, also known as The Mother Church. She consulted with attorneys familiar with Massachusetts statutes in order to find a legal means to incorporate her church that would place its corporate government on a solid basis without encouraging undue attachment to her personal authority. The new charter provided a powerful centralized structure in the form of a five-member board of directors responsible for management of the church's affairs; it also fostered the practice of democratic self-government already established in the branch churches outside of Boston that were affiliated with the growing church movement. All members of these branches were invited to apply for concurrent membership in The Mother Church.

Eddy was henceforth designated as the Discoverer and Founder of Christian Science. To her mind, this title expressed the scientific aspect of her work—emphasizing her role in formulating and articulating its religious teachings in much the same way

Eddy, Mary Baker

that scientific laws and principles are formulated and articulated, but not created, by those who discover them.

In October of 1893, the building of the new church edifice was begun in Boston's Back Bay area, with the cornerstone of the church laid in May of 1894 and the first service held on December 30, 1894. Eddy took the unusual step of ordaining the Bible and *Science and Health*, rather than human ministers, as pastors of the church. When she published the *Manual of the Mother Church* in 1895, setting forth the rules by which the church was to be governed, she made provisions in its bylaws for the election of lay readers who would read texts from the Bible and from *Science and Health* relating to twenty-six topics she set forth.

The texts were selected by a special committee; the resulting lesson sermons were studied daily by individual members and were read Sundays at Christian Science church services throughout the world. These changes were instituted by Eddy in order to avoid the adulteration of her teachings through personal preaching. In this way, she believed that the healing message contained in the Bible and in her book would speak directly to all who attended her church without the injection of personal opinion or conflicting interpretations.

In 1898, Eddy established a board of education to provide for the formal instruction of students in Christian Science by those who were approved to serve as teachers. She also established a Board of Lectureship to which practitioners (ordained healers within the church) and teachers of Christian Science were appointed. These lecturers were responsible for preparing and delivering public lectures on Christian Science in order to introduce and clarify its teachings to those unfamiliar with the religion. The Christian Science Publishing Society was created through a deed of trust and was charged with the responsibility for publishing and distributing *Science and Health* and Eddy's other books as well as *The Christian Science Journal* and the newly founded periodical, *The Christian Science Weekly* (renamed *The Christian Science Sentinel* in 1899). In 1902, Eddy completed work on her final major revision of *Science and Health*; it was the 226th edition of the book known as the Christian Science textbook.

Although she enjoyed the relative peace and seclusion of her New Hampshire estate, known as Pleasant View, Eddy faced bitter personal attacks in the popular press during the early twentieth century that threatened to undermine her church. These articles reflected the sensational "yellow journalism" of the period. Few pieces were more damaging than those published by Joseph Pulitzer, whose *New York World* newspaper claimed that Eddy was near death from cancer and that her alleged fortune of $15 million was being wrested from her control. Refusing to meet with Pulitzer's reporters, Eddy granted audience to representatives of several other leading newspapers and press associations. After answering three brief questions concerning her health, Eddy gave evidence of her well-being by departing to take her daily carriage ride.

Despite Eddy's efforts to disprove the rumors concerning her health, her son George was approached by the publishers of the *New York World* and was encouraged, on the basis of the paper's erroneous accounts of his mother's welfare, to begin legal proceedings to determine Eddy's mental competence and ability to conduct business affairs connected with her church. Although funded by Pulitzer's newspaper fortune, this lawsuit ultimately collapsed after a panel appointed to determine Eddy's competence held a one-hour interview and established that she was in full possession of her mental faculties.

Refusing to back down in the face of these personal attacks, Eddy was prompted to establish a trust for her property in order to preserve its orderly transfer to the church after her death. More important, Eddy was impelled to launch an enormous new undertaking: She directed the Trustees of the Publishing Society to establish a daily newspaper to be known as *The Christian Science Monitor*, which began publication in 1908. By bringing national and international events into clearer focus for its readers, *The Christian Science Monitor* would fulfill Eddy's vision of its purpose: to combat the apathy, indifference, and despair that were common responses to world affairs through its spiritually enlightened, problem-solving journalism. After witnessing the fruition of her long-cherished hopes, Eddy died quietly in her sleep on toward the end of 1910.

SIGNIFICANCE

Regardless of one's perspective on the validity of her religious beliefs, Mary Baker Eddy clearly led a remarkable life—one full of extraordinary success despite the prejudices that confronted her as a woman attempting to establish a spiritually minded religious movement during an age of rampant materialism. Novelist and humorist Mark Twain, who was one of Eddy's most outspoken critics, once remarked that she was "probably the most daring and masterful woman who has appeared on earth for centuries."

A pragmatic and capable administrator who inspired her followers by her example of single-minded dedication, Eddy was equally comfortable in her role as a religious thinker—one who refused to compromise her conscience "to suit the general drift of thought" and was convinced of the importance of maintaining the intellectual and spiritual purity of her writings. Her church remains an active presence in the United States and throughout the world, and her book *Science and Health* was recognized by the Women's National Book Association in 1992 as one of seventy-five important works by "women whose words have changed the world."

—*Wendy Sacket*

FURTHER READING

Eddy, Mary Baker. *Mary Baker Eddy: Speaking for Herself*. Boston: Writings of Mary Baker Eddy, 2002. Includes two of Eddy's books: her memoir, *Retrospection and Introspection*, first published in 1891, and *Footprints Fadeless*, a defense of one of her critics, written in 1901-1902, and published here for the first time. Jana K. Reiss, religion editor for *Publisher's Weekly*, provides an introduction, analyzing Eddy's writings and placing Eddy's life and work in the context of late nineteenth century American religion and society.

Gill, Gillian. *Mary Baker Eddy*. Reading, Mass.: Perseus Books, 1998. Feminist biography. Gill portrays Eddy as a powerful woman who broke free from conventional gender roles to introduce radical new ideas. While acknowledging Eddy's faults, Gill is generally sympathetic, emphasizing her subject's gifts as a religious leader, administrator, and promoter of Christian Science.

Gottschalk, Stephen. *The Emergence of Christian Science in American Religious Life*.

Berkeley: University of California Press, 1973. Although its examination of Christian Science from the perspective of intellectual history may make it less easily accessible to general readers, this work sets forth the distinctive contributions Christian Science has made to American theology and culture.

Orcutt, William Dana. *Mary Baker Eddy and Her Books.* Boston: Christian Science Publishing Society, 1950. Written by a distinguished bookmaker who worked closely with Eddy from 1897 to 1910 and helped design the oversize subscription edition of *Science and Health* that was released in 1941, this memoir provides an intriguing window on Eddy's career as an author.

Peel, Robert. *Mary Baker Eddy: The Years of Discovery.* New York: Holt, Rinehart and Winston, 1966.

⎯⎯⎯. *Mary Baker Eddy: The Years of Trial.* New York: Holt, Rinehart and Winston, 1971.

⎯⎯⎯. *Mary Baker Eddy: The Years of Authority.* New York: Holt, Rinehart and Winston, 1977. Written by a Harvard-educated scholar who had unprecedented access to church archival materials, this monumental three-volume biography remains the definitive work on Eddy's life. Although Peel was himself a Christian Scientist, his work gives evidence of his conscientious effort to provide "a straightforward, factual account free from either apologetics or polemics."

Satter, Beryl. *Each Mind a Kingdom: American Women, Sexual Purity, and the New Thought Movement, 1875-1920.* Berkeley: University of California Press, 1999. Focusing on the New Thought Movement in general, and Eddy's Christian Science in particular, Satter describes American women's intellectual and psychological relationships to progressive social movements and self-improvement cults during the late nineteenth and early twentieth centuries. She concludes that participation in these movements gave disenfranchised middle-class white women a way to escape their homes and refashion society and gender roles.

Thomas, Robert David. *"With Bleeding Footsteps": Mary Baker Eddy's Path to Religious Leadership.* New York: Alfred A. Knopf, 1994. Trained in the theories of psychoanalysis, Thomas brings this psychological perspective to bear on his study of Eddy's character and behavior. Despite his serious, scholarly approach, Thomas fails to provide a complete assessment of Eddy's significance as a religious leader and seems to fall short of bringing his subject fully alive. Nevertheless, this biography is useful as one of the few fair-minded studies of Eddy to have appeared since Peel's three-volume work, cited above.

Marian Wright Edelman

❝ *If we don't stand up for children, then we don't stand for much.* **❞**

Attorney and social reformer

Edelman created the Children's Defense Fund, an advocacy and public education association dedicated to improving conditions for children in the United States.

Born: June 6, 1939; Bennettsville, South Carolina
Also known as: Marian Wright (birth name)
Areas of achievement: Education; social reform

Early Life

Marian Wright Edelman (EH-dehl-muhn) was born in Bennettsville, South Carolina, to Arthur Jerome Wright and Maggie Leola Bowen Wright. Her father, a Baptist minister, said that "service is the rent we pay for living." Hence, helping others was the basic duty of all people and an essential part of her early family life. Her parents taught by example. They built a home for the elderly in which Marian cleaned and cooked. Her parents reared five of their own children and cared for twelve foster children over the years.

Marian's education emphasized international understanding. After she completed high school at Marlboro Training High School, she attended Spelman College in Atlanta, Georgia. During her junior year, she received a Merrill Scholarship to study at the University of Paris and at the University of Geneva during the academic year 1958-1959. In the summer of 1959, she participated in a student exchange study tour of East Germany, Poland, Czechoslovakia, and the Soviet Union. These experiences broadened her perspective on humanity. She returned to the United States unable to accept the indignities of segregation, under which she had grown up and lived.

In 1960, Marian received her bachelor's degree from Spelman College as the valedictorian of her class. During that same year, black college students were conducting sit-in demonstrations at college campuses throughout the South. Her own participation in a sit-in at Atlanta's city hall led her to be arrested along with fourteen other students. Marian's civil rights activism, coupled with her international experiences and her family's commitment to service, shaped her life. Instead of choosing to pursue graduate work in Russian studies and traveling abroad, she decided to become a lawyer and use the law to effect social change.

While she pursued higher education, she continued learning from other cultures through educational service. Her achievements led to her becoming a John Hay Whitney Fellow from 1960 to 1961 at Yale University. During the summer of 1962, she worked in Crossroads Africa, a work project in the Ivory Coast, West Africa. Wright eventually received an LL.B. degree from Yale University in 1963. With her law degree in hand, Wright was poised to launch her career as a civil rights attorney.

Edelman, Marian Wright

Marian Wright Edelman. (AP/Wide World Photos)

Life's Work

From 1963 to 1964, Marian Wright worked in New York City at the headquarters of the National Association for the Advancement of Colored People (NAACP), where she served as a staff attorney for the NAACP Legal Defense and Educational Fund. Because the NAACP was working in cooperation with other civil rights groups on the Voter Education Project in Mississippi, Wright moved to Mississippi, where she became the first black woman to be admitted to the bar. Because she had to work with federal law, she also became a member of the bar in Washington, D.C., and in Massachusetts. From 1964 to 1968, she served as the director for the NAACP Legal Defense and Educational Fund in Jackson, Mississippi, where she successfully defended the Head Start Program from political attacks, helped to get student demonstrators out of jail, became involved in school desegregation issues, and risked injury and arrest in the process.

As part of her Head Start activities, Wright served on the board of the Child Development Group of Mississippi, a representative for one of the largest Head Start projects in the United States. Her advocacy for the poor of Mississippi led her to give testimony before the Senate and to work as a liaison between the Poor People's Campaign and Congress. In the course of this work, Wright came in contact with Peter Edelman, a Jewish lawyer who served as an assistant to Senator Robert F. Kennedy. Wright married Peter D. Edelman on July 14, 1968. Theirs was one of the first interracial marriages to take place in Virginia after the state's antimiscegenation laws had been declared unconstitutional. The couple eventually reared three sons: Joshua, Jonah, and Ezra.

In 1968, Marian Wright Edelman toured Eastern Europe, India, Israel, East Africa, and Southeast Asia. From 1968 to 1973, she served as coeditor with Ruby G. Martin of the Washington Research Project of the Southern Center for Public Policy, headquartered in Washington, D.C. The project used litigation to promote equal employment opportunity, monitored various federal programs in such areas as child care and school desegregation, and worked with community groups. This organization became the parent organization of the Children's Defense Fund (CDF), which became incorporated in 1973. In 1971, Edelman and her husband moved to Boston, from where she continued to travel regularly to Washington, D.C., as a partner of the Washington Research Project. She became a trustee of Yale University, the second woman to serve in this capacity in the university's 270-year history. She also served from 1971 to 1973 as director of the Harvard University Center for Law and Education, part of the Office of Economic Opportunity's legal services program. The organization emphasized reform in education through research and action related to the legal implications of educational policies.

In 1973, Edelman became a founder and the president of the CDF, the advocacy and public education association for children's issues that has become one of the best-known and best-connected of all lobbies, with an annual budget of $10 million and staff of more than 120. Soon, as the director of the nation's most effective organization for children's issues such as teen pregnancy, prenatal care, early childhood education, health services, child care, adoption, child labor, and child welfare, Edelman became known as "the children's crusader." Through CDF, Edelman has sought to make it "un-American" for any child to grow up poor, lacking adequate health care, food, shelter, child care, or education.

To allow Edelman to spend more time at her organization's headquarters, she and her family returned to Washington, D.C., in 1979. As the spokesperson for CDF, Edelman has avoided the politics of confrontation, choosing instead to forge alliances with other groups that seek to lessen the effects of poverty, injustice, inadequate health care, insufficient education, and family violence.

During the course of her tenure as director of CDF, Edelman has testified about the human and public costs the United States would face if it continued to fail to provide adequate funds and resources to meet the needs of American children and families. Such problems became greater in the 1980's as increasing numbers of children and families faced poverty as a result of economic recession, structural change in the economy, stagnating wages, tax and budget policies that favored the well-to-do, lack of state enforcement of child support payments, and greater dependency on welfare by the growing number of female-headed households. Edelman uses statistics and personal testimony to demonstrate that children have become the poorest Americans and will become a permanent "underclass" if public policy fails to address the needs outlined by CDF. Her passion is also mixed with optimism, since she not only stresses the problems but also provides remedies to build the broadest constituency to protect the children and alleviate poverty through education, legislation, and welfare reform.

Edelman, Marian Wright

Edelman has been a member of numerous committees addressing social, educational, and public policy, such as the advisory council of Martin Luther King, Jr., Memorial Library, the advisory board of Hampshire College, the Presidential Committee on Missing in Action (1977), the Presidential Committee on International Year of the Child (1979), and the United Nations International Children's Emergency Fund (UNICEF). She has also served on many boards of directors, such as those of the Eleanor Roosevelt Institute, the Carnegie Council on Children (1972-1977), and the Martin Luther King, Jr., Memorial Center. She has served as trustee for the March of Dimes, the Joint Center for Political Science, the Yale University Corporation (1971-1977), and the Aetna Center. In 1980, she became the chair of the Spelman College Board of Trustees, becoming the first African American and the second woman to serve in that role. Through the years, Edelman has worked closely with First Lady Hillary Rodham Clinton, a friend since 1969 and former staff attorney for the CDF. After the election of Bill Clinton as president, Edelman consulted with the First Lady on national health care issues and legislation but indicated that she did not want any administrative appointment.

Her outstanding contributions have been recognized with many awards. Edelman has been the recipient of sixty-eight honorary degrees from such institutions as Smith College, Columbia University, Swarthmore College, Rutgers University, Georgetown University, and Yale University. Named one of the Outstanding Young Women of America in 1966, Edelman continued to be recognized for her outstanding achievements. She received the *Mademoiselle* magazine award (1965), the Louise Waterman Wise Award (1970), the National Leadership award from the National Women's Political Caucus (1980), the Black Women's Forum award (1980), and the Eliot Award of the American Public Health Association (1987). She was named a MacArthur Foundation Fellow in 1985. Edelman also was honored with the Albert Schweitzer Humanitarian prize from Johns Hopkins University (1987), the Hubert Humphrey Civil Rights award, and the AFL-CIO award (1989). In 1991, the Jackie Robinson Foundation recognized her decency and dedication to working on the behalf of children.

Significance

Edelman's leadership in shaping programs and legislation to improve life for American children, made her one of the nation's most effective lobbyists for the young. She argued that conditions must be changed to provide a better environment for the development of the nation's future leaders. In the course of her work, she also contributed significantly to the efforts to obtain equal rights for all citizens, particularly African Americans and women.

—Dorothy C. Salem

Further Reading

Atkins, Norman. "Marian Wright Edelman." *Rolling Stone*, December 10, 1992. This interview examines the personality behind Edelman's public career.

Bouton, Katherine. "Marian Wright Edelman." *Ms.*, July/August, 1987. Describes Edelman's attempts to juggle career and family while leading the CDF.

Edelman, Marian Wright. *Families in Peril: An Agenda for Social Change*. Cambridge, Mass.: Harvard University Press, 1987. This book compares the status of black and white children and families in America. It discusses problems resulting from inadequate attention and a lack of public policies and programs to deal with these issues.

_____. *Lanterns: A Memoir of Mentors*. Boston: Beacon Press, 1999. A tribute to the people who helped shaped Edelman's life, including her parents, teachers, and civil rights activists Martin Luther King, Jr., and Fannie Lou Hamer.

_____. *The Measure of Our Success: A Letter to My Children and Yours*. Boston: Beacon Press, 1992. Edelman presents a blend of personal advice, homilies, and analysis of experiences in this work, which was on best-seller lists for several weeks.

Jones, Arthur. "A Voice for the Poor in D.C." *National Catholic Reporter*, March 24, 2000. A profile of Edelman that focuses on her efforts to help poor people in the United States.

Kaus, Mickey. "The Godmother." *New Republic*, February 15, 1993. This article provides a critical look at some of the basic arguments put forth by Edelman during her leadership of the Children's Defense Fund.

THOMAS ALVA EDISON

" *Opportunity is missed by most people because it is dressed in overalls and looks like work.* "

Inventor

Edison was perhaps the greatest inventor in world history. His incandescent electric lights transformed electrical technology; his myriad other inventions included a stock ticker, duplex and quadraplex telegraphs, the phonograph, a telephone transmitter, the motion picture camera, and the storage battery. He symbolized the ingenious, prolific, heroic, and professional American inventor in an age of invention, innovation, and industrialization.

Born: February 11, 1847; Milan, Ohio
Died: October 18, 1931; West Orange, New Jersey
Areas of achievement: Invention and technology; telecommunications

EARLY LIFE

Thomas Alva Edison (EH-dih-suhn) grew up in the midwestern industrial heartland of the United States during his country's transformation from an agrarian to an industrial nation. The seventh and last child of Samuel and Nancy (née Elliot) Edison, he was reared in Port Huron, Michigan, near Detroit. He found formal schooling disagreeable, so his mother, a former teacher, tutored young Tom at home. Gifted with a natural inquisitiveness, a love of science and experimentation, and access to the Detroit Free Library, he largely educated himself.

As a teenager, Edison worked, first selling newspapers and candy on the train between Port Huron and Detroit and later as a telegraph operator in the Midwest. In both jobs he managed to find time to perform various chemical and electrical experiments and to continue his lifetime reading habit. By 1868, he had moved to Boston, where he came under the intellectual influence so strong in that city at the time. There his reading of Michael Faraday's work on electricity, with its heavy emphasis on experimentation and conceptualization of physical models, strengthened his own strong preference for applied science with its testing of hypotheses, its pragmatic approach to problems, and its interest in practical application. Inventing for profit became a goal for Edison as he directed his genius toward the industrial and economic climate of post-Civil War America.

Seeking fame and fortune, Edison moved to New York City in 1869, having neither a job nor money. A combination of luck and acumen at the Law's Gold Indicator Company resulted in his appointment as plant superintendent. Edison's working in Wall Street during an age of enterprise provided him with the basis for his first commercially successful invention, an improved stock ticker. His additional improvements of stock ticker technology brought Edison forty thousand dollars for his patent rights, a princely sum in 1870. With a small fortune and some fame, Edison turned to electrical technology, an arena that consumed much of his life's work.

Life's Work

Like so many of his fellow pioneers in the world of electrical invention, Edison was well versed in telegraphy. His many years as a first-rate telegraph operator, his familiarity with electrical devices and experiments, and his vision of an industrial, urban America directed his various endeavors. In the period from 1872 to 1874, he turned his attention to duplex and quadruplex telegraphy, the process of sending two or four simultaneous signals, respectively, over a single wire. His commercial success with these two processes led him to improvements with the telephone, itself a special type of telegraph.

In 1876, Edison sought and found a more efficient transmitter for the telephone. His carbon button device in the mouthpiece provided a stronger signal that would travel farther on transmission lines. With this success, he demonstrated his legendary ability to improve existing inventions. In this same year, he moved to Menlo Park, New Jersey, and established a research-and-development laboratory complete with support personnel and several workshops. Edison realized the central role of systematic inquiry for new enterprises, and Menlo Park became the prototype for the industrial research laboratories that have been so important for innovation in a technological society.

The phonograph was another Edison invention with its origins in telegraphy. The embossed paper tape that recorded the dots and dashes of telegraph messages gave off a musical sound when Edison moved the tape quickly through a repeater mechanism. From this stimulus he devised a tin-foil-covered cylinder that would record vibrations of sound entered through a recording diaphragm. A quickly conceived idea became a patented reality in 1877, although the phonograph required substantial modification

Edison, Thomas Alva

Thomas Alva Edison.
(Library of Congress)

before it became a commercial success. Edison's ability to invent a "talking machine" enhanced his reputation as a genius. His most prolific years of work on the phonograph came in the period 1887-1890, when he developed the wax-coated flat record and separate recording and playback components.

Success with the early phonograph led Edison to another challenge in the world of electricity: an incandescent electric lighting system. From 1878 to 1882, he and his Menlo Park staff devoted much of their time to the invention and innovation of a system that would subdivide the electric arc light. In this task, Edison was an entrepreneur as well as a pioneer developer of a new technology. He used the full resources of the Menlo Park laboratory and workshops to attack the problems of incandescent lighting and to seek commercially successful solutions to those problems, which required many painstaking hours of research and development; he relied on the best talent in Menlo Park, the scientific method of inquiry, and the systematic empirical approach to problem-solving.

When Edison began his quest to provide a workable lighting system, he built on an awareness of arc lighting developments and on the achievements of other inventors seeking an incandescent system. He realized that he needed a high-resistance lamp filament that would burn for several hours, an efficient generator, a distribution network with wires, switches, meters and fuses, and a central power station. A heavy reliance on a skilled and knowledgeable staff provided the successful lighting elements: a carbonized cotton filament, the "long legged Mary Ann" generator, and the prototype

Edison, Thomas Alva

Pearl Street central station. He set his sights on the marketplace, used the familiar terminology and methods of gas illumination in his system, and displayed his entrepreneurial talents by promoting his own system, a promotion helped greatly by his reputation as an inventive genius (a reputation which Edison made no attempt to dispel). So successful was he in this enterprise that to generations of Americans, Thomas Edison was *the* inventor of the electric light.

Although Edison's business acumen was greater than most people believed, his chief interest was not the ledger book, and he soon tired of the business of electric lighting and turned to other areas of invention. By 1892, the Edison General Electric companies became part of a larger conglomerate known simply as the General Electric Company. With his name no longer associated with the operation, Edison lost interest in electric lighting developments and sold his stock in General Electric. He now had millions of dollars to use for new inventive challenges.

By 1887, Edison had moved his laboratories to West Orange, New Jersey, in a more extensive physical plant. With this move, he could engage in large-scale invention and innovation, as he did during the 1880's and 1890's with two major projects: the motion picture camera and a magnetic ore separation process. The former was a commercial success; the latter was an economic disaster.

Although he began his work on the motion picture camera in 1887, Edison performed most of the developmental work on it in the years from 1889 to 1891. His invention of a camera that took a series of still photographs in rapid succession resulted from mechanical insight rather than any electrical or chemical knowledge that was so important in almost all of his other inventions. That he could successfully devise a practical motion picture camera through the strength of his mechanical ability attests his inventive talent.

From 1894 to 1899, Thomas Edison devoted his attention to another chiefly nonelectrical project: magnetic ore separation. Sensing that a market for low-grade Eastern iron ore existed if it could be extracted cheaply, he invested several years and millions of dollars in creating huge ore-crushing machines. These machines would pulverize the ore deposits, and the resulting powder would pass by electromagnets that separated the ore from the dross. Although a technical success, the process never could compete with the low-cost ores of the Mesabi range; Edison found himself deeply in debt by 1900 and finally abandoned the scheme.

At the turn of the century, Edison returned to electrical technology with his invention of a durable storage battery. From 1899 to 1909, he and his West Orange technical staff developed an alkaline-iron-nickel storage battery as an improvement over the widely used lead-acid battery. Edison envisioned this lighter, more durable battery for use in the growing automobile industry, especially in electric cars. By the time Edison had a commercially successful battery available in 1909, however, electric cars had lost favor with the public, which preferred the vehicles powered by internal combustion engines that were being promoted by men such as Henry Ford. The Edison battery proved unreliable for intermittent automobile uses, was ineffective in cold temperatures, and never replaced the lead-acid storage battery in motor car applications. Edison's battery did find successful use in marine and railroad applications that required a durable, long-lived battery.

Edison, Thomas Alva

The storage battery was Edison's last major invention. In 1914, a fire destroyed most of the West Orange laboratories; World War I diverted his attention as he served as chairman of the Naval Consulting Board to direct the nation's inventive talent into the war effort. As he grew older, Edison spent the winter months at his home in Fort Myers, Florida, and established a modest laboratory there. In 1927, he began work trying to create artificial rubber but did not complete that endeavor. His fertile mind was active until his death at West Orange, New Jersey, on October 18, 1931.

SIGNIFICANCE

With the death of Thomas Alva Edison, the United States lost a legendary and heroic inventor. The example of his life and personality—simplicity, pragmatism, hard work, and self-education linked to inventive genius—appealed to the egalitarian spirit of Americans in an age of enterprise. Edison was a self-made man whose mental capacity, ambition, and dedication brought him success in the tradition of the American spirit of private enterprise. In an age of invention and industrialism, he stood as a symbol of the modern spirit in the United States with his contributions of electrical inventions and innovations: duplex and quadraplex telegraphy, incandescent lighting, telephone transmitter, phonograph, motion picture camera, and storage battery. These contributions alone guarantee his place among great Americans.

Thomas Edison the heroic inventor is as much myth as reality. His strong determination to conquer a problem or task and his ability to work long hours in his laboratory are characteristic of the lone inventor, but Edison was much more complex than might be suggested by the familiar image of the simple genius at work alone. He was among the foremost professional American inventors. His success was a result in large measure of his prescience about changes in an urban, industrial America and the need for new technological systems to serve that new society.

Edison's technique matched his vision; he excelled at improving on existing designs, assessing the commercial potential of a device. He also relied heavily on a systematic and rational approach to invention and innovation and on a highly trained staff, as his Menlo Park and West Orange laboratory complexes attest. Edison's early use of the industrial research laboratory provided a model for American industry in the twentieth century. Further, Edison's talent for understanding complex processes, for seeing the need for technological systems, and for focusing on practical application mark him as a highly organized professional who was a pioneer inventor-innovator and entrepreneur. Just as his image as a heroic inventor appealed to the average American of his time, so his success as a professional inventor who held nearly eleven hundred patents should appeal to students of American technological, social, and economic history.

—*Harry J. Eisenman*

FURTHER READING

Baldwin, Neil. *Edison: Inventing the Century*. New York: Hyperion, 1995. Reprint. Chicago: University of Chicago Press, 2001. Critically acclaimed comprehensive biography, providing information on Edison's personal life and career. Baldwin argues that Edison embodied the American potential for technological change; his book describes the cultural context of Edison's inventions.

Edison, Thomas Alva

Conot, Robert. *A Streak of Luck*. New York: Seaview Books, 1979. A full-scale biography of Edison. Conot examines Edison's personal life and technological achievements and treats Edison's successes and failures in a thorough and objective manner.

Dyer, Frank Lewis, and Thomas Commerford Martin. *Edison: His Life and Inventions*. 2 vols. New York: Harper & Brothers, 1910. The first authorized biography of Edison. Limited because it was published during Edison's lifetime. Praises Edison and lacks objectivity.

Israel, Paul. *Edison: A Life of Invention*. New York: John Wiley & Sons, 1998. Israel draws on Edison's notebooks to describe Edison's working methods, portraying him as a tireless experimenter who labored to create his many inventions.

Jehl, Francis. *Menlo Park Reminiscences*. 3 vols. Detroit: Edison Institute, 1936. Although written by an Edison associate and very subjective, this is an excellent source of material on the workings of the Edison laboratories and of Edison himself. Many useful illustrations.

Jenkins, Reese V. "Elements of Style: Continuities in Edison's Thinking." In *Bridge to the Future: A Centennial Celebration of the Brooklyn Bridge*, edited by Margaret Latimer, Brooke Hindle, and Melvin Kranzberg. New York: New York Academy of Sciences, 1984. Jenkins explores the fascinating subject of style as a factor in Edison's inventions; well worth considering.

Jonnes, Jill. *Empires of Light: Edison, Tesla, Westinghouse, and the Race to Electrify the World*. New York: Random House, 2003. Explains how the three inventors sought to create businesses that would provide safe, reliable electricity. Jonnes describes the inventions and careers of Edison, Tesla, and Westinghouse and relates how they worked with bankers, lawyers, and financiers to create electrical "empires."

Josephson, Matthew. *Edison: A Biography*. New York: McGraw-Hill, 1959. An excellent full-scale biography of Edison that treats his professional and personal life in detail. Contains cogent discussions of Edison's inventions, innovations, and relationships with financial figures such as Jay Gould and J. P. Morgan.

Albert Einstein

❝ *I am convinced that [God] does not play dice.* **❞**

German-born American physicist

Einstein was the principal founder of modern theoretical physics, and his theory of relativity fundamentally changed the understanding of the physical world. His stature as a scientist, together with his strong humanitarian stance on major political and social issues, including nuclear energy and weaponry, made him one of the outstanding thinkers of the twentieth century.

Born: March 14, 1879; Ulm, Germany
Died: April 18, 1955; Princeton, New Jersey
Areas of achievement: Physics; mathematics; social reform

Early Life

Albert Einstein (IN-stin) was born in Ulm, Germany, to moderately prosperous Jewish parents. His early childhood did nothing to suggest future greatness; he was late learning to speak, and his parents feared that he might be backward. He was apparently fascinated at the age of five by the mysterious workings of a pocket compass, and at the age of twelve he became enthralled by a book on Euclidean geometry. In his childhood, he also learned to play the violin and so acquired a love of music that was to last throughout his life.

In 1888, Einstein was sent to the Luitpold gymnasium in Munich, but he disliked the regimented and authoritarian atmosphere of the school. Even at this young age he seems to have exhibited the independence of mind, the ability to question basic assumptions and to trust in his own intuition, which were to lead him to his brilliant achievements. He left the gymnasium in 1895, without gaining a diploma. His father tried to send him to a technical school in Zurich, but he failed the entrance examination, in spite of high scores on mathematics and physics. The following year he was more successful, and in 1900 he received the diploma that qualified him to teach. To his disappointment, however, he failed to obtain a teaching position at the school.

In 1901, Einstein became a Swiss citizen. (He had renounced his German citizenship in 1896.) In 1902, after temporary positions at schools in Winterthur and Schaffhausen, he secured a post as a technical expert in the Swiss patent office in Berne, where he was to remain for seven years. In the following year, he married Mileva Maric, a friend from his student days in Zurich, and in 1904 the first of their two sons was born.

Einstein's first scientific paper had been published in 1901, and he had also submitted a Ph.D. thesis to the University of Zurich. While he was working quietly in the patent office, however, isolated from the mainstream of contemporary physics, there was little to suggest the achievements of 1905, which were to shake the scientific world to its core.

Life's Work

In 1905, Einstein published three major papers, any one of which would have established his place in the history of science. The first, which was to bring him the Nobel

Einstein, Albert

Prize in Physics in 1921, explained the photoelectric effect and formed the basis for much of quantum mechanics. It also led to the development of television. The second concerned statistical mechanics and explained the phenomenon known as Brownian motion, the erratic movement of pollen grains when immersed in water. Einstein's calculations gave convincing evidence for the existence of atoms.

It was the third paper, however, containing the special theory of relativity, that was to revolutionize understandings of the nature of the physical world. The theory stated that the speed of light is the same for all observers and is not dependent on the speed of the source of the light, or of the observer, and that the laws of nature (both the Newtonian laws of mechanics and Maxwell's equations for the electromagnetic field) remain the same for all uniformly moving systems. This theory meant that the concept of absolute space and time had to be abandoned because it did not remain valid for speeds approaching those of light. Events that happen at the same time for one observer do not do so for another observer moving at high speed in respect of the first. Einstein also demonstrated that a moving clock would appear to run slow compared with an identical clock at rest with respect to the observer, and a measuring rod would vary in length according to the velocity of the frame of reference in which it was measured.

In another paper published in 1905, Einstein stated, by the famous equation $E = mc^2$, that mass and energy are equivalent. Each can be transferred into the other because mass is a form of concentrated energy. This equation suggested to others the possibility of the development of immensely powerful explosives.

Such was Einstein's achievement at the age of twenty-six. There had not been a year like it since Newton published his *Principia* in 1687. The scientific world quickly recognized him as a creative genius, and in 1909 he took up his first academic position as associate professor of theoretical physics at the University of Zurich. After two more positions, one in Prague and the other in Zurich, he became a member of the Prussian Academy of Sciences and moved to Berlin in 1914.

In the meantime, Einstein had been working to extend the special theory of relativity to include new laws of gravitation, and the general theory of relativity was published in 1916. It was one of the greatest intellectual productions ever achieved by one person, and its picture of the universe as a four-dimensional space-time continuum lies at the foundation of all modern views of the universe. The theory stated that large masses produce a gravitational field around them, which results in the curvature of space-time. This gravitational field acts on objects and on light rays; starlight, for example, is deflected when passing through the gravitational field of the sun.

In 1919, the general theory received experimental confirmation from a team of British astronomers. Suddenly, the world awoke to the implications of Einstein's work, and he found himself internationally celebrated as the greatest scientist of the day. During the early 1920's, he traveled extensively in Europe, the Far East, and the Americas, hailed everywhere as genius, sage, and hero. With his untidy shock of hair—formerly black, now graying—rising from a high forehead, his deep brown eyes, and small moustache, he made a striking figure. It was not only his superior intellect that aroused public recognition and respect but also his simple good nature, nobility, and kindliness. However, Einstein, always modest, was genuinely astonished at the attention he received.

Einstein, Albert

It was during his travels in the 1920's that the other great concerns of Einstein's life came to the fore. A man of deep humanitarian instincts, he did not isolate himself from the turbulent political events around him. During World War I, he had spoken out against militarism and nationalism. Now, as a famous person, he once more took up the cause of pacifism, expressing his opinion openly, caring nothing for popularity. Einstein's other lasting concern was the promotion of Zionism, and his tour of the United States in 1921 was undertaken in part to raise funds for Hebrew University. These activities made him a target for fierce abuse from the Nazis, and even outside Germany his radical political views made him a controversial figure.

When Hitler came to power in 1933, Einstein was on his third visit to the United States, and he resolved not to return to Germany. After brief stays in Belgium and England, he left Europe for the last time, to become a professor at the Institute for Advanced Study at Princeton. He continued to lend his support to the cause of justice and freedom, helping Jewish refugees whenever he could, and he modified his former pacifism in the face of the threat of Nazi domination. In 1939, he was persuaded to write a letter to President Franklin D. Roosevelt, alerting him to the military potential of atomic energy. (Einstein played no part, however, in the research that led to the development of the atomic bomb, which merely verified the truth of his famous equation.) After the war, he remained tirelessly devoted to the cause of world peace and proposed a world government in which all countries were to agree to forfeit part of their national sovereignty.

Albert Einstein.
(Library of Congress)

Einstein, Albert

His later scientific career took two main directions. First, he was so deeply convinced of nature's fundamental simplicity that he labored unsuccessfully for thirty years in an attempt to construct a unified field theory. Second, he could not accept one of the fundamental results of quantum theory, that the interaction of subatomic particles could be predicted only in terms of probabilities. "God does not play dice with the world," he remarked. Many of his colleagues thought him stubborn, but nevertheless he remained a revered figure; his reputation as a genius who also possessed wisdom and saintliness never left him, neither in life nor in death.

Significance

Einstein's scientific achievements place him alongside such figures as Copernicus, Galileo, and Newton, as one who vastly enlarged the scope of human knowledge about the physical universe. In this respect he is a universal figure and belongs to no country. It is perhaps appropriate, however, that Einstein, a German Jew to whom destiny had decreed a nomadic existence, eventually found a permanent home in the United States. His links with his adopted country—he became a U.S. citizen in 1941—are profound. He was the most illustrious of the hundreds of intellectuals who fled from Europe before World War II, and his presence at the newly formed Institute for Advanced Study, which marked a new period of development for American research and education, played a key role in attracting other eminent scholars.

Einstein had always viewed the United States as a bulwark of democracy and individual freedom, and in the debates that divided the country in the postwar decade—particularly the Cold War and the use of nuclear energy—his was a consistent voice for sanity and decency in human affairs. He spoke out for freedom of thought and speech in the McCarthy era, when he feared that the United States was betraying its own ideals, and he continued to urge scientists to consider the social responsibilities of their work in the atomic age. In his final year, he and a group of leading scientists signed a statement, known as the Russell-Einstein Manifesto, warning about the terrible consequences of nuclear war. This led to the Pugwash Conference on science and world affairs in 1957, in which for the first time scientists from East and West met to discuss nuclear arms. A series of influential conferences followed, and the Pugwash movement has continued its activities ever since.

—*Bryan Aubrey*

Further Reading

Bernstein, Jeremy. *Einstein*. New York: Viking Press, 1973. First published in *The New Yorker* magazine, this biography includes a historical survey of the scientific issues of Einstein's life. No index.

Brian, Denis. *The Unexpected Einstein: The Real Man Behind the Icon*. Hoboken, N.J.: J. Wiley, 2005. Based on interviews with friends and associates, this biography demystifies Einstein to present a realistic portrait of his life, thoughts, and personality.

Clark, Ronald W. *Einstein: The Life and Times*. New York: World, 1971. Lengthy, authoritative, and readable. Gives a balanced treatment of Einstein's life, although the author tends to see Einstein as an idealist who was out of his depth when he entered practical politics.

Einstein, Albert. *Out of My Later Years*. 1950. Rev. ed. Westport, Conn.: Greenwood Press, 1970. Collection of Einstein's writings, including articles, letters, appeals, and miscellaneous papers, from 1934 to 1950, on the philosophical, political, social, and scientific issues of the period.

Einstein, Albert, and Leopold Infeld. *The Evolution of Physics*. 1938. New ed. New York: Simon & Schuster, 1961. Covers the period from the rise of the mechanical philosophy to relativity and quanta. Einstein's clarity of thought and expression is apparent throughout, and this remains one of the best popular expositions of his thought. No mathematics.

French, A. P., ed. *Einstein: A Centenary Volume*. Cambridge, Mass.: Harvard University Press, 1979. Beautifully designed, lavishly illustrated. Includes personal reminiscences from Einstein's friends and colleagues; expositions of many aspects of his scientific, political, and educational thought; and extracts from his writings.

Isaacson, Walter. *Einstein: His Life and Universe*. New York: Simon & Schuster, 2007. Isaacson, the prominent biographer of Benjamin Franklin and other subjects, discusses how Einstein's love for intellectual and individual freedom and his rebellious nature formed his scientific imagination.

Robinson, Andrew, et al. *Einstein: A Hundred Years of Relativity*. New York: Harry N. Abrams, 2005. One of the better books released to commemorate the one-hundredth anniversary of Einstein's scientific paper outlining the theory of relativity. This volume includes essays by prominent physicists, including Stephen Hawking and Freeman Dyson, who discuss Einstein's theories and influence. It also features photographs of Einstein bequeathed by him to Hebrew University in Jerusalem.

Sayen, Jamie. *Einstein in America: The Scientist's Conscience in the Age of Hitler and Hiroshima*. New York: Crown, 1985. A well-researched, detailed account of Einstein's nonscientific activities from 1933 to 1955. Gives political and historical background on issues such as Palestine, the Cold War, and McCarthyism.

Schwartz, Joseph. *Einstein for Beginners*. New York: Pantheon Books, 1979. Amusing, entertaining, comic-book format, useful for those with no scientific background. Clear explanation of special relativity, and some biographical background. Illustrated by Michael McGuiness.

Dwight D. Eisenhower

> " *A people that values its privileges above its principles soon loses both.* "

President of the United States (1953-1961)

During World War II, Eisenhower served with distinction as Allied commander for the invasions of North Africa, Italy, and France. He won the presidential elections of 1952 and 1956 and guided the United States through eight years of relative peace and prosperity.

Born: October 14, 1890; Denison, Texas
Died: March 28, 1969; Washington, D.C.
Also known as: Dwight David Eisenhower (full name); Ike (nickname)
Areas of achievement: Government and politics; military

Early Life

Although born in Texas, where his parents lived briefly, Dwight D. Eisenhower (IZ-ehn-how-ur) grew up in the small town of Abilene, Kansas. The Eisenhowers were a close-knit family and belonged to the Brethren Church, part of the heritage of ancestors who had immigrated to Pennsylvania from Germany during the eighteenth century. The third of seven sons (one of whom died as an infant), Dwight enjoyed a secure childhood, completed high school, and worked in a creamery for two years before entering West Point on the basis of a competitive examination. West Point appealed to him because it offered a free college education.

As a cadet, Eisenhower excelled at football until a knee injury ended that career. He proved a conscientious but not exceptional student and was graduated sixty-first in a class of 164. At graduation in 1915, he stood five feet eleven inches tall and weighed 170 pounds. His classmates remembered and respected "Ike," as did his boyhood friends, as likable, honest, and confident, a person with a quick temper but a quicker infectious grin. He had an expressive face, blue eyes, and light brown hair that thinned and receded when he was a young man.

Eisenhower's early military years were uneventful except for his marriage in 1916 to Mamie Geneva Doud of Denver, Colorado. The two had met in Texas during his first assignment at Fort Sam Houston. They became parents of two sons, the first of whom died as a child.

Life's Work

During the 1920's and 1930's, Eisenhower demonstrated exceptional organizational skill and an ability to work with others. In 1926, Eisenhower, who had been merely an average student at West Point, finished first among 275 in his class at the Army's elite Command and General Staff School. When General Douglas MacArthur served as the Army's chief of staff, Eisenhower assisted him, and then served as his senior assistant in the Philippines. MacArthur once evaluated Eisenhower as the most capable officer in the Army.

Eisenhower's personality and his performance during maneuvers in the summer of

Eisenhower, Dwight D.

1941 impressed the Army's chief of staff, General George C. Marshall. Both in 1941 and in 1942, Eisenhower won two promotions, jumping from lieutenant colonel to lieutenant general. In June, 1942, Marshall appointed Eisenhower European Theater Commander. The next year, as general, Eisenhower became Supreme Allied Commander and won fame as the leader of the multinational invasion of Europe in June, 1944.

After accepting Germany's surrender, Eisenhower served as the Army's chief of staff. He retired from the Army in 1948 and became president of Columbia University. His book *Crusade in Europe*, published the same year, sold millions of copies and gave him financial security. Two years later, President Harry S. Truman recalled Eisenhower to active duty as Supreme Commander of the North Atlantic Treaty Organization (NATO) forces.

In May, 1952, Eisenhower again retired from the Army to seek the Republican Party's nomination for president, an office that leaders in both parties had urged on him for years. With his decisive victory in the November election, Eisenhower embarked on a second career, one even more important than the first.

As president, Eisenhower set his primary foreign policy objective as maintaining the international role the United States had assumed during the previous decade. More specifically, he intended to end the fighting in Korea, reduce military spending, and lessen the intensity of the Cold War while still adhering to the policy of containment. Militarily, Eisenhower pursued a policy of strategic sufficiency rather than superiority. This policy, as well as a reduction of the capacity to fight limited wars, made possible cuts in the defense budget.

In 1953, Eisenhower approved an armistice in Korea and the next year rejected the advice of his secretary of state and the chairman of the Joint Chiefs of Staff, among others, and refused to intervene in the French war in Indochina. The United States took the lead, however, in establishing the Southeast Asia Treaty Organization as an attempt to accomplish in a region of Asia what NATO had accomplished in Europe. During this same period, Eisenhower also approved Central Intelligence Agency covert activity that helped overthrow the governments of Iran and Guatemala and thereby contributed to the growing acceptance of undemocratic action in the name of freedom.

In 1955, he helped terminate the post-World War II occupation of Austria and then, at Geneva, Switzerland, became the first president in a decade to meet with Soviet leaders. That same year and again in 1956, Eisenhower reacted to crises in the coastal waters of the People's Republic of China, in Hungary, and in Suez in a manner that helped prevent these crises from escalating into greater violence.

On the domestic side, Eisenhower followed a moderate path. He accepted the New Deal programs and even expanded those covering labor, Social Security, and agriculture. Although he cut the budget of the Tennessee Valley Authority and reduced federal activity and regulations regarding natural resources, Eisenhower championed the nation's largest road-building project (the Federal Aid Highway Act of 1956) and federal development of the Saint Lawrence Seaway. He also approved spending increases in health care. Fiscally, Eisenhower cut taxes and controls and each year balanced or nearly balanced the budget. The nation's gross national product, personal income, and

Eisenhower, Dwight D.

Dwight D. Eisenhower.
(Library of Congress)

house purchases all climbed. Inflation proved negligible, averaging 1.5 percent per year. Fundamental to Eisenhower's public philosophy was his belief that only a sound economy could sustain a credible, effective foreign policy.

In the presidential election of 1956, Americans gave Eisenhower a second, even greater, landslide victory over his Democratic opponent Adlai E. Stevenson, despite Eisenhower's major heart attack in 1955 and his operation for ileitis in 1956. Voters approved his moderate policies and, like the friends of his youth and the military personnel with whom he worked, responded positively to his famous grin. His dislike of politics and his lifelong refusal to discuss personalities in public also struck responsive chords. Even his hobbies of golf, fishing and hunting, bridge and poker, and cookouts embodied widespread American values.

Eisenhower's second term continued the basic policies and themes of the first. He steadfastly resisted demands from Democrats and from conservative Republicans to increase defense spending, although he expanded the ballistic missile program after the Soviets launched the world's first human-made earth-orbiting satellite (Sputnik) in 1957. In 1958 (in Quemoy) and in 1958-1959 (in Berlin), Eisenhower again handled crises with deliberation. After he hosted the visit of Soviet leader Nikita S. Khrushchev, Eisenhower looked forward to a Paris summit meeting in May, 1960, and to a

Eisenhower, Dwight D.

visit to the Soviet Union as his final contribution to promoting peace. On the eve of the conference, the Soviets shot down an American spy plane over Soviet territory. The U-2 incident, named for the plane, ruined the conference, canceled Eisenhower's planned visit to the Soviet Union, and dashed his hopes to improve relations between the two superpowers.

Domestic highlights of Eisenhower's second term included his ordering troops to Little Rock, Arkansas, to maintain order while the high school racially integrated its classes. In the same year, 1957, Eisenhower signed the first civil rights act in eighty-two years. Important symbolically, the act produced little change in the lives of black Americans. The same proved true of another civil rights act in 1960. In response to *Sputnik*, Eisenhower established the National Aeronautics and Space Administration (NASA) and approved the National Defense Education Act, providing the first substantial federal aid to higher education in almost a century.

Criticism of Eisenhower dealt mostly with three subjects. First, he refused to exercise any public leadership in response to Senator Joseph McCarthy's excessive and unsubstantiated accusations of disloyalty directed against numerous Americans, including General Marshall. Second, after the U.S. Supreme Court ruled in 1954 that separate-but-equal facilities were unconstitutional, Eisenhower refrained from lending his moral or political support for implementation of the ruling or for promotion of civil rights in general. The third area of criticism concerned his sparse defense budget and the limited range of responses it permitted in times of crisis. Eisenhower's confidence and public support, however, kept him from altering his positions because of such criticism.

In his presidential farewell address, Eisenhower warned the nation of the threat to democracy from the influence of the military-industrial complex, which benefited from massive military budgets. He retired to his Gettysburg, Pennsylvania, farm and wrote his memoirs. Most contemporary observers agreed that, had the Constitution permitted and had he been willing to run, Eisenhower easily would have won a third term.

SIGNIFICANCE

Eisenhower, the career military officer, curtailed defense spending, pursued a foreign policy that emphasized conciliation rather than conflict, and presided over eight years of peace. An advocate of gradual domestic change, Eisenhower watched his most prominent appointee, Chief Justice of the United States Earl Warren, use his position and influence to bring sweeping changes to society. As a Republican president, Eisenhower, who disliked politics and favored limitations on the terms of senators and representatives, proved the most able politician of his generation. He adhered to definite policies, faced a Democratic Congress for six of his eight years in the White House, and suffered domestic and foreign setbacks, yet he gave the country eight years of economic growth and prosperity and left office with undiminished popularity.

Eisenhower obviously was a capable, complex man, but the key to his success seems to have been his ability to radiate straightforward honesty and uncomplicated common sense. The events of the decades following his presidency—the international arms race, war, riots, Watergate, inflation, declining standard of living, and uncontrol-

Eisenhower, Dwight D.

lable budget deficits—have greatly enhanced respect for Eisenhower's accomplishments. Indeed, according to many, he joined the ranks of the nation's ten greatest presidents.

—*Keith W. Olson*

FURTHER READING

Ambrose, Stephen E. *Eisenhower.* 2 vols. New York: Simon & Schuster, 1983-1984. Volume 1 is a comprehensive assessment covering Eisenhower's life and career before he entered the White House. Based on an unequaled mastery of archival material, Ambrose provides an insightful and readable narrative. The book is especially strong on the influences that shaped Eisenhower's personality and career. The book's highlight is Eisenhower's tenure as Supreme Allied Commander during World War II. Volume 2 presents a detailed chronology of Eisenhower's presidency.

Boyle, Peter G. *Eisenhower.* New York: Pearson/Longman, 2005. In examining the major issues during the Eisenhower presidency, Boyle concludes that Eisenhower was an effective leader, although he failed to groom a successor and to provide leadership to the Republican Party.

Burk, Robert F. *The Eisenhower Administration and Black Civil Rights.* Knoxville: University of Tennessee Press, 1984. The most important book about Eisenhower and civil rights. Although Burk concentrates on events, he also discusses Eisenhower's attitudes and beliefs. The bibliographical essay is especially valuable.

Divine, Robert A. *Eisenhower and the Cold War.* New York: Oxford University Press, 1981. A clear, brief summary of several problems and themes in Eisenhower's foreign policy. In four essays (dealing with the presidency, Asia and massive retaliation, the Middle East, and Russians) Divine offers a favorable view of Eisenhower and of his handling of international crises.

Eisenhower, David. *Eisenhower: At War, 1943-1945.* New York: Random House, 1986. This massive study (nearly one thousand pages long) provides an indispensable account of Eisenhower's wartime leadership. The author (who is the grandson of his subject) emphasizes Eisenhower's awareness of long-range strategic considerations that would shape the postwar era.

Eisenhower, Dwight D. *The Eisenhower Diaries.* Edited by Robert H. Farrell. New York: W. W. Norton, 1981. This 445-page volume presents the diary that Eisenhower started in 1935 and continued sporadically until late in life. Among other things, the diary records Eisenhower's frustration with individuals whom, as a matter of policy, he refrained from criticizing publicly. Farrell's introduction is excellent.

Griffith, Robert. "Dwight D. Eisenhower and the Corporate Commonwealth." *American Historical Review* 87 (February, 1982): 87-122. A long, interpretative article that analyzes and synthesizes the components of Eisenhower's political philosophy (view of society, responsibility of government, role of economics) and the influence of this philosophy on his domestic and foreign policies. Griffith also describes the influences that shaped Eisenhower's philosophy.

Mayer, Michael S. "With Much Deliberation and Some Speed: Eisenhower and the

Brown Decision." *Journal of Southern History* 52 (February, 1986): 43-76. An assessment that portrays Eisenhower's civil rights record as more complex and, at times, more ambiguous than previous scholars have judged it to be. This article is broader in its concerns than the title suggests and is valuable for its account of Eisenhower's view of equality and African Americans.

Wukovits, John. *Eisenhower*. New York: Palgrave Macmillan, 2006. Part of a series on great generals, this volume focuses on Eisenhower's contributions to warfare, analyzing his military career before and during World War II.

CHRIS EVERT

" If you can react the same way to winning and losing, that's a big accomplishment.... "

Tennis player

Chris Evert burst upon the American tennis scene in the summer of 1971 at the U.S. Open as the first of the modern teenage stars. During the two decades that followed, she became one of the great champions of the sport and one of the most popular players that tennis has ever known.

Born: December 21, 1954; Fort Lauderdale, Florida
Also known as: Christine Marie Evert (birth name); Chris Evert Lloyd; Chrissie; Ice Maiden (nickname); Ice Princess (nickname)
Area of achievement: Sports

EARLY LIFE
Chris Evert (EH-vehrt) was born on December 21, 1954, in Fort Lauderdale, Florida, to James Evert, the manager of a tennis center, and Colette Evert. Chris was the second of their five children. All the Evert children learned to play tennis, but Chris displayed a special aptitude for the game. Her parents, however, did not direct her toward a professional career in the sport. Jimmy Evert did teach his daughter the two-handed backhand stroke that became her trademark because young Chris lacked the strength to execute a backhand with only one hand. From an early age, Chris stressed discipline and practicing to perfect her game. Her father was a major influence on her professional life and approach to tennis.

She began to attract the attention of top tennis players when she was fifteen. In the autumn of 1970, at a small tournament in Charlotte, North Carolina, the Carolinas International Tennis Classic, Evert beat two top-ranked players. Her most notable triumph was over Margaret Smith Court, the number-one woman player in the world, who had just won the Grand Slam the preceding year. The score was 7-6, 7-6. Evert lost to Nancy Richey in the final, but she was now a rising young star on the circuit.

During 1971, Evert continued to beat some top players in the tournaments that she entered. She won the Virginia Slims Masters in St. Petersburg, Florida, in April and

Evert, Chris

then was selected for the American Wightman Cup team to compete against Great Britain. She won two matches and was named the most valuable player in the competition.

Her true emergence as an international star occurred on the large public stage at the United States Open at Forest Hills in late August. Though still just sixteen, she won her first-round match easily. Facing defeat and elimination in a second-round match against Mary Ann Eisel of the United States, Evert rallied from a match point against her in the second set to win in three exciting sets, 4-6, 7-6, 6-1. Evert captivated the savvy New York crowd of avid tennis fans. She defeated two more players to reach the semifinals against the reigning queen of American women's tennis, Billie Jean King. King defeated her 6-3, 6-2 and went on to win the tournament. For the spectators there and for the national television audience, Evert was the story of the United States Open in 1971. *The New York Times* called her a "Cinderella in sneakers." She became a celebrity player and remained popular during the two decades of her career that followed.

LIFE'S WORK

Evert's career as a tennis star included so many victories and records that they cannot be easily summarized in a brief space. She entered thirty-four Grand Slam tournaments between 1971 and 1983 and made the semifinals in every one of them. From 1974 through 1986, she won at least one Grand Slam tournament every year. She was invincible on clay from August of 1973 through May of 1979, when she won 125 consecutive matches on her favorite surface. She was never ranked lower than fourth in the world throughout her career. She won 1,309 singles matches as against only 146 losses. In doubles, her record was 119 wins and 39 losses. Her career earnings totaled nearly $9 million.

Evert was especially dominant in the Grand Slam matches at the height of her career. She won the United States Open four years in a row between 1974 and 1978 and won additional titles there in 1980 and 1982. She won 101 matches at the Open, a record for both men and women. Her appeal to the New York crowds never faded, and it was appropriate that she played her last major professional match at that tournament in 1989.

The Australian Open was a tournament that Evert entered only five times. Yet she was a finalist in each of the tournaments, winning in 1982 and 1984. One of her victories came in 1982 against her friend and traditional rival Martina Navratilova, in a match that went three sets, 6-3, 2-6, 6-3. She outlasted Helena Sukova in the 1984 final, 6-7, 6-1, 6-3.

The red clay courts at Roland Garros Stadium for the French Open were a friendly surface for Evert throughout her career. She won the tournament seven times, in 1974, 1975, 1979, 1980, 1983, 1985, and 1986. Her last two victories were at the expense of Navratilova, and each one went the full three sets. In 1985, Evert triumphed 6-3, 6-7, 7-5, and a year later the score was 2-6, 6-3, 6-3. These were two of the most exciting encounters in the storied rivalry of these excellent tennis players. They reestablished Evert as a credible challenger to Navratilova and helped her end her playing career on a high note.

Chris Evert.
(National Archives)

Although Evert won Wimbledon three times, she did not excel in this prestigious tournament to the extent that she did in the French Open or U.S. Open. The fast grass court surface was less suited to her baseline game. The sensational British tabloids dubbed her the "Ice Maiden" and emphasized personal gossip in their intensive and often intrusive coverage of her annual appearances. The British fans, for their part, did not always appreciate the intense concentration that characterized her playing style. Despite these handicaps, she won her first Wimbledon title in 1974, two years after her first appearance in the tournament, with a victory over the Russian player Olga Morozova, 6-0, 6-4. Two years later, she triumphed again, defeating Evonne Goolagong Cawley, 6-3, 4-6, 6-1. Navratilova defeated Evert twice in Wimbledon finals, in 1978 and 1979, and Cawley also beat Evert in 1980. Evert won her third and last Wimbledon in 1981. She then lost three more finals to Navratilova, in 1982, 1984, and 1985.

Two rivalries with top players marked Evert's long career. During the 1970's, she often met the great champion of women's tennis, Billie Jean King, in key matches of top tournaments. The rivalry that most affected Evert during the 1980's, however, was the contest she waged with Navratilova for the top ranking in the women's game. In the cases of both King and Navratilova, the difference in approach to the game gave these matches great charm. Both King and Navratilova played an attacking style of serve-and-volley tennis. Evert's game, however, was built on her devastatingly accurate ground strokes hit from the baseline. Her most lethal weapon was her two-handed backhand, but her forehand, drop-shots, and lob were equally important in keeping her opponents off balance. Along with the excellent technical execution of her strokes, which good footwork and racquet preparation set up, she added tremendous concentration, discipline, anticipation, and tactical control of points to her game.

The challenge that Navratilova brought helped prolong Evert's tennis career. Navratilova's dominance pushed Evert to add new dimensions, such as a greater use of net play, to her game. The matches between these two great players attracted large television audiences and became legendary in the sport. Despite their strong desire to beat the other, the two women forged an unlikely friendship out of their confrontations. That sense of mutual respect enhanced the moments when they faced each other across the net. When their professional rivalry ended in 1988, Navratilova had won forty-three matches while Evert had prevailed in thirty-seven. As Evert noted, the two women had been by themselves in the locker room on championship Sundays over a period of sixteen years. They had dealt with that responsibility in a mature and understanding manner.

When Evert retired at the end of the 1989 season, her career of almost two decades was one of the longest and most memorable in the history of women's tennis. Evert brought a personal charisma to tennis that has also been reflected in her life off the court. In 1974, she was engaged to the popular men's player Jimmy Connors. Their twin victory at Wimbledon made headlines as the "Love Double," but they ended their engagement later that year. In April of 1979, Evert married John Lloyd, a British tennis player whose talent did not match that of his wife. The strains of life on the professional tennis circuit took their toll. Lloyd lacked the drive and commitment to excellence that motivated Evert. As a result, their marriage ended in divorce in 1986. In 1988, Evert married Andy Mill, a former Olympic skier in Boca Raton, Florida, in a civil ceremony with Navratilova and other women tennis players in attendance. The couple had three children: Alexander James, born in 1991; Nicholas Joseph, born in 1994; and Colton Jack, born in 1996. In 2005, she said of her husband that he was "a keeper." To a reporter writing a book about her famous matches with Navratilova, she confided her hopes that she and Mill could grow old together with their three boys. In December, 2006, however, she and Mill were divorced in Florida because of what were called in the newspapers "irreconcilable differences." Evert's friendship with the Australian golfer Greg Norman was mentioned as an element in the divorce.

After her retirement in 1989, Evert continued to have an active involvement with tennis. She sponsored an annual pro-celebrity charity tournament and participated in other fund-raising tennis programs. She served as an expert and well-informed television commentator for the French Open, Wimbledon, and the 1992 Barcelona Olympics. She collaborated on two autobiographical books, and she was a contributing editor to a tennis magazine, writing articles on various aspects of how to play the game. She continued as a leader in the Women's Tennis Association. With her brother John, she also opened the Evert Tennis Academy in Boca Raton. She was involved in charitable work to help at-risk children and to combat the HIV-AIDS epidemic. She told an interviewer in 2004 that her involvement in these varied activities had a single underlying purpose—to get to know herself as a human being. Years after her retirement from competition, she remained one of the icons of women's tennis, instantly recognized by fans around the world.

Significance

Evert's impact on the game of women's tennis has been as significant as that of any other player in the history of her sport in the twentieth century. She became the most popular figure in women's tennis at the time of her rise to prominence in 1971, and she sustained that level of acclaim. Her disciplined, precise style of tennis attested to her commitment and determination on the court. As she wrote in her autobiography *Chrissie* (1982), "I love tennis, I love the competition, the sheer challenge of playing to perfection." At the same time, she was dignified and sporting in her demeanor toward opponents. Her professionalism and dedication made her a leader in the development of women's tennis. She did much for the Women's Tennis Association as an officer, but as a star player and celebrity she helped to lift the game to heights of popularity in the United States it would not otherwise have attained. The Women's Sports Foundation named her the Greatest Woman Athlete of the preceding twenty-five years in 1985. A poll taken by American Sports Data in 1991 showed that she was the most widely known athlete in the nation. Her distinguished place in the history of American sports is secure.

—Karen Gould

Further Reading

Brown, Gene, ed. *The Complete Book of Tennis*. New York: Arno Press, 1980. A history of tennis based on accounts from *The New York Times*, this book offers a good survey newspaper coverage of Evert's major matches as she rose to international stardom during the 1970's.

Collins, Bud. *My Life with the Pros*. New York: E. P. Dutton, 1990. A very lively memoir by a reporter and broadcaster who covered Evert throughout her career and who later worked with her as a commentator on televised tennis matches. A valuable source for the inside perspective on her impact as a tennis star.

Feinstein, John. *Hard Courts: Real Life on the Professional Tennis Tours*. New York: Villard Books, 1991. Though the subject of his book is the 1990 tennis year, Feinstein has much to say about Evert's impact on the women's game.

Howard, Johnette. *The Rivals: Chris Evert vs. Martina Navratilova, Their Epic Duels and Extraordinary Friendship*. New York: Broadway Books, 2005. An in-depth analysis of this famous tennis rivalry with much new information about Evert's career and personality.

King, Billie Jean, and Cynthia Starr. *We Have Come a Long Way: The Story of Women's Tennis*. New York: McGraw-Hill, 1988. An engaging history of the women's game written by one of Evert's most famous rivals. King makes some perceptive remarks about the popular response to Evert and the reaction of her fellow

women tennis players to Evert's stardom.
Lloyd, Chris Evert, with Neil Amdur. *Chrissie: My Own Story.* New York: Simon & Schuster, 1982. A forthright memoir of her tennis career up to 1982, with comments about the place of tennis in her family, her approach to the game, and how she dealt with her celebrity status.
Lloyd, Chris Evert, and John Lloyd, with Carol Thatcher. *Lloyd on Lloyd.* London: Willow Books, 1985. Written in England with her first husband, this book gives a vivid picture of Evert's life during the mid-1980's and shows how the marriage of two professional players affected their careers and ultimately led to their divorce.
Lumpkin, Angela. *Women's Tennis: A Historical Documentary of the Players and Their Game.* Troy, N.Y.: Whitston, 1981. This overview of the role of women in tennis considers Evert's effect on the game and provides references to many of the articles written about her during the 1970's.
Schwabacher, Martin. *Superstars of Women's Tennis.* Philadelphia: Chelsea House, 2000. Evert's career receives a chapter in this look at the major figures of women's tennis.
Wade, Virginia, with Jean Rafferty. *Ladies of the Court: A Century of Women at Wimbledon.* New York: Atheneum, 1984. This survey of women at Wimbledon has a very good chapter on Evert's victories in this prestigious championship.

LOUIS FARRAKHAN

" *There really can be no peace without justice. There can be no justice without truth. And there can be no truth, unless someone rises up to tell you the truth.* **"**

Minister and civil rights activist

As leader of the Nation of Islam, one of the most influential black nationalist organizations in the United States, Farrakhan has focused his work on the most serious social and economic issues of the African American community. A highly controversial figure, he has been accused of anti-Semitism, sexism, and racism. To many, he is a hero for championing African American causes.

Born: May 11, 1933; Bronx, New York
Also known as: Louis Eugene Walcott (birth name); Louis Abdul Farrakhan (full name)
Areas of achievement: Religion and theology; social reform

EARLY LIFE
Louis Farrakhan (FEH-reh-kahn) was born Louis Eugene Walcott in the Bronx, New York, to an immigrant from the West Indies. His mother named him after his stepfather and the birth father of Farrakhan's older brother. Farrakhan was raised by his mother in Roxbury, Massachusetts, in a supportive West Indian community. He studied the vio-

lin privately at the age of five and regularly attended an Episcopalian church. He did well in school and was one of only a few black students to secure entry to the city's highly prestigious Boston Latin School. He transferred after a year to a different (though still prestigious) high school with a higher percentage of African Americans and became a popular presence on the high school track team.

Farrakhan continued with his music, singing in Boston nightclubs while keeping up with classical violin. He performed on the violin on the nationally telecast *Ted Mack Original Amateur Hour* and attended a small all-black college in Winston-Salem, North Carolina. He returned to Boston to marry a local woman and resumed a career as a club musician.

Life's Work

Farrakhan's major work has been with the Nation of Islam (NI), originally a separatist organization of Black Muslims with a distinctly conservative orientation. He was introduced to the NI in 1955, when he heard its then-leader, Elijah Muhammad, speak in Chicago. Farrakhan joined the group and was soon appointed the minister of its mosque in Boston. He then obtained various leadership posts in New York, including that of the official spokesperson for Muhammad. When Muhammad died in 1975, his son succeeded him and introduced a strong sense of moderation into the organization. The changed NI became much more tolerant of whites and focused on various forms of outreach to all communities, not just black.

Farrakhan vigorously disagreed with this change in the NI's orientation and focus and so formed a new group in 1978 that was much closer to the original movement's ideology and activities. Part of the work of Farrakhan's newly minted NI was to re-establish a security force with a significant percentage of former criminals as its staff. Indeed, the NI has received millions of dollars from the U.S. government to provide security services for housing projects in major cities in the United States.

Farrakhan developed the NI largely by reaching out to the media, which exhibited a great deal of interest in the more controversial aspects of his leadership. He made numerous public statements that could be considered nothing other than slurs against the American Jewish community. He is on record remarking that Judaism is a "gutter religion" and, according to a news report, once praised Adolf Hitler as a "great man." He has also attacked Israel for its policies toward Arabs and repeated the canard that American Jews control the American media as well as the country's financial sector. In Farrakhan's view, those who criticize him for making inflammatory and derogatory public remarks are themselves guilty of perpetuating a racist, antiblack system. His critics, however, allege that incitement stirred up against Jews has also spilled over to other ethnic groups, including claims that Korean businesses have exploited American blacks.

Under Farrakhan, the NI has taken a conservative position on a number of key moral issues. For example, interracial relationships are condemned as a remnant of slavery and as impossible until the economic and social discrepancies between the different racial groups are resolved. Homosexuality is similarly regarded as a perversion resulting from white society's emasculation of the black male, with the resulting feelings of denigration expressed by black females. The death penalty is supported for a variety of sexual offenses, including adultery, rape, and interracial relations.

The reconstituted organization has been active in antidrug campaigns in the black community and in the fight against urban crime. One of the highlights of Farrakhan's leadership was his organizing of the 1995 Million Man March in Washington, D.C., aimed at strengthening a sense of solidarity among black men. The march featured a dual message: atonement for American blacks for failing to control their community's destiny and resolve internal fractionalizations and for the U.S. government for fostering a slavery mentality and advocating white supremacy. Actual attendance estimates for the march varied from 400,000 to more than 1 million marchers, heralding a major demonstration of black unity. Critics, however, claimed the march was a watershed in serving to distance blacks from other racial groups. Whereas many in other religious and racial groups might previously have viewed Farrakhan as a fringe purveyor of hatred and discord, the Million Man March brought him more into the mainstream as a champion of black pride and interests.

Farrakhan himself, however, kept up and even nurtured his controversial profile following the Million Man March. He has since held dialogues with leaders of countries long regarded as terrorist states, and in 1996 he conducted a World Friendship Tour to Libya, Iran, Iraq, Sudan, and Syria. In Iran he was quoted as saying that the United States was the "great Satan."

Nation of Islam ideology includes prominent discussion of a future with an apocalyptic-type war (or Armageddon) between the races, a consequence of increasingly hostile interracial relations. In the messianic era, the NI states, wicked nations and governments will be destroyed. All elements of the devil will cease to exist, and a New Jerusalem era will be ushered in, with blacks in charge of an idyllic society that will suffer from none of society's present ills.

In 1999, Farrakhan was diagnosed with prostate cancer, and in 2003 he started a foundation to fight this disease. On February 25, 2007, he told a huge gathering at the NI's annual Saviour's Day convention at Ford Field in Detroit that his "time is up." This appearance was followed by his stay in a Washington, D.C., hospital for the treatment of complications from prostate surgery. He struck a somewhat conciliatory tone in his message, suggesting that his adherents engage in cooperative efforts with members of other faiths. At the same time, however, he stressed the continued development of black pride and unity.

Significance

Farrakhan has been a galvanizing force both for African Americans and for black Muslims, helping to build black consciousness and self-identity. However, he has done so at the expense of purveying a sense of distrust and animosity toward whites, other ethnic groups (especially Jews), and women. Although he has worked against the Nation of Islam's potential adoption of a more moderate political course with other institutional and political entities, Farrakhan nevertheless managed to change the image of the organization from that of a radical fringe group to that of a mainstream movement for civil rights and social reform.

—Eric Metchik

FURTHER READING

Alexander, Amy, ed. *The Farrakhan Factor*. New York: Grove Press, 1998. An edited volume of essays that examine Farrakhan's political ideology and his political work.

Farrakhan, Louis. *A Torchlight for America*. Chicago: FCN, 1993. An extensive exposition of Farrakhan's philosophy and prescriptions for moral reform and for reform of the U.S. economy, health care system, and education. Main points in each chapter are illustrated by statistical tables.

Gardell, Mattias. *In the Name of Elijah Muhammad: Louis Farrakhan and the Nation of Islam*. Durham, N.C.: Duke University Press, 1996. A scholarly exposition of the history of the Nation of Islam, with discussion of Farrakhan's seminal leadership role. Extensive bibliography, including both published and unpublished (interviews, speeches, FBI files) sources.

Peterson, Jesse Lee. *Scam*. Nashville, Tenn.: WND Books, 2003. A critical analysis of the sociological dynamics and the current state of leadership in the black community in the United States.

Singh, Robert. *The Farrakhan Phenomenon*. Washington, D.C.: Georgetown University Press, 1997. An analysis of Farrakhan's career in the context of polarization and schisms within and among different racial groups in the United States. Bibliography, index.

BETTY FORD

> *A woman . . . told us she was forever getting herself into trouble. 'But I just keep coming back,' she said. . . . Showing up for life. Being blessed with the rebirth that recovery brings.*

First Lady of the United States (1974-1977)

Ford was a popular, outspoken First Lady of the United States. In the White House, she was an advocate for a number of women's issues. She was diagnosed with breast cancer soon after becoming First Lady, which led her to join the emerging women's health movement. After leaving Washington, D.C., she founded and chaired the Betty Ford Center, an internationally known institution for the treatment of substance abuse.

Born: April 8, 1918; Chicago, Illinois
Also known as: Elizabeth Ann Bloomer (birth name)
Areas of achievement: Women's rights; mental health; public health

EARLY LIFE

Betty Ford was born as Elizabeth Ann Bloomer, the third child and only daughter of William and Hortense Bloomer. When Ford was two years old, the family moved to Grand Rapids, Michigan, where she had a comfortable upbringing. Ford's early years

Ford, Betty

were full of friends, family, and social activities. Tragedy, however touched her at age sixteen when her father died. At his funeral, she learned that her father had been an alcoholic.

A lifelong love of dance began when Ford started taking lessons at the age of eight. For two years during high school, she attended the well-respected Bennington School of Dance in Vermont, where she became acquainted with modern dance innovator Martha Graham. Ford aspired to dance in Graham's regular company and, at the age of twenty, she moved to New York to pursue that goal. Though talented, she was not invited to join Graham's main group. Her mother, who was uncomfortable with the idea of her daughter living alone in New York, encouraged Ford to return to Grand Rapids, and she did.

LIFE'S WORK

Ford worked at a local department store as a fashion coordinator and also taught dance. In 1942, she was married to William Warren, a man she had known for years. Like her father, Warren was an alcoholic. The marriage ended in divorce five years later.

In 1947, Betty met Gerald Ford, a lawyer who also was from Grand Rapids. Their romance progressed and they were married on October, 15, 1948. Ford was elected to the U.S. House of Representatives less than one month later. The couple set up house-

Betty Ford. (NARA)

keeping near the capital and Ford became a political wife. She was active in the Congressional Club, gave tours to visiting constituents, and campaigned when her husband was running for reelection.

The Ford family grew quickly: Between 1950 and 1957, the couple had four children. Ford's husband was away from home for as many as 258 days a year doing congressional business or supporting fellow Republicans. The burden of raising the family fell almost exclusively on Ford, and it took a toll. Recurring physical problems from a pinched nerve in her neck as well as low self-esteem led her to consult a psychiatrist, who she saw for a number of years.

In 1973, the Fords had decided that they would retire to Grand Rapids after one more term in the House. Then, President Richard M. Nixon named Gerald Ford to succeed the disgraced Spiro Agnew as vice president of the United States in October, 1973. Less than one year later, on August 9, 1974, Gerald Ford became president after Nixon left office after his impeachment. Betty Ford became First Lady of the United States.

After five years of Pat Nixon's formality, Ford was a breath of fresh air. She wanted to be an active First Lady, and it was apparent that she intended to speak her mind—frequently, and to the displeasure of her husband's West Wing staff.

Ford's abbreviated tenure in the White House kept her from developing an ongoing White House program or project. Building on a lifetime as a homemaker and political partner, she became an advocate for women and women's concerns. At least part of her activity was unintentional. Shortly after becoming First Lady she was diagnosed with breast cancer. She made the conscious decision to tell the public about her cancer and subsequent radical mastectomy. She said, "My feeling was if I had it, others had it, and if I said nothing, their lives would be gone." The announcement came at a time when breast cancer was rarely discussed in public. After leaving the hospital and completing chemotherapy, Ford continued to be an advocate for regular mammography exams and for health education. Her advocacy was a part of the emerging women's health movement in the 1970's.

The First Lady became a vocal supporter of the Equal Rights Amendment (ERA) as well. The ERA had already been passed by thirty-four state legislatures, but four others were needed for passage at the federal level as an amendment to the U.S. Constitution. Ford made telephone calls and wrote notes to members of the state legislatures where votes were pending. She aroused the ire of anti-ERA forces that were annoyed with her lobbying efforts. She asserted that she was only expressing her opinion, but she finally backed away from active support when it seemed that her efforts might affect her husband politically.

Ford encouraged her husband to appoint women to government positions. Taking her views into consideration, President Ford named Carla Hills to serve as secretary of housing and urban development. Anne Armstrong was appointed U.S. ambassador to the Court of St. James. Ford was also hopeful that her husband would nominate the first woman to the U.S. Supreme Court, but when he had the opportunity, he named John Paul Stevens instead.

A defining moment for Ford occurred in August, 1975, when she appeared on the CBS television program *60 Minutes*. The program coincided with the anniversary of

Ford, Betty

the Ford administration's first year in office. The First Lady startled interviewer Morley Safer with her enthusiastic support for *Roe v. Wade* (1973). She also told Safer that she would not be surprised if her children tried marijuana, and she would not be shocked if her daughter had an affair. The public reaction was immediate, and much of it was negative. Over time, however, public opinion reversed and Ford saw her popularity rise.

Ford's popularity rose so much that a campaign button from the 1976 presidential election read "I'm Voting for Betty's Husband." Unfortunately, her husband was defeated by Jimmy Carter in the 1976 elections.

After leaving the White House, the family grew increasingly concerned with Ford's drinking and dependence on prescription drugs. They conducted an "intervention" to help her face her problems. She entered a rehabilitation program in California and was so grateful for the help she had received that she founded the Betty Ford Center in Rancho Mirage, also in California, for the treatment of substance abuse. Over the years, the center became one of the most well-known treatment centers in the world, partly because of the center's name. Ford stepped down as the chair of the board of trustees in 2005 and was succeeded by her daughter, Susan Ford.

SIGNIFICANCE

As one scholar observed, Ford's legacy was more in her example than in the success or failure of the causes she supported. Well liked by Americans who admired her candid, personal style, she was an active First Lady who was in touch with the times. Her public policy forays achieved mixed but well-publicized results.

Perhaps Ford's greatest achievement in the White House was that she brought breast cancer out of the closet, so to speak. Her openness about breast cancer most likely saved lives and is credited with contributing to what was a burgeoning women's health movement in the 1970's. After leaving the White House, she confronted her own demons and faced the realities of her substance abuse. Her status as a public figure—indeed, a celebrity—helped the nation talk openly about two previously taboo subjects: breast cancer and substance abuse.

One of the more popular and well-respected First Ladies, Ford's personal tragedies and challenges have enlightened and improved the lives of Americans. One scholar referred to her as "an American hero," a well-deserved title.

—*Myra G. Gutin*

FURTHER READING

Ford, Betty, with Chris Chase. *The Times of My Life*. New York: Harper, 1978. Ford's autobiography follows her from childhood through the tumultuous events of 1974-1977, when she served as First Lady, and through her successful treatment for alcohol and drug dependency.

Greene, John Robert. *Betty Ford: Candor and Courage in the White House*. Lawrence: University Press of Kansas, 2004. The most comprehensive and thoughtful discussion of Ford, this book incorporates primary and secondary materials as it assesses her effectiveness in the White House and in the years after.

Gutin, Myra G. "Betty Ford." In *The President's Partner: The First Lady in the Twen-*

tieth Century. Westport, Conn.: Greenwood Press, 1989. Classifying Ford as a political surrogate and independent activist, this study looks at Ford's speeches, media relations, and social activities while serving as First Lady.
Gutin, Myra G., and Leesa E. Tobin. "'You've Come a Long Way Mr. President': Betty Ford as First Lady." In *Gerald R. Ford and the Politics of Post-Watergate America,* edited by Bernard J. Firestone and Alexej Ugrinsky. Vol. 2. Westport, Conn.: Greenwood Press, 1993. This chapter discusses Ford as a political spouse and White House activist. Focuses special attention on her speeches, media relations, and her appearance on *60 Minutes.*
Tobin, Leesa E. "Betty Ford as First Lady: A Woman for Women." *Presidential Studies Quarterly* 20 (Fall, 1990): 761-767. Written by the Ford Library archivist responsible for processing the papers of the First Lady and her staff, this article describes their significance in understanding women's issues in the 1970's.
Weidenfeld, Sheila. *First Lady's Lady: With the Fords at the White House.* New York: Putnam's, 1979. Weidenfeld, who served as Betty Ford's press secretary, discusses her years with the First Lady in chronologically arranged entries.

BENJAMIN FRANKLIN

> *They who can give up essential liberty to obtain a little temporary safety deserve neither liberty nor safety.*

Statesman, scientist, and philosopher

Franklin helped shape most of the important political, social, and intellectual developments in eighteenth century America. He became a veritable symbol of the United States by the end of his life, both at home and abroad, and he remains an influential folk hero.

Born: January 17, 1706; Boston, Massachusetts
Died: April 17, 1790; Philadelphia, Pennsylvania
Areas of achievement: Government and politics; diplomacy; invention and technology; literature

EARLY LIFE

Among Benjamin Franklin's English ancestors, one had owned a bit of land only twelve miles from the English ancestral seat of the Washingtons. Franklin's father, Josiah, had repudiated the Church of England and left England for Boston in the 1680's; Franklin's mother's forebears had arrived somewhat earlier. When Franklin was born in 1706, the modest household was already teeming with children, for he was a tenth son—and, incidentally, the youngest son of the youngest son for five generations back. The salient facts of Franklin's life were extraordinary from the start.

Although his father was a struggling tradesman (a candle maker and soap boiler), there was much in the way of reading, thinking, and discussing as well as hard work in his home. Franklin learned to read when very young, and by the age of twelve he had progressed through the Bible, the works of John Bunyan, Plutarch's *Parallel Lives* (105-115), and certain essays of Daniel Defoe and of Boston's Cotton Mather. He had very little formal schooling, and his family could not afford to send him to Harvard College.

Instead, an effort was made to bring him into the family business. He disliked the work, and he hated the smell. At that point, an older brother, James, returned from London, where he had been trained as a printer. Thus, the restless, bright, bookish twelve-year-old Benjamin Franklin was apprenticed to his high-spirited brother, who in 1721 started a newspaper, *The New England Courant*. It was the fourth newspaper in the colonies. These years were supremely important in shaping the man who later became so famous. He learned a trade that would bring him profits and prominence. He had access to many books, especially those loaned by patrons and friends. He discussed and debated matters with men who loitered in the shop and also with friends after hours. The principal subjects were the two that would be commonly avoided centuries later: religion and politics. He worked hard at learning to write, and he experienced the thrill of seeing his first piece, an anonymous letter to the editor, in print. When the pugnacious James got into trouble with the authorities and was jailed, his brother, then sixteen, functioned as the paper's editor.

The brothers often quarreled, and the younger Franklin, a mere apprentice, was often treated severely. He resented this and decided to run away, arriving in Philadelphia in October, 1723, munching on a large roll, with one Dutch dollar and a copper shilling in his pocket. The scene became a memorable passage in the memoir he later wrote, which included the fact that his future wife happened to see him and laughed at the ridiculous sight he made. He soon found work, for he was an excellent printer, and he soon found adventure as well. An eccentric governor of the province, William Keith, proposed that Franklin go to England to purchase equipment for a new printing business Keith hoped would outdo all competition. He would send letters of credit and letters of introduction.

Franklin was in London by Christmas, 1724, but no letters came from the governor. The eighteen-year-old did find work, however, in a printing house, and as always he read intensively and grappled with ideas. After setting type for a religious book, he became convinced that the author was all wrong. In response, Franklin composed and printed a pamphlet that set forth a radical refutation. He later regarded this as a mistake, but it did gain him some attention and some new acquaintances, a few of them prominent writers of the day.

Franklin returned to Philadelphia in 1726 and was soon employed again in his old shop. Before long, he left the shop to form a new business with a partner, on credit. By dint of very long hours of work, ingenious planning, and excellent workmanship, they survived—barely. Then the partner wanted to leave, and Franklin, borrowing money, bought him out. By July, 1730, he was the sole proprietor of a promising business, which included the printing of a newspaper begun the year before, *The Pennsylvania Gazette*. Six weeks later, he married Deborah Read, the daughter of his first landlady. Though she was uneducated (thus never an intellectual companion), she was frugal, industrious, and loving. Franklin, at twenty-four, had become a solid Philadelphia burgher.

Franklin, Benjamin

LIFE'S WORK
The foundation of Benjamin Franklin's renown was his success as a businessman. Both he and Deborah worked very hard, and they lived frugally for some time. It was, however, more than routine drudgery, for new projects were always appearing: Franklin established a stationery shop; Deborah collected and prepared rags for the paper makers; he imported books in both English and foreign languages; he printed almanacs for those who compiled them, and then decided to compile his own. *Poor Richard's Almanack*, begun in 1732 and published between 1733 and 1758, was ultimately to become the best known of the many that were printed in eighteenth century America. Franklin enjoyed borrowing and reworking phrases from his reading and sometimes wrote new adages, which delighted his readers. For many, he and his fictional wise man, Richard Saunders, became one. The central themes of Richard's concern were thrift, industry, and frugality, and Franklin at the time appeared to be practicing what "Poor Richard" preached.

Political connections quickly became an important feature of Franklin's business success. He printed much of the provincial government's work: laws, records of legislative voting, and even the new paper currency in favor of which Franklin had argued in his first political pamphlet, *A Modest Enquiry into the Nature and Necessity of a Paper Currency* (1729). He became clerk of the Pennsylvania Assembly in 1736. The following year, he secured an appointment as postmaster for Philadelphia, a position that gave him immediate access to the latest news—very helpful in his newspaper business. Later, he was deputy postmaster general for all the colonies (1753-1774), and under his administration the governmental department showed a profit. He was always heavily involved with public affairs and often managed to influence their course.

It was during his years as a businessman that Franklin's remarkable flair for civic improvement by private initiative appeared. In 1727, he founded a discussion group, or club, of tradesmen, clerks, and mechanics, which he called the Junto. Often Franklin would first propose to his friends at the Junto for discussion an idea for a public project and then follow his proposal with an article in his newspaper. Soon the project would be under way. He was prominent in the founding of a circulating library, a fire company, a hospital, and an academy that evolved into the University of Pennsylvania, among many other projects. Ever the keen observer of daily life in his beloved city, he was always alert to possibilities for improvement.

Franklin was also a particularly astute observer of nature, and this ultimately led him to the forefront of certain branches of the sciences of his day. On an early transatlantic voyage, he kept careful records of temperatures, of the flora and fauna of the sea, of the positions of the Moon and the stars; later he made a map of the Gulf Stream. He believed that knowledge must be useful, and actual inventions came out of many of his studies, including the improved Franklin stove, bifocal spectacles, a glass harmonica (a musical instrument for which even Wolfgang Amadeus Mozart wrote music), and other gadgets.

His main interest, though, was electricity. His famous kite experiment in 1752 demonstrated the identity of lightning and electricity and gave him an international reputation. He was, as always, interested in practical application, which in this case became the lightning rod. Nevertheless, he was also responsible for naming the concept of po-

Franklin, Benjamin

larity, negative and positive, to describe the behavior of electricity.

In 1748, Franklin was able to retire from business, expecting to devote himself to his favorite scientific pursuits. Public affairs, however, became the dominant force throughout the remainder of his life. When the threat of war with France led to a gathering of delegates at Albany in 1754, Franklin was there representing Pennsylvania. He proposed a plan for an intercolonial union that the Albany Congress approved, only to see it rejected by both the various colonial governments and the imperial authorities in London. Franklin always believed that if these governments had not been so shortsighted, the American Revolution might have been avoided. In 1757, as a result of a quarrel between the Pennsylvania Assembly and the proprietors of the colony, he was sent to London as spokesman for the assembly, the members of which wanted the authorities there to intervene. In this he achieved a partial success. While in England, he received honorary degrees from St. Andrews and Oxford. He was very happy in England and seriously considered a permanent move, but he came home to Philadelphia in 1762.

Another political quarrel in Pennsylvania led to Franklin's return to England in 1764, where he soon became involved in efforts to forestall the new imperial policies toward the colonies, which Americans regarded as outrageous. For ten years, Franklin was torn between his profound pride in America and things American, and his enthusiasm for English culture. As the foremost American of his day, he was looked to for the preservation of American rights: He became an agent for Georgia, New Jersey, and Massachusetts, as well as the Pennsylvania Assembly. As Anglo-American relations deteriorated, Franklin revealed in private his growing conviction that the American colonists' claims were sound and that their resistance was justified, while he continued to make every diplomatic effort possible for accommodation.

Early in 1774, however, news arrived of the destruction of tea at Boston Harbor, in an act known as the Boston Tea Party. This was quickly followed by a mighty personal attack on Franklin, occasioned by his part in obtaining and circulating certain letters written by Governor Thomas Hutchinson of Massachusetts, the contents of which inflamed opinion against Hutchinson and led to a petition for his recall. Franklin was dismissed by the royal government from his postal appointment and subjected to a searing public humiliation before a committee of the Privy Council (January, 1774). For another year he tried in many ingenious ways to achieve a reconciliation, but to no avail. He sailed for America in March, 1775.

When Franklin arrived home, the Continental Congress, which had first convened during the preceding fall, was now into its second session at Philadelphia. The deliberations were becoming extremely anxious because the unthinkable had happened: Actual fighting had broken out with British soldiers at Lexington and Concord. Franklin was made a member of the congress the day after he arrived, and he immediately undertook important work. He drew up a plan of colonial union, something similar to an early version of a national constitution. He organized a post office and became postmaster general. He served on a number of important committees, including one that in 1776 was to draft the Declaration of Independence. He was, at the age of seventy, the oldest signer. Toward the end of that year, he was sent by the congress, along with Arthur Lee and Silas Deane, to solicit French support for the American cause.

Franklin was well known in France. He had visited that country before, but more important was his reputation as a scientist, writer (Poor Richard's witticisms had been translated), and apostle of the latest ideas of the Age of Reason. He played the part well, with fur hat and simple clothes, a genial manner, and appropriate bons mots (witticism), and he exuded the spirit of liberty—a veritable backwoods Socrates spreading the truths of nature. Following the American victory at Saratoga (October, 1777), the French became receptive to American suggestions, and by February of 1778, France had become a formal ally. This meant that France was now at war with Great Britain.

Franklin became the sole American ambassador in September of 1778 and, as always, found many interests beyond his principal work. He managed, nevertheless, to keep French-American relations good; France provided America with material aid, an army, and, in the crucial autumn of 1781, a navy. After the British defeat at Yorktown (October, 1781), peace negotiations with Britain began. Franklin was joined by John Adams and John Jay in the final talks, but on several occasions the wily old Philadelphian's role was decisive. It was an excellent treaty for Americans, gaining them a formal acknowledgment of independence and generous boundaries.

When Franklin returned to Philadelphia in September, 1785, he was nearly eighty years old. Yet he was chosen president of the executive council of Pennsylvania, and he became the president of an antislavery society. He was chosen as a Pennsylvania delegate to the Philadelphia Convention, which drew up the U.S. Constitution in 1787, and he gave his prestigious support to its ratification. His last public act was signing a petition to Congress for the abolition of slavery. He died on April 17, 1790.

Significance

Benjamin Franklin's life was so varied and his achievements so diverse that it seems as though there were several Franklins, though one tends to overlap the other. The most familiar is the successful businessman who rose from humble circumstances to dine with kings, substantially by his own efforts. His life symbolized the rags-to-riches success of a self-made man, a theme of great importance in American thought. His version of his life, as presented in the didactic *The Autobiography of Benjamin Franklin* (1791) and in the sayings of Poor Richard, stressed thrift, industry, and frugality, which were important elements of his own Puritan heritage, rendered in secular, easily understood forms. His zest for useful knowledge became the main style of American science and technology, yet he had great respect for learning and for intellectual curiosity, and he believed that educational opportunity was indispensable for a great future nation.

He was civic-minded from the start. He demonstrated what could be done by private, voluntary community effort to care for human needs, but he also stressed the importance of alert participation in the prevailing political system. His style was egalitarian, tolerant, and democratic before such a style was expected and common; yet he understood well the importance of dignity and deference in human affairs. Americans, during his later years, repudiated kings and hereditary aristocrats, but they also yearned for heroes. Franklin provided them with a hero unlike any other known before.

—*Richard D. Miles*

Franklin, Benjamin

FURTHER READING

Aldridge, Alfred Owen. *Benjamin Franklin: Philosopher and Man*. Philadelphia: J. B. Lippincott, 1965. An effort to explain Franklin's human qualities as much as his achievements, this is a judicious, authoritative biography by an author who has done much to expand knowledge of Franklin and who has written extensively about him.

Cohen, I. Bernard. *Franklin and Newton*. Cambridge, Mass.: Harvard University Press, 1966. In this reprint of the excellent 1956 study of eighteenth century scientific thought, Cohen, a historian of science, places Franklin in the context of prevailing notions about scientific method. He appreciates Franklin as a scientist without overstating the case. Especially good depiction of human qualities that affect scientific work.

———. *Science and the Founding Fathers: Science in the Political Thought of Jefferson, Franklin, Adams, and Madison*. New York: W. W. Norton, 1995. Cohen explains how Franklin and other Founding Fathers were affected by the Age of Reason, seeking to discover the links between scientific principles and constitutional government.

Conner, Paul W. *Poor Richard's Politics: Benjamin Franklin and His New American Order*. New York: Oxford University Press, 1965. A systematic discussion of Franklin's political ideas. This is a thoughtful, well-informed book, filled with materials regarding Franklin's intellectual world. Strong effort to arrive at balanced judgments about Franklin as a thinker.

Crane, Verner W. *Benjamin Franklin and a Rising People*. Boston: Little, Brown, 1954. A succinct, extremely informative, and reliable work, which is especially strong on philosophical, social, and political ideas.

Franklin, Benjamin. *The Autobiography of Benjamin Franklin*. Edited by Leonard W. Labaree et al. New Haven, Conn.: Yale University Press, 1964. Franklin's memoirs (the word "autobiography" was not used in the eighteenth century) have been printed a bewildering number of times, and most readers may well believe that they are familiar with them. It is one of those classics, however, that deserves repeated readings, even though it presents only one of several sides of Franklin's life.

Granger, Bruce I. *Benjamin Franklin: An American Man of Letters*. Ithaca, N.Y.: Cornell University Press, 1964. A skilled presentation of Franklin's literary achievements. Each chapter is devoted to a kind of writing, such as essays, letters, and almanacs. Strong claims are made for Franklin, many of them persuasive.

Isaacson, Walter. *Benjamin Franklin: An American Life*. New York: Simon & Schuster, 2003. In this best-selling popular biography, Isaacson depicts Franklin as "the founding father who winks at us." Clearly written, well researched, and an enjoyable read.

Lopez, Claude-Anne. *Mon Cher Papa*. New Haven, Conn.: Yale University Press, 1966. An unusually charming account of Franklin's life in France during the American Revolution by one of the editors of the Franklin papers. The author does a good job of dispelling some of the myths about Franklin and makes a strong case for his greatness as a diplomat.

Middlekauff, Robert. *Benjamin Franklin and His Enemies*. Berkeley: University of

California Press, 1996. Middlekauff presents Franklin as a man of passionate anger who drew the enmity of William Penn, the "founder" of Pennsylvania, and John Adams, among others.

Morgan, Edmund S. *Benjamin Franklin.* New Haven, Conn.: Yale University Press, 2002. Morgan focuses on Franklin's public life, detailing his activities as a politician and diplomat.

Srodes, James. *Franklin: The Essential Founding Father.* Washington, D.C.: Regnery, 2002. Srodes describes Franklin's evolution from "striving craftsman to daring diplomat, spy, and national master builder" in generally favorable terms.

Stourzh, Gerald. *Benjamin Franklin and American Foreign Policy.* Chicago: University of Chicago Press, 1954. A searching, learned analysis of some major features of Franklin's thought. Begins with a review of prevailing currents of thought in the eighteenth century, such as the Great Chain of Being and the belief in progress and reason, then describes how Franklin developed such materials in the course of his diplomatic career.

Van Doren, Carl C. *Benjamin Franklin.* New York: Viking Press, 1938. A magisterial biography, massive and still impressive. This is the kind of book to which one might turn for reliable information about nearly anything regarding Franklin's life. An excellent literary achievement containing profound, extensive scholarship.

JOHN C. FRÉMONT

" *Today we have in this country the abuses of a military dictation without its unity of action and vigor of execution.* **"**

Explorer and military commander

Frémont's exploits as an explorer helped to propel the American nation westward toward Oregon and California. When the continental nation he helped to create was faced with civil war, he fought to maintain the Union and end slavery.

Born: January 21, 1813; Savannah, Georgia
Died: July 13, 1890; New York, New York
Also known as: John Charles Frémont (full name)
Areas of achievement: Exploration; military

EARLY LIFE

When John Charles Frémont (FREE-mahnt) was born, his parents were not married. In 1811, Ann Beverly Whiting had left her elderly husband John Pryor to run away with Charles Frémon, a young French emigrant who taught dancing and French. For several years the struggling Frémon family traveled the South, but after the father died they settled in Charleston, South Carolina, where John Charles grew to maturity.

At the age of fourteen, Frémont clerked in the law office of John W. Mitchell, who

Frémont, John C.

soon sent the young man to Dr. John Roberton's academy. In 1829, Frémont entered the junior class of the College of Charleston. Showing promise, he nevertheless fell behind in his studies from a lack of diligence as well as the distraction of a young love. In 1831, the faculty reluctantly dismissed him for "incorrigible negligence," three months short of his graduation.

In 1833, saved from obscurity by Joel Poinsett, former minister to Mexico, Frémont taught mathematics on the USS *Natchez* on a South American cruise and then earned an appointment in 1835 as professor of mathematics in the Navy. He nevertheless declined this position to join Captain William G. Williams in surveying part of a proposed railroad route from Charleston to Cincinnati. This first assignment earned for him a second as Williams's assistant in 1836-1837, surveying the lands of the Cherokee Indians in Georgia. Frémont showed little concern for the forced removal of the Cherokees across the Mississippi, but he did discover a longing to pursue a life in unexplored lands.

With the help of Secretary of War Poinsett, Frémont was assigned in 1838 to assist Joseph Nicolas Nicollet, a respected French scientist mapping the region between the Mississippi and Missouri Rivers. He was commissioned a second lieutenant in the United States Topographical Corps and from Nicollet received valuable experience in frontier survival, as well as rigorous training in mapmaking and scientific observation. As Nicollet's protégé, Frémont stood ready to replace the gravely ill scientist on future missions.

Bright and inquisitive, Frémont already possessed the knowledge of surveying, mathematics, and natural sciences, as well as the impulsiveness, that would shape his later career. Bearded and slightly but sturdily built, he was able to endure great physical and personal hardships. His dark hair, olive skin, and piercing blue eyes attracted the friendship and affection of men and women alike. In 1841, he won the lifelong admiration and love of the young and talented Jessie Benton, acquiring not only a bride but also another powerful benefactor in her father, Senator Thomas Hart Benton of Missouri.

Life's Work

Frémont received his first independent assignment in 1841 to survey the Des Moines River region. On his return, he secretly married Jessie, soon benefiting from his family connection with Senator Benton: Advocates of American expansion, led by Benton, were eager to encourage immigration to the Oregon country, and Frémont was thus given command of his first western expedition, assigned to examine part of the trail to Oregon while gathering information useful to immigrants and the government.

In Missouri, Frémont enlisted Kit Carson as his guide and set off from the Kansas River in June, 1842. Following the Platte to the Sweetwater River, he went on to cross the Rocky Mountains at South Pass in Wyoming, later describing the route as no more difficult than the ascent up Capitol Hill. He then explored the headwaters of the Green River in the Wind River Range, unfurling an American flag atop one of its loftiest peaks. Returning, Frémont led six men in a collapsible boat down the Platte. When the current became swift and dangerous, he rashly decided to run the rapids, resulting in an accident that destroyed much of his equipment and part of the expedition's records.

Frémont's second expedition of 1843-1844 was more ambitious. With a large, well-equipped party (including an unauthorized howitzer cannon), he was to complete his survey of the overland trail all the way to Oregon. Setting off in May, the explorer first sought a new pass through the Colorado mountains but soon rejoined the Oregon Trail. Crossing at South Pass, he pushed on to the British forts in the Oregon country, finally reaching Fort Vancouver on the Columbia. On this expedition, Frémont made the first scientific investigation of the Great Salt Lake; his reports inspired Brigham Young to lead his Mormon followers to settle there and make the region bloom, as Frémont had predicted.

From Oregon, Frémont embarked on a perilous journey southward, exploring and naming the Great Basin and then attempting a risky winter crossing of the Sierra Nevada into California, successfully leading his men to Sutter's Fort in the Sacramento Valley. Inspired in part by American interest in the Mexican province of California, Frémont's adventures intensified American passions to possess this valuable Pacific prize. Returning via the old Spanish Trail, Utah Lake, and Bent's Fort on the Arkansas River, Frémont emerged in August, 1844, a national celebrity.

With Jessie's valuable help, Frémont prepared reports of his first and second expeditions that captured the excitement and promise of the new land. Congress ordered the reports published for public distribution, providing immigrants a guide for western travel. The popular reports helped to dispel the notion that the Plains region was an arid wasteland, showed the Oregon Trail passable, and praised the fertile valleys of Oregon and California.

With a well-armed party of sixty men, the brevet captain's third expedition would place him in California just as relations with Mexico worsened. Starting in June, 1845, the party followed the Arkansas and then crossed the central Colorado Rockies. Frémont paused to examine further the Great Salt Lake, then led his party across the desert to the west. While the main party followed a safer route, Frémont led a smaller group directly across the Great Basin and then attempted another winter crossing of the Sierra. Encountering less difficulty than on the previous trip, he arrived once again at Sutter's Fort, eager to play a role in California's future.

Frémont's formidable force earned the suspicion of Mexican officials, who ordered the party to leave the province. Although war with Mexico was months away, Frémont defied the order, raised the American flag, and prepared for a confrontation. When none developed, he slowly moved toward Oregon but retraced his steps after the arrival of a messenger from Washington. Marine Lieutenant Archibald Gillespie had carried important dispatches to Consul Thomas O. Larkin at Monterey, directing him to conciliate the native Californians to accept American rule. Gillespie repeated these instructions to Frémont and relayed news of trouble with Mexico. Frémont misinterpreted the government's instructions to mean that he should return to California and act to protect American interests there. After a bloody clash with Indians, he returned to the Sacramento Valley, assuming command of the "Bear Flag" revolt of American settlers in June, 1846.

Frémont's actions secured Northern California for the United States, but were con-

Frémont, John C.

trary to the government's wishes to win the province peacefully with the aid of its citizens. Once hostilities with Mexico began, American naval forces seized the ports of Monterey and San Francisco in July, 1846. Frémont's frontiersmen and settlers then formed the "California Battalion" to assist Commodore Robert F. Stockton in securing Southern California. San Diego and Los Angeles were quickly occupied, but a revolt by Californians forced the Americans to retake the south. Assembling a large force in the north, Frémont arrived too late to join in the battle for Los Angeles, but he did accept (without authority) the Californians' surrender at Cahuenga.

In January, 1847, Stockton appointed Frémont governor of California. This position embroiled the current lieutenant colonel in a bitter dispute over proper authority between the commodore and General Stephen Watts Kearny, who had arrived from Santa Fe only to be bloodied by Californians at San Pasqual. As governor in Los Angeles, Frémont recognized Commodore Stockton's authority while unwisely resisting General Kearny's commands, resulting in his arrest and return east virtually a prisoner. In a celebrated court-martial defense, he won public sympathy, but in January, 1848, was found guilty of mutiny, disobedience, and conduct prejudicial to military order. He was sentenced to dismissal from the service. President James K. Polk disallowed the mutiny conviction but upheld the lesser charges while suspending the punishment. Frémont spurned Polk's gesture and resigned his commission instead, ending his career as an explorer for the United States Army.

To regain his injured honor, Frémont organized a privately funded fourth expedition in late 1848. Intended to locate suitable passes for a central railroad route to the Pacific, the expedition attempted a midwinter passage of the severe San Juan Mountains in southern Colorado. Disregarding the advice of mountain men and perhaps misled by his guide "Old Bill" Williams, Frémont plunged into the snowy mountains, only to find disaster. Cold and starvation eventually took the lives of ten of his thirty-three men, while a few survivors may have resorted to cannibalism. Frémont withdrew to Taos, New Mexico, sending a relief party to his surviving men. With a smaller party, he pushed on to California by the Gila River route, arriving in early 1849.

Frémont's fortunes revived once more as gold had just been discovered in California. In 1847, he had directed Consul Larkin to buy a tract of land near San Francisco; instead Larkin had secured a large grant in the interior. At first apparently worthless, the Mariposa grant yielded immense wealth in gold and became the Frémonts' California home. Then in December, 1849, Frémont was selected one of California's first United States senators, serving a short term from 1850 to 1851 as an antislavery Democrat.

Not chosen to lead one of the five government parties surveying the best route for a Pacific railroad, Frémont in late 1853 undertook his fifth and final expedition to prove the superiority of a central route. On this venture, Frémont found less hardship in attempting another winter crossing of the Colorado mountains. Crossing into Utah, however, his men were again on the brink of starvation, whereupon he swore them not to resort to cannibalism. The party was finally saved in February, 1854, when it arrived at a Mormon settlement in Parowan. The route was not adopted for a Pacific railroad.

As tension grew between North and South, Frémont emerged as a candidate for president in 1856, first for the Democratic Party and then for the newly organized Republican Party. Hostile to slavery, he favored the Republican position, opposing slavery's westward expansion, and in June, 1856, accepted the first presidential nomination of the young party. In the general election, he faced both Democrat James Buchanan and the candidate of the Know-Nothing Party, Millard Fillmore. The "Pathfinder" made few campaign utterances, but his illegitimate origins and false campaign charges that he was a Catholic virtually overshadowed his opposition to the spread of slavery to Kansas. While he carried eleven free states, lack of campaign organization and money in politically critical states such as Pennsylvania and Indiana probably cost him the election. Perhaps Frémont was not the best man to lead his nation in time of crisis, but his popularity helped to establish the Republican Party and thus contributed to the election of Abraham Lincoln four years later.

After his disappointing defeat, Frémont temporarily retired to private life, absorbed in developing the Mariposa, by now encumbered with debt. When the Civil War erupted in April, 1861, he was in Europe on business. Born a Southerner, he did not hesitate to support the Union in its greatest crisis. On his own authority he purchased arms and ammunition for the Union in England and France and then returned home to accept an appointment as a major general commanding the Western Department based in St. Louis.

Beginning in July, 1861, Frémont's challenging task was to pacify the divided state of Missouri while raising an army to undertake an offensive down the Mississippi. He received little support from Washington, and his duties were overwhelming. Although he reinforced the strategic Illinois town of Cairo, he did not act quickly enough to aid Nathaniel Lyon, who was defeated and killed at Wilson's Creek on August 10. Charges of favoritism and corruption in government contracts haunted Frémont's command, but most controversial was his sudden order of August 30, declaring martial law in Missouri, threatening to shoot captured guerrillas, and freeing the slaves of rebel masters.

While antislavery advocates praised Frémont's emancipation edict, Lincoln feared its effect on the border states and directed him to modify the order. The general stubbornly refused to heed Lincoln, forcing the president to reverse the measure publicly. With Frémont's command assaulted by powerful political enemies, Jessie went east to present his case, but her stormy interview with Lincoln did more harm than good. As Frémont sought to lead his troops to victory in southwestern Missouri, Lincoln removed him from command of the Western Department in November, 1861.

Outcry over Frémont's removal induced Lincoln to appoint him in March, 1862, to command the newly formed Mountain Department, designed to capture an important railroad at Knoxville, Tennessee. Abandoning this effort, Frémont was also outmarched by Stonewall Jackson in the Virginia Valley Campaign of 1862. At the Battle of Cross Keys on June 8, Frémont proved ineffective against Confederate troops, and when Lincoln added Frémont's force to the command of John Pope, Frémont asked to be relieved. In 1864, Frémont was nominated to the presidency by some Democrats and radical Republicans dissatisfied with Lincoln. At first accepting the nomination, he soon feared a Democratic victory and withdrew from the race, helping to ensure Lincoln's reelection.

As the war came to an end, Frémont lost much of his wealth as well as control of his

Frémont, John C.

beloved Mariposa. His ambitions turned to railroad finance, as he still hoped to realize his dream of a Pacific railroad. He became involved with unscrupulous business associates, however, squandering the remainder of his fortune and a good portion of his reputation when the Southwest Pacific failed in 1867 and the Memphis & El Paso did so in 1870.

From 1878 to 1883, Frémont served as governor of Arizona Territory. With Jessie's help he wrote his memoirs, published in 1887. Belated gratitude from his nation came in April, 1890, when he was restored to his rank as major general and placed on the retired list with pay. Death came in New York in July, 1890, from a sudden attack of peritonitis.

Significance

Frémont's exploits as an explorer exemplified the restless energy and unbounded ambition of mid-nineteenth century America. Proud and self-reliant, Americans resented restraints and the rulings of authority. Frémont's career also reflected the lack of discipline and wisdom born of experience that led the young and sometimes careless American people into such tragedies as the brutal treatment of American Indians, the war on Mexico, and the spilling of brothers' blood in the Civil War. Like his nation, Frémont climbed heights of adventure and opportunity but also found failure, conflict, and injustice.

Frémont never claimed to be a "Pathfinder"; his mapping expeditions usually followed paths already worn by fur traders and early immigrants. Nevertheless, his romantic journeys spurred American expansion to the Pacific, his reports encouraging western immigration while providing travelers with useful information. Frémont's mapping and scientific work rivaled that of earlier explorers, improving knowledge of the vast interior region from the Rockies to the Sierra, while helping to clarify the true natures of the Continental Divide and the Great Basin.

As politician, soldier, and financier, Frémont found less glory. His unauthorized actions in the California revolt remain controversial, while his service during the Civil War provoked charges of political opportunism and military ineffectiveness. His mining and railroad schemes typified the boom period of American industrial expansion but left him almost destitute. His death in 1890 coincided with the end of the romantic age of the American West, where he left his name and his mark.

—*Vernon L. Volpe*

Further Reading

Chaffin, Tom. *Pathfinder: John Charles Frémont and the Course of American Empire*. New York: Hill & Wang, 2002. Well-written, comprehensive, and balanced biography, describing Frémont's varied life and career. Includes information on his expeditions, relationships with allies and adversaries, and his marriage to Jessie Benton Frémont.

Egan, Ferol. *Frémont: Explorer for a Restless Nation*. Garden City, N.Y.: Doubleday, 1977. By focusing on Frémont's career to 1854, this work praises his accomplishments more than most.

Frémont, Jessie Benton. *The Letters of Jessie Benton Frémont*. Edited by Pamela Herr and Mary Lee Spence. Urbana: University of Illinois Press, 1993. Collection of 271 of Jessie Frémont's letters, fully annotated by the editors. The letters reveal her relationship with her difficult husband and her outspokenness on abolition and other issues.

Frémont, John Charles. *Memoirs of My Life*. Chicago: Belford, Clarke, 1887. Frémont's memoirs are the only source for much of the available information on his personal life as well as his career. An intended second volume was not published.

Goodwin, Cardinal L. *John Charles Frémont: An Explanation of His Career*. Stanford, Calif.: Stanford University Press, 1930. This is perhaps the most critical account of Frémont's life. It views the explorer as a "drifter" who entered into corrupt financial dealings.

Harlow, Neal. *California Conquered: War and Peace on the Pacific, 1846-1850*. Berkeley: University of California Press, 1982. Much of this work examines Frémont's controversial role in the California conquest. It also discusses his dispute with Kearny and subsequent arrest.

Jackson, Donald, and Mary Lee Spence, eds. *The Expeditions of John Charles Frémont*. 3 vols. Champaign: University of Illinois Press, 1970-1984. This multivolume collection of documents is an invaluable source of information for Frémont's expeditions. It includes his reports, important correspondence, and the record of his court-martial.

Nevins, Allan. *Frémont: Pathmarker of the West*. 2 vols. New York: Frederick Ungar, 1961. Perhaps the best study of Frémont, this work by a famous American historian portrays the explorer as a flawed hero of American expansion.

Roberts, David. *A Newer World: Kit Carson, John C. Frémont, and the Claiming of the American West*. New York: Simon & Schuster, 2000. An account of Frémont's expeditions in the Western United States from the early 1840's until the beginning of the Civil War. Describes Carson's role in the expeditions and the relationship of the two men.

Rolle, Andrew. *John Charles Frémont: Character as Destiny*. Norman: University of Oklahoma Press, 1991. A psychological examination of Frémont's character, resulting in a generally unflattering biography.

Betty Friedan

❝ *It is easier to live through someone else than to become complete yourself.* **❞**

Writer and feminist

Friedan's book The Feminine Mystique *(1963) energized an untold number of women and helped spark the second wave of the feminist movement. Although Friedan became a leader in the continuing struggle for women's rights, she also was a controversial figure. She later advocated against radical feminism and sexual politics and argued instead for unity with men in common struggle for gender equality.*

Born: February 4, 1921; Peoria, Illinois
Died: February 4, 2006; Washington, D.C.
Also known as: Betty Naomi Goldstein (birth name)
Area of achievement: Women's rights

Early Life

Betty Friedan (free-DAN) was born Betty Naomi Goldstein in Peoria, Illinois, to jeweler Harry Goldstein and former journalist Miriam Horowitz Goldstein. Friedan recalled that her mother gave up a career in journalism to be a homemaker and mother. This, Friedan believed, explained her mother's enthusiastic encouragement of her daughter's journalistic endeavors in high school, college, and beyond.

Friedan graduated from Smith College in 1942, summa cum laude, and later did graduate work at the University of California, Berkeley, studying with the famous child psychologist Erik Erikson. She received a fellowship for her studies and was about to accept a second, which would have allowed her to complete a doctorate, when she quit school. She decided that becoming an academic was too "tame"; she preferred the more active world of reporting. Accordingly, she returned to New York City, where she worked as a reporter for *The Federated Press*, a labor news service. It was wartime, and women were encouraged to fill jobs while men were overseas as soldiers. In 1946 she became a reporter for *U.E. News*, a weekly union paper.

Once the war ended, however, women were expected to give up their jobs so that returning veterans could find work. Friedan lost her reporting position and had to take a position as a researcher. This was a "woman's job," which involved doing the research and often much of the writing for articles that were then published under the male authors' bylines.

In the postwar era, women also were expected to return to their traditional domestic roles—to get married, settle down, and have children. Thus began a time when women were presented with idyllic visions of being "happy housewives" at home in the suburbs raising families and caring for their homes and husbands. In 1947, Friedan accepted this vision and married Carl Friedan, an advertising executive; they had three children: David, Jonathan, and Emily. Friedan had, however, kept her job, taking a year's maternity leave after her first child's birth. When she requested her second leave, however, she was fired.

Friedan now tried to live up to the ideals of the day, working hard to find the so-called feminine fulfillment her mother had never found in domestic life. Eventually moving to a house in Rockland County, New York, Friedan reared her family, but she also continued to write, contributing articles to several magazines for women.

LIFE'S WORK

A popular topic in the media of the postwar period was the idea that women's education was not preparing them adequately for their roles as women. That is, women went to colleges where they received educations they would never be able to apply in careers, since their proper role as women was to be housewives. Too much education was making them discontent with this role in life. The focus was on the inappropriateness of women's education, but Friedan began to see that what was wrong was not education but the role expectations that limited the choices of educated women.

Based on a 1957 survey of her classmates from Smith College, Friedan wrote an article for *McCall's* magazine on the issue of women and education, but her work was rejected by the male editor as too unbelievable. She was then asked to write the same story for *Ladies' Home Journal*, but the article that was published revealed the opposite of what Friedan had originally written. *Redbook* also considered and refused to do the story. Friedan realized that she would have to write a book to get her ideas into print, because her ideas threatened the very identity and existence of magazines geared to women.

In her first book, *The Feminine Mystique* (1963), Friedan coined the now-famous phrase "feminine mystique" to describe the prescribed female role of the postwar years. Although reviewers were largely hostile or cautious, the book caused shock waves throughout the country among readers, because thousands of American women identified with the "nameless, aching dissatisfaction" that she described. Friedan's readers were to become part of the energy that would instigate the second wave of the feminist movement, beginning in the late 1960's.

By 1966, Friedan, sensing that words were not enough to make change, began putting her energies into organizing for women's rights. In that year, she attended a conference in Washington, D.C., of all the state Commissions on the Status of Women. The delegates, who shared their frustrations at having state and local governments dismiss their concerns, soon organized what was to become the National Organization for Women (NOW). Friedan wrote NOW's statement of purpose. The organizing conference of the new group was held in October of 1966, with about three hundred members, and Friedan was elected the first president, a post she held until 1970 (one year after her divorce in May, 1969). In 1969 she also cofounded the National Association for the Repeal of Abortion Laws (now known as NARAL Pro-Choice America) with Bernard Nathanson.

Continuing her activism, Friedan became a major organizer of the Women's Strike for Equality, which took place on August 26, 1970, the fiftieth anniversary of the date women won the right to vote. During this time, Friedan joined the debates over sexual politics. She was opposed to a feminist politics that condemned males as oppressors of women and girls, that embraced notions of female separatism, and that supported lesbian sexuality as a political issue. She argued that sexual politics was divisive and that it diverted attention from what she considered the real political and economic issues of most women.

In 1971, Friedan helped organize and served as the co-convener of the National Women's Political Caucus (with Gloria Steinem and Bella Abzug). The caucus was formed to encourage and support women and prowomen candidates for public office. By 1972, however, Friedan was beginning to back out of political activism, focusing her energies on writing, speaking, and teaching. In that year, she was invited to teach as a visiting professor at Temple University. This was followed by invitations to teach at Yale in 1974 and at Queens College of the City University of New York in 1975. It was around this time as well that Friedan was exploring what she called the "second stage," defined by her as the sex-role revolution that must include men. This new focus was reflected in her course titles at Temple, Yale, and Queens: "The Sex-Role Revolution, Stage II."

In 1975, Friedan was named Humanist of the Year by the American Humanist Association, and she received an honorary doctorate of humane letters from Smith College. The following year saw the publication of her second book, *It Changed My Life: Writings on the Women's Movement* (1976). In this book Friedan described her work over the previous years and included a journal of her experiences. Her third book, *The Second Stage* (1981), further explored her growing concern with the need to overcome the polarization between women and men and to achieve the human wholeness that she saw as the ultimate promise of feminism. In addition, she was concerned about a damaging myth she saw growing in American culture—that of the superwoman who could have it all: career, marriage, and family. Her book argued that the time for reacting against male dominance and focusing on work outside the home was passing as women's goals were being won. Women now needed to begin to unite with men in building a new society of male-female equality.

Although a logical extension of Friedan's previous work, *The Second Stage* unleashed a great controversy. Many feminists turned on Friedan, saying that she had betrayed the women's movement by buying into popular ideas about the importance of the traditional family and the need to gain the approval of men. Moreover, she was faulted for focusing on the problems of middle-class white women and neglecting women of color and the poor. By the early 1990's, however, she insisted that while she still considered herself a feminist, she was not concerned with women as a separate special interest group.

Friedan's next book was *The Fountain of Age* (1993), which she wrote to face her own denial and dread of aging. However, in the process of her research she found a major contradiction between the typical view that aging is a time of loss and debility and the realities of the lives of the aging people she interviewed. She notes that for women the aging process is changing because of differences in the way women are defining themselves (a change she helped bring about with her leadership in the feminist movement). She developed the phrase "fountain of age" (a play on "fountain of youth") to describe the new generativity experienced by both women and men as they grow older.

Friedan, Betty

Betty Friedan.
(Library of Congress)

Friedan held a variety of academic appointments. She became Distinguished Visiting Professor and director of the New Paradigm Project at Cornell University and also taught at New York University, the University of Southern California, and Mount Vernon College as the George Mason Professor of Social Evolution. She also lectured worldwide. Beyond academia she organized and directed the First Women's Bank and Trust.

In her 2000 autobiography *Life So Far*, Friedan described her married life as stormy to the point of physical battles. Her husband Carl once said much the same when, following the couple's divorce, he admitted, in describing Friedan, "It took a driven, superaggressive, egocentric almost lunatic dynamo to rock the world the way she did. Unfortunately, she was the same person at home, where that kind of conduct doesn't work. She simply never understood this." Friedan was well known among colleagues for her abrasiveness, fits of temper, and tendency to monopolize the spotlight. According to Germaine Greer, a writer and feminist who did not share Friedan's philosophy, Friedan also was very feminine and dressed in stylish clothes.

Friedan divided her time at homes in Washington, D.C., and Sag Harbor, New York. She died at her Washington home on February 4, 2006, from congestive heart failure. It was her eighty-fifth birthday.

Friedan, Betty

Significance

Friedan's effect on the American women's movement, and on American culture, is immeasurable. Indeed, her name, along with that of Gloria Steinem, has become synonymous with feminism in the United States. Friedan first gave voice to the dissatisfaction of housewives caught in the postwar ideology of the feminine mystique, then cofounded and led feminist organizations such as NOW. In her later years she focused first on the second stage and then on aging. She always was willing to be controversial, to follow her own star, and always spoke for many who identified with her insights. On a practical level, Friedan worked successfully with others for economic parity with men, and for gender-neutral language, maternity leave, abortion rights, and child-care centers for working women.

Biographer David Horowitz suggested that it was less Friedan's experience as a housewife than it was her youthful communist sympathies, evidenced by her journalistic work for labor unions, that led her to reject the mid-century stereotype of American womanhood. Whatever her inspiration, historians regard *The Feminine Mystique* as among the most influential nonfiction books of the twentieth century. More than three million copies of the book have been sold, and it has been translated into numerous languages. Although a flamboyant, divisive figure, Friedan continued to personify women's struggle for equity, even after her death.

—*Eleanor B. Amico*

Further Reading

Behm, Barbara. *Betty Friedan: Speaking Out for Women's Rights*. Milwaukee, Wis.: Gareth Stevens, 1992. This book discusses Friedan's views of women's rights and her impact on the women's movement.

Friedan, Betty. *It Changed My Life: Writings on the Women's Movement*. New York: Random House, 1976. Perhaps the most autobiographical of Friedan's books, this work documents her activism in the women's movement and provides various entries from her journal.

Hennessee, Judith. *Betty Friedan: Her Life*. New York: Random House, 1999. Hennessee portrays Friedan as a "woman of paradoxes," a feminist who did not like women. The biography covers her youth and early ambitions, including her desire to be an actor, but focuses on the women's movement and her ongoing conflicts with leading feminists such as Gloria Steinem and Bella Abzug.

Horowitz, Daniel. *Betty Friedan and the Making of the Feminine Mystique*. Amherst: University of Massachusetts Press, 1998. Horowitz contends that many of Friedan's ideas came from her study of humanistic psychology and from her participation in the labor movement of the 1940's.

Sherman, Janann, ed. *Interviews with Betty Friedan*. Jackson: University Press of Mississippi, 2002. A collection of published interviews with Friedan conducted over the course of her career. Part of the Conversations with Public Intellectuals series.

William Lloyd Garrison

> *I am in earnest, I will not equivocate, I will not excuse, I will not retreat a single inch, and I will be heard.*

Journalist and abolitionist

A crucial figure in the abolition of American slavery and the coming of the Civil War, Garrison combined Protestant evangelicalism, Jeffersonian liberalism, and Quaker humanism into a radical antislavery doctrine that called for the immediate end of the institution of slavery.

Born: December 10, 1805; Newburyport, Massachusetts
Died: May 24, 1879; New York, New York
Also known as: An Old Bachelor
Areas of achievement: Civil rights; social reform; evangelism; journalism

Early Life

In his 1913 biography of William Lloyd Garrison (GAR-rih-suhn), John Jay Chapman described his subject's emergence as a radical abolitionist in 1830 as a streaking, white-hot meteorite crashing into the middle of Boston Commons. However, little in Garrison's background would have foretold of his career as a professional reformer and founder of a radical antislavery movement. His parents, Abijah and Frances (Fanny) Maria Lloyd Garrison, had once lived simply and obscurely in wealthy Newburyport, Massachusetts. By the summer of 1808, however, President Thomas Jefferson's embargo had nearly destroyed New England's merchant marine, inflicting immense suffering upon lower middle-class sailing masters such as Abijah.

During that same summer, the Garrisons' five-year-old daughter died from an accidental poisoning. Abijah Garrison could not withstand the pressure and grief of this period. He took to heavy drinking and then deserted his struggling family of three. The childhood of young William Lloyd was then an even greater ordeal, and he often had to beg for food from the homes of Newburyport's wealthy residents.

In 1815, Lloyd, as he was called, was apprenticed to a Maryland shoemaker, but the young boy simply lacked the physical strength to do the work. In 1817, Lloyd found himself back in Newburyport, alone and apprenticed to a cabinetmaker. That work also proved unsuitable. When he was thirteen, his luck began to change when he secured an apprenticeship with the editor of the Newburyport *Herald*. Lloyd feared another failure, but within weeks he displayed remarkable skill and speed. The editor quickly made him shop foreman. Garrison had found his life's work.

After mastering the mechanics of the trade, Lloyd was eager to print his own writing. Like Benjamin Franklin a century before, he submitted editorials under a pseudonym (Garrison used "An Old Bachelor") that his boss liked and published. "An Old Bachelor" gained much attention, even from conservative political leaders. In 1826, with a loan from his former employer, Garrison purchased his own newspaper, which he immediately named the *Free Press*. Seeking respectability and entrance into the ruling elite of Massachusetts, Garrison advocated the conservative politics and social ideas of the Federalist Party. The *Free Press* became bellicose in its political stands, denouncing everything that smacked of Jeffersonian democracy. During his brief tenure at the paper, Garrison discovered the poet John Greenleaf Whittier, published his first poetry, and also made some oblique criticisms of the institution of slavery, but he revealed nothing that gave the slightest indication of what lay only four years in the future.

Following this relatively conservative initiation into his journalistic career, Garrison became more and more strident in his style and radical in the opinions he voiced in editorials, to the extent that he lost subscribers, defaulted on his loan, and lost his paper. In 1828, he drifted to the *National Philanthropist*, a temperance paper, and attacked dancing, theatergoing, dueling, and gambling. The fiery editor denounced war and began to display a more thoroughgoing disdain for the institution of slavery by decrying a South Carolina law outlawing black education. Garrison soon repeated his familiar pattern and within six months found himself without a job. He managed to secure a position at the *Journal of the Times* in Bennington, Vermont, and there railed at intemperance and advanced his ideas concerning peace and gradual emancipation.

In 1829, Garrison had become radicalized on the issue of slavery, about one year after reading Benjamin Lundy's newspaper, the *Genius of Universal Emancipation*. Garrison had met Lundy, a Quaker abolitionist, in 1828 and had adopted his views on the gradual emancipation of American slaves. On July 4, 1829, again unemployed, Garrison delivered his first antislavery speech, indicting the North for its racism and declaring that gradual emancipation was the only possible way to end slavery. Then, after reading the works of black Americans such as David Walker and English abolitionists such as James Cropper, Garrison decided to dedicate his life to ending what he viewed as the greatest abomination in American history. He went to work for Lundy and moved back to Baltimore, Maryland, where he coedited the *Genius of Universal Emancipation*.

Before the end of 1829, Garrison had abandoned gradual emancipation—Lundy had not—and called for the immediate end of slavery. He lashed out against slaveholders and even against New Englanders who countenanced the institution. On April 17, 1830, he was confined to a Baltimore jail for criminal libel against a New England merchant. Word of Garrison's imprisonment circulated throughout the North and eventually reached the ears of the wealthy New York merchants and reformers, Arthur and Lewis Tappan. They bailed Garrison out of jail and paid his fines. He wandered back to Boston and decided to set up a new paper there.

On October 16, 1830, Garrison advertised a series of public lectures on the subject of slavery and the American Colonization Society. The ACS, established in 1817, claimed to oppose slavery and favored black uplift and the evangelization of Africa, but Garrison sought to expose it as a tool of the slaveocrats who actually perpetuated slavery. At the October lectures, Garrison denounced the ACS as a racist organization that intended to expel free black Americans if they refused to leave voluntarily. Boston's liberal and conservative clergy alike reacted to the lectures with disgust. Other thinkers, such as Samuel Joseph May, a renegade Unitarian minister and reformer, Bronson Alcott, a Transcendentalist educator and May's brother-in-law, and Samuel E. Sewall, May's cousin, became captivated by Garrison's moral vigor and earnestness. They instantly converted to radical abolitionism and pledged to aid the young editor. Emergence of the *Liberator* the following year established Garrison as the leader of the radical antislavery movement.

LIFE'S WORK

William Lloyd Garrison stood about five feet six inches tall. His slender, almost fragile frame supported a massive bald head, and his powerful blue eyes were framed by tiny, steel, oval-shaped spectacles. Although relentless on the lecture platform, in private Garrison comported himself with great dignity and grace. Like many reformers, he married late. While lecturing in Providence, Rhode Island, in 1829, he met Helen Benson, the daughter of the Quaker philanthropist, George Benson. Timid in the presence of women and lacking a stable career, Garrison initiated a long courtship, finally marrying Helen on September 4, 1834.

On January 1, 1831, Garrison published the first issue of the *Liberator*. It angered Northerners as irrational and incendiary and struck fear in slaveholders as an uncompromising condemnation. Garrison, as a pacifist, eschewed violent rebellion, but his strident language—something entirely new in the long history of American antislavery thought—inaugurated a new era in American history. He denounced slavery as sin, called upon all true Christians immediately to abandon it no matter what the cost to the Union, and blasted those who thought slavery might be gradually abandoned. What, gradually stop sin? Tell a man to rescue his wife from a rapist gradually? Garrison thundered. Why complain of the severity of my language, he cried, when so unutterable an evil abounded. Ignoring his critics, Garrison lashed out: "I *will be* as harsh as truth, and as uncompromising as justice. . . . I will not excuse—I will not retreat a single inch—AND I WILL BE HEARD."

Garrison's antislavery appeal fused the evangelical fervor of the Second Great Awakening, which had begun during the 1790's, with the long-standing Quaker opposition to slavery. He had tapped an essential root of American thought, and if he could convince Americans that slavery was, in fact, sin, then they would have to accept his second proposition that it be immediately abandoned. Southerners understandably recoiled from his rhetoric, but they were horrified when, eight months after appearance of the *Liberator*, Nat Turner turned Virginia inside out by fomenting a slave rebellion and killing dozens of whites, including women and children. Southerners connected the two events, blamed Garrison for the killings, put a price on his head, and demanded that Massachusetts suppress the newspaper and its editor.

In January, 1832, Garrison and twelve men—antislavery apostles—founded the New England Anti-Slavery Society. In June, he published his influential *Thoughts on African Colonization* (1832), and, for the next three years, Garrison and his associates dedicated themselves to destroying the credibility of the American Colonization Society. He helped found the American Anti-Slavery Society on December 4, 1833. Between 1833 and 1840, two hundred auxiliaries of the American Anti-Slavery Society were organized from Massachusetts to Michigan with about 200,000 members. They sent antislavery agents throughout the North to whip up controversy and support for the cause.

The growth of radical antislavery thought caused great consternation. Between

1830 and 1840, abolitionists suffered from personal and physical abuse. Rocks, bricks, and the contents of outhouses were thrown at them. They were denounced as anarchists who would destroy the Union if it suited their whim. In 1836, southern states requested Governor Edward Everett of Massachusetts to suppress Garrison and his friends. On November 7, 1837, Illinois abolitionist editor Elijah P. Lovejoy was assassinated by a rampaging mob determined to destroy his newspaper, the *Alton Observer*. The attacks on abolitionists and the murder of Lovejoy sparked unprecedented sympathy for the antislavery advocates, who could now justifiably claim that abolitionism and a defense of a free press and free speech were inseparable.

To Garrison, abolitionism was only the most important of a collection of reforms, from women's rights to temperance, connected by a liberal Christian faith in a benevolent God and the rejection of all forms of force and violence. In 1836, Garrison learned of two extraordinary women from Charleston, South Carolina. Sarah and Angelina Grimké, born into a slaveholding family, had rejected their home and human bondage, converted to Quakerism, and moved north. In 1837, Garrison arranged a speaking tour for them in New England. Huge crowds turned out for the sisters, who risked their reputations to ignore the social restrictions against women speaking in public. Indeed, during the course of their tour, the Grimkés became ardent exponents of women's rights, having seen how prominent clergymen denounced their violation of women's restricted sphere. Garrison supported the sisters and opened up the Massachusetts Anti-Slavery Society to women, urging his conservative colleagues to do the same.

Garrison's support for women's rights brought howls of protest from other abolitionists, who urged him to avoid "extraneous" issues and stick to antislavery work. He refused to compromise and answered his critics by becoming even more radical. At the September, 1838, meeting of the American Peace Society, Garrison, May, and Henry C. Wright, a radical Garrisonian, attempted to gain the society's acceptance of nonresistance thought. They wanted to outlaw as utterly unchristian all forms of war, force, and violence, even denying one's right to defend oneself. When faced with an attacker, according to nonresistance thought, one could only respond with Christian meekness and manifestations of love. Garrison, May, and Wright all claimed that they had personally disarmed robbers or criminals with love. Conservatives refused to accept the new doctrine or to permit women to participate in their society, and they left the meeting. In response, Garrison and his friends formed the New England Nonresistance Society to spread what they saw as true Christian principles.

Garrison's extreme ideas fractured his own Massachusetts Anti-Slavery Society in 1839 and the American Anti-Slavery Society in 1840. Although the antislavery movement seemed to be crumbling, Garrison responded in typical fashion. While many of the best young male abolitionists avoided Garrison's organizations and went into politics, Garrison damned the political system. In 1842, he advocated the dissolution of the Union. The nation had become so corrupt, so dominated by slave power that no hope existed for slavery's end so long as the South remained in the Union.

Although Garrison's critics argued that no hope for the end of slavery existed if the South left the Union, Garrison ignored them. In 1843, the *Liberator* adopted its most radical stand yet. The "compact which exists between the North and the South is 'a covenant with death, and an agreement with hell'—involving both parties in atrocious criminality; and should be immediately annulled." On March 17, 1843, Garrison began placing the slogan "NO UNION WITH SLAVE-HOLDERS!" on the masthead of his newspaper, where it remained until the Civil War.

Split over women's rights and nonresistance ideas, the antislavery movement nearly ended by the mid-1840's. Little money flowed in, and few Americans could accept disunionism, no matter how much they hated slavery. Passage of the Fugitive Slave Act in 1850 boosted the American Anti-Slavery Society's prospects, because most Northerners came to hate the law as an infringement of constitutionally protected rights. As the nation moved toward civil war during the 1850's, Garrison increased his attacks on slavery, the Constitution, and the Union.

With the firing on Fort Sumter in April, 1861, Garrison supported Abraham Lincoln and the Union cause. Although many of his associates thought the South ought to leave the Union peacefully, Garrison saw the war as perhaps the only opportunity to end slavery, even if it did violate his peace principles. He thus supported the Lincoln administration's war policy, all the while urging the president to abolish slavery. When Lincoln signed the Emancipation Proclamation in 1863, Garrison was ecstatic, and when the nation adopted the Thirteenth Amendment, abolishing slavery, in 1865, he felt vindicated. Believing his life's purpose fulfilled, Garrison retired from activism, though he continued to support the Republican Party and causes such as temperance and women's rights. He died in New York City on May 24, 1879.

SIGNIFICANCE

Although Garrison harbored some racial prejudice, he was a pioneer of racial justice. He argued that racism and slavery worked hand-in-hand and that Northern prejudice and Southern intransigence shared equally in the responsibility for perpetuating slavery. Garrison's message of racial justice and abolitionism threatened the nation's class system, which exploited Northern free blacks as well as Southern slaves and endangered the tenuous bonds that had kept the Union together since the formation of the Constitution. Public reaction to Garrison did not change until passage of the Emancipation Proclamation in 1863. Before the war's end, he became a prophetic figure to Americans. The Boston mobs that tried to lynch him in 1834 raised statues to him in 1865. Modern historians have recognized Garrison's indispensable role in the ending of American slavery and have hailed him for his simple claim that the Declaration of Independence ought to speak for everyone, black and white, male and female.

—*Donald Yacovone*

FURTHER READING

Chapman, John Jay. *William Lloyd Garrison*. New York: Moffat, Yard, 1913. A sympathetic early biography by the son of one of Garrison's associates.

Friedman, Lawrence J. *Gregarious Saints: Self and Community in American Abolitionism, 1830-1870*. New York: Cambridge University Press, 1982. Representative of the best modern studies of the abolitionist movement. Gives an inside look at the subtle distinctions the reformers made on a variety of topics related to voting, the Constitution, and how distinct groups of reformers sprang up around charismatic figures such as Garrison, Gerrit Smith, or the Tappan brothers.

Garrison, William Lloyd. *The Letters of William Lloyd Garrison*. Edited by Walter M. Merrill and Louis Ruchames. 6 vols. Cambridge, Mass.: Harvard University Press, 1971-1981. The best way for the student to become acquainted with Garrison is to read the activist's own work. These are copiously annotated personal and public letters that fully display the thinking and the sometimes idiosyncratic personality of the *Liberator*'s chief editor.

_____. *William Lloyd Garrison and the Fight Against Slavery: Selections from "The Liberator."* Edited with an introduction by William E. Cain. Boston: Bedford Books of St. Martin's Press, 1995. Includes forty-one selections from the newspaper dealing with issues related to slavery. The introduction provides historical background on slavery and the abolition movement in the United States and the events in Garrison's career.

Kraditor, Alieen S. *Means and Ends in American Abolitionism: Garrison and His Critics on Strategy and Tactics, 1834-1850*. New York: Pantheon Books, 1969. Far and away the best book on Garrison's movement and thought. Kraditor fully explores the controversy of the "woman question" and argues convincingly that, in order for Garrison to gain acceptance of a minimum of antislavery thought, he had to remain more radical than the nation and many of his antislavery brethren.

Merrill, Walter M. *Against Wind and Tide: A Biography of William Lloyd Garrison*. Cambridge, Mass.: Harvard University Press, 1963. A thorough and often critical examination of the abolitionist's career. The text emphasizes Garrison's personality, which could be extremely abrasive and unforgiving. The author recognizes, however, that it took an abrasive personality to challenge the foundations of American society.

Perry, Lewis. *Radical Abolitionism: Anarchy and the Government of God in Antislavery Thought*. Ithaca, N.Y.: Cornell University Press, 1973. The most sophisticated treatment of antislavery thought, concentrating on Garrison and his nonresistance colleagues. Perry examines the origins of Garrison's thinking and connects it to wider trends in Western Christian thought.

Rogers, William B. *"We Are All Together Now": Frederick Douglass, William Lloyd Garrison, and the Prophetic Tradition*. New York: Garland, 1995. Describes how Douglass and Garrison drew on the tradition of biblical prophecy in their struggle against slavery, intemperance, and the oppression of women and minorities.

Stewart, James B. *Holy Warriors: The Abolitionists and American Slavery*. New York: Hill & Wang, 1976. A good, readable survey of the antislavery movement, emphasizing Garrison's role and the religious nature of the movement that stemmed from the influence of the Second Great Awakening.

Thomas, John L. *The Liberator: William Lloyd Garrison—A Biography*, Boston: Little, Brown, 1963. The best study of Garrison; it appreciates his central role in the movement but remains critical of his tactics and personality. Thoroughly researched and more detailed than Merrill's biography.

MARCUS GARVEY

❝ *The whole world is my province until Africa is free.* **❞**

Jamaican civil rights leader

Combining his talents of effective journalism and charismatic oratory, Garvey organized the first black mass-protest movement in the history of the United States. His work inspired not only later slogans such as "black power" and "black is beautiful" but also the founding of black nationalism in the United States in the 1960's.

Born: August 17, 1887; St. Ann's Bay, Jamaica, British West Indies
Died: June 10, 1940; London, England
Also known as: Marcus Moziah Garvey (full name)
Areas of achievement: Civil rights; social reform; oratory; journalism

EARLY LIFE

Marcus Garvey (GAR-vee) was born in St. Ann's Bay, Jamaica, British West Indies. His parents, Marcus and Sarah Garvey, were both blacks of African descent. As such, the family, including young Marcus, suffered under the racial caste system prevalent in Jamaica at the time—a system that relegated "pure" blacks to a lower socioeconomic status than either mulattoes or whites. This fact may explain why Garvey subsequently would emphasize black racial purity, denouncing mulattoes as mere pawns or tools of whites.

During his childhood and adolescence, Garvey was precocious, an avid reader, a gifted speaker, and a bright student. His formal education, however, did not extend beyond his fourteenth year. Family financial difficulties forced him to quit school and accept employment as a printer's apprentice, an experience that would later prove to be invaluable to his career in journalism and to the movement he came to lead. Nevertheless, Garvey's failure to complete a formal education seriously influenced his thinking and behavior for the remainder of his life, explaining, in part, his future antagonism toward the intellectual community in general and black intellectuals in particular.

As a young black journalist in the early twentieth century, Garvey became increasingly aware of and concerned with the humiliating plight of fellow blacks throughout the Caribbean. Moreover, through extensive reading, research, and travel, including a trip to England, where he was influenced by a number of African nationalists, Garvey finally came to believe that white discrimination against and exploitation of black people were serious worldwide problems that demanded an immediate solution. Toward this end, he decided to become a leader of his race to unite blacks throughout the world in a nation and government of their own.

LIFE'S WORK

Following his two-year sojourn in England, Garvey returned to Jamaica in 1914, where he established the Universal Negro Improvement and Conservation Association and African Communities League, usually called the Universal Negro Improvement Association (UNIA). The initial goals of UNIA centered on universal black uni-

Garvey, Marcus

fication, the enhancement of black racial pride worldwide, and black development of and control over the continent of Africa. Achieving only moderate success in Jamaica, Garvey decided to seek support for his infant organization in the United States. He arrived in New York on March 23, 1916, and quickly proceeded to establish a branch of UNIA in Harlem, which had a relatively large West Indian enclave. Two years later, he founded a newspaper, *Negro World*, which became the propaganda arm of UNIA. Coupled with a lengthy and flamboyant speaking tour throughout the United States, Garvey's editorials in *Negro World* succeeded in attracting thousands of native converts to UNIA. In a matter of months, thirty branches of the organization were established throughout the country. By 1920, Garvey claimed to have four million followers and, in 1923, six million. Although these figures were probably exaggerations, even Garvey's most critical opponents admitted that there were at least a half million members in UNIA at its height.

At the heart of Garvey's ideology was his fervent desire to mobilize the black peoples of Africa, the West Indies, the Americas, and elsewhere, for the spiritual, historical, and physical redemption of Africa and Africans, at home and abroad. "The faith we have," he declared, "is a faith that will ultimately take us back to that ancient place, that ancient position that we once occupied, when Ethiopia was in her glory." Notwithstanding this pronouncement, it is mistaken to suppose that Garveyism was simply another "Back to Africa" movement. Garvey was realistic enough to appreciate that a mass black exodus to Africa, in the physical sense, was impossible. Although he did believe that black leaders had an obligation to return to their ancestral homeland to assist in its development and liberation from white colonialists, his basic argument revolved around the concept of a spiritual return to Africa for the majority of American blacks. He maintained that white racism in the United States had created a sense of self-hatred in blacks and that the only way to purge themselves of self-contempt was through a spiritual identification with Africans and Africa. By stressing Africa's noble past, Garvey declared that American blacks should be proud of their ancestry and, in particular, proud of their blackness. Concurrently, American blacks should strive to achieve black community pride, wealth, culture, and independence in the United States by creating and maintaining a nation-within-a-nation. The struggle for African redemption, he stated, did not call for blacks to surrender their domestic struggle for political justice and economic independence.

In 1921, Garvey established a provisional government-in-exile for Africa, with himself as president. In addition, he established a black cabinet, a black army (the Universal African Legion), attired in resplendent uniforms, a corps of nurses (the Universal Black Cross Nurses), and even an African Orthodox Church, with a black God and a black Christ. Earlier, Garvey had created the Negro Factories Corporation (NFC), an experiment designed to promote black economic independence by providing loans and technical assistance to aspiring black small businessmen. The NFC reflected Garvey's acceptance of Booker T. Washington's late nineteenth century philosophy of black self-help as a stepping-stone to genuine black emancipation. Although the NFC rarely had enough working capital, it did succeed in establishing a number of independent black businesses, including a restaurant, a chain of cooperative grocery stores, and a publishing house.

Garvey's pet project was his Black Star Line, a steamship company designed to engage in commerce with and transportation to Africa. Garvey was convinced that a black-owned-and-operated "link" with the African motherland would not only promote black self-help and economic opportunity but also visibly enhance black pride and self-awareness. Thousands of urban blacks heeded the call, buying up more than a half million dollars of Black Star Line stock (inexpensively priced at five dollars a share and limited to black investors) during the first year of the company's existence. The fact that Garvey and his associates purchased (many say were hoodwinked into purchasing) ships that were hardly seaworthy did not detract from the enthusiasm this venture generated among the black urban masses. Financially, however, the Black Star Line proved to be a disaster for the UNIA. The organization was unable to raise enough money to repair steamships that, in some cases, were beyond repair. By late 1921, the company was more or less defunct.

The elaborateness, flamboyance, and, above all, the promise and the dream of Garveyism, coupled with Garvey's own charismatic personality, had a profound effect on the black urban masses, who were drawn to their "messiah" as if he were a magnet. On the other hand, black intellectuals denounced Garvey as a buffoon (he often wore elaborate academic gowns and uniforms) and a demagogue. W. E. B. Du Bois, for example, described him as "a little, fat black man, ugly, but with intelligent eyes and a big head ... the most dangerous enemy of the Negro race in America." For his part, Garvey shunned intellectuals such as Du Bois, whom he called a "lazy dependent mulatto," as

Marcus Garvey.
(Library of Congress)

Garvey, Marcus

well as the black bourgeois establishment, which, in his mind, had betrayed the black race by cooperating with whites.

Garvey's sincere but inept management of the Black Star Line finally put an end to his meteoric rise. In 1922, he was indicted on mail-fraud charges concerning the sale of Black Star Line stock. Convicted in 1923, he was imprisoned for two years and then, in 1927, deported as an undesirable alien. In his absence, Garveyism (or Black Zionism) in the United States lost much of its appeal. Moreover, faced with a decade of economic depression during the 1930's, most urban blacks became much more concerned with their own personal survival than with the grandiose schemes of a deported Jamaican.

Unable to resurrect the UNIA in Jamaica, Garvey moved to London in 1935. Following several bouts with pneumonia in the late 1930's, Garvey suffered two severe strokes in 1940. He subsequently died in relative obscurity in London on June 10, 1940. Garvey was fifty-two years old.

Significance

Regarded by some as an egotistic, self-serving charlatan and by others as a black messiah or a black Moses, Garvey proved to be the embodiment of pent-up black nationalism in the United States during the early twentieth century. By organizing the first black mass-protest movement in the history of the United States, and by emphasizing self-help, black pride, racial purity, and the resurrection of a great black empire in Africa, Garvey unwittingly became the spiritual founder of many black nationalist movements of subsequent years. Organizations such as the Black Muslims and the Black Panthers and slogans such as "black is beautiful" and "black power" would later emerge as manifestations of a revived Garveyism.

—*Robert R. Davis, Jr.*

Further Reading

Blaisdell, Bob, ed. *Selected Writings and Speeches of Marcus Garvey*. Mineola, N.Y.: Dover, 2004. A collection of Garvey's speeches and writings, including "Declaration of the Rights of the Negro Peoples of the World" and "Africa for the Africans."

Brisbane, Robert H. *The Black Vanguard: Origins of the Negro Social Revolution, 1900-1960*. Valley Forge, Pa.: Judson Press, 1970. Contains a well-written, lengthy chapter on the Garvey era, placing Garvey in the mainstream of American black radicalism.

Cronon, Edmund David. *Black Moses: The Story of Marcus Garvey and the Universal Negro Improvement Association*. Madison: University of Wisconsin Press, 1962. Generally considered the most authoritative, scholarly account of Garvey and Garveyism, Cronon's book is balanced, well documented, and especially well written. Contains both a bibliographical essay and a list of primary and secondary references.

Garvey, Amy Jacques. *Garvey and Garveyism*. New York: P. F. Collier, 1970. Useful, firsthand reminiscences by Garvey's second wife and widow. Especially good for the postdeportation era in the West Indies and London.

Garvey, Marcus. *Philosophy and Opinions of Marcus Garvey*. Edited by Amy Jacques Garvey. 1923-1925. Reprint. New York: Atheneum, 1969. This is one of several reprinted volumes of Garvey's original writings edited by his widow. A supplemental volume (*More Philosophy and Opinions of Marcus Garvey*) was published by Frank Cass (London) in 1977.

Levine, Lawrence. "Marcus Garvey and the Politics of Revitalization." In *Black Leaders of the Twentieth Century*, edited by John Hope Franklin and August Meier. Urbana: University of Illinois Press, 1982. This indispensable essay offers an analytical overview of the Garvey movement and its legacy.

Sundiata, Ibrahim. *Brothers and Strangers: Black Zion, Black Slavery, 1914-1940*. Durham, N.C.: Duke University Press, 2003. Describes how Garvey's United Negro Improvement Association worked with the government of Liberia to resettle American blacks in Africa. However, his plan ran into difficulties when confronted with the realities of Liberia's racial and class divisions and labor abuses.

Toppin, Edgar A. *A Biographical History of Blacks in America Since 1528*. New York: David McKay, 1971. Based on a series of articles originally appearing in *The Christian Science Monitor* in 1969, Toppin's work contains both a chronological chapter on black American history during the Garvey era and, more important, a formal biographical essay on Garvey himself.

Vincent, Theodore G. *Black Power and the Garvey Movement*. Berkeley, Calif.: Ramparts Press, 1971. Stresses the historical link between Garveyism and American black radicalism in general and shows how Garvey paved the way for subsequent black protest groups in the United States.

BILL GATES

> *Success is a lousy teacher. It seduces smart people into thinking they can't lose.*

Computer developer, entrepreneur, and philanthropist

Gates cofounded Microsoft Corporation, the world's largest software company. He served as Microsoft's chair, CEO, and chief software architect. With his wife, Melinda Gates, he established the largest charitable organization in the world.

Born: October 28, 1955; Seattle, Washington
Also known as: William Henry Gates III (full name)
Areas of achievement: Computer science; telecommunications; invention and technology; business; philanthropy

EARLY LIFE

Born in Seattle, Washington, Bill Gates was the second of three children and only son of Bill Gates, Sr., an attorney, and Mary Gates, a University of Washington regent. As a baby, Gates often rocked himself, a trait for which he became well known as an adult. Brilliant and intellectually curious, Trey, as his family called him, reportedly read the lion's share of his family's encyclopedia at age seven or eight.

Gates, Bill

Bill Gates. (AP/Wide World Photos)

Gates preferred skiing and activities with the Boy Scouts over team sports, and he was extremely competitive during family card games. Small in stature and socially awkward as a child, he was frequently teased by his classmates, which prompted him to assume the role of class clown. His parents sent him to a psychologist when he was in the sixth grade because of his stubborn, rebellious nature.

In the seventh grade, Gates transferred to Lakeside School, an elite private institution. It was at Lakeside that he first used a computer, which was actually a teletype machine connected by telephone to a mainframe computer in a local office of General Electric. He spent endless hours in the computer room, writing his first software program, a game of tic-tac-toe, at age thirteen. He formed a close friendship with Paul Allen, a like-minded student two years his senior. Gates, Allen, and several others formed the Lakeside Programmers, a club that earned money by writing payroll and traffic data programs. Gates surprised some classmates by landing the lead role in a school play.

Gates entered Harvard University in 1973 as a prelaw major, but he remained focused on computers. He frequently skipped his classes and studied at the last minute for exams. On the social side, he became friends with fellow student Steve Ballmer and often participated in all-night poker games.

Life's Work

The turning point in Gates's life occurred when he was in his second year at Harvard. While Allen was visiting him on campus, Allen discovered a magazine article featuring the first microcomputer, the Altair 8800, which was manufactured by Micro Instrumentation and Telemetry Systems (MITS). However, the computer lacked software. Sensing a groundbreaking opportunity, Gates and Allen informed MITS that they had software for the computer, even though such was not the case. For approximately five weeks during the winter of 1975, the pair worked around the clock to adapt a program from Beginners All-purpose Symbolic Instruction Code (BASIC). After Allen successfully demonstrated the program at MITS's New Mexico headquarters, the company agreed to distribute it with the Altair 8800 pursuant to a royalties agreement. It was under these circumstances that Gates and Allen established their business, Micro-Soft, later known as Microsoft Corporation.

While Allen temporarily went to work for MITS, Gates took a leave of absence from Harvard, briefly returned, then permanently dropped out and moved to New Mexico, where Micro-Soft was based. Known to work sixteen-hour days, Gates raced his car around the nearby desert to relieve stress. In 1979, Gates relocated the business to Bellevue, Washington, a Seattle suburb. Through the promise of stock options, he persuaded his Harvard friend, Ballmer, to join the company in a top position.

In 1980, International Business Machines (IBM) asked Microsoft to write a program for its new personal computer (PC). At the time, it was commonly believed that software played a subservient role to hardware. However, Gates had a contrary opinion. He purchased an existing operating system for $75,000 and adapted it for IBM's PC. Called the Microsoft Disk Operating System, or MS-DOS, it was sold with every IBM PC. Pursuant to the licensing agreement, Microsoft was also entitled to sell its software to other companies. The operating system quickly became the computer industry standard. By the end of 1982, Microsoft sold approximately $32 million worth of software.

Gates was left in charge of Microsoft when Allen left the company in 1983 because of health concerns. Early on, Gates had often been underestimated because of his youthful, unkempt appearance. As Microsoft grew and Gates matured, he acquired a reputation as a savvy businessman and a ruthless competitor, the latter of which resulted in numerous enemies. Known for recruiting the brightest college graduates, Gates often sat in on interviews. His employees dressed casually and had flexible hours, but the work environment was intense and competitive. Gates himself continued to work long hours and had little time for vacations. He was often rude and arrogant, and he did not easily tolerate those whose technological knowledge failed to match his. However, he preferred sweaters to suits and only agreed to a reserved parking spot so he could leave on time for the airport.

Under Gates's leadership, Microsoft continued to expand its product offerings, with sales topping $140 million in 1985. In 1986, Microsoft's shares were traded on the stock exchange. While it would take him nine more years to attain the status of the world's wealthiest individual, in no time he became the planet's youngest billionaire. By 1987, Microsoft became the planet's largest software company. It was a point of pride that Gates had never borrowed money from his family to finance his business.

Gates's immense wealth did not slow him down. In 1990, he launched the operating system Windows 3.0, which was a huge success because it allowed several different applications to run at the same time and was more user-friendly with its point-and-click mouse. Gates continued to release new versions of Windows, with each version an improvement over the last. Initially failing to recognize the importance of the Internet, Gates subsequently released Internet Explorer (IE), Microsoft's Web browser, with the operating system Windows 95. IE would become the dominant Web browser.

Although Gates devoted long hours to Microsoft, he still found time to have several girlfriends, most notably businesswoman Ann Winblad, with whom he still maintains a friendship. In 1987, Microsoft hired a manager, Melinda French, who attracted his attention. They were married in Hawaii on January 1, 1994, and soon had three children. The family has lived in a forty-five-room house on Lake Washington in Medina that cost $50 million to build.

On May 18, 1998, the U.S. Department of Justice and twenty states commenced an antitrust suit against Microsoft, alleging, among other things, that Microsoft bullied other companies into using Microsoft's Web browser over that of competitors. Gates did not personally testify at the trial. Instead, attorneys played his taped deposition, during which he denied knowledge of important company matters. His reputation suffered somewhat because many did not believe that he had been unaware of Microsoft's business dealings. Although the trial judge ordered Microsoft to be split into two companies, the order never took effect because of a reversal on appeal and because of a settlement by the parties.

Gates was Microsoft's chair and chief executive officer (CEO) until 2000. At that time, Ballmer became CEO while Gates remained chair and assumed the title of chief software architect. On June 15, 2006, Microsoft announced that, effective July, 2008, Gates would no longer be involved in the company's daily operations. However, he would retain the role of chair, as well as advise the company on certain projects under development.

Gates's job will change because of his desire to devote more time to the Bill & Melinda Gates Foundation, a philanthropic organization he formed with his wife in 2000. The foundation is dedicated to improving health and education, as well as reducing poverty. It supports work throughout the United States and in more than one hundred countries. In March, 2007, it had an endowment of $33.4 billion.

SIGNIFICANCE

While the industry was still in its infancy, Gates envisioned widespread use of computers and recognized the critical importance of software. His products made it easier for the average person to use a computer and for businesses to communicate with one another. These factors, in turn, made it easier to access information on a previously unimaginable scale.

Coupling astute business sense with superior technological knowledge, Gates embodies the traits that are necessary to survive and thrive in the modern global economy. Dedicated to philanthropic work, he has challenged others to donate a larger percentage of their fortune to charitable causes. Notwithstanding one's opinion of Gates as a person, his influence on the world cannot be denied.

—Diane S. Carter

Further Reading
Brinkley, Joel, and Steve Lohr. *U.S. v. Microsoft*. New York: McGraw-Hill, 2001. Provides a comprehensive account of the lawsuit against Microsoft at the trial level and presents background information on the judge, attorneys, and key witnesses. Photographs.
Gates, Bill. *The Road Ahead*. New York: Penguin Books, 1995. Gates reflects on the status of the "information highway" twenty years after he and Paul Allen wrote their groundbreaking program for the Altair 8800. Includes Gates's personal history, as well as his predictions for the future. Photographs.
Klein, Maury. *The Change Makers*. New York: Henry Holt, 2003. Maintains that Gates belongs to an elite group of entrepreneurs, which includes Andrew Carnegie, Thomas Alva Edison, and Henry Ford. Proposes that Gates and the others each pursued a vision that triggered major cultural and social changes and inspired an industry.
Lowe, Janet. *Bill Gates Speaks*. New York: John Wiley & Sons, 1998. Depicts Gates as an individual who has had a great impact on twentieth century daily life. Discusses Gates's management style, his charitable contributions, and his heroes. Time line of important events.

Lou Gehrig

> **"** *Today I consider myself the luckiest man on the face of this earth.... I might have been given a bad break, but I've got an awful lot to live for.* **"**

Baseball player

Gehrig was the bulwark of the New York Yankees baseball dynasty of the 1920's, including the famed Murderer's Row team of 1927. He played in 2,130 consecutive major-league games, an endurance record unsurpassed until 1995.

Born: June 19, 1903; New York, New York
Died: June 2, 1941; New York, New York
Also known as: Henry Louis Gehrig (full name), the Iron Horse
Area of achievement: Sports

Early Life
Lou Gehrig (GEHR-ihg) was born in New York's Upper East Side. His parents, Heinrich and Christina Gehrig, were German immigrants whose two other children died at a very young age. They spoke no English on their arrival in New York, and their lives were filled with deprivation and poverty. Lou's father was never able to work consistently at his craft and often drank beer and played pinochle at the neighborhood tavern. Lou's mother was the dominating force of his life. She worked at many jobs, such as domestic, cook, and laundress, and Lou often helped and ran her errands. Christina

Gehrig, Lou

Gehrig's driving ambition was to provide Lou with an education so that he might become an engineer and escape the cycle of poverty that had engulfed her and her husband.

As he grew up on the East Side, Lou was a profoundly shy "momma's boy." He wore hand-me-down clothes and spoke with a German accent, leading his peers to taunt him. This formative period of his life left him with a lack of self-confidence that he would never overcome completely. His mother, however, emphasized the idea that hard work and dedication to his studies were keys to success in America. Lou was so proud of his perfect attendance record in elementary school that he would not allow pneumonia to keep him out of school.

Gehrig was a good and attentive student, but he excelled in sports. His father once gave him a right-handed catcher's mitt for Christmas. Although he was a southpaw, Gehrig was very proud of the glove and played ball with neighborhood children. He was big and awkward, not a natural-born baseball player. Yet his father helped him to build up his physique and muscle coordination, and Gehrig became very active in school sports, particularly track, shot put, and baseball. His proudest moment occurred when he helped his team win New York's Park Department League baseball championship.

At the High School of Commerce, and despite his mother's fears that sports would distract her son from his studies, Gehrig became the star of the school's basketball, soccer, and baseball teams. Commerce's soccer team, for example, won the city's championship three consecutive years. Gehrig played first base for the baseball team and became the team's leading slugger. During his senior year, the baseball team won the city's championship, which entitled them to play Lane High School, the champions of Chicago. Gehrig hit a grand-slam home run to help his team emerge victorious.

Gehrig's baseball exploits at Commerce enabled him to enter Columbia University in 1921 on an athletic scholarship. His parents were employed at a fraternity house, and Gehrig helped out by waiting on tables. When he had some spare time, he played baseball with members of the fraternity. He inadvertently jeopardized his scholarship, however, when he signed a contract with the New York Giants under manager John McGraw, who sent him to Hartford, Connecticut, in the Eastern League. When Gehrig's professional contract became known, Columbia University officials attempted to strip him of his amateur status. Friends intervened on behalf of Gehrig, however, and his amateur ranking was restored on the condition that he sit out his freshman year.

Life's Work

By this time, Gehrig was six feet tall with massive shoulders and weighed two hundred pounds. He played fullback on Columbia's football team and pitched and played first base on the baseball team. He was called "Columbia Lou" as his hitting exploits received increasing attention from fans. During the spring of 1923, Paul Krichell, a scout for the New York Yankees, was so impressed with Gehrig's hitting that he predicted that he would become another Babe Ruth. Gehrig was offered a bonus and a contract to complete the 1923 season with the Yankees. The money was so good that even his mother approved of his withdrawal from Columbia. Thus, at the age of twenty, Gehrig began his professional baseball career.

During the early 1920's, Yankee manager Miller Huggins sought to build a nucleus for a baseball dynasty. Babe Ruth was the heart of the team, and Gehrig found it difficult to find a place for himself. First base was Gehrig's position, but veteran Wally Pipp was at the height of his career and had a lock on it. Accordingly, Gehrig spent most of the 1923 and 1924 seasons in Hartford, where he hit well over .300 and drove out sixty-one home runs over two years.

In 1925, Gehrig's break finally came. On June 1, 1925, he pinch-hit for the shortstop. On June 2, 1925, Pipp was hit in the head by a fastball during batting practice and was unable to start the game. Huggins inserted Gehrig into the starting lineup, and Pipp never played first base for the Yankees again. Gehrig started every game for fourteen years, a total of 2,130 consecutive games. He became the Iron Horse of the New York Yankees.

Gehrig enjoyed a solid rookie year. He hit .295, with twenty home runs, twenty-three doubles, nine triples, and sixty-eight runs-batted-in (RBI's), for a seventh-place team. In 1926, the Yankees won the American League pennant, and Gehrig proved to be a major factor in that season with a .313 average, 107 RBI's, and twenty triples. Gehrig hit cleanup, between Ruth and outfielder Bob Musil. In 1927, that trio formed part of Murderer's Row, perhaps the greatest baseball team in history. The team's statistics were awesome: a 110-44 won-lost record, a .307 team batting average, and an earned run average of 3.20.

What also caught the fans' imagination were the exploits of Ruth and Gehrig. For good or ill, Ruth was the dominant personality on the team. In many ways, he was an oversized boy who challenged authority to its limits. Gehrig, in contrast, was the organization man, obedient, quiet, noncontroversial, and hardworking. Gehrig's quiet, passive personality may explain his inability to escape Ruth's shadow fully. In 1927, Gehrig hit .373 and Ruth .356; Gehrig led the league with 175 RBI's, and Ruth came in second. Yet Ruth led Gehrig in slugging percentage; in the most spectacular race of all, he and Gehrig were neck and neck for the home-run title. Finally, in the last weeks of the season, Ruth pulled ahead to hit sixty home runs, a record that was to last until Roger Maris of the Yankees hit sixty-one in 162 games in 1961. Few people recall that Gehrig finished second with forty-seven home runs.

During the early 1930's, the Yankees were once again in the process of reconstructing their team under manager Joe McCarthy. Ruth was desperately unhappy under McCarthy's discipline, and age began to blunt his skills. By 1935, Ruth was gone, traded to the Boston Braves. Gehrig thrived under McCarthy and, at last, emerged from Ruth's shadow. Moreover, he became more independent of his mother when he married Eleanor Twichell of Chicago late in December, 1933. Eleanor Gehrig provided her husband with a happy and contented home life. The results were obvious: In 1934, Gehrig had his best year, winning baseball's coveted Triple Crown: forty-nine home runs, 165 RBI's, and a .363 batting average.

Gehrig's days in the Yankee sun, however, were few. In 1935, his performance did not match that of 1934. In 1936, the Yankees acquired center fielder Joe DiMaggio from the Pacific Coast League, and DiMaggio would dominate the team through the 1940's. Even so, 1936 was one of Gehrig's best years, as he hit .354 and led the league in home runs (forty-nine). He came through again in 1937, with 159 RBI's, thirty-

Gehrig, Lou

seven home runs, and a .351 average. The following year, however, was extremely disappointing. Only thirty-four years old, he appeared to be on the decline, although his .295 batting average and 114 RBI's were quite respectable. His defensive play at first base was below his usual standards; he played in constant pain, pain so severe that he had to leave games in the late innings. Gehrig suspected that he had lumbago, but his doctors diagnosed the problem as a gallbladder condition. He was treated on that basis during the winter months.

The 1939 spring training season in St. Petersburg, Florida, revealed that Gehrig was very ill. His muscle coordination had deteriorated over the winter. During the early part of the regular season, Gehrig had only four hits in twenty-eight times at bat for a .143 average. Finally, in Detroit in early May, he requested that McCarthy take him out of the lineup, thus terminating his legendary consecutive-game streak. Gehrig later flew to the Mayo Clinic in Rochester, Minnesota, where doctors diagnosed his condition as amyotrophic lateral sclerosis, an incurable and deadly form of paralysis. At the insistence of his wife, Eleanor, doctors did not inform Gehrig of the implications of his disease.

Gehrig ultimately returned to the Yankees as a coach for the remainder of the 1939 season. On July 4, 1939, the team held a Lou Gehrig day in Yankee Stadium, and more than sixty thousand fans came out to honor the Iron Horse. Gehrig was deeply moved by the fans' display of affection and respect; in a heartfelt speech, he declared that he was "the luckiest man on the face of this earth." Eleanor made the last days of Gehrig's life as useful and happy as possible. She arranged to have New York mayor Fiorello La Guardia appoint Gehrig as a member of the parole board. They attended as many cultural events as they could. Finally, on June 2, 1941, Gehrig died at home, quietly, at ten o'clock in the evening, only two weeks short of his thirty-eighth birthday.

SIGNIFICANCE

Gehrig played in 2,164 major-league games, of which 2,136 were at first base, nine in the outfield, and one at shortstop. He had 8,001 official at bats and collected 2,721 hits, including 525 doubles, 162 triples, and 493 home runs. He hit a home run every 6.2 times at bat. His lifetime batting average was .340. He scored 1,888 runs, batted in 1,191 runs, struck out 789 times, and walked to first base 1,528 times. His lifetime slugging percentage was .632. In World Series play, his record was equally impressive. Gehrig played in thirty-four World Series games; in 119 at bats, he had forty-three hits, of which eight were doubles, three were triples, and ten were home runs. He scored thirty runs and knocked in thirty-five runs against the best teams that the National League had to offer. His career World Series batting average was .361, and his slugging percentage, .731.

For all their impressive effect, these statistics do not reveal Gehrig the human being. He represented the American dream to hard-pressed citizens of the late 1920's and 1930's. He was an inspiring role model for the American youth in a way that Babe Ruth could never have been. He represented basic American values that were the bedrock of the baseball mystique: honor, sportsmanship, duty, and work. However, Gehrig fulfilled this role without visible effort. It was as much a part of his character and personality as were the grace and dignity of his play in a child's game. He never complained that life had been unfair to him. The courage and humility of his last days were so inspiring that amyotrophic lateral sclerosis became popularly known as Lou Gehrig's disease. In 1939, the Baseball Writers Association of America did him honor by waiving the required waiting period to vote Gehrig into baseball's Hall of Fame.

—*Stephen P. Sayles*

FURTHER READING

Allen, Mel, and Ed Fitzgerald. *You Can't Beat the Hours: A Long, Loving Look at Big League Baseball, Including Some Yankees I Have Known*. New York: Harper & Row, 1964. A general and popular account of the New York Yankees by their radio broadcaster of a quarter century. Covers the team from the era of Ruth and Gehrig to the era of Mantle and Maris. A very readable and entertaining book.

Anderson, Dave, Murray Chass, Robert Creamer, and Harold Rosenthal. *The Yankees: The Four Fabulous Eras of Baseball's Most Famous Team*. New York: Random House, 1979. A fascinating account of the Yankee dynasties from the perspectives of the dominating players of each era. Many photographs.

Eig, Jonathan. *Luckiest Man: The Life and Death of Lou Gehrig*. New York: Simon & Schuster, 2005. A balanced and interesting profile of Gehrig, including information about his relationships with his family, wife, and Babe Ruth.

Fleming, G. H., ed. *Murderer's Row*. New York: William Morrow, 1985. A collection of photographs, newspaper clippings, and articles by the major sportswriters of the 1920's, linked by Fleming's commentary to form a day-by-day narrative of the 1927 season. A major theme is the home-run duel between Ruth and Gehrig.

Gehrig, Eleanor, and Joseph Durso. *My Luke and I*. New York: Thomas Y. Crowell, 1976. A moving, personal account of the public and private lives of Lou and Eleanor Gehrig. Particularly revealing are insights into Gehrig's personality, the rivalry between Gehrig's mother and his wife for his affections, and the stability of Gehrig's life following his marriage.

Kashatus, William C. *Lou Gehrig: A Biography*. Westport, Conn.: Greenwood Press, 2004. This biography of Gehrig also focuses on his wife, Eleanor, who devoted her life to finding a cure for amyotrophic lateral sclerosis.

Rubin, Robert. *Lou Gehrig: Courageous Star*. New York: G. P. Putnam's Sons, 1979. An admiring popular biography of the Iron Horse. Written by a Miami newspaper sportswriter. Emphasizes the impact of Gehrig's formative years and his struggle to emerge from the shadow of Babe Ruth, only to be overshadowed by the young Joe DiMaggio.

Sultans of Swat: The Four Great Sluggers of the New York Yankees. New York: St. Martin's Press, 2006. Using sports reporting from *The New York Times*, the book re-creates the careers of Gehrig, DiMaggio, Ruth, and Mantle.

GERONIMO

> " *I was no chief and never had been, but because I had been more deeply wronged than others, this honor was conferred upon me, and I resolved to prove worthy of the trust.* "

Native American leader

Through two decades, Geronimo was the most feared and vilified person in the Southwest, but in his old age he was placed on display as a freak attraction at fairs and expositions. His maligned and misunderstood career epitomized the troubles of a withering Apache culture struggling to survive in a hostile modern world.

Born: June, 1829?; near present-day Clifton, Arizona
Died: February 17, 1909; Fort Sill, Oklahoma
Also known as: Goyathlay (birth name)
Area of achievement: Native American affairs

EARLY LIFE

Although the precise date and location of Geronimo's (jeh-RAHN-ih-moh) birth are not known, he was most likely born in around June, 1829, near the head of the Gila River in a part of the Southwest then controlled by Mexico. Named Goyathlay (One Who Yawns) by his Behonkohe parents, the legendary Apache warrior later came to be called Geronimo—a name taken from the sound that terrified Mexican soldiers allegedly cried when calling on Saint Jerome to protect them from his relentless charge.

Geronimo's early life, like that of other Apache youth, was filled with complex religious ritual and ceremony. From the placing of amulets on his cradle to guard him against early death to the ceremonial putting on of the first moccasins, Geronimo's relatives prepared their infant for Apache life, teaching him the origin myths of his people and the legends of supernatural beings and benevolent mountain spirits that hid in the caverns of their homeland.

Through ritual observances and instruction, Geronimo learned about Usen, a remote and nebulous god who, though unconcerned with petty quarrels among men, was the Life Giver and provider for his people. "When Usen created the Apaches," Geronimo later asserted, "he also created their homes in the West. He gave to them such grain, fruits, and game as they needed to eat. . . . He gave to them a climate and all they needed for clothing and shelter was at hand." Geronimo's religious heritage taught him to be self-sufficient, to love and revere his mountain homeland, and never to betray a promise made with oath and ceremony.

Geronimo grew into adulthood during a brief period of peace, a rare interlude that interrupted the chronic wars between the Apache and Mexican peoples. Even in times of peace, however, Apache culture placed a priority on the skills of warfare. Through parental instruction and childhood games, Geronimo learned how to hunt, hide, track, and shoot—necessary survival skills in an economy based on game, wild fruits, and booty taken from neighboring peoples.

Geronimo also heard the often-repeated stories of conquests of his heroic grandfather Mahko, an Apache chief renowned for his great size, strength, and valor in battle. Like his grandfather, Geronimo had unusual physical prowess and courage. Tall and slender, strong and quick, Geronimo proved at an early age to be a good provider for his mother, whom he supported following his father's premature death, and later for his bride, Alope, whom he acquired from her father for "a herd of ponies" stolen most likely from unsuspecting Mexican victims. By his early twenties, Geronimo (still called Goyathlay) was a member of the council of warriors, a proven booty taker, a husband, and a father of three.

LIFE'S WORK

In 1850, a band of Mexican scalp hunters raided an Apache camp while the warriors were away. During the ensuing massacre, Geronimo's mother, wife, and three children were slain. Shortly after this tragedy, Geronimo had a religious experience that figured prominently in his subsequent life. As he later reported the incident, while in a trancelike state, a voice called his name four times (the magic number among the Apache) and then informed him, "No gun can ever kill you. I will take the bullets from the guns of the Mexicans, so they will have nothing but powder. And I will guide your arrows." After receiving this gift of power, Geronimo's vengeance against Mexicans was equaled by his confidence that harm would not come his way.

While still unknown to most Americans, during the 1850's, Geronimo rose among the ranks of the Apache warriors. A participant in numerous raids into Mexico, Geronimo fought bravely under the Apache chief Cochise. Although wounded on several occasions, Geronimo remained convinced that no bullet could kill him. It was during this period that he changed his name from Goyathlay to Geronimo.

War between the U.S. government and the Apache first erupted in 1861 following a kidnapping-charge incident involving Cochise. The war lingered for nearly a dozen years until Cochise and General Oliver Otis Howard signed a truce. According to the terms of the agreement, the mountain homeland of the Chiricahua (one of the tribes that made up the Apache and Geronimo's tribe) was set aside as a reservation, on which the Chiricahua promised to remain.

Following Cochise's death in 1874, the United States attempted to relocate the Chiricahua to the San Carlos Agency in the parched bottomlands of the Gila River. Although some Apache accepted relocation, Geronimo led a small band off the reservation into the Sierra Madre range in Mexico. From this base, Geronimo's warriors conducted raids into the United States, hitting wagon trains and ranches for the supplies needed for survival.

In 1877, for the first and only time in his life, Geronimo was captured by John Clum of the United States Army. After spending some time in a guardhouse in San Carlos, Geronimo was released, being told not to leave the reservation. Within a year, however, he was again in Mexico. Although a fugitive, he was blamed in the American press for virtually all crimes committed by Apache "renegades" of the reservation.

Upon the promise of protection, Geronimo voluntarily returned to the San Carlos

Agency in 1879. This time, he remained two years until an unfortunate incident involving the death of Noch-ay-del-klinne, a popular Apache religious prophet, triggered another escape into the Sierra Madre. In 1882, Geronimo daringly attempted a raid into Arizona to rescue the remainder of his people on the reservation and to secure for himself reinforcements for his forces hiding in Mexico. This campaign, which resulted in the forced abduction of many unwilling Apache women and children, brought heavy losses to his band and nearly cost Geronimo his life. The newspaper coverage of the campaign also made Geronimo the most despised and feared villain in the United States.

In May, 1883, General George Crook of the United States Army crossed into Mexico in search of Geronimo. Not wanting war, Geronimo sent word to Crook of his willingness to return to the reservation if his people were guaranteed just treatment. Crook consented, and Geronimo persuaded his band to retire to San Carlos.

Geronimo, however, never adjusted to life on the reservation. Troubled by newspaper headlines demanding his execution and resentful of reservation rules (in particular, the prohibition against alcoholic drink), Geronimo in the spring of 1885 planned a final breakaway from the San Carlos Agency. With his typical ingenuity, Geronimo led his 144 followers off the reservation. Cutting telegraph lines behind him, he eluded the cavalry and crossed into Mexico, finding sanctuary in his old Sierra Madre refuge. Although pursued by an army of five thousand regulars and five hundred Apache scouts, Geronimo avoided capture until September, 1886, when he voluntarily surrendered to General Nelson Miles. (He had agreed to a surrender to General George Crook in March but had escaped his troops.)

Rejoicing that the Apache wars were over, the army loaded Geronimo and his tribesmen on railroad cars and shipped them first to Fort Pickens in Florida and then to the Mount Vernon Barracks in Alabama. Unaccustomed to the warm, humid climate, so unlike the high, dry country of their birth, thousands of the Apache captives died of tuberculosis and other diseases. In 1894, after the government rejected another appeal to allow their return to Arizona, the Kiowa and Comanche offered their former Apache foes a part of their reservation near Fort Sill, Oklahoma.

Geronimo spent the remainder of his life on the Oklahoma reservation. Adapting quickly to the white man's economic system, the aged Apache warrior survived by growing watermelons and selling his now infamous signature to curious autograph seekers. Although the government technically still viewed him as a prisoner of war, the army permitted Geronimo to attend, under guard, the international fairs and expositions at Buffalo, Omaha, and St. Louis. In 1905, Theodore Roosevelt even invited him to Washington, D.C., to attend the inaugural presidential parade. Wherever Geronimo went, he attracted great crowds and made handsome profits by selling autographs, buttons, hats, and photographs of himself.

In February, 1909, while returning home from selling bows and arrows in nearby Lawton, Oklahoma, an inebriated Geronimo fell from his horse into a creek bed. For several hours, Geronimo's body lay exposed. Three days later, the Apache octogenarian died of pneumonia. As promised, no bullet ever killed him.

Significance

The Industrial Age of the late nineteenth century altered the life patterns of American farmers and entrepreneurs, women and laborers. No groups, however, were more affected by the forces of modernization than were the Native American Indians. Geronimo's tragic career as warrior and prisoner epitomized the inevitable demise of an ancient Apache culture trapped in a web of white man's history.

Although a stubbornly independent and uncompromising warrior, Geronimo symbolized to countless Americans the treacherous savagery of a vicious race that could not be trusted. Highly conscious of his wrath and unrelenting hatred, the American public never knew the deeply religious family man who yearned to abide in his mountain homeland.

During his last twenty-three years of captivity, the legend of Geronimo grew, even as the public's hatred of the once-powerful Apache mellowed into admiration. Always a good provider, Geronimo established for himself a profitable business by peddling souvenirs and performing stunts at Wild West shows. A living artifact of a world that no longer existed, Geronimo became the comic image of the tamed American Indian finally brought into white man's civilization.

—*Terry D. Bilhartz*

Further Reading

Adams, Alexander B. *Geronimo: A Biography*. New York: G. P. Putnam's Sons, 1971. A well-researched history of the Apache wars that contains much material on Mangas Coloradas, Cochise, and other warriors as well as Geronimo. Replete with documentation of the connivance, blunders, and savagery that characterized the removal of the Apache from their homelands, this biography exposes the limitations of General Nelson Miles and the inexperience of the white leadership in Indian affairs.

Betzinez, Jason, with Wilbur Sturtevant Nye. *I Fought with Geronimo*. Harrisburg, Pa.: Stackpole Books, 1960. Another firsthand narrative account of the Apache wars written by the son of Geronimo's first cousin. Includes stories told more than a half century after the event. An entertaining primary source, but it must be used with caution.

Brown, Dee. "Geronimo." *American History Illustrated* 15 (May, 1980): 12-21; 15 (July, 1980): 31-45. The best article-length introduction to the life of Geronimo. A lively and sympathetic overview of the career of this clever Apache warrior.

Clum, Woodworth. *Apache Agent: The Story of John P. Clum*. Boston: Houghton Mifflin, 1936. Reprint. Lincoln: University of Nebraska Press, 1978. A story of the only man who ever captured Geronimo. Written from the notes of John Clum, a man who hated Geronimo with a passion. Biased yet entertaining account.

Cozzens, Peter, ed. *Eyewitnesses to the Indian Wars, 1865-1890: The Struggle for Apacheria*. Harrisburg, Pa.: Stackpole Books, 2001. This book is the first in a five-volume series containing army reports, diaries, news articles, and other contemporaneous accounts of Indian Wars. This volume focuses on military campaigns against the Apaches, with Part Five, "Chasing Geronimo, 1885-1886," containing accounts of Geronimo's escape and eventual surrender.

Davis, Britton. *The Truth About Geronimo*. New Haven, Conn.: Yale University Press, 1929. Reprint. Lincoln: University of Nebraska Press, 1976. An entertaining narrative filled with humorous and thrilling incidents written by an author who spent three years in the United States Army attempting to locate and capture this Apache warrior.

Debo, Angie. *Geronimo: The Man, His Time, His Place*. Norman: University of Oklahoma Press, 1976. The best of the many Geronimo biographies. Carefully researched and documented, this balanced account portrays Geronimo neither as villain nor as hero but as a maligned and misunderstood individual trapped in an increasingly hostile environment. Highly recommended.

Faulk, Odie B. *The Geronimo Campaign*. New York: Oxford University Press, 1969. A reassessment of the military campaign that ended with the surrender of Geronimo in 1886. Includes much information collected by the son of Lieutenant Charles B. Gatewood, who arranged the surrender and was one of the few white men Geronimo trusted.

Geronimo. *Geronimo: His Own Story*. Edited by S. M. Barrett and Frederick Turner. New York: Duffield, 1906. The personal autobiography dictated by Geronimo to Barrett in 1905. A chronicle of Geronimo's grievances, in particular against the Mexican nationals. Includes informative sections on Apache religion, as well as methods in dealing with crimes, ceremonies, festivals, and appreciation of nature.

Kraft, Louis. *Gatewood and Geronimo*. Albuquerque: University of New Mexico Press, 2000. A biography of Geronimo and Lieutenant Charles B. Gatewood, a cavalryman posted in Arizona who was criticized by the military and civilians for his equitable treatment of Apaches.

LRC - Batavia HS
Batavia, IL 60510